D0415523

OLYMPIC CITIES

City Agendas, Planning, and the World's Games,
1896–2012

LIVERPOOL JMU LIBRARY

3 1111 01163 5529

LIVERPOOL JOHN MOORES UNIVERSITY
Aldham Roberts L.C
TEL 0151 231 3701/3634

Planning, History and Environment Series

Editor:

Professor Dennis Hardy, Middlesex University, UK

Editorial Board:

Professor Gregory Andrusz, London, UK

Professor Arturo Almandoz, Universidad Simón Bolivar, Caracas, Venezuela

Professor Nezar AlSayyad, University of California, Berkeley, USA

Professor Robert Bruegmann, University of Illinois at Chicago, USA

Professor Meredith Clausen, University of Washington, Seattle, USA

Professor Jeffrey W. Cody, Getty Conservation Institute, Los Angeles, USA

Professor Robert Freestone, University of New South Wales, Sydney, Australia

Professor Sir Peter Hall, University College London, UK

Professor Peter Larkham, University of Central England, Birmingham, UK

Professor Anthony Sutcliffe, Nottingham, UK

Technical Editor

Ann Rudkin, Alexandrine Press, Marcham, Oxon, UK

Published titles

Of Planting and Planning: The making of British colonial cities by Robert Home

Planning Europe's Capital Cities: Aspects of nineteenth-century urban development by Thomas Hall

Politics and Preservation: A policy history of the built heritage, 1882–1996 by John Delafons

Selling Places: The marketing and promotion of towns and cities, 1850–2000 by Stephen V. Ward

Changing Suburbs: Foundation, form and function edited by Richard Harris and Peter Larkham

The Australian Metropolis: A planning history edited by Stephen Hamnett and Robert Freestone

Utopian England: Community experiments 1900–1945 by Dennis Hardy

Urban Planning in a Changing World: The twentieth experience edited by Robert Freestone

Twentieth-Century Suburbs: A morphological approach by J.W.R. Whitehand and C.M.H. Carr

Council Housing and Culture: The history of a social experiment by Alison Ravetz

Planning Latin America's Capital Cities, 1850–1950 edited by Arturo Almandoz

Exporting American Architecture, 1870–2000 by Jeffrey W. Cody

Planning by Consent: The origins and nature of British development control by Philip Booth

The Making and Selling of Post-Mao Beijing by Anne-Marie Broudehoux

Planning Middle Eastern Cities: An urban kaleidoscope in a globalizing world edited by Yasser Elsheshtawy

Globalizing Taipei: The political economy of spatial development edited by Reginald Yin-Wang Kwok

New Urbanism and American Planning: The conflict of cultures by Emily Talen

Titles published 2006

Remaking Chinese Urban Form: Modernity, scarcity and space. 1949–2005 by Duanfang Lu

Planning Twentieth Century Capital Cities edited by David L.A. Gordon

Titles published 2007

Olympic Cities: City agendas, planning, and the world's games, 1896–2012 edited by John R. Gold and Margaret M. Gold

Planning the Megacity: Jakarta in the twentieth century by Christopher Silver

Ordinary Places, Extraordinary Events: citizenship, democracy and urban space in Latin America edited by Clara Irazábal

Designing Australia's Cities by Robert Freestone

OLYMPIC CITIES

City Agendas, Planning and the
World's Games, 1896–2012

edited by

John R. Gold

and

Margaret M. Gold

Routledge
Taylor & Francis Group

LONDON AND NEW YORK

First published in 2007
by Routledge, 2 Park Square, Milton Park, Abingdon, Oxfordshire OX14 4RN

Simultaneously published in the USA and Canada
by Routledge
270 Madison Avenue, New York, NY 10016

Routledge is an imprint of the Taylor & Francis Group, an informa business

© 2007 Selection and editorial material John R. Gold and Margaret M. Gold; individual
chapters: the contributors

Typeset in Aldine and Swiss by PNR Design, Didcot
Printed and bound in Great Britain by TJ International Ltd, Padstow, Cornwall

This book was commissioned and edited by Alexandrine Press, Marcham, Oxfordshire

All rights reserved. No part of this book may be reprinted or reproduced or utilised in any
form or by any electronic, mechanical or other means, now known or hereafter invented,
including photocopying and recording, or in any information storage or retrieval system,
without permission in writing from the publishers.

The publisher makes no representation, express or implied, with regard to the accuracy of the
information contained in this book and cannot accept any legal responsibility or liability for
any errors or omissions that may be made.

British Library Cataloguing in Publication Data

A catalogue record of this book is available from the British Library

Library of Congress Cataloging in Publication Data

Gold, John Robert.
Olympic cities : city agendas, planning, and the world's games, 1896-2012 / edited by John R.
Gold and Margaret M. Gold.
p. cm. — (Planning, history, and the environment series)
Includes bibliographical references and index.
ISBN 978–0–415–37406–4 (hbk : alk. paper) — ISBN 978–0–415–37407–1 (pbk : alk. paper)
1. City planning—History. 2. Municipal government—History. 3. Municipal services—
History. 4. Olympics—History. 5. Olympics—Planning. 6. Olympics—Management—
History. I. Gold, Margaret M. II. Title.
HT166.G614 2007
307.1'21609—dc22
2007014022

ISBN10: (hbk) 0–415–37406–5
ISBN10: (pbk) 0–415–37407–3
ISBN10: (ebk) 0–203–09887–0

ISBN13: (hbk) 978–0–415–37406–4
ISBN13: (pbk) 978–0–415–37407–1
ISBN13: (ebk) 978–0–203–09887–5

For David Pepper

Contents

Preface

Many people have early memories of Olympic competitions. In our case, the first direct memories stemmed from grainy black-and-white television pictures that came from the 1960 Summer Games in Rome. Distant Melbourne in 1956 was well beyond the reach of live television, but Rome, courtesy of Eurovision, was now within range. From a parochial perspective, things were not going well for the British team, which was hardly surprising given that they came from a country where sports came under the control of patrician administrators, who seemingly believed that training was tantamount to cheating. Suddenly, a bespectacled and somewhat emaciated-looking athlete called Don Thompson won the 50 kilometres walk. Although, being a road race, his efforts were mostly off camera, the images of his triumphant entry into the stadium remained a staple of the station's broadcasting for several days.

Television coverage, however, did not focus solely on the sporting competitions. The BBC, then the only British television station covering the Olympics, took the opportunity to present news features and documentaries about the city of Rome. Predictably, the sights of the classical city received coverage, but the programme makers gave a sense of the modernity alongside tradition. What caught the eye of news teams, and subsequently the attention of historians, was that the Games' organizers had gone beyond their obligations to invest in facilities that were directly related to the Olympics. Panoramas of the recently-constructed districts containing those facilities, glimpses of developments in the city's transport systems, and discussion of the creation of an Olympic Village that would house Romans after it had accommodated competitors and officials gave the sense that the Games would leave a lasting impact on Rome.

It was an early pointer to a future in which cities eagerly sought the nomination to host the Olympics for reasons almost as much associated with general urban development as with seeking the prestige associated with staging this most expensive of all major sporting and cultural festivals. In this respect, host cities increasingly gained the support of the Olympic movement, itself concerned about the growing scale and expense of the Games. The pursuit of what became known as 'legacy' – whether measured in terms of the promotion of sport or long-term investment in new buildings and infrastructure – routinely became an important ingredient in calculations about the benefits of staging the Games. Ensuring that the legacy is unequivocally *positive*, however, is a challenge. The variable fortunes of cities in staging the event, for reasons connected with what went on both within and outside the stadium, is a subject of the closest scrutiny amongst commentators interested in the history of the Games. Moreover, even Olympic festivals that apparently pass off well can subsequently appear less satisfactory once the longer term reality of empty and decaying stadia, underused transport links or badly conceived regeneration schemes become apparent.

This book draws on the expertise of an international group of authors to examine comparatively the experience of Olympic cities. In doing so and in examining the balance sheet of success and failure, we identify the unfolding process by which festivals ostensibly steeped in tradition are continually invented and reinvented to meet changing times and needs. The period in which we are interested covers the full span of Olympiads from the revival of the Games in 1896 to the view ahead, as manifested in construction projects unfolding for Beijing 2008 and London 2012. Understandably, the focus is on the Summer Games as the largest and most visible of the Olympic festivals, but we also recognize the interrelationships between the Summer Games and the other manifestations of Olympic celebration – the Winter Games, Cultural Olympiads and the parallel Paralympics.

This book adopts a multilayered approach to its subject matter, with the chapters arranged into three main parts. It opens with surveys of the broad historical trends in staging the Games, followed by chapters that scrutinize significant themes arising from cities acting as host, and then provides a representative selection of city portraits – understandably concentrating on the period from the 1960s onwards when host cities became more interested in using the Olympics as a catalyst for development. Adopting a tripartite structure that seeks both thematic insight and chronological coverage inevitably means revisiting the same festivals at several points in the text but from different angles and perspectives. In addition, the correct balance between allowing authors scope for initial context and removing unnecessary repetition by employing cross-references is difficult to achieve, but we hope that the results are acceptable. Certainly, we would like to express our sincere gratitude to our contributors for their patience with the editorial process and for their willingness to redraft material to benefit the book as a whole.

Certain elements of standardization and conventions deserve some clarification. Statements of expenditure frequently occur in local currencies and exchange rates at points in the past are not always easy to obtain, especially when sources are unclear about precise dates. Where possible, we have attempted to use pound Sterling or US equivalents, and all sums where dollars are shown without qualification relate to the US currency. In addition, anyone familiar with using Olympic documentation, especially Official Reports, will realize that there are often different versions available. We have retained the linguistic version used by our contributors in cited references, even though this means that different language versions of the same publication might be listed separately in the consolidated bibliography. Finally, Olympic sport is a realm in which institutional acronyms abound. Although we have tried throughout to provide names of bodies in full wherever they first occur in a chapter, there is also a full listing of abbreviations at the start of this text.

As ever, we have incurred a variety of debts in the process of preparing this book. Dennis Hardy and Ann Rudkin supplied the stimulus to develop the initial idea and Graeme Evans supplied valuable contacts. The International Planning History Society supplied an invaluable opportunity to gather an initial group of contributors together at its Biennial Meeting in Barcelona in 2004. In connection with that event and subsequent valuable discussions, we would like to thank Jo Foord, Graeme Ford, Sarah Loy and Kat Martindale. The School of Social Sciences and Law at Oxford Brookes University and the Business School at London Metropolitan University provided finance and other assistance to facilitate our work. We would particularly like to acknowledge the assistance of the British Olympic Association for allowing us access to source materials and Martin McElhatton, Chief Executive of Wheel Power, for sparing generous amounts of time to show us round the Stoke Mandeville Stadium. Iain, Josie and Jenny tolerated the things that did not happen in order to allow us time and space to complete this text. Finally, we have great pleasure in dedicating this book to David Pepper, a man for whom sport occupies its proper place in life.

John and Margaret Gold
West Ealing
June 2007

The Contributors

Michael Barke is Reader in Human Geography at Northumbria University, Newcastle upon Tyne. His research interests include the study of socio-economic change in southern Spain, the historical geography of North East England and place promotion in the United Kingdom. His publications include *Tourism in Spain: Critical Issues* (CAB International, 1996).

Brian S. Chalkley is Professor of Geography at the University of Plymouth and Director of the Higher Education Academy National Subject Centre for Geography, Earth and Environmental Sciences (GEES). His teaching and research focus on geographical education, urban planning and the infrastructural implications of the Olympic Games.

Jon Coaffee is a Senior Lecturer in Spatial Planning and Urban Regeneration at the University of Manchester and a member of the Centre for Urban Policy Studies in the University's School of Environment and Development. His research interests revolve around the interplay of regeneration, urban management and security policy. He is the author of *Terrorism, Risk and the City* (Ashgate, 2003).

Ian G. Cook is Professor of Human Geography at Liverpool John Moores University and Head of the Centre for Pacific Rim Studies. He is the joint editor/author of seven books of which the most recent are *The Greening of China* (China Intercontinental Press, Beijing, 2004) and *New Perspectives on Aging in China* (Nova Science Publishers, New York, 2007).

Stephen J. Essex is Reader in Human Geography at the University of Plymouth. His teaching and research focuses on tourism and the infrastructural implications of the Olympic Games. He has co-authored a number of journal articles on the urban impacts and planning of both the Summer and Winter Olympic Games with Professor Chalkley.

Graeme Evans is Professor of Urban Cultures and Regeneration and Director of the Cities Institute at London Metropolitan University where he leads research projects under the Engineering and Physical Sciences Research Council's Sustainable Urban Environments programme. His book *Cultural Planning: An Urban Renaissance?* (Routledge, 2001) was the first to consider culture and city planning from both historic and contemporary perspectives.

Beatriz Garcia is the Director of Impacts 08, a longitudinal research programme into the impact of Liverpool becoming European Capital of Culture, jointly developed by the University of Liverpool and Liverpool John Moores University. An urban sociologist by training, her recent projects assess the legacy of cultural programming within the Olympic Games (Barcelona 1992 onwards), the Commonwealth Games (Manchester 2002), and the European Capital of Culture (Glasgow 1990, Liverpool 2008). She is an advisor to the London 2012 Culture, Ceremonies and Education team and co-editor of *Culture @ the Olympics*.

John R. Gold is Professor of Urban Geography at Oxford Brookes University and a member of the University's Institute for Historical and Cultural Research. He is the joint editor of five books and author/joint author of a further nine books of which the most recent are *Cities of Culture* (Ashgate, 2005) and *The Practice of Modernism: modern architects and urban transformation, 1954–72* (Routledge, 2007).

Margaret M. Gold is Senior Lecturer in Arts and Heritage Management at London Metropolitan University and a member of the University's International Institute for Culture, Tourism and Development. She is the joint author of *Imagining Scotland* (Scolar Press, 1995) and *Cities of Culture* (Ashgate, 2005).

Lorraine Johnston is a post-doctoral researcher in the School of Social Sciences at the University of Manchester. Her research interests are in strategic public sector management and local regeneration.

Paul Kitchin is the course leader of the MA in Sport Management at London Metropolitan University's North Campus. His current research interests focus on the role of the Internet in assisting CRM/CEM, consumer behaviour in participation sports and studying aspects of Olympic legacy delivery.

Monika Meyer-Künzel is head of the department of Urban Development and Urban Ecology at the Leibniz-Institute of Ecological and Regional Development Dresden, and a member of the Deutsche Akademie für Städtebau und Landesplanung. Her main fields of work are urban development and mega-events.

Daniel Latouche is Research Professor of Political Science in the Centre for Urban and Cultural Studies of the National Institute of Scientific Research (Montréal). He is the author of numerous books on issues of ethnocultural relations, constitutional design, forecasting and urban economic development. His recent interests deal with territorial planning in West Africa, the contribution of urbanism to ethnic accommodation, the impact of artistic and cultural clusters, and 'cultural adjustment' as a contributor to modernity.

Francisco-Javier Monclús is Professor of Urbanism at the Polytechnical University of Catalonia, Barcelona. He was Convenor of the 11th International Planning History Society Conference in 2004 and since 2005 has worked as Planner for the Consortium Zaragoza Expo 2008. He is co-editor of the journal *Perspectivas Urbanas* and his books include the *Atlas Histórico de Ciudades Europeas* (CCCB,

1994–1996), *Culture, Urbanism and Planning* (Ashgate, 2006) and *El Urbanismo de las Exposiciones Internacionales* (Ediciones UPC, 2006).

George Revill is Senior Lecturer in Geography at the Open University. His research interests include cultural histories of travel and transport and the study of music, landscape and national identity. Publications include *Representing the Environment* (Routledge, 2004, with John R. Gold) and *Railway* (Reaktion, 2008). He is chair of the Landscape Research Group.

Stephen V. Ward is Professor of Planning History at Oxford Brookes University. He is a former President of the International Planning History Society and Editor of the Journal *Planning Perspectives*. His books include *Selling Places* (Routledge, 1998), *Planning the Twentieth-Century City* (Wiley, 2002) and *Planning and Urban Change*, second edition (Sage, 2004).

Acknowledgements

The editor, contributors and publisher would like to thank all those who have granted permission to reproduce illustrations. We have made every effort to contact and acknowledge copyright holders, but if any errors have been made we would be very happy to correct them at a later printing.

In particular we are grateful to the following for permission to reproduce photographs:

Barcelona City Council: 13.6
CCCB-Salvat: 13.2, 13.3, 13.4, 13.5
Jon Coaffee: 9.1, 9.2, 9.3
Colegio de Arquitectos de Catalunya: 13.1
Ian Cook: 16.1
Beatriz García: 14.1, 14.2, 14.3, 14.5
Gerkan, Marg and Partners: 10.5
Lu Jiewen: 16.2, 16.3
Monika Meyer-Künzel: 10.3

The following illustrations are either from historic postcards or now defunct publishing houses for which no successor could be traced: 2.1, 2.2, 2.3, 2.4, 2.5, 2.6, 4.1, 10.1, 10.2, 10.4, 11.1, 11.2.

All remaining photographs were taken by the editors.

List of Acronyms

The list below contains an alphabetical listing of acronyms used substantively in the text rather than simply for bibliographic purposes:

ACOG	Atlanta Committee for the Olympic Games
AOBC	Athens 2004 Olympic Bid Committee
AOSC	Athens Olympic Sports Complex
ATHOC	Athens Organizing Committee for the Olympic Games
BBC	British Broadcasting Corporation
COJO	Comité d'Organisation des Jeux Olympiques
CONI	Comitato Olimpico Nazionale Italiano
COOB	Barcelona Olympic Organizing Committee
FIFA	Fédération Internationale de Football Association
IBC	International Broadcast Centre
ICC	International Coordinating Committee of the World Sports Organizations
IOC	International Olympic Committee
IPC	International Paralympic Committee
ISMGF	International Stoke Mandeville Games Foundation
ISOD	International Sports Organization for the Disabled
LDA	London Development Agency
LOCOC	London Organizing Committee for the Olympic Games
OCOG	Organizing Committee for the Olympic Games
SOCOG	Sydney Organizing Committee for the Olympic Games
TOK	Transfer of Olympic Knowledge
TOP	The Olympic Programme
TOROC	Organizing Committee of the XX Turin 2006 Olympic Winter Games
WWF	World Wildlife Fund

Chapter 1

Introduction

John R. Gold and Margaret M. Gold

On the evening of 4 November 2004 Dora Bakoyannis, the Mayor of Athens, rose to address a public meeting at the London School of Economics. Her talk was entitled 'What makes an Olympic City?' and she might reasonably have expected her audience to listen attentively to a commentary on the Greek experience of staging the recent Twenty-Eighth Summer Olympic Games. After all, London was then mounting an enthusiastic bid for the right to host the 2012 Games, even if its campaign seemed tinged with defeatism. Paris was the strong favourite to win the contest and Madrid the likely runner-up. Any pointers to themes that might help to tip the balance and curry favour with the International Olympic Committee (IOC) would presumably be welcome. The speaker, however, scarcely reached the end of her first sentence before a group of Greek students stormed the platform, while their colleagues in the upper tier of seating tossed leaflets down to the audience below. After some confusion, those on the platform unfurled a three-metre-long hand-painted banner. It read: '18 Dead Workers make a Good Olympic City'.

For those wondering what the commotion was about, an associated web site from a radical organization based in Thessaloniki supplied more information. The commentary argued that: 'it took 18 dead workers for these games to happen. And this is not all that Mrs Bakoyannis doesn't want you to know. Below are some highlights of Athens's Olympic experience and the true legacy that the games have brought to the city' (IMC, 2005). The ensuing list asserted that the Greek authorities had used the occasion 'as the perfect excuse to attack all unwanted social groups and detain them, so that they wouldn't ruin the country's image. Immigrants, junkies, political activists and gypsy populations were amongst those who experienced the true face of the "Olympic city"'. According to the protesters, the results included constructing a special prison for holding troublemakers in the former US Army base at Aspropirgos that 'is now part of the city's legacy of the Games' and building a set of lavish, but unwarranted, sports arenas that would see little subsequent use, especially for sports barely practised in Greece. More generally, they argued that the long-term consequences of staging the Games included reinforcement of trends towards the militarization of urban space, environmental damage and destruction of heritage.

It was a telling example of the way that hosting the Olympic Games continues to divide opinion before, during and after the event. For those on the left of Greek politics, the Olympics aroused deep suspicions about the intentions of the ruling classes, who were seen as using the Games as an opportunity to advance systematic repression of minority groups and political activists. More generally, the security measures around the Games aroused mistrust, from both left and nationalist right of the political spectrum, of the Greek government's contacts with the United States and NATO. Besides having made expensive purchases of surveillance equipment from large American defence corporations, the Greek government had authorized a series of military exercises to test the authorities' readiness for the Games. These, notably, had invited foreign participation. Four hundred members of the US special operations forces, for instance, had joined the Greek armed forces in an exercise lasting from 10 to 23 March 2004 that tested preparedness for suicide bombings, chemical and biological attacks, and plane hijackings (Levy, 2004).

By contrast, such measures and precautions were readily justified, indeed presented as essential, by the Greek government. The Olympics are an event with which the Greeks have a unique cultural connection and successful stewardship of the 2004 Games was a matter of national pride. As with any modern host city, the Athenian authorities were continually mindful of the risk of international terrorism. The era of the 'Games-as-target' had begun at Munich 1972,[1] when hostage taking by the 'Black September' Palestinian group eventually resulted in the death of eleven Israeli athletes and officials, five of the eight terrorists and a German police officer. A pipe bomb, later established to be the work of anti-abortionists, had exploded at Atlanta in 1996. Closer to home, the murder of the British Defence Attaché Stephen Saunders as he drove to work in Athens on 8 June 2002 and an explosion at Piraeus on 29 June 2002, attributed to the Greek revolutionary Marxist group N17, had opened questions about the security for Athens 2004. According to a written reply to a question in the Westminster Parliament, a team of Metropolitan Police officers, sent from London by the British government to participate in the investigations into the murder of Brigadier Saunders, would remain in Athens to assist 'more widely [in] helping Greece fight the terrorism menace of N17'.[2] Other countries expressed their concerns both publicly and through diplomatic channels. In an atmosphere already dramatically changed by Al-Qaeda's attacks on the United States on 11 September 2001, there was an inevitable tendency for the Greek authorities to react in a way that reassured the international community and stressed that decisive plans were in hand to deal with any further threat.

Reinventing the Olympics

In many respects, there was nothing remarkable about finding the Olympics embroiled in such matters, since they consistently evoke issues that span domains beyond the sporting arena. To some extent, that is true by definition since the Olympics always had an intrinsic cultural dimension. The ancient Games, as chapter 4 shows, were not just sporting festivals, but represented a gathering of all the people (*panegyris*) and featured art, oratory, music and poetry as well as athletics. When revived in 1896, the founders of the modern Olympics sought to revive a semblance of this sense of the *panegyris* by adopting a pan-cultural approach that regarded sports, the arts, technology and culture as mutually enriching and interrelated aspects of human life. From the outset, therefore, cultural programmes that might serve to enhance the lives of the societies that staged the modern Games were attached to the Olympic festivals – even if chosen host cities chose to downplay this dimension (see chapter 4).

This breadth of interpretation was merely a taste of what was to come. The Olympics, as we stress at many points in this book, are highly versatile festivals that can embrace many agendas, absorb new ideas and priorities, and adapt to changing times. On the sporting front, the Games soon came to embrace events that either had a primarily regional appeal or had no ancient equivalent – as with the introduction of the Winter Games in 1924 (see chapter 3). From 1948 onwards, there were the beginnings of a qualitative shift in philosophy, with appropriation of the Olympic spirit to cover sporting competitions for athletes with disabilities. This development, which culminated in the establishment of the Paralympics as a parallel yet integrated festival, challenged the core notion of the Olympics as a celebration of bodily perfection, while retaining the ethos of participation and competition (see chapter 5).

Other developments had rather less to do with the founding ideals of the revived Games or the present-day requirements of the IOC. The early festivals saw organizers treat the Olympics as an adjunct to the fairground, employing them as an additional but subsidiary attraction for the programmes of International Expositions (World's Fairs). Paris 1900 witnessed the Olympics treated as an indistinguishable component of the Exposition Universelle. The organizers of St Louis 1904 followed the same formula, adding sports of their own choosing such as college football (gridiron), local cross country championships, professional events, the national championships of the American Athletic Union of the United States, and 'automobiling' (*Anon*, 1904, pp. 3, 48). From the mid-1930s, host nations seized the opportunity to use the Olympics as flagship events that would act as advertisements for their countries and regimes. Berlin 1936, for instance, served as a platform for Hitler's Germany to put an acceptable face on the Third Reich's political regime and to mask its endemic theories of racial supremacy. Tokyo 1964 was an important medium for conveying Japan's credentials as a modern country and for signifying its re-emergence on to the international stage after the Second World War.

From the late 1960s through to the 1980s, the Summer Games regularly took centre stage in the realm of international relations as competing nations made use of the limelight afforded by the Olympics to mount politically-inspired boycotts. Guttmann (2002, p. 141) noted the case of the Egyptian shot putter Youssef Nagai Assad, who qualified for three Olympics but never had the chance to participate in his event. In 1972, his government ordered their competitors home from Munich to show solidarity with the Palestinian cause. Four years later, the team returned to Egypt from Montreal without taking part in the Games in order to support the Non-Aligned Nations' protest against New Zealand's rugby ties with South Africa (even though rugby was not then an Olympic sport).[3] In 1980, Assad again lost his opportunity to compete when the Egyptian government chose to join the American-led boycott of the Moscow Games, mounted in protest at the Soviet Union's invasion of Afghanistan. Ironically, Assad was too old for selection for Los Angeles in 1984 when Egypt did at last participate, albeit in a Games overshadowed by a Soviet-inspired retaliatory boycott.

Yet perhaps the most striking reinvention of the Olympics was as catalyst for urban development in the face of changing economic circumstances. Use of the Games to reinvigorate sluggish or declining urban economies was essentially a product of new thinking from late-1970s, when growing awareness of the pervasiveness of deindustrialization led city planners to take action to stimulate new sources of employment. Given clear recognition that urban regeneration through traditional production-based approaches looked progressively more implausible, they became interested in alternative strategies that relied on service industries and consumption to supply the locomotive of growth. These strategies rested on two bases. First, they involved municipal authorities adopting a more entrepreneurial stance, forming partnerships with the private sector to integrate 'a traditional local boosterism … with the use of local government powers to try and attract external sources of funding, new direct investments or employment sources' (Harvey, 1989, p. 7; Hall and Hubbard, 1998). Secondly, they looked to the cultural sector – including sport, tourism, entertainment, media and creative design – as particularly valuable channels for promoting development and expansion. The resulting programmes mostly involved small-scale initiatives, but the more ambitious councils of larger cities directed their attention to attracting a select group of large-scale, prolonged and spectacular festivals that simultaneously offered the opportunity to bring about local change while raising the international profile of the city.

These festivals are best known as 'mega-events' (Roche, 1992, 2000; Spezia, 1992), although sometimes also termed 'meta-spectacles' (Bergmann, 1999, p. 13), 'hallmark events' (Hall, 1989), 'landmark events' (Hiller, 1990) or 'world festivals' (Proudfoot et al., 2000). Some are held each year in the same home city, as is common with international arts festivals. Others, which are of particular interest here, have no permanent home and are the subject of competition between cities seeking to act as hosts. Of these a few, like American football's Super Bowl, are national events that command large enough domestic interest to sustain the title of mega-event. Super Bowl XXXVII in San Diego, for example, injected an estimated $367 million into the local economy in 2003 (Matheson, 2006, p. 26). Rather more of these festivals find cities acting as hosts for events that have a continental remit (e.g. the Asian Games or European Nations Cup), or intercontinental basis (e.g. the Commonwealth Games or cricket's World Cup), or that attract near-universal participation (e.g. soccer's World Cup or the now-fading International Expositions).

These events are normally under the stewardship of an internationally constituted body, such as the Fédération Internationale de Football Association (FIFA), located in Zurich, which runs soccer's World Cup or the Paris-based Bureau International des Expositions that gives its official seal of approval to World's Fairs. These bodies generally draw support from member nations through having a central secretariat or executive responsible to a body of national delegates. The precise mechanisms by which they make decisions about awarding the right to stage events, however, vary from organization to organization. In some instances, as with FIFA's stewardship of soccer's World Cup, the sponsoring body awards the event to a specific nation, which then allocates it to appropriate venues. For other events, the controlling organization directly awards the right to stage festivals to candidate cities, often after stiff competition between potential hosts.

Stage and Legacy

The Summer and, increasingly, the Winter Games are leading examples of the type of ambulatory, city-based mega-events that have proliferated over the last 150 years. In the early days, hosting the Olympics meant little more than assuming responsibility for providing the necessary venues for competitions and for Games-related activities. Nevertheless, even at this stage the city became the *stage*, with Olympic festivities serving as the focal point of celebrations that spread beyond the confines of the stadium, perhaps also drawing in preliminary or post-Games events. From the time that Organizing Committees started to provide purpose-built stadia, there were certain economic benefits that invariably accrued to the host city. These included a medium-term stimulus to the construction industry, a brief tourist boom, and a short-term boost in employment at Games venues and in administration. These might generate sufficient returns to help defray the costs of staging the events and, in some instances, to generate a modest surplus.

As the scale of the Games themselves increased over time, so the ambitions of those that planned these events widened. Their wish to make statements about the technological prowess and modernity of the host nation led to the adoption of larger, more spectacular and inherently more expensive stadia. From the mid-1950s onwards, concern for *legacy* became an ever more important aspect of staging the Olympics. Mega-events like the Olympics involve large-scale investment that, if applied properly, can bring about long-term benefits for the host city. This strategy became particularly popular once the organizers of Barcelona 1992 provided a much-admired model of how to achieve mega-event-driven urban regeneration. City planners routinely integrated the Olympics into general exercises intended to have a material impact on the long-term future of their cities by offering a broad package of benefits. *Inter alia*, these included boosting a city's economy, improving its international standing, repositioning it in the global tourist market, promoting urban regeneration, revamping transport and service infrastructures, creating vibrant cultural quarters, establishing a network of high-grade facilities that could serve as the basis for bids for future events, and gaining a competitive advantage over rivals.

The main problem is that there is no guarantee that these alluring longer-term gains will materialize, as the experience of many host cities readily testifies. The Olympics in Sydney 2000 and Athens 2004 provided festivals that were highly praised at the time but saw both cities saddled with the legacy of underused stadia and supporting facilities – a problem that has intensified with the extension of Olympic status to a range of sports that have a far-from-universal appeal. The anticipated publicity benefits may also be eroded by global coverage. Preparations for Olympic festivals in recent years, for example, have proceeded against a backdrop of investigative journalism readily attuned to exploit rumours of delays, financial problems, labour disputes, structural problems, managerial incompetence and corruption. The press boost the atmosphere of crisis by arguing that the cost will be double or treble the original estimate, that the stadia and infrastructure will not be ready in time, that terrorists will target the event, and that the Olympics have diverted resources away from other, more deserving causes. After the event, critical scrutiny falls on conversion and disposal of the Olympic sites, with empty stadia and unpopular housing schemes taken as signs of poor planning and mismanagement.

Needless to say, the roots of this negativity towards the Olympics and their legacy are frequently not just journalistic mischief. Organizing Committees make mistakes – an almost inevitable state of affairs given that the ambulatory character of the Olympics means that new and untried Committees employing *ad hoc* administrative arrangements are assembled for each Games. Moreover, the re-conceptualization of the Olympics as a vehicle for general urban development rests on a seldom-admitted gamble played with, and for, high stakes. It involves committing enormous amounts of public money and varying amounts of private funds over the course of six or seven years to plan the sites, construct stadia, develop transport and other infrastructures, and adjust the sites to their post-Games condition with whatever amount of associated regeneration is desired. Quite apart from the financial returns only accruing at the end of the cycle – requiring the organizers to bear substantial medium-term budgetary deficits – the requisite large-scale capital construction projects accord to the profile of what are termed 'megaprojects'. Defined as prestige schemes involving large-scale and high-risk investment over a lengthy period, megaprojects notoriously suffer heavy cost overruns, often fail to deliver the supposed benefits and regularly provoke financial crises (Flyvbjerg et al., 2003). Indeed, the Olympics may suffer more in this respect than other megaprojects by virtue of having an immutable deadline for completion. When works run behind timetable, this can add further cost pressures by forcing organizers to instigate high-cost emergency building programmes, with round-the-clock working and additional contractors, in order to get laggard projects back on schedule.

In addition, large capital projects like the Olympics characteristically benefit some groups in society rather than others. Leaving aside issues involving corruption, the choice of locations for stadia and associated facilities from a range of possibilities inevitably leads to locational decisions for investment that have implications at local, regional and national levels. Certain districts will benefit from new sources of employment, rising property values, and the development of high-speed transport routes. Other districts will experience clearance to make way for stadia and infrastructure, or will suffer prolonged pollution, noise nuisance from construction work, a degree of blight that depresses property values, and sometimes displacement of the existing population. Efforts to place a more agreeable face on a city may lead to superficial beautification rather than fundamental regeneration. All these elements can be drawn into narratives which maintain that resources have been consciously allocated with political objectives in mind.

The question of cultural politics also has significance. Organizing Committees routinely drew their members and support from the Establishment, tending, intentionally or otherwise, to ignore cultural diversity. This was particularly apparent, for instance, in Opening Ceremonies, always prominent media for communicating messages about the host nation. These tended to present notions of nationhood and religiosity from the perspective of dominant groups. More recently, acceptance of multiculturalism, or at least the pragmatic necessity of gaining the cooperation of minority groups, has offered inclusiveness to groups previously seen as marginal.

The organizers of the Sydney Olympics in 2000, for example, bore in mind the problems that arose at the Australian Bicentennial in 1988, when the celebration of European conquest led to severe inter-communal frictions. Part of the adopted solution was to broaden the constituent basis of support for the Olympics, making efforts to gain the involvement of community leaders. Another element lay in seeking to change modes of representation, with images of nationhood adjusted to include the various groupings that comprised the multicultural Australia of the twenty-first century. One specific problem lay in tackling prevalent negative and stereotypic representations of Aboriginal peoples. The Olympic Opening Ceremony, therefore, commenced with an enacted encounter between indigenous and white Australians, emphasizing the antiquity of indigenous culture, its diversity, myths, legends and spirituality. The Aborigines emerged as environmentally-wise managers of the land, in contrast to the approach of what the Official Report described as the European period of 'vitality and violence' (SOCOG, 2000b). Later in the ceremony, the Aboriginal athlete Cathy Freeman was selected to receive the relay-run Olympic torch to light the cauldron of the Olympic flame in the stadium.

Aims

Selection by the IOC as an 'Olympic city' invites the host to contribute to a process that is now more than a century old, but in continual evolution. The Olympic city gains the right to stage a festival carefully wrapped in the trappings of historical precedent, but which also possesses a remarkable malleability that has allowed the event to survive repeated crises and emerge, by the start of the twenty-first century, as unquestionably the 'World's Games'.[4] Olympic cities, however, are partners in the staging of the Olympics rather than nominees that run a festival crafted by its sponsoring body. Each recipient city shapes the Games to greater or lesser extent and contributes to the body of customs and practices associated with the Olympics. Equally, the Games have an impact upon the host cities, not least because those cities and the Olympic movement alike increasingly seek to ensure that the festival should bequeath a positive legacy. In a process of continual adaptation and change, the Olympics and host cities have enjoyed a symbiotic relationship.

This book explores that relationship, examining the experience of Olympic cities and the balance sheet of success and failure from the revival of the Games in 1896 to the plans for the London Olympics in 2012. As such, it has three main aims. First, it examines the city's role in *staging* the modern Games, a word that covers the full spectrum of activity from initial selection of sites to final modification of these sites to their post-festival condition. Secondly, it explores the underlying *agendas* that host cities have brought to bear on staging the Games, recognizing the different blends of social, political, cultural and economic aspirations that have emerged over time. Finally, it recognizes that, despite being an exceptional event in the life of a specific city, the business of staging the Games is now commonly related to the wider *planning* process. In this respect, we focus particularly on issues concerned with legacy, including infrastructural development and urban regeneration projects, which are now regarded as central to the process of planning for the Olympics.

At the outset, three further points are important in understanding the scope and coverage of this book. First, while giving understandable prominence to the Summer Games as by far the largest, most prestigious and visible of the Olympic events, we seek a more comprehensive approach. The Olympics are not a single event. The advent of the Winter Olympics in 1924 and the gradual convergence of the Paralympics with both the Summer and Winter Games have added further strands to the Olympic sporting competitions. In addition, as noted above, the revival of the modern Games predicated a cultural festival to exist alongside the sports events. Each of these strands merits coverage as intrinsic parts of the experience of being an Olympic city.

Secondly, the prevailing focus is historical. This does not mean that we have confined the scope of the book purely to dealing with the past since later chapters deal with Olympics that, at the time of writing, are yet-to-come. What this volume does stress, however, is the value of seeing even these forthcoming Games as the product of a chain of events that reaches back into the late nineteenth century and has been steadily developing since that time. This is not simply a matter of recognizing that the Olympics are events clothed in the past, with specified traditions that future host cities will perforce incorporate in their ceremonial content. Rather, the staging of the Olympics invites historical analysis. Continuity between Games arises from each new Organizing Committee scrutinizing the experience of previous Committees, with transfer of knowledge from one to another facilitated by the IOC's own procedures (see chapter 6). In addition, each new host city prepares its Olympic festivals in the sure and certain knowledge that its efforts will be compared to those of predecessors and will, in turn, provide a new point of comparison.

Thirdly, and related, we have endeavoured throughout to counter the trend towards what is sometimes termed 'presentism' – the tendency by modern historians to see the past in the light of, and in support of, their current beliefs (e.g. Fischer, 1971; see also Bourne, 2006). Seen from the standpoint of the present, two possible meta-narratives emerge. One construes both the general history of the Games and the more specific history of the relationship between the Olympics and their host city as the inevitable triumph of visionary ideas. The other, heavily influenced by the cultural turn in the social sciences, views the modern Olympics as being at a key moment of reformulation, with the underlying philosophy arguably tending towards some new, postmodern state. Neither view, however, is wholly satisfactory. Any book that views the Olympics through a historical lens inescapably encounters a flow of events quite unlike a strip cartoon moving tidily from frame to frame. Quite simply, the unpredictable highs and lows of the experience of Olympic cities resist the imposition of simple categorizations or single-strand narratives.

Structure

As befits the multi-stranded nature of the narratives that surround the Games, therefore, the ensuing chapters divide into three main sections, each of which offers different perspectives on the Olympics. Part I contains four parallel but complementary essays that look chronologically at the progress of the individual Olympic festivals from inception to the early twenty-first century. Chapter 2 provides an overview of the relationship between the Summer Olympics and their home cities, acting as a general framework for the city case studies found later in the book as well as adding coverage of Summer Games, particularly from the early years, which are not tackled there. After examining the circumstances behind the revival of the Olympics, it traces seven phases in the history of staging the festival from the opening Games in Athens 1896 to their distant successor in 2004. In a similar vein, Chapter 3 identifies a four-phase framework for analysing the role of the Winter Olympics, albeit still relatively limited, in changing and modernizing the built environment of its host cities. Chapter 4 examines the cultural dimension of the Games and its growth to embrace not just the Summer Games but the

Winter Games. Recent developments have seen the cultural festivals growing in scale, particularly in response to interest in the potentially positive contribution of culture to the urban legacy of both Summer and Winter host cities. Chapter 5 examines the Paralympic Games. It charts their development from small beginnings as a competition for disabled ex-servicemen and women in England in the late 1940s to the present day ambulatory international festivals for athletes with disabilities, which now take place in the Olympic city immediately after both the Summer and Winter Games.

Part II provides surveys of four key aspects of activity involved in planning and managing the Olympics. Chapter 6 examines the crucial area of finance, adopting a business-historical perspective to identify past growth and potential trends in development of income streams and the major sources of expenditure. Chapter 7 deals with city marketing, recognizing the importance of the Olympics in global place promotion and particularly in securing the bid in the first place. The ensuing chapter 8 switches attention to the question of spectacle. Its main focus is less with the content of spectacle than with the problems that cities encounter in accommodating that spectacle. It is argued that the search for spectacle has potentially serious pitfalls linked to such questions as democratic governance, city and regional economic debt, and security. Chapter 9 then reviews the association between the Olympics and urban renewal and regeneration. After surveying the regenerative impact of Summer Olympics on host cities between 1896 and 1980, it highlights the development of holistic and citywide models of regeneration adopted from 1992 onwards, along with recent concerns about the environmental implications of the Games for the host city.

Part III offers eight portraits of Olympic cities, arranged in chronological order. Chapter 10 discusses the various phases in development of the Olympic sports complex in Berlin and its subsequent problematic history in light of the postwar division and eventual reunification of the city. Chapter 11 recalls the first occasion that the Games were held in a developing nation, analysing the way that the bid was won and the economic and political consequences of the 1968 Olympics for Mexico City. Chapter 12 deals with Montreal 1976, widely recognized as a watershed in modern Olympic history for the scale of its financial mismanagement and the lasting burden upon the city. By contrast Barcelona 1992 provides perhaps the most celebrated example of employing the Olympic Games as part of successful urban development strategy. The account in Chapter 13 provides a detailed picture of the planning of the Barcelona Games, showing how calculations about the Olympics as place promotion strategy and as catalyst for urban regeneration preoccupied planners as much as the conduct of the Games themselves.

The remainder of Part III deals with the first four Games of the twenty-first century, past and future. Chapter 14 focuses attention on cultural policy and planning, exploring the way that the cultural programme was organized at Sydney 2000, the way in which the city was experienced during the Olympic fortnight, and the types of images that the city projected to the rest of the world prior to and after the Games. The ensuing chapter 15 analyses the Games' return to Athens in 2004, discussing the serious delays incurred by belatedly switching from a nucleated to a dispersed locational policy for Olympic facilities. It also highlights the lip-service paid to the much heralded goal of environmental sustainability. Chapter 16 deals with the plans for Beijing 2008 and the facilities now appearing, recognizing not only the urban dimension of this Games but their significance within wider processes of development taking place within the People's Republic of China. Chapter 17 looks further ahead to London 2012, a Games in which the prospect for regeneration of a deprived and environmentally blighted area of East London was as much part of the bidding process as the image of an inclusive and spectacular Olympic festival.

That chapter's emphasis on the importance of legacy is carried through into the Afterword, which shows how concern with longer-term impact has become of primary concern in debate about the Olympics. At a time when the Games have grown to bloated proportions, imposing financial and organizational burdens completely out of proportion to what commonsense might suppose was appropriate for a brief sporting festival, concern for legacy has become an inevitable touchstone of the bidding process and a continuing mantra for those who seek to justify the necessary virement of funds to see the project through to conclusion.

Notes

1.   When specific Games are mentioned in abbreviated form in this book, the convention is to use the city name followed by the date.

2.   Written Reply by Mike O'Brien MP to questions on 'Foreign and Commonwealth Affairs', Hansard, 338(176), 11 July 2002.

3.   Although rugby union did feature in Olympic Games before 1924.

4.   It is important to distinguish this commonly applied aphorism for the Olympics from the 'World Games', a multi-sport event staged at four-yearly intervals since 1981 by the International World Games Association and covering sports not represented in the Olympics, such as billiards, netball, surfing and body-building. These aspire, yet unconvincingly, to equal or even exceed the importance of the world championships that are organized individually by each individual participant federation.

Part I

The Olympic Festivals

Chapter 2

Athens to Athens: the Summer Olympics, 1896–2004

John R. Gold and Margaret M. Gold

Yet let us all together to our troops,
And give them leave to fly that will not stay;
And call them pillars that will stand to us;
And, if we thrive, promise them such rewards
As victors wear at the Olympian games

William Shakespeare[1]

Knowledge about the Olympic Games and its significance for ancient Greek society had never faded from the European consciousness, despite the centuries that had elapsed since the prohibition of the festival in 393 AD. Shakespeare's matter-of-fact reference to the Games illustrates the point that the Olympic idea 'was a shared, not isolated reference' in the arts throughout Western Europe (Segrave, 2005, p. 22); indeed, as Littlewood (2000, p. 1179) observed, the Olympics were 'probably the one' among the 'incalculable influences of the Greeks in the modern world … of which the general public [were] the most aware'. Much the same applied to Olympia, the place with which the Games were associated. As the English theologian Richard Chandler (1766, p. 308) remarked, its name would 'ever be respected as venerable for its precious era by the chronologer and historian', for whom:

> [it] had been rendered excessively illustrious by the power and reputation of its ancient princes, among whom were Œnomaus and Pelops; by the Oracle and temple of the Olympian Jupiter; by the celebrity of the grand *Panegyris* or general assembly held at it; and by the renown of the *Agon* or Games, in which to be victorious was deemed the very summit of human felicity. (*Ibid*., p. 303)

Yet despite its reputation, no one was certain as to Olympia's exact whereabouts.

Despite being indicated on maps since 1516, when the Venetian cartographer Battista Palnese referred to it as 'Andilalo',[2] the passage of time meant that 'Olympia has since been forgotten in its vicinity' (*Ibid.*, p. 308).

Matters changed in the 1770s when travellers ventured to the Peloponnesus on the west coast of Greece, then an obscure corner of the Ottoman Empire, in search of this important place. For example, towards the end of a trip in 1776 sponsored by the Society of Dilettanti, Richard Chandler and his companions took local advice as to where Olympia might have been. There was little immediately apparent on arriving there. Two earthquakes had levelled the buildings, already in ruins, in the sixth century AD (Fellmann, 1973, p. 109). Periodic flooding by the two rivers (Cladeos and Alpheios) that meet there had subsequently deposited a layer of alluvium several metres thick. Yet despite the site appearing 'almost naked', closer inspection revealed some wall footings and a massive capital from a Doric column that had recently emerged from the river mud. The latter, Chandler correctly inferred, was a fragment of the Temple of Jupiter (Zeus). He made further deductions about a depression occupied by a pestilential pool: 'At a distance before it was a deep hollow, with stagnant water and brickwork, where, it is imagined, was the Stadium' (Chandler, 1766, p. 308). From these fragments, Chandler provided a mind's eye account of classical Olympia, drawing on ancient descriptions to outline the grandeur of buildings, temples and stadium that had made this 'no inconsiderable place'.

Chandler attached no special significance to these observations within his travelogue, but the rediscovery of the site brought new waves of visitors. Surveys carried out for Lord Spencer Stanhope in 1807 revealed an imposing complex replete with temples, gymnasia, stadium, hippodrome and accommodation (Stanhope, 1824). Noticeably, Stanhope's account extended to the ruined city of Elis, the prime settlement of the *polis* in which the festival site was situated, and recognized the links between the two. Adopting a similar approach to his subject matter, William Leake (1830, I, pp. 23–44) described Elis as the 'place of ordination and preparation for the *athletæ* of the Olympic Games' (*Ibid.*, II, p. 220) and the point from which participants set out in procession to traverse the distance (36 kilometres) to Olympia. The journey, complete with ceremonies of ritual purification *en route*, took place before the start of each Games (see also S.G. Miller, 2003, p. 9). The complex of permanent structures at Olympia also contained buildings that served the Elis-based civil government's need for political administration rather than having religious or sports functions (Crowther, 2003; see also Drees, 1968). These were early and intriguing recognitions of the close relationship between host city and Games.

Understandably, discovery of the ruins prompted campaigns for archaeological work since, as Leake (1830, I, p. 44) observed, 'there is every reason to believe that the most interesting discoveries in illustration of the arts, language, customs and history of Greece, may yet be made by excavations at Olympia'. The first fruits of those campaigns were small-scale digs by English and then French archaeologists in the early nineteenth century, but these encountered Greek sensitivities about removal of artefacts. The third set of excavations, however, proved decisive. Licensed by the Greek Parliament after negotiations between the Greek and German governments to ensure that artefacts did not leave the country, the excavations between 1875 and 1881 by a team from the Imperial German Archaeological Institute provided systematic analysis of the core of the site and vital insights as to its usage (Kyrieleis, 2003).

The reports coming from the excavations aroused excitement beyond archaeological circles. Historians and other scholars eagerly devoured news emerging from Olympia and reflected on the mystique of the Games and place of sport in classical Greek society. Their interest was not simply antiquarian. Some saw the achievements of the past as offering parallels for the modern age. For example, in a public lecture Sidney Colvin, the Director of Cambridge University's Fitzwilliam Museum, enthused over the new archaeological findings, but wistfully remarked that:

> It has been said that Englishmen and ancient Greeks are much like one another in two respects. One is their ignorance of all languages except their own, and the other is their love of physical sports. We have our Epsom and our Grand National, our games of cricket and football, our rowing and our running matches, and we despise Frenchmen and foreigners, generally, with the most impartial disdain; but somehow we don't make of our athletic sports so much as these ancient Greeks did. (Colvin, 1878, p. 7)

Colvin primarily had in mind the link between sport and art, seeing the Games as bridging the sacred and secular and creating a vital exemplar for contemporary cultural life. Others also felt that the ancient Games *per se* had an important ethos that might be revived and recaptured. Their model was that of a peaceful yet competitive sporting festival that brought nations together notwithstanding the pressures of a turbulent external environment.

This chapter provides a brief review of the principal phases in the development of that festival, as expressed in the evolution of the Summer Games. It opens by discussing the revival of the modern Olympics, before providing an overview of the intricate history of cities staging the Summer Games from Athens 1896 through to the official return of the Olympics to the Greek capital in 2004 (see table 2.1). We then identify seven main phases in the development of the relationship between the city and the Games. The first (1896–1906) traces the way that the nascent Olympics narrowly survived negative associations with the fairground, with two sets of Games held in Athens a decade apart offering a more positive path forward that intimately involved city and stadium. The next phase (1908–1936) saw local Organizing Committees devote mounting resources to preparing stadia and associated facilities. By the time of the 1936 Berlin Games, the Olympics had started to gain a consensual content with ingredients broadly replicated by each succeeding festival, although remaining an event that gave the home nation scope to mould the associated spectacle according to its own needs. After the war and a brief series of lower-key events framed by Austerity (1948–1956), the Olympics witnessed growing acceptance of the economic importance and general promotional significance of the event for the host cities. The fourth phase (1960–1976) saw host cities viewing the Olympics as catalyst for initiating

Table 2.1. Cities bidding for the Summer Olympic Games, 1896–2012.

Games	Year awarded	Host city	Other candidates
1896	1894	Athens	London
1900	1894	Paris	
1904	1901	St Louis★	Chicago
1908	1904	London†	Berlin, Milan, Rome
1912	1909	Stockholm	
1916	1912		Berlin, Alexandria (Egypt), Budapest, Cleveland, Brussels
1920	1914	Antwerp	Amsterdam, Atlanta, Brussels, Budapest, Cleveland, Lyon, Havana, Philadelphia
1924	1921	Paris	Los Angeles, Atlantic City, Chicago, Pasadena, Rome, Barcelona, Amsterdam, Lyon
1928	1921	Amsterdam	Los Angeles
1932	1923	Los Angeles	
1936	1931	Berlin	Barcelona, Buenos Aires, Rome
1940	1936		Tokyo, Helsinki. Rome
1944	1939		London, Athens, Budapest, Lausanne, Helsinki, Rome, Detroit
1948	1946	London	Baltimore, Lausanne, Los Angeles, Minneapolis, Philadelphia
1952	1947	Helsinki	Amsterdam, Chicago, Detroit, Los Angeles, Minneapolis, Philadelphia
1956	1949	Melbourne	Buenos Aires, Chicago, Detroit, Los Angeles, Mexico City, Minneapolis, Montreal, Philadelphia
1960	1955	Rome	Budapest, Brussels, Detroit, Lausanne, Mexico City, Tokyo
1964	1959	Tokyo	Brussels, Detroit, Vienna
1968	1969	Mexico City	Buenos Aires, Lyon, Detroit
1972	1966	Munich	Detroit, Madrid, Montreal
1976	1970	Montreal	Los Angeles, Moscow
1980	1974	Moscow	Los Angeles
1984	1978	Los Angeles	Teheran
1988	1981	Seoul	Nagoya (Japan)
1992	1986	Barcelona	Amsterdam, Belgrade, Birmingham, Brisbane, Paris
1996	1990	Atlanta	Athens, Belgrade, Manchester, Melbourne, Toronto
2000	1993	Sydney	Berlin, Beijing, Manchester, Istanbul (Brasilia, Milan, Tashkent withdrew)
2004	1997	Athens	Buenos Aires, Cape Town, Istanbul, Lille, Rio de Janeiro, Rome, San Juan, St. Petersburg, Seville, Stockholm
2008	2001	Beijing	Bangkok, Cairo, Havana, Istanbul, Kuala Lumpur, Osaka, Paris, Seville, Toronto
2012	2005	London	Paris, Madrid, Moscow, New York

★ The nomination was originally to Chicago.
† The nomination was originally to Rome.

Source: Partly based on Buchanan and Mallon (2001).

major infrastructural and related works; a period that ended with the misfortunes of Montreal 1976. After an interlude when the Games became dominated by late-Cold War ideological issues with rather less attention to regeneration (1980–1984), the success of the strategies introduced at Los Angeles 1984 and Barcelona 1992 heralded a new phase of commercialism and regeneration programmes (1988–1996). The final phase (2000–present) found cities actively competing to host a festival designed to leave a perceptible but sustainable physical legacy.

Revival

The idea of appropriating the title 'Olympic' had long appealed to organizers of sporting events (Redmond, 1988; Buchanan and Mallon, 2001). Robert Dover, described as an 'English captain and attorney' (*Anon*, 1910, p. 453), established a 'Cotswold Games' on his estate in 1604, largely as a protest against Puritan proscriptions of sporting pastimes and other frivolities (Mandell, 1976, p. 29). The festival that contemporary writers described as 'Mr Robert Dover's Olimpick Games upon the Cotswold Hills' included 'cudgel-playing, wrestling, running at the quintain, casting the ball and hammer, hand-ball, gymnastics, rural dances and games, and horse-racing, the winners in which received valuable prizes' (*Anon*, 1910, p. 453). The Cotswold Games lasted until 1644, although were briefly revived during the reign of Charles II, with a separate 'Olympics', largely devoted to dog racing, occurring at Hampton Court Palace in 1679.[3]

During the first half of the nineteenth century, a series of separate initiatives consciously sought to use Olympic sport to cement nationalist or pan-national aspirations. The Scandinavian Olympic Games of 1834 and 1836, founded at Ramlösa (Sweden) by the sports educator Gustav Johan Schartau, were designed as national festivals for the 'strong sons of Scandinavia' (Øresundstid, 2003). The Anglophone community in Montreal staged an Olympics in 1844 to assert their identity against the Francophone majority. The influential Much Wenlock Games, founded by Dr William Penny Brookes, grew from an initially limited affair to subsequent grander aims. Founded in October 1850 and still held annually, they aimed 'to promote the moral, physical and intellectual improvement of the inhabitants of the Town and neighbourhood of Wenlock' (WOS, 2006). Gradually, Brookes's vision expanded, most notably assisting the establishment of a National Olympian Association (NOA) in the 1860s. This eventually foundered, particularly due to opposition from the Amateur Athletic Club – an aristocratic and elitist group founded in 1866 to counter the NOA. Nevertheless, during its brief lifespan the NOA stimulated a brief flowering of athletics events in British cities, including the London Olympics – which attracted 10,000 spectators to Crystal Palace between 31 July and 2 August 1866.

Understandably, there was considerable interest in reviving the Olympics in Greece. Having achieved political independence in 1830, groups within the country campaigned to restore the Games as a symbol of their re-emerging nationhood (see chapter 15). In 1859, an Olympic sports festival took place in Athens, assisted by sponsorship from Evangelis Zappas, a wealthy expatriate Greek landowner living in Romania (see also chapter 15). The so-called 'Zappas Games', held again in 1870 and 1875, constituted a different scale of competition and spectacle than other events previously styled as 'Olympian'. The 1870 meeting, for example, attracted 30,000 spectators to watch Greek athletes compete in the partially restored Panathenian stadium.

Historians, however, show considerable selectivity in relation to these events. Official versions of Olympic history typically styled them as 'pseudo-Olympics' (Redmond, 1988); interesting as expressions of the desire to create prestige sporting competitions, but not representing progenitors of the revived Games as developed by the IOC under Baron Pierre de Coubertin's leadership.[4] This selectivity had an ideological purpose since, by emphasizing the originality of Coubertin's vision and downplaying the contribution of others, it privileged the IOC's claims for ownership of the Games. The traditional treatment of the personal relationship between Pierre de Coubertin and William Penny Brookes is a case in point. Historical accounts recognize that the two men actively corresponded and that Brookes had staged a special Autumn version of the Wenlock Games in Coubertin's honour when he visited England in October 1890, which featured award ceremonies and pageantry that greatly impressed Coubertin (Young, 1996, p. 78). The 1866 London Olympics, by contrast, received no mention in official Olympic histories; nor do Brookes's speeches in which he proposed an international basis for the Games and advocated that they had a permanent home in Athens (Young, 1998, p. 31; Toohey and Veal, 2000, p. 29). Brookes, therefore, emerged as the organizer of a small rural sporting festival rather than one of the lynchpins of the Games' revival.

The ideological dimension was even stronger in the disparagement of Greece's attempts to reinstate the Games. Downgrading the significance of the Zappas Games denied approval to any proprietorial claims by Greece to the revived Olympics, even though they were clearly based on a classical festival held on Greek soil for almost 1,200 years. In one sense, this ran counter to the mood of the times which favoured folk revival and saw collectors scouring the margins of Western nations in a nationalistic search for the 'authentic' roots of folk culture (Gold and Revill, 2006). Instead, the founders of the Olympics perceived their task as resuscitating an event that represented the quintessence of ancient cultural achievement to which Western civilization in general, rather than the late nineteenth-century Greek state, was heir. That outlook, in turn, imbued the modern Olympics with an internationalist stance, able continually to move to new host cities without loss of purpose, rather than needing to return permanently to Greece as a geographic hearth that would give the revived Games authenticity. Ceding control to the Greeks would have interfered with the freedom of action to pursue that policy.

Yet recognition of alternative precursors scarcely detracts from the importance of Coubertin's role in campaigning for the revival of the Olympics and, subsequently for his formative influence on the Games' early development. Commentators (e.g. Mandell, 1976; MacAloon, 1981) rightly identify Coubertin's contribution as a reformer who gradually moved beyond specific concern with promoting sports education within France as a medium for fostering national regeneration to addressing the 'democratic and international' dimension of sport. On 25 November 1892, his speech at the Sorbonne in Paris exhorted a somewhat sceptical audience to aid 'this grandiose and salutary task, the restoration of the Olympic Games' (quoted in Müller, 2000, p. 297).[5] Coubertin repeated his exhortation, with greater success, at an international Sports Congress that he organized in 1894, which supported the re-establishment of the Games and laid down key principles for organizing them.

To summarize its recommendations, the revived Olympics would reintroduce the ancient Games' four-yearly cycle, but would be ambulatory rather than based at a permanent site. They would be open to amateur sportsmen and should comprise modern rather than classical sports, although there was no definitive list of which sports to include or exclude. The Congress initiated the process of constructing a Charter of 'fundamental principles, rules and by-laws' to run the Games, normally known as the Olympic Charter. Central to its outlook was the notion of 'Olympism', the humanistic philosophy that mediated the cultural construction of the revived Games and guided the development of the supporting ceremonial content that steadily accumulated in subsequent years (see chapter 4). Finally, the Congress founded the IOC to exercise control and to select the host cities, but local Organizing Committees would plan the Olympics,[6] with the first two Games scheduled for Athens in 1896 and Paris in 1900. Both were pragmatic choices (Young, 1987, p. 271). The Congress accepted the inevitable by recognizing that Athens's symbolic associations made it the only city that could effectively launch the modern Olympics, notwithstanding resistance to Greek claims to ownership of the Games and giving serious consideration to London given its advantages regarding access and venues. The choice of Paris for 1900 reflected Coubertin's hope to capitalize on the International Exposition taking place that year and to draw spectators to the newly established Games.

Surviving the Fairground (1896–1906)

The first distinct phase of development saw a sequence of four Summer Games, in which the fortunes of the Olympics fluctuated profoundly. Athens 1896 proceeded against a difficult political and economic background that made preparations problematic and led to the first airing of a perennial question: should money be spent on the Olympics as a prestige project in light of competing needs? In this instance, one side, led by Prime Minister Charilaos Tricoupis, argued against the Games for economic reasons; the other, led by Opposition leader Theodorus Delyannis and supported by the monarchy, sympathized with the Games as a prestigious project that might reflect well on Greek identity and international standing (MacAloon, 1981, p. 182). The latter won the day, with the necessary finance raised through a mixture of public funds, appeals for subscriptions, private sponsors and the first special issue of Olympic postage stamps (*Ibid.*, p. 196; see also chapter 6).

Athens 1896 set an early pattern of low expenditure, pressing into service the existing Zappeion Building and the restored Panathenian stadium, with new construction restricted to a velodrome, shooting gallery and seating for the swimming events (Davenport, 1996, pp. 4–5; Gordon, 1983). This policy posed some problems. The Panathenian stadium, for instance, successfully held crowds of more than 50,000 and accommodated a modern running surface, but its traditional elongated horseshoe shape with accentuated curves at each end, hindered athletic performance (figure 2.1). Nevertheless, the revived festival worked well. The Games, symbolically opening on Greek Independence Day (6 April), attracted 245 athletes from 14 countries to compete in 45 events. The Opening Ceremony filled the stadium, with spectators occupying the surrounding hillsides and streets swelling the audience to an estimated 80,000–120,000.

The city beyond the stadium readily embraced the Games. The Athenian authorities decorated the streets, illuminated the Acropolis and arranged an entertainments programme that included torchlight processions, parades, fireworks, an orchestral concert by the Athens Philharmonic Orchestra and a performance of Sophocles's *Antigone* (Mallon and Widland, 1998). The marathon, introduced for the first time, added spectacle, provided a link with tradition[7] and supplied an important, if invented, symbol. Spectators lined the route through the Greater Athens region and filled the stadium to see the finish. Its popularity, enhanced by the victory of a local man, Spiridon Louis, not only brought a new

Figure 2.1. The Panathenian stadium, Athens during the 1896 Olympic Games.

fixture to the athletics calendar,[8] but also served to provide a focus that stressed the unity of city and Olympics.

Although small scale by contemporary standards, the 1896 Games showed that the modern Olympics had considerable potential as a coherent framework for a new international festival. By contrast, the two succeeding Games came perilously close both to derailing the Olympic movement and to downgrading the relationship between host city and Games to inconsequentiality. In both cases, the reason lay in the conflict between the nascent Games and larger, more important International Expositions. At Paris 1900, the connection between the events was the conscious, if misguided policy of associating the second Games with the 1900 Paris Exposition Universelle. Coubertin believed that the Olympics could capitalize on the Fair's many visitors and festive backdrop and, in particular, wanted to build a replica of Olympia, with temples, stadia, gymnasia and statues and an archaeological display.[9] The organizers, however, remained unmoved by this idea. Disputes over the control of the sporting element resulted in the Olympic movement effectively withdrawing, with a new committee appointed to plan the Exposition's Games (Mallon, 1998, p. 6). The Olympics became an International Games rather than a true Olympics. They were of indeterminate length, given that they lacked Opening or Closing Ceremonies and that the organizers haphazardly added events to the programme, some of which, like fishing in the River Seine (Harlan, 1931, p. 88), did not conform to Olympic standards. Indeed some competitors in tournaments connected with the Exposition never realized that they had entered Olympic competitions. For example, Michel Theato, the marathon winner, only learned in 1912 that he was the 'gold medallist' at the 1900 Olympics (Mallon, 1998, p. 9).

Compared with the considerable impact that the Exposition had on Paris – with a 543 acre (219 hectare) fairground located in the heart of the city in the Avenue Alexandre III and the Bois de Vincennes – the Olympics scarcely registered a presence. There was no stadium or running track. The track and field events were staged at the Racing Club of France's grounds in the Bois de Bologne, but the owners refused permission to remove any trees. As a result, discus and javelin throws often landed in wooded areas. The 500 metre (546 yard) grass running track sloped and undulated. Rigid former telegraph poles served as hurdles. The organizers hastily constructed a grandstand, but a row of trees obscured the track from spectators (Howell and Howell, 1996). Wholly overshadowed by the Exposition, the movement that had shown 'so much promise in 1896 seemed to have collapsed by 1900' (*Ibid.*, p. 17).

The next Summer Games at St Louis proved equally inimical to the revival of the Olympics. The IOC had strongly backed selection of a North American city and chose Chicago in May 1901 to stage the 1904 Games. Spoiling tactics by the organizers of St Louis's Louisiana Purchase International Exposition, however, led the IOC reluctantly to revise that decision even if it was inevitable that the Olympics 'would only be a sideshow attraction to the much larger international exposition' (Barnett, 1996, p. 19). Their fears had justification. The Exposition itself brought considerable kudos to St Louis, created an extensive fairground from the wooded Forest Park, and allowed much needed improvement works to the erstwhile heavily polluted and flood-prone Des Peres River. By contrast, the Olympics left little trace. There was at least a stadium, capable of seating 10,000 spectators, although with a one-third mile (536 metres) track instead of the standard quarter-mile circuit of the time, and 'something approaching' an Opening Ceremony on 14 May 1904 (Mallon, 1999a, p. 11). The programme, however, supplied little sense of continuity, with sporting competitions held at irregular intervals through to November, with scarcely any distinction between 'Olympic' sports and other competitions. In addition, the festival was tarnished by the infamous 'Anthropology Days' (12–13 August 1904) when African, Asian and Native American competitors competed in racially motivated athletic contests that denigrated their performances and gave succour to theories of white supremacy. Following hard on the heels of the 1900 debacle, St Louis 1904 threatened the continuance of the modern Olympics (Barnett, 1996, p. 23).

In the event, it took a sporting festival not usually reckoned as part of Olympic history – the 1906 Intercalated Games held in Athens – to secure the future (Young, 1996, p. 166; Mallon, 1999b, p. 5). This was the first, and only, product of a tactical compromise made in 1897, when a Coubertin-inspired initiative offered Greece the opportunity to hold a series of Intercalated Games at four-yearly intervals in non-Olympic years. Greece's defeat in the first Greco-Turkish War (1897) had left the country bankrupt (Davenport, 1996, p. 10), but improved economic circumstances allowed the staging of an Intercalated Games by 1906. This returned to the Panathenian stadium, with more extensive and eye-catching rituals and accompanying festivities than those staged in 1896. The sporting festival once more spilled over into the city, in a manner that contrasted with the experience of Paris and St Louis. The streets and buildings of Athens were again decorated, the city's squares staged evening concerts and there was a sustained programme of entertainments. The international press was more in evidence than at previous Games, although the eruption of Mount Vesuvius (4 April) and the San Francisco earthquake (18 April) detracted from the coverage that the Games received (Mallon, 1999b, p. 6). Nevertheless, the Intercalated Games effectively rescued the Olympics from its disastrous flirtation with the fairground and initiated a period in which host cities actively welcomed the Olympic Games as a premier and prestigious sporting event that merited purpose-built facilities.

Olympics by Design (1908–1936)

Just as the eruption of Vesuvius in April 1906 detracted from the coverage of the Athens Intercalated Games, so, arguably, did it put paid to its successor as the severe strains that recovery from the devastation placed on the Italian economy led to Rome abandoning its attempt to hold the 1908 Games.[10] In November 1906, the IOC formally confirmed the transfer to London (Mallon and Buchanan,

2000, p. 3). Here too, the Games were linked to an International Exposition – the 1908 Franco-British Exhibition of Science, Arts, and Industry held to celebrate the recent Entente Cordiale between the two nations. This large-scale event, occupying a 140 acre (56 hectare) plot of former agricultural land at Shepherd's Bush (West London), seemed at first glance to pose precisely the same threat of eclipsing the Games as at Paris and St. Louis. That this did not happen was due largely to the Exhibition Organization Committee agreeing to construct a stadium specifically for the Olympics in return for 75 per cent of the proceeds. The largest stadium of its day, its enormous concrete bowl enclosed athletics and cycle tracks, a 100 metre swimming pool, platforms for wrestling and gymnastics and even archery. Dressing rooms, restaurants and emergency services were located under the stands (figure 2.2). The foundation stone of the White City stadium, so-called because the Exhibition Buildings were finished in gleaming white stucco, was laid on 2 August 1907 and the stadium was inaugurated on the opening day of the adjoining Exhibition (14 May 1908). It held 93,000 spectators, with 63,000 seated. A newly opened station at Wood Lane, on an extension of the Central London Railway from its terminus at Shepherd's Bush, supplied both the Exhibition and Olympics with direct connections to central London.

London 1908 left a considerable legacy for the Olympic movement by developing the spectacle of the festival and supplying the basis for 'a compact and independent Olympic festival' (Wimmer, 1976, p. 22). Yet while it allowed the Games to prosper as an event in its own right, London 1908 gained the less desirable legacy of a huge and largely unwanted stadium. The White City remained almost completely unused for two decades before passing to the Greyhound Racing Association in 1927. Although serving as the home of British athletics

Figure 2.2. The White City stadium, Shepherd's Bush, London, 1908.

between 1933 and 1971, it languished further during the 1970s before demolition and redevelopment in 1985 for offices and housing.

The 1912 Games in Stockholm saw the Olympics move to a far smaller city.[11] Partly as a result, the Stockholm Organization Committee found it easier to create a festival that integrated city and stadium. The design of the stadium, built in the grounds of the royal Djirgaden (Zoological Gardens), assisted that aim. More modest than the White City, it seated 22,000 people, with stands arranged around a quarter mile (400 metre) running track (figure 2.3). From the outset, it was intended to be multipurpose, a decision that Coubertin applauded:

> The Gothic Stadium ... seemed to be a model of its kind. You could see it turned into a banquet hall, a concert hall, or a dance hall, and yet on the following morning always ready once again for carrying on with the contests. You could see how in a single night it got covered with ready-made squares of lawn, how hurdles were being put up, and how it decked itself with blossoming brushwood for the riding tournaments. All this was achieved without any ado, any delay, any blunder. While in London it had proved impossible for the life of the great city to be in any way affected by the proximity of the Olympic Games, Stockholm turned out to be thoroughly imbued with them. The entire city participated in its efforts to honour its foreign guests, and one had something like a vision of what the atmosphere must have been like in Olympia in the ancient days ... (Quoted in Wimmer, 1976, p. 27)

The stadium's evening entertainments included military concerts, displays of Scandinavian sports, gymnastic displays, fireworks and illuminations. The city provided street decorations, opera, theatre, a two-day aquatic festival, the

Figure 2.3. The American team entering the stadium during the Opening Ceremony of the Olympic Games, Stockholm, 1912.

usual round of receptions and banquets, and played reluctant host to the artistic competitions that were a cherished part of Coubertin's vision of linking sport and the arts. For the first time, too, the organizers took steps to publicize the Games internationally, through the Olympic movement, the Swedish diplomatic service and advertisements in national newspapers of other countries. The makings of the promotional activity that typified later Olympics Games had started to emerge.

The next Games took place eight years later. Hidebound by its observance of the four-year cycle of Olympiads despite the inconvenient reality of the First World War, the IOC retained the fiction of a sixth Olympiad in 1916. Although six cities in the, as yet non-belligerent, USA (Chicago, Cleveland, Newark, New York, Philadelphia and San Francisco) had offered to act as hosts to avoid disrupting the series, the IOC maintained that it had awarded Berlin the right to stage the 1916 Olympics and could not withdraw a nomination without that city's agreement. As the German Olympic Committee remained adamant that Berlin held the nomination, the sixth Olympiad was never held and the Games resumed their four-year cycle with the seventh Olympiad in Antwerp in 1920.

Awarded at an IOC meeting in Lausanne in April 1919 as much as a political act of moral support for Belgium than as a sporting event, Antwerp 1920 used the quickly renovated Beerschot stadium. Shortage of resources and materials meant that the standard of facilities was much poorer than at Stockholm, with constant rain leaving the running track pitted and rutted. A canal at Willebroek near Brussels, used for the rowing events, provided an industrial setting so ugly that Coubertin called it 'anti-Olympic' (Renson, 1996, p. 57). There were few associated festivities in the city. Yet despite the austerity, Antwerp 1920 recorded a deficit of 626 million Belgian francs, prompting accusations of acute financial mismanagement and leaving the organizers accused of treating the event as 'a symbol of conspicuous consumption' (Renson, 1996, p. 59).

The responsibility of consolidating the progress made at London and Stockholm therefore passed to the Organization Committees of the two ensuing Games. Paris 1924 represented the first occasion on which the growing prestige of the Olympics led to serious international competition among cities to act as hosts. Four American cities (Los Angeles, Atlantic City, Chicago and Pasadena) and five European (Rome, Barcelona, Amsterdam, Lyons and Paris) expressed interest in staging the Olympics (Welch, 1996, p. 61). The return to Paris proceeded with assurances that, unlike 1900, the organizers would treat the Olympics as an important international event. Rather than employ the Pershing stadium, which staged the 1919 Inter-Allied Games,[12] the Organization Committee decided in June 1922 to construct a purpose-built stadium at Colombes. The Stade Olympique Yves-du-Manoir had seating for 20,000 spectators, standing room for an additional 40,000 (Welch, 1996, p. 64) and would remain the main venue for national soccer and rugby matches until the opening of the Parc des Princes in 1972. Paris 1924 saw the birth of the concept of the Olympic Village at Rocquencourt, although the barrack-like accommodation with few services had 'very little to do with what was

Figure 2.4. Water polo competition in progress, the Olympic Pool, Amsterdam, 1928.

to be the first Olympic village' at Los Angeles 1932 (Muñoz, 1997, p. 30). Paris also witnessed the first significant dissatisfactions about the growing size of the Games, given that the scatter of the Olympic venues around the Paris region necessitated long bus journeys for most competitors.

The 1928 Amsterdam Games favoured the now familiar idea of clustered Olympic sites. Although the athletes were housed on ships in the harbour rather than in a specially constructed Village (Goldstein, 1996), the Dutch employed the 'Cité Olympique' idea of bringing the stadium and associated facilities together in a sporting complex. The new athletics stadium, built on reclaimed marshland, had seats for 40,000, with the other venues having a capacity of a further 30,000. The open-air swimming pool was located next to the main stadium (figure 2.4), with adjacent gymnasia for boxing, wrestling and fencing. Concerns were again expressed about the growing size of the Games, although the target was now the 'excessive festivities', with proposals that there should be reforms to allow only those that 'the reception of authorities and officials demanded' (Organizing Committee, 1928, p. 957).

The two final interwar Games completed the Summer Olympics' development into a high-status international festival that would play an important part in the lives of host cities. Los Angeles 1932 was an Olympiad conceived in the American boosterist tradition, resolutely advancing the city's economic and cultural interests against rivals. The city gained the right to stage the 1932 Olympics in 1923, but faced severe funding problems in the wake of the 1929 Wall Street Crash, with the federal government refusing to contribute. The Games' survival rested on the city issuing bonds and capitalizing on connections with the private sector, most notably the film industry which actively promoted the Olympics. Yet perhaps the key to encouraging participation lay in making the Games affordable to competitors by assisting travel and in constructing the first true Olympic Village, an innovation that combined economy with the spirit of Olympism.[13] The Official Report of the Games (TOC, 1933, pp. 235, 237) waxed lyrical about the symbolism of the Village and intermixing of peoples, to the extent that the observers recommended the Organizing Committee for the Nobel Peace Prize for their work in promoting the fellowship of the Games through the nations' athletes living peacefully side-by-side (Stump, 1988, p. 199).

With heavy subsidies for food and accommodation, 1,500 athletes from 34 nations competed at Los Angeles 1932 despite the problems of the international economy. Apart from the auditorium for the indoor competitions, most of the stadia were at Olympic Park (the former Exposition Park). The Memorial Stadium, the last Olympic arena to use the old-fashioned modified U-shape (Wimmer, 1976, p. 39), was created by refurbishing and enlarging the Coliseum into a venue with a seated capacity of 105,000. The swimming stadium and the State Armoury, which staged the fencing competitions, were built nearby. The Olympic Park also housed the Los Angeles Museum of History, Science and Art, which held more than 1,100 exhibits from the 32 countries that supplied entries for the Olympic Art Competition. The organizers added another important innovation by coordinating the decoration of the Olympic venues and the city using streamers and bunting in the official colours of blue, yellow, black, green and red. Flags of the competing nations, Olympic banners and large insignia hung across the main streets. The organizers also encouraged the owners of buildings and businesses to buy specially manufactured materials to embellish their buildings.

Despite economic stringencies, the Games achieved an operating surplus, with 1.25 million people paying $1.5 million to watch events over the 16 days of the Games. Tourist agencies put together packages featuring the Olympics and the scenic attractions of southern California. Sixty-two conventions were attracted to Los Angeles, enabling their delegates to enjoy the Games and further boosting the local economy at a time of continuing economic depression (TOC, 1933, p. 215). A visiting journalists' programme dealt with several hundred reporters from around the world in the three years leading up to the Games (*Ibid.*, p. 211); a strategy that maximized the possibility of favourable coverage. Not surprisingly, the 1932 Games left the city eager to repeat the exercise, with repeated candidacy before the Olympics finally returned in 1984 (see below).

Berlin 1936, the final Summer Games before the Second World War, was a landmark in political as well as sports history. The background to the Berlin Games, as chapter 10 shows, resonates with the history of Germany in the interwar period. Berlin, the host city, bid unsuccessfully for both the 1908 and 1912 Games, had seen the cancellation of the 1916 Games for which it held the nomination, and saw its further ambitions placed in abeyance until Germany was readmitted to the Olympic movement in time for the 1928 Games in Amsterdam. In May 1931, the

IOC awarded the 1936 Games to Berlin as an act of reconciliation, but the choice proved problematic with Hitler's rise to power. The Nazis' initial hostility to the financial burden and avowed internationalism of the Games seemed likely to bring rapid cancellation, but subsequent reappraisal of the classical origins of the Games to align them with National Socialist ideas of German origins[14] quickly brought enthusiastic support. This led to concern within the Olympic movement that the Games would be hijacked by the Nazi leadership for propaganda purposes (Hart Davis, 1986).

Certainly the creation of the stadium, the surrounding complex and other Olympic venues proceeded with wider ideological and propaganda goals in mind. As chapter 10 shows, the regime vetoed Werner March's original plans for expansion of the 1913 stadium, already approved by the IOC, favouring instead a proposal for a 110,000-seater stadium with a steel- and stone-clad structure. The stadium would lie at the heart of the Reichsportsfeld, soon to become the world's largest sports complex, complete with swimming and diving pools (with seating for 18,000), facilities for lawn tennis, hockey, equestrian sports, the House of German Sports (Deutschland Halle) for boxing, fencing, weightlifting, wrestling, the Reich Academy of Physical Education, accommodation for female competitors and the Maifeld Parade Ground (figure 2.5). Located in a peripheral area of Berlin but well connected into the city's U-bahn rail system, the site became the focus of attention throughout Germany in the period leading up to and including the Games for a regime that appreciated and mobilized the opportunity for powerful spectacle. Berlin was specially decorated throughout the Games and codes of behaviour issued to present the best possible impression to visitors, with careful concealment of explicit aspects of racial policies. After the Games, the city and state

Figure 2.5. Aerial view of the Reichssportfeld, Berlin, 1936.

gained the infrastructural legacy of a sports complex and parade ground that could be used for military purposes and for future National Socialist celebrations.

Austerity (1948–1956)

The bidding process after 1945 revived the pattern set in the interwar period. American cities, with their ingrained city rivalries, featured prominently, with formal bids for the 1948 Games from Baltimore, Los Angeles, Minneapolis and Philadelphia as well as informal interest from several other potential US contenders. There was a feeling, however, that the United States was too far away for affordable travel in these austere years (Voeltz, 1996, p. 103). Therefore, after conducting a postal ballot, in 1946 the IOC officially awarded the Fourteenth Summer Olympics to London.[15]

The next two years proved far more difficult economically than the British had anticipated when agreeing to host the Games, with few surplus resources available (Holt and Mason, 2000, pp. 27–29). The organizers quickly abandoned any idea of laying on stunning spectacle and custom-built stadia in favour of existing sports facilities. The Empire Stadium at Wembley, built for the 1924 British Empire Exhibition, became the Olympic Stadium. There was no Olympic Village, with athletes housed instead in Royal Air Force accommodation at Uxbridge, a convalescents' camp in Richmond Park, Southlands College in Wimbledon, and convenient school premises (Organizing Committee, 1948). The organizers borrowed sports equipment from the Armed Forces or from manufacturers on a lend-and-return basis. The Board of Trade adjusted rationing regulations for participants and new Tourist Voucher Books made it easier for foreign visitors to spend money in British shops. Yet despite the difficulties, the London Games successfully relaunched the Olympics after the traumas of war. The city was not *en fête* as Berlin or Los Angeles had been, but the Games undoubtedly lifted the mood of postwar Britain and recorded a profit of £30,000. Visitor numbers to London in 1948 were a post-war record, with hotels enjoying a bumper season (Holt and Mason, 2000, p. 31).

The two succeeding Games followed London's low-key approach. Helsinki had held the nomination for the Twelfth Summer Olympics in 1940, after the Japanese withdrew, and had built a stadium, swimming and diving arena, and a competitors' village in anticipation of that event. The organizers renovated and expanded the sporting facilities for the 1952 Games (figure 2.6), with the aid of a $1.25 million grant from the Finnish government, but the Olympic Village posed greater problems. The one originally constructed at Käpylä, 6 kilometres from the city centre, had long since been converted to public housing. The increased size of the Games required new accommodation not just at Käpylä, but also at new sites (Otaniemi and Töölö). The situation was further complicated by the Soviet Union's demands for a separate village for the socialist bloc's athletes (Hornbuckle, 1996, p. 117). In response, the organizers allocated the Otaniemi

Figure 2.6. The Olympic stadium, Helsinki, 1952.

site to the USSR and its allies, placing competitors literally as well as figuratively into two ideological camps.

Melbourne 1956 was the last Summer Olympics developed under conditions of postwar financial stringency. The city's bid for the Games (MIC, 1948) projected an image of a prosperous, developed and well-equipped 'city of culture', with the promise of a new Olympic stadium complex on the banks of the Yarra River east of the Melbourne Cricket Ground (MCG). Once Melbourne won the Games, the organizers decided to reduce costs by modifying the MCG and restricting construction of major new buildings to the swimming pool and velodrome. Available spaces at the local university, museum, art school and public library displayed the four associated art exhibitions – on architecture, painting, graphics and literature. The Olympic Village was built as a cheap housing project in the suburb of Heidelberg, using the existing system of government loans. These buildings, however, presented so many subsequent construction and social problems that the Games might well have been 'a force for urban degeneration rather than regeneration' (Essex and Chalkley, 1998, p. 194).

Catalyst (1960–1976)

Although important for their host nations, the financially straited 1948–1956 Games made little lasting impact on the Olympic cities. By contrast, Rome 1960 threw off the pall of Austerity and propelled the Games into the modern era. The city's Olympian aspirations stretched back many years. Rome, as noted above, initially held the nomination for the 1908 Games and, under Mussolini, had lobbied hard for the right to stage the 1940 Olympics. Indeed, Rome 1960 effectively capitalized on two districts developed by the Fascist regime with international festivals in mind. The first, the Foro Italico in the north of the city, already offered two imposing arenas: the Stadio dei Marmi, built in 1932, and the Stadio Olimpico, built in 1936. The second district was EUR, so-called because it was initially designed to supply a spectacular setting for the (cancelled) 1942 Esposizione Universale di Roma. Located to the south of the city, it was only partially developed before the Second World War, but its monumental and spacious qualities made it an ideal place for the core of the Olympic facilities. These included the Palazzo dello Sport (Sport Palace), the Velodrome, the Piscana delle Rose (swimming pool) and the Fontane Sports Zone training area. Ten other venues were scattered throughout the city, with several using sites with classical associations to underline the Games' pedigree. The vaults of the Basilica of Maxentius built in 303 AD, for instance, housed the Greco-Roman and free wrestling contests, while the Caracalla Baths (217 AD) staged the gymnastics.

These 'Olympic areas' made a permanent contribution to the city's sporting and cultural life. The Village at Campo Paroli provided private sector housing (Wimmer, 1976, p. 202; see also Muñoz, 1997) and the city also gained from infrastructural improvements undertaken with the Games in mind. These included new roads and bridges built to connect the Village to the main Olympic sites, modernization of the airport, improvement of the telephone, telegraph and radio networks, and initiatives to expand hotel accommodation. The Rome Olympics also had a major impact on financing the Games. Core funding came from the Italian soccer pools, the Totocalcio, but now supplemented for the first time by sales of television rights. Broadcasters had refused to pay for rights at Melbourne, arguing that covering the Games was akin to televising news and should be similarly free to the broadcaster. The organizers of the Rome Olympics, however, managed to convince the major television networks that the Games were a proprietorial commodity for which payment was necessary. The American Columbia Broadcasting System (CBS) paid $600,000 for US television rights, with Eurovision subscribing another $540,000. It marked another significant step towards realizing the economic potential of the Games and ensured that, when leaving aside wider infrastructural improvements, the Rome Olympics ran at a profit.

Tokyo 1964 followed Rome's example by embarking on major redevelopment projects before the Games, merging the specific proposals for the Olympics into the city's 10-year development plan. Aiming to cater for Tokyo's infrastructural needs up to the year 2000, the combined works cost $2.7 billion and included housing, hotel developments, harbour improvements, a monorail system, water supply, sewage disposal and a public health programme (Essex and Chalkley, 1998, p. 195). The city had 30 Olympic sites, with 13 major facilities concentrated into three districts: the Meiji Olympic Park, which contained the Olympic Stadium; the Yoyogi Sports Centre, which housed the swimming competitions; and the

Komazawa Sports Park. Accommodating participants in six Olympic Villages ensured, at least in principle, that competitors and officials had no more than a 40-minute journey to reach their venues (Organizing Committee, 1964, p. 114). Hoteliers received grants to remodel their premises for Western tourists, with a further 1,600 visitors lodged on ships in Tokyo harbour. Importantly, Tokyo saw the introduction of an approach concerned with the 'look' of a city during the period of the Olympic festival. This represented more than the old approach of simply decking the city in flags, but instead saw conscious attempts to unify the disparate sporting and Olympic infrastructure into a cohesive whole through design of signage, dressing the venues and decorating the streets. As a result of an open competition, the Japanese designer Yusaku Kamekura won a contract to provide visually consistent designs for all the ephemeral elements of the Games – symbols, signs, pamphlets, posters, tickets, decorations and even the colour scheme used for the city and at Olympic venues (Yew, 1996, p. 176).

The 1968 Games in Mexico City saw Latin America, and more specifically a developing nation, host the Olympics for the first time. Set against a background of political tension and sports boycotts, the Olympics stretched Mexico's resources and contributed to domestic unrest in the months leading up to the Games. The organizers' approach was to use existing sports facilities and blend them with new venues by means of a common 'look', in the manner pioneered by Tokyo, to supply a sense of visual unity (see chapter 11 for details). Despite troubled beginnings, the Mexico City Games finished with a favourable balance sheet. Costing $175 million, much of which was expended on facilities with a lifespan that extended well beyond the festival, the Olympics were considered to have covered their costs. For some observers, the 1968 Games represented an important moment of achievement and harmony for the Mexican nation that fully justified the cost (e.g. Arbena, 1996), but others argued that money diverted into the Olympics had exacerbated the divide between Mexico City's rich and poor. Before the Games, for example, the city chose to transfer $200 million from the social services budget to city improvement projects in an elaborate urban and national re-imaging campaign. Not only did this have a detrimental long-term impact on the city's provision for the poor; it also prompted protest demonstrations that left no less than 325 dead (Lenskyj, 2000, pp. 109–110).

The ability of the Olympics to polarize opinion would escalate steadily over the next decade. In their different ways, Munich 1972 and Montreal 1976 created crises for the Olympic movement: the former due to problems over security and the latter finance. Initial planning for both events, however, proceeded unproblematically with an upbeat view that emphasized the Olympics' apparently risk-free character; seemingly guaranteeing host cities advantageous international attention and endless prospects for undertaking urban development. Partly because of this mood, the 1970s Games were lavish affairs, with huge expenditure on iconic facilities and distinctive urban quarters.

The return of the Olympics to Germany in 1972 inevitably raised the spectre of 1936. The powerful militaristic and nationalist images still associated with that Olympics encouraged the Munich organizers to stage a 'Carefree Games' (Organizing Committee, 1972, p. 28). Their bid to the IOC emphasized Munich's claim to embrace international and modern cultures; a rich hearth of 'the arts and Muses' that offered four orchestras, 23 museums, 17 theatres, and an artistic tradition that embraced global as well as local and national scales (*Ibid.*, pp. 24, 28). At the same time, Munich in the early 1970s was in the throes of rapid economic and demographic growth, with severe pressures on services and physical infrastructure. Preparation for the Games, therefore, also addressed the host city's broader planning goals, fitting Olympic developments alongside schemes designed to restore and pedestrianize Munich's historic centre, to improve and extend public transport, construct 145 miles (233 kilometres) of expressways, provide underground parking, and build new retail and hotel accommodation (Essex and Chalkley, 1998, p. 195).

The location for the new Olympic Park in the north of the city was a derelict area long earmarked for redevelopment. Originally flat, its surface was bulldozed into a gently rolling landscape, with a hill created from wartime rubble and a small lake formed by damming the Nymphenburg Canal. The organizers then placed the athletes' warm-up facilities, the swimming pool, many smaller sports venues, restaurants, a theatre, the Olympic Village, press centre and stadium around the lake. The 80,000-seater Olympic stadium was an innovative tent-roofed structure designed by Gunter Behnisch and Frei Otto. The Olympic Village, which housed 10,000 athletes, was designed for conversion into a 'self-sustaining' community for single people and middle- and lower-income families – groups who found it difficult to find accommodation in the city (Essex and Chalkley, 1998, p. 195; Organizing Committee, 1972, p. 125). Trams, an underground rail line and a rapid transit provided physical links between the complex and the city centre. Symbolic links were added by attention to the 'look' of the city. Coordinated by a German designer Otl Aicher, the city adopted a holistic design policy towards decorations for the city, venues and orientation of visitors. Besides choosing colours felt to resonate with Olympic values, the dominant colour of blue was chosen to symbolize peace with the 'aggressive' colour red deliberately avoided (Organizing Committee, 1972, p. 269; Yew, 1996, p. 213).

Viewed in organizational and financial terms, the Twentieth Summer Games were critically regarded as a success. They generated a working profit, with marketing and television rights producing over $12 million for the IOC and international federations. Munich and Bavaria gained lasting publicity benefit (Brichford, 1996, p. 151). Other aspects of their legacy proved more difficult. Despite the efforts to promote the 'carefree' theme, Munich 1972 brought the Olympics face-to-face with the realities of security. The massacre of the Israeli athletes and officials on 5 September effectively destroyed the Organizing Committee's attempts to stage a light-hearted, non-nationalistic Olympics. It also ensured that future host cities faced a bill for security measures of a wholly different order, recognizing the Olympics' new, and unwanted, status as a prime target for international terrorism (see chapter 9).

The ensuing Games were a landmark in Olympic history for being ill-conceived and poorly planned. Although intended as a 'modest Games', Montreal 1976 produced a final shortfall of $1.2 billion, primarily caused by cost overruns on over-ambitious buildings. Admittedly, the times were not propitious. The Games took place against a background of severe world recession and inflation that profoundly affected costings, especially those concerning the surfeit of transport infrastructural projects associated with the Olympics. Nevertheless, as chapter 11 makes clear, a large measure of the blame rested with the counterproductive machinations of the political regime led by Jean Drapeau and the flawed design of the Olympic complex, particularly the stadium. The organizers ditched the notion of providing an orthodox open-air Olympic stadium in favour of a design that might be used all-year round. As the Olympic movement would not countenance a covered stadium for athletics, it was decided to build a new stadium with a retractable roof – understandably at much greater cost (Killanin, 1983, p. 123). The

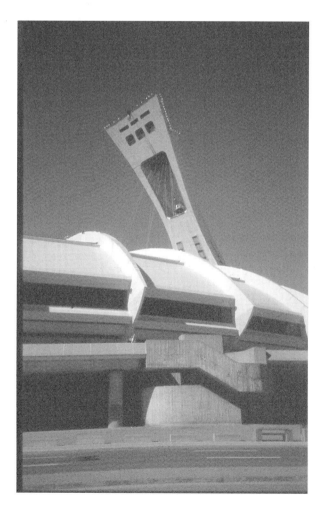

Figure 2.7. Olympic stadium, Montreal 1976 (architect Roger Taillibert).

chosen design by the French architect Roger Taillibert, architect of the critically acclaimed Parc des Princes in Paris, exacerbated the problems by embracing an unmistakeable monumentality. Most notably, it featured an innovative system for opening and closing the roof involving a 575 foot (190 metre) tower, inclined at 45 degrees, which supported the roof on 26 steel cables (figure 2.7). This radical conception produced problems that plagued construction. In fact, the infamous roof was not completed until 1987 and quickly became unusable. It was an episode that led, in the fullness of time, to a stadium with an impressive observation tower and a non-retractable roof.

Other buildings produced their share of problems. Difficulties with subsoil meant the velodrome needed new foundations to support its roof (Organizing Committee, 1976, pp. 16–17). The adjacent Olympic Village lodged participants in four architecturally innovative ziggurat structures, around 19 storeys high at their tallest points, which proved difficult to service. Among the infrastructural investment projects was the remote, expensive and unnecessary international airport at Mirabel, which closed three decades later without achieving any useful function. In addition, labour problems caused the loss of 155 working days in the 18 months leading up to the Games. Lack of proper operational planning and failure to sequence the construction process led to delays and bottlenecks. Round the clock working was introduced at great expense to meet the Games deadline, but it still proved impossible to complete all the facilities. In May 1976, emergency work began to erect temporary installations for several sports rather than continue with the intended venues. It all contributed to an event that inevitably presented a 'kaleidoscope of contradictory narratives and outcomes' (Kidd, 1996, p. 153).

Ideological Games (1980–1984)

1980 and 1984 were essentially rival Olympics, staged by two superpowers to show the superiority of their ideological systems, but which left less mark on their host cities than the Games of the previous two decades. Moscow and Los Angeles were the only candidates for the 1980 games and, after the withdrawal of a half-hearted bid from Teheran, Los Angeles was the sole formal bidder for 1984. With an eye to the lessons of the Montreal Games, both sets of organizers made virtues out of economy and pragmatism. The Organizing Committee for the Moscow Games made much of rejecting the recent trend towards gigantism, leaving behind expensively maintained and underused sports facilities. Rather they 'sought efficiency', building only 'essential' installations that would 'not remain monuments to vanity' but would be 'in constant use for the benefit of the Soviet People' (Organizing Committee, 1980, p. 43). They therefore planned to use Moscow's existing sports facilities wherever possible, employing temporary grandstands and ensuring that any new structures would be designed as multi-purpose venues. The main ceremonies and the track and field competitions, for example, centred on the renovated Lenin Stadium (built originally in 1956).

Given the nature of the command economy, the authorities subsumed preparations for the Olympics into the city's planning strategy (the General Plan for the Development of Moscow 1971–1990) and the state's tenth Five-Year Plan of Economic and Social Development. The former adopted decentralist principles, dividing Moscow into eight functional zones, each with a population of between 600,000 and 1.2 million and their 'town public centres' and subsidiary centres, to achieve a 'balance between labour resources and employment opportunities' (Lappo *et al.*, 1976, pp. 138–140). The Olympics provided the opportunity to improve access to sporting, cultural and entertainment facilities for those living within these zones by designing new venues for use once the Games were over (Promyslov, 1980, p. 230). The main Olympic facilities were distributed into six main areas, with the Village in a seventh. Located in the south west of the city, the Village comprised 18 blocks, each 16 storeys high, arranged in groups of three with associated communal catering facilities, entertainment, shopping and training facilities. After the Games, the Village would become a self-contained neighbourhood complete with cultural and sporting facilities (*Ibid.*, pp. 245–246). This dispersal posed logistic problems, but there was little need for new road construction given the low levels of private car ownership at this time. Infrastructural improvement was primarily confined to building new media centres and renovating the city's three airports, with a new international air terminal added to Sheremetyevo International Airport. The authorities also renovated historic buildings (especially churches), planted trees, and commissioned new hotels, cafés and restaurants. In a distant echo of Berlin 1936, Moscow was unusually free of banners expressing party slogans, posters and even the Intourist guides desisted from propaganda during the Games.[16]

Notwithstanding the rhetoric of virtuous utilitarianism, the regime could not resist the urge to display Soviet technological expertise in designing large structures. This contributed to the organizers commissioning the world's largest indoor arena in north Moscow for the basketball and boxing competitions. Capable of seating up to 45,000 spectators, it could be used either as a single space or divided into two separate auditoria, allowing it to serve as a multipurpose space for sports, political and cultural events after the Games (Promyslov, 1980, pp. 236–237).

Yet the most significant manifestation of Cold War ideological conflict stemmed from the US-led boycott, staged as part of a package of measures taken in response to the Soviet intervention in Afghanistan. This reduced participation to 80 competing nations from 121 at Munich and even 92 at boycott-hit Montreal, with many other nations sending weakened teams. Not surprisingly, a Soviet-led boycott of the subsequent Los Angeles Games, ostensibly over the security of athletes and officials, saw 14 socialist countries miss the Los Angeles Games in 1984.

Like Moscow, Los Angeles sought economy in staging the Games, with the organizers' commitment to funding the Games without the public funds available in the USSR resulting in an event that added fine-tuned commercialism to cost-consciousness. This meant using volunteers wherever possible and making maximum use of existing facilities. The Los Angeles Memorial Coliseum was refurbished as the Olympic stadium, with just four new venues required – for rowing, cycling, swimming and shooting. Each attracted high levels of sponsorship. The McDonald's Swim Stadium, for example, was built in Olympic Park for the University of Southern California. The Southland Corporation, parent company of the 7-11 chain of convenience stores, funded the velodrome on the California State University site. Fuji Film sponsored the shooting range. The three Olympic Villages used sites on university campuses (University College at Los Angeles, University of Southern California and the University of California at Santa Barbara), with the accommodation later available for students (Burbank *et al.*, 2001, pp. 76–77). This emphasis on named sponsorship and private finance introduced a measure of commercialism that the Olympic movement then felt powerless to resist. Rather more serious perhaps was the lack of intimacy caused by using existing facilities scattered around the sprawling, car-based Los Angeles city region rather than creating a nucleated Olympic Park. Some effort to create a sense of place came from decking the city in standardized colours to create a 'festive federalism' (Yew, 1996, p. 288), although it was recognized that only so much could be achieved by design.

Where Los Angeles 1984 scored most heavily was its success in changing ideas about Olympic finance. Los Angeles's commercial approach dramatically altered the prospects for other prospective host cities. The Games made a profit of $225 million that was channelled into American sports bodies and programmes. Local universities gained major new facilities. The event injected an estimated $2.4 billion into the Southern Californian economy.[17] After the events of the 1970s, the act of being host to the Olympics was fully restored as the pinnacle of ambition for cities with global aspirations.

Shifting Horizons (1988–1996)

Seoul's decision to seek the 1988 Games was less inspired by that logic – which had yet to re-emerge when the city gained the nomination in 1981 – than by the success of Tokyo 1964, which the Koreans believed had altered perceptions of the Japanese and helped Japan join the ranks of the developed world in the cultural, social, diplomatic and economic fields. The Games would provide a positive context for international scrutiny, show the economic transformation and political progress within Korea, and establish dialogue with Communist and non-aligned nations. It also provided an opportunity to regenerate Seoul. The South Korean capital faced severe environmental, economic and demographic problems for which staging the Olympics seemed to offer a means to short-circuit the process of replanning and reconstruction.

The organizers concentrated the Olympic facilities in the Seoul Sports Complex, built in the Chamshil area on the south bank of the Han River around 13 kilometres south of central Seoul, with another six venues at the Olympic Park, just over 3.5 kilometres to the east. The South Korean government had originally commissioned the Seoul Sports Complex in 1977, when the country lacked the facilities even to host the Asian Games. The 59 hectare site contained a major stadium, which became the 100,000 capacity Olympic stadium, as well as a 50,000-seater venue for the exhibition sport of baseball. The complex was linked to the Olympic Expressway, which connected the airport with Seoul's downtown. The Olympic Park provided the venues for the cycling, weightlifting, fencing, tennis, gymnastics and swimming events. The Olympic Village comprised blocks of flats of various heights (6–24 storeys) clustered in groups around common open spaces. In total 5,540 units were built, which were sold after the Games as private housing for upper middle-income families (Kim and Choe, 1997, pp. 197–198). During the construction of the Park, the discovery of the earthen walls of a fortress from the Baekje Kingdom (18 BC–660 AD) led to the designation of a historic park within the masterplan (*Ibid.*, p. 208).

Beyond the Olympic Park, the authorities conducted a programme of repairing historic monuments, including palaces and shrines, tree planting, and improvements to streets, drainage and power supply. Two new urban motorways linked the airport to the Olympic sites and improved east–west traffic flows in the city. The authorities built new Metro lines and expanded the airport. Seoul's planners instigated the Han River Development Project, which combined anti-flood measures, water treatment for the heavily polluted river, habitat regeneration and the creation of a series of recreational areas. Temporary measures that applied for the duration of the Games included encouraging dust-producing firms along the marathon route and around Olympic venues to switch to shorter working hours or night-time operation, and advising public bath houses to take holidays on days of key events.

The strategies chosen to improve the city's built environment and infrastructure, however, drew international criticism for paying greater attention to urban form than social cost. Ideas of improvement centred on the removal of slums and the creation of modernistic, often high-rise, developments for high-income residential or commercial use. Traditional walking-scale urban forms (*hanoks*), built at high density with narrow streets and passageways, were bulldozed for commercial redevelopment. Laws covering preservation and conservation were not introduced until 1983 and, even then, only the oldest historic buildings with connections to the Yi dynasty benefited. Clearance continued in areas without that historic cachet (Kim and Choe, 1997, pp. 209, 212).

Barcelona 1992 would take the regeneration theme further and supply a model that is a benchmark for prospective Olympic cities. The Games took place against a political background of brief-lived optimism about the world order and had no significant security problems. In conditions that allowed the potential of the Olympics to act as a vehicle for urban development to shine through, Barcelona launched a challenging package of regenerative measures that countered years of neglect under the Franco regime (Maloney, 1996, p. 192). This was not an entirely new strategy, since the city had used earlier international festivals to address urban planning goals. The 1888 Universal Exhibition in the Parc de la Ciutadella to the east of the old medieval centre and the International Exhibition of 1929 on Montjuic to the west, for example, had both resulted in urban improvements and enhanced the city's cultural institutions, open space and transport (Hughes, 1996; see also chapter 13).

The Olympics were seen in a similar light. Barcelona had previously bid to host the Games for 1924, 1936 and 1972. Selected at the IOC meeting in 1986 over Paris, the only other credible candidate, Barcelona's bid claimed that 88 per cent of the necessary facilities for the Games *per se* were already 'available'.[18] The Olympic Stadium was an updated and renovated version of that used for the 1929 International Exhibition. Ten other venues came from refurbishments to existing facilities, with 43 other facilities used very much in their existing state (Essex and Chalkley, 1998, p. 198). The promoters emphasized that only 15 new venues would be required. Altogether, less than 20 per cent of the total expenditure for the 1992 Games went on sports facilities (Varley, 1992, p. 21), with the lion's share of the investment devoted instead to urban improvements. Barcelona's planners concentrated the Olympic facilities in four areas located in a ring around the city, roughly where the outer limits of the nineteenth-century city met the less structured developments of the second half of the twentieth century. These were: the Vall d'Hebron in the north (cycling, archery, and accommodation for journalists); the Diagonal (football, polo and tennis); the Montjuic (the major Olympic site including the 60,000-seater stadium, the Sant Jordi Sports Palace, and the swimming and diving pools); and Parc de Mar, which housed the Olympic Village (figure 2.8). Large-scale investment in the city's transport systems,

Figure 2.8. The Olympic Village for Barcelona 1992. Many of the 15,000 participants were housed in the two tower blocks, which were intended for conversion after the Games to a hotel and offices.

substantially stimulated by the Olympics, served to link sites together. The Metro system was extended, the coastal railway rerouted, the airport redesigned and expanded, and the telecommunications systems modernized.

Barcelona codified the changing nature of the criteria by which to judge whether or not a Summer Games had been a success. The spectacle of the Games delighted the Olympic movement and television audiences were captivated by images from the outdoor pool, showing divers performing against the panoramic backdrop of the city beyond. Economically, the Olympics *per se* performed less well. Cost overruns ate into the projected $350 million surplus such that the Games barely broke even (a mere $3.8 million surplus). The innovative Sant Jordi Sports Palace, for example, may have supplied stunning architecture but cost $89 million rather than the estimated $30 million. Construction costs on the ring road were 50 per cent more than the estimated $1 billion. The cultural Olympiad also spawned heavy losses, despite trading on Barcelona's rich heritage in the arts and architecture (Hargreaves, 2000, p. 106).[19] Inflation and adverse movements in foreign currency rates also severely increased costs. Unemployment rose by 3 per cent in the city immediately after the Olympics, prices soared and business taxes rose 30 per cent (Maloney, 1996, p. 193). Nevertheless, critical opinion remained highly positive with regard to the wider regenerative impact on Barcelona. The city had deployed the Games as part of a conscious long-term development strategy that existed before obtaining the nomination to stage the Olympics and continued afterwards. It represented a major transformation in the fortunes of Olympic cities just 16 years after the debacle of Montreal.

Atlanta 1996, by contrast, would renew questions about staging the Games, particularly regarding commercialism. Unusually for Olympic practice, a private consortium undertook the organization, with heavy representation of and deference to business interests. Funding came from sponsorship, broadcasting rights and merchandizing which, when combined with ticket sales, raised $1.72 billion (Burbank *et al.*, 2001, p. 94). In addition, the Federal government expended nearly $1 billion on infrastructure, housing, safety and security, with smaller amounts spent by the state of Georgia and the city (*Ibid.*, p. 116). Most of the spending on the Games and on infrastructure took place in central Atlanta's 'Olympic Ring' – an area around 3 miles (5 kilometres) in radius that contained 16 of the 25 Olympic facilities and most of the urban improvements. The Atlanta Committee for the Olympic Games (ACOG) made use of existing facilities such as the Georgia Dome and Omni Arena, coupled with facilities at Atlanta's universities. The Georgia Institute of Technology, for example, provided sites for the Olympic Village, a new aquatic centre (swimming, diving and water polo) and boxing. ACOG commissioned a new but temporary Olympic Stadium in the Summerhill district in the south of the Olympic Ring. This was tied in with a longer-term plan to develop baseball in the city. The Olympic Stadium was located next to the Atlanta Fulton County Stadium, which was used for the baseball competition. Built to seat 85,000 spectators, the Olympic Stadium was scheduled for partial demolition after the Games to create a new 47,000-seater stadium (Turner Field) for the Atlanta Braves, with the Fulton County Stadium demolished to provide parking space (Larson and Staley, 1998, p. 281). Neighbourhoods near Olympic sites experienced beautification, with projects designed to improve central city streets and upgrade 12 pedestrian corridors that linked the venues. This work included widening pavements, burying power-lines, installing new street furniture, tree planting, history panels, signage, and the redesign of five parks and plazas.

Atlanta disappointed those who looked for more from the Games that marked the centenary of the modern Olympics. The conduct of the Games and the quality of ceremonial content led Tomlinson (1999, p. 69) to describe it as 'an elongated event of tattiness and tawdriness'. Concentrating so many facilities at the centre of the city placed pressure on the transport systems. Traffic congestion, slow journey times, and long queues to use the shuttle buses added to the difficulties for athletes, officials and spectators reaching venues (Larson and Staley, 1998, p. 278). The organizers' claims that Olympic sites were within walking distance of one another proved meaningless given the excessive summer temperatures. The repeated systems failures of the results service, the arrogance of officials, poor relations with the press, the large numbers of unauthorized street vendors, aggressive sponsorship and rampant commercialism undermined Atlanta's desire to stage a modern and efficient event. The city's policy towards regenerating two areas close to the Olympic sites encountered particular condemnation. One, the Techwood

Figure 2.9. Centennial Park, Atlanta 1996. The photograph shows the creation of a new public open space in the heart of the downtown area.

and Clark Howell public housing district to the south of the Georgia Institute of Technology, was demolished and replaced by a mixed gated community, effectively replacing poorer tenants with more affluent residents. The other, a rundown housing and industrial area near the Georgia World Congress Centre (GWCC), was cleared to create Centennial Park as an area where visitors and spectators could congregate during the Games and where entertainment could be provided (figure 2.9). Clearance here and in nearby Woodruffe Park removed more than 16,500 of Atlanta's poorest inhabitants to make way for the stadium. The additional loss of a hostel and three shelters displaced around 10 per cent of Atlanta's homeless (Burbank et al., 2001, p. 112). Aggressive use of city ordinances that criminalized anti-social behaviour and measures to remove the homeless physically evicted 'undesirables' from the vicinity of the Games (Lenskyj, 2000, pp. 138–139).

The passage of time has eroded the force of some of these criticisms. For example, Atlanta's policy towards the stadium fully acknowledged the realities of post-Games use and spared the city being saddled with expensive and underused venues, as was subsequently the case with Sydney and Athens. The central area was remodelled and Centennial Park stands as a memorial to the Games. The Olympics raised Atlanta's profile as a sporting venue, even if it failed to enhance its broader image as a cultural centre. Nonetheless, the distaste for commercialism persisted, with the IOC stating that the Games would never again be entrusted to an entirely privately-run organization (Whitelegg, 2000, p. 814). Even a century after the revival of the modern Olympics, the formula for staging a successful event remained downright elusive.

Towards Sustainability

Although chosen as Australian nominee for candidate city in March 1991, Sydney's bid for the Olympics had actually been in gestation since the late 1960s (see chapter 14). The city drafted feasibility plans for both the 1972 and 1988 Games, with the latter envisaging an Olympic Park at Homebush Bay, approximately 9 miles (14 kilometres) upstream from Sydney's city centre. Originally tidal wetlands and scrub, Homebush Bay at different times had housed Sydney's racecourse, a saltworks, the country's largest abattoir, the state brickworks and a naval munitions store. In the 1930s, the bay had regularly spawned algal blooms through contamination from waste products from the slaughterhouses and from depositing household and industrial waste in landfill sites. Work had begun in the 1980s to clean up and redevelop the area, but a successful Olympic bid would help regenerate the remainder of the site, tackle its severe environmental problems, supply the city with a replacement for the Royal Agricultural Society's outmoded Showground at Moore Park, and provide a cluster of modern world-class sports facilities. Any bid would involve the state and federal governments as funding agencies and as the owners of the land, as well as the city of Sydney.

Sydney gained the nomination for the 2000 Games in September 1993 against competition from Beijing, Manchester, Berlin and Istanbul, with a key element in its candidacy being the promise to concentrate the Olympic venues in one central park, which would eventually have a built core surrounded by parkland. The main Olympic venue, named Stadium Australia, was built using public funds, sponsorship and sale of corporate packages. Designed to hold 110,000 spectators during the Games, its capacity would be reduced to 80,000 for its subsequent life as a rugby and Australian Rules football stadium. The other major stadia at Homebush were the Hockey Centre, Superdome (basketball and artistic gymnastics), International Athletics Centre (warm-up facilities), Tennis Centre, the Aquatic Centre (swimming and diving) and the Archery Park. The adjacent Olympic Village would accommodate all participants at a single centre for the first time. It comprised a mixed development of apartments and town houses, arranged into three precincts and designed to ecologically sustainable guidelines. Provision of a school and commercial precinct looked ahead to the area's post-Games future as a residential suburb of Sydney. The other Olympic facilities, particularly those associated with rowing and sailing, were located within the Sydney city-region at a maximum distance of 60 miles (100 kilometres) from Homebush Bay.

Planning for the Games embraced different agendas. First, responding to the growing mood of environmentalism the bid claimed these would be a 'Green Games' expressing environmental responsibility in use of resources and design of facilities. Secondly, the Sydney Games were a national project, celebrating the 'entire continent of Australia' rather than just the host city: a strategy also adopted at Melbourne 1956. Thirdly, capturing the Games would allow the organizers to highlight the profound changes that had taken place in the 44 years since Melbourne. As noted in chapter 1, the need to recognize the multicultural identity of Australia placed requirements on the framing of the programme, especially those sections relating to the Cultural Olympiad and ceremonial aspects.

One indicator of the IOC's sense of relief at the success of the resulting Games came with the IOC President Juan Antonio Samaranch, resurrecting the statement that 'these have been the best Games ever', a description that he had pointedly omitted at the Closing Ceremony of Atlanta 1996. An early study of impact by the Australian Tourist Commission revealed that 75 per cent of the Americans surveyed had seen pictures and stories concerning Australia as a holiday destination as part of the Olympic coverage and half reported that they were more interested in Australia as a destination (Morse, 2001, p. 102). Locally, the Games passed off well. Potential demonstrations about homelessness, the plight of Aborigines, ticketing, and the claimed misuse of public funds did not occur. An economic analysis (Haynes, 2001) argued that the total cost of the Games at A$6.5 billion was roughly neutral in that it was covered by an equivalent amount in extra economic activity in Australia between 1994–1995 and 2005–2006, of which A$5.1 billion would accrue in New South Wales. For this price, Sydney had achieved the regeneration of a severely blighted industrial region, gained significant improvements to infrastructure, improved its tourist standing, and gained world-class sport facilities. For the

Olympic movement, it again showed the value of a festival largely held at a central venue rather than the dispersal of Atlanta.

With the passage of years, however, second thoughts began to appear. Questions are asked about the nature of the cultural legacy (see chapter 14). Environmentalists have continued to question whether the decontamination of the toxic waste site had been fully tackled (Berlin, 2003). The main problems, however, concern the stadia. There are relatively few events that require a venue of Olympic proportions and other modern stadia in Sydney operating before the Games were perfectly capable of handling almost all of them (Searle, 2002, p. 857). Stadium Australia, latterly the Telstra stadium, operated consistently at a loss from the moment that it was handed over for post-Games use. In November 2006, the group running the stadium defaulted on its debts and was taken over by its bankers (Askew, 2006).

Similar types of problem cloud the legacy of Athens 2004, although any Games involving Greece inevitably involved circumstances unique to that country. As chapter 15 shows, the reconstruction of Athens and the return of the Olympics were parallel themes in the consciousness of the Greek people during the nineteenth century and continued to have resonances in the late twentieth century. The city's successful bid in 1997 for the 2004 Olympics claimed that most of the competition venues and almost all the training venues were already in place, with the makings of an Olympic Stadium and Park in the complex already constructed for the 1982 European Athletics Championships. The subsequent decision to revisit the plans and make drastic alterations, in particular exchanging the nucleated Olympic centres for a more dispersed approach, undermined the timetable to the point where completion on time hung in the balance.

The immediate impact of the Games was a profound psychological lift for the country and agreement that tourism had benefited from transformation of the city centre, the creation of an Archaeological Park in Athens, and investment in the city's hotels, cultural sector and public transport. Yet, as with Sydney, wider questions about *sustainability* quickly surfaced. In the narrower sense, critics focused on the way in which the environmental guidelines for the Olympics were, at best, perfunctorily observed. In the more general sense of sustainable development, profound doubts surround the potential use of the Olympic facilities. Despite its architecturally sophisticated buildings being intended as a symbol of the new Athens, the Olympic Sports Complex at Maroussi remains heavily underused and off limits to the public except when soccer matches are held at the stadium. The Faliro and Helleniki complexes have also struggled to find alternative uses. All continue to lose money as borrowing and maintenance costs have still to be met. The evidence suggests that pre-Games plans for post-Games use of Olympic facilities contained a strong dose of wish fulfilment. Presented with this evidence, the questions of how to turn the lavish and large-scale facilities required for the Summer Olympics into sustainable legacy for the host city now preoccupy planners of future Olympics almost as much as issues linked to the preparation of the Games themselves.

Notes

1 Spoken by Prince George, later Duke of Clarence, in William Shakespeare (1593) *Henry VI*, Part 3, Act II, Scene III, lines 52–56.

2 Although there was a nearby village called Andilalo – the name means 'village of the echo' – it is just as possible that the name simply relates to the spot where the remarkable reverberating echo found at Olympia occurs (see Leake, 1830, vol. 1, p. 31).

3 The event was mentioned in a letter dated 30 April 1679, written by Colonel Edward Cooke in London and addressed to the Duke of Ormond, Viceroy of Ireland, in Dublin. *Source: Notes and Queries*, Tenth Series, X (22 August 1908), p. 147.

4 Baron Pierre de Coubertin (1863-1937), a French educational reformer, was the key figure behind the movement that founded the IOC (see note 6).

5 This came at the end of a speech made at a Jubilee event to celebrate the fifth anniversary of the founding the Union of French Sports Associations.

6 At the outset, the IOC was a small, conservative and entirely male-dominated body, heavily under the sway of Coubertin, comprising prominent sportsmen and titled individuals whose social status might lend weight to the embryonic organization. The first committee comprised 15 members from 12 countries. By 1904, this had increased to 32 members, of whom 17 had aristocratic or civil titles (eight counts, three barons, two princes, a knight, a professor, a general and a bishop). To Coubertin, that social background seemed to suggest people whose impeccable background and private means would insure their impartiality. To later commentators, it would provide the recipe for cronyism and an unrepresentative self-perpetuating oligarchy (e.g. Simson and Jennings, 1992; Lenskyj, 2000).

7 The marathon made connection with ancient legend, with the story of the runner who brought news of the Greek victory over the Persians from Marathon to Athens in 490 BC. In reality, however, the race had no parallel in ancient Greek practice, where races rarely exceeded 5 kilometres.

8 Athletes returning from the Athens Games established the Boston Marathon the following year (Lovett, 1997, p. xii).

9 Mallon (1998, p. 5) points out that Coubertin had previously suggested a recreation of Olympia for the 1889 Universal Exposition in Paris, with some sporting events.

10 There may well have been an element of pretext here: it is now suggested that the Italians were preparing to withdraw from the Games before the eruption occurred (Mallon and Buchanan, 2000, p. xxxvii).

11 With a population in 1900 of 300,624 compared with Greater London's 1901 figure of 6.5 million.

12 Named after General John Pershing, the Commander-in-Chief of the American Expeditionary Force, the Pershing stadium was built by the Americans on land donated by the French.

13 This prefabricated encampment was for male athletes. Female athletes were housed in the Chapman Park Hotel as it was thought they required a rather more permanent type of residence (TOC, 1933, p. 292).

14 It was suggested, for example, that ancient Greece was partly settled by early Germanic migrants during the Neolithic period (Arnold, 1992, p. 32).

15 The Games of the twelfth and thirteenth Olympiads were not celebrated because of the war.

16 M. Binyon, 'The way the Games were won', *The Times*, 4 August 1980.

17 Although accusations of commercial excesses galvanized the IOC into taking control of sponsorship through TOP (The Olympic Programme). For all the disdain of commercialism, the IOC now found itself in the position of inviting corporations to pay tens of millions of dollars to become worldwide Olympic sponsors.

18 *Financial Times*, 15 October 1986.

19 This was partly through facing the competing attractions of Expo 92 in Seville and having Madrid as 1992 European City of Culture.

Chapter 3

The Winter Olympics: Driving Urban Change, 1924–2002

Stephen J. Essex and Brian S. Chalkley

The delay in establishing a separate Winter Olympic Games until 1924, almost 30 years after the revival of the Summer Games, reflected the fact that winter sports were not included in the original conception of the Olympics. Pierre de Coubertin objected to their inclusion partly because of Scandinavian fears that to do so would have possible detrimental effects on their traditional sports festivals, such as the Nordic Games and Holmenkollen Week.[1] However, as the popularity of winter sports spread, the movement to include them in the Olympic programme gathered pace. Some of the early Summer Games included figure skating (London 1908, Antwerp 1920) and ice hockey (Antwerp 1920) in their programmes. In 1924, a separate winter sports week was held at Chamonix six months before the Summer Games in Paris. On the success of this winter sports week, the IOC amended its Charter in 1925 to establish the Winter Olympics, with Chamonix retrospectively designated as the first Winter Games. Until 1948, the country hosting the Summer Games also had the opportunity to stage the Winter Games. Thereafter, the selection of the host for the Winter Games was subject to a separate competition decided by a vote of IOC members, but the event was staged in the same year as the Summer Games. From 1992, further change occurred, with the Summer and Winter Games now held alternately every two years in order to maximize the profile of the Olympics and its television revenue (Borja, 1992).

Perhaps the clearest possible evidence that potential hosts now perceive major benefits to be derived from staging the event is seen in the remarkable growth in the number of candidates for the Winter Olympics (Essex and Chalkley, 1999). The total number of potential bids for the Winter Games rose considerably after 1992. Thirty-one locations expressed an interest in hosting the Winter Games of 2002, with 24 potential bids for the Games of 2010 and, well ahead of schedule, nine bids for the 2014 event. Indeed, it seems that some places are willing to go to any length, including unethical behaviour and discarding fair play, to secure the event.

Candidate cities have, in recent years, spent millions of dollars on entertainment and gifts to impress IOC members. These practices culminated in the serious bribery allegations over the decision to locate the Winter Games in Salt Lake City in December 1999. The Salt Lake Bid Committee, making their second bid and determined to secure the event, allegedly made payments to IOC members for holidays, medical treatment and members' children while at university or working in America, in return for support (Booth, 1999; Lenskyj, 2000; Toohey and Veal, 2000, p. 232). This controversy led to reforms in the selection process for all Olympic hosts as well as in the composition of the IOC.

This chapter reviews the role of the Winter Olympics in changing and modernizing the built environment of its hosts, together with a consideration of the changing organization and funding of the event over time. Certain features, of course, remain relatively fixed. The construction or refurbishment of sports facilities have been a constant requirement on hosts throughout the history of the Winter Games, albeit with different outcomes based on local circumstances. The range of sports facilities required for the event is normally standard, although the detailed specifications may change. The main sports venues for the Winter Olympics include a stadium, slopes for slalom and down-hill ski runs, cross-country ski-trails, bob-sled and luge runs, and an indoor ice arena. The scale of provision of associated infrastructure, such as the Olympic Village, Media Centre, hotels and transport, reflect the increasing popularity and interest in the event. The impact on host cities, however, involves greater degrees of change. In this respect, there are inevitable comparisons to draw with the Summer Games, which, as chapter 2 indicated, have witnessed the progression from the minor impact of the early Games to a more responsive, entrepreneurial and business-led approach to urban planning through Olympic-led development (see also Essex and Chalkley, 1998, 2002; Chalkley and Essex, 1999). The key questions addressed here are whether the Winter Olympics have had the same trajectory of development impacts on host centres and whether the role of the public sector in the planning and management of the event has contracted in deference to the emergence of more entrepreneurial approaches.

To answer these questions, this chapter draws on the Official Reports of the Organizing Committees to identify four phases in the development of the event and in the changing scale of impacts (Essex and Chalkley, 2004). These phases, respectively, are characterized as ones of minimal infrastructural transformations (1924–1932), emerging infrastructural demands (1936–1960), tool of regional development (1964–1980), and large-scale transformations (1984–present). While business interests have always been instrumental in galvanizing a desire to stage the Games throughout the period under consideration here, the public sector has traditionally organized and funded much of the infrastructural investment for the Winter Olympics, as well as accumulating the main debts. Moreover, although private sources of capital, such as television rights and sponsorship, have emerged since 1984, the public sector remains pivotal for the organization of the event.

Minimal Infrastructural Transformations, 1924–1932

The first three Winter Olympics (see table 3.1) were characterized by relatively low levels of interest and participation. The events were staged in settlements with populations of about 3,000, with less than 500 athletes competing in each of the Games. Nevertheless, the motivations of the hosts in staging the Games allude to some interest in the development prospects, especially given the emerging enthusiasm for winter sports tourism. Chamonix, in the Haute-Savoie department of eastern France, appears to have been volunteered as the host by the French Olympic Committee, which was no doubt cognisant of the need to have world-class facilities to develop winter sports. Similarly, the local Chamber of Commerce was not slow to recognize the economic advantages for the town created by the

Table 3.1. Winter Olympic Games, 1924–2006.

Games	Host city	Host nation	Other candidates
1924	Chamonix	France	–
1928	St. Moritz	Switerland	Davos, Engelberg, (Switzerland)
1932	Lake Placid	USA	Montreal (Canada), Bear Mountain, Yosemite Valley, Lake Tahoe, Duluth, Minneapolis, Denver (USA)
1936	Garmisch-Partenkirchen	Germany	St Moritz (Switzerland)
1948	St Moritz	Switzerland	Lake Placid (USA)
1952	Oslo	Norway	Cortina (Italy), Lake Placid (USA)
1956	Cortina	Italy	Colorado Springs, Lake Placid (USA), Montreal (Canada)
1960	Squaw Valley	USA	Innsbruck (Austria), St Moritz (Switzerland), Garmish-Partenkirchen (Germany)
1964	Innsbruck	Austria	Calgary (Canada), Lahti/Are, (Sweden)
1968	Grenoble	France	Calgary (Canada), Lahti/Are (Sweden), Sapporo (Japan), Oslo (Norway), Lake Placid (USA)
1972	Sapporo	Japan	Banff (Canada), Lahti/Are (Sweden), Salt Lake City (USA)
1976	Innsbruck	Austria	Denver (USA), Sion (Switzerland), Tampere/Are (Finland), Vancouver (Canada)
1980	Lake Placid	USA	Vancouver-Garibaldi (Canada): withdrew before final vote
1984	Sarajevo	Yugoslavia	Sapporo (Japan), Falun/Göteborg (Sweden)
1988	Calgary	Canada	Falun (Switzerland), Cortina (Italy)
1992	Albertville	France	Anchorage (USA), Berchtesgaden (Germany), Cortina (Italy), Lillehammer (Norway), Falun (Sweden), Sofia (Bulgaria)
1994	Lillehammer	Norway	Anchorage (USA), Öestersund/Are (Sweden), Sofia (Bulgaria)
1998	Nagano	Japan	Aoste (Italy), Jaca (Spain), Öestersund (Sweden), Salt Lake City (USA)
2002	Salt Lake City	USA	Öestersund (Sweden), Quebec City (Canada), Sion (Switzerland)
2006	Turin	Italy	Helsinki (Finland), Klagenfurt (Austria), Poprad-Tatry (Slovakia), Sion (Switzerland), Zakopane (Poland)

Source: Compiled by the editors from IOC (2007).

popular interest in the Games. Funding of the first Winter Olympics appears to have been shared equally between the public and private sectors. In 1928, the Games in St Moritz were led by the local authority and assisted the consolidation of the resort as an international winter sports destination.

Although the initial idea to stage the Winter Olympics in Lake Placid in 1932 came from the American Olympic Committee in 1927, it was the Lake Placid Club, which owned existing sports facilities in the area, that investigated the feasibility of the event. The decision to bid for the Games was only made after a representative of the Lake Placid Club had visited a number of European resorts and the St Moritz Olympics of 1928 to convince himself, on behalf of the community, that Lake Placid could match the highest standards abroad and secure longer-term benefits from the investments required. The Lake Placid Chamber of Commerce set up a guarantee fund of $50,000 to support the bid in July 1928, but it was New York State that provided the main funding for infrastructural requirements for the event. The involvement of New York State eased the concerns of some local residents about the magnitude and responsibility of the task (LPOOC, 1932, p. 43). The organization of the event was a partnership between New York State, Essex County Park Commission, North Elba Town Board, North Elba Park Committee and Lake Placid Village Board (*Ibid.*, p. 74). In 1932, the substantial funding from New York State led to the establishment of the New York State Olympic Winter Games Commission to ensure that the money was spent wisely (*Ibid.*, p. 60), which is a model that has been followed in other Games.

Many organizers of the early Winter Olympics were especially aware of the long-term viability of facilities when deciding whether to stage the Games, mainly because of the small size of the potential host settlements and their limited capacity to sustain expensive, high order facilities. The skeleton[2] was a good example. The eastern Swiss resort of St Moritz, which staged the 1928 Games was able to make use of the existing Cresta Run, first constructed in 1885, for the event. The organizers of the subsequent Games at Lake Placid 1932, however, questioned whether the cost ($25,000) of a similar facility could be justified.[3] Believing that such an outlay would bequeath the resort an expensive and unviable legacy, the event was eliminated from the programme at Lake Placid. The skeleton was only re-introduced seventy years later at Salt Lake City (Utah) in 2002.

In contrast to this prudence, the American organizers were criticized for the extravagance of building an indoor ice rink very late in the preparations. The plan was not supported by the State of New York because of the proposed costs ($375,000). The organizers were responding to a suggestion by the IOC President that such a facility would provide an alternative venue for events in the case of bad weather (which had so badly disrupted the St Moritz Games 1928) and would also be a tangible and physical memorial to the event. The required finance was eventually raised by forcing the hand of the town authorities. The site for the rink was already cleared and, with the prospect of a derelict site in the middle of town, the authorities were forced to fund the construction via a bond issue (Ortloff and

Ortloff, 1976, p. 77). According to the organizers, the indoor ice rink proved its worth by providing an alternative venue for events affected by the unseasonably warm weather and so prevented the programme from being disrupted (LPOOC, 1932, p. 154).

The construction of Olympic Villages or new hotels was certainly not justified in this phase because of fears of over-provision. Instead, existing accommodation within a wide geographical catchment area was used and, if necessary, 'winterised'. Hotel and cottage owners in the vicinity of Lake Placid were urged to 'winterise' their summer accommodations by the organizers of the Games of 1932 to house the expected 10,000 visitors. Eventually accommodation in Montreal, which was three and a half hours from Lake Placid, had to be used to cater for the demand (LPOOC, 1932, p. 112).

Despite its small scale, some Olympic-related developments that were proposed for early Winter Games could still raise environmental protests. In March 1930, a local action group (the Association for the Protection of the Adirondacks) brought a successful legal action against a proposed Olympic bobsled run for the Lake Placid Games on environmental grounds and because building on state land was unconstitutional. As a result, a less sensitive site was found at South Meadows Mountain, later renamed Mount Van Hoevenberg (*Ibid.*).

Emerging Infrastructural Demands (1936–1960)

The second phase bears many of the hallmarks of the first phase: host centres were generally small (less than 13,000 residents) and had been offered as hosts by a combination of National Olympic Committees, Sports Federations and local authorities. The funding of the infrastructural investment was predominantly public sector. The key difference was that, by 1936, there was substantial growth in the number of participating countries and athletes. Investment in Olympic-related infrastructure continued to be constrained by the same factors of long-term viability as in the first phase, but with the added pressures created by the temporary influx of larger numbers of competitors and spectators. Initial plans for an Olympic Village at Cortina d'Ampezzo in northern Italy for the Winter Games of 1956 were abandoned after opposition from local hoteliers who feared the effect of an increase in the town's accommodation capacity on their businesses (CONI, 1956, p. 267). The award of the 1960 Games to Squaw Valley, according to the organizers, had transformed a remote mountain valley into a 'throbbing city' (California Olympic Commission, 1960, p. 27). The development of the Olympic Village for Squaw Valley 1960 was out of scale with the small local community, but was considered necessary because of the number of athletes now requiring accommodation and that local hotel capacity was required for officials and journalists (Chappelet, 1997, p. 83). Yet, it was only a temporary construction as the town's small population (*c*.4,000) meant there was no viable post-Olympic use.

The main exception in this phase was the Norwegian capital Oslo, which hosted the Winter Olympics of 1952. With a resident population of 447,100, the city was by far the largest centre to have accommodated the Games. The larger population created new opportunities for the type of facilities provided, as the post-Olympic viability and future use was more assured. In the period before 1960, Oslo was also the only host to have built an Olympic Village, albeit it was dispersed in various locations around the city with planned post-Olympic uses such as student halls of residence, a hospital and an old people's home (Organisasjonskomiteen, 1952, pp. 23, 42). However, new infrastructural requirements were also created by the increased size of the hosts. For example, larger urban centres were often at some distance from competition sites. Large numbers of athletes and spectators had to be moved considerable distances to isolated locations in difficult terrains and within limited time-frames, sometimes compounded by adverse weather conditions. Investment in transport infrastructure, such as new roads, bridges and ski-lifts, became essential to the operation of the Oslo Games of 1952 and subsequent events.

Tool of Regional Development (1964–1980)

The third phase (1964–1980) is characterized by a number of definite shifts: an expansion of the number of athletes, an increase in the population of the host centres and the emergence of regional development and modernization as a key motivation for staging the Games. Four of the five hosts during this period had populations of more than 100,000, with one having more than one million. Only one, Lake Placid 1980, had a level of population similar to those of previous phases. Both private development companies and local authorities recognized the potential of the Winter Olympics for justifying major infrastructural investment as part of broader modernization programmes. Television revenue was also emerging as an important source of income during this phase, which began to shift the onus of the funding from the public sector to the private sector, although the local public sector remained central to the organization of the event. The Innsbruck Games of 1964 received $597,000 from television rights, while the Lake Placid Games of 1980 were able to command $15.5 million.

Partly because of their increased size, the Winter Olympics were recognized as a tool of regional development from the 1960s. The Innsbruck Winter Games of 1964 was used as a showcase for Austrian businesses, especially those related to ski equipment (Espy, 1979, p. 90). The modernization of the Isère Department was accelerated by the Grenoble Games of 1968 (Borja, 1992) and as a means of remodelling its planning system after a period of rapid growth (1946–1968) (COJO, 1968, p. 46). The Sapporo Games of 1972 were viewed by the Japanese government as a unique economic opportunity to invigorate the northern island of Hokkaido (Borja, 1992). Most of the spending was on investment in the urban infrastructure, with less than 5 per cent of capital improvements for these Games expended on sports facilities (Hall, 1992, p. 69).

With the choice of host centres with larger populations after 1960, the post-Games viability of a purpose-built Olympic Village became more assured, usually as a residential area of the host settlement or a student hall of residence for a local university or college. For example, the Olympic Village at Grenoble was built in a Priority Urbanization Zone and subsequently was used as an 800-room university hall, a 300-room hostel for young workers and a tower block with 52 apartments (COJO, 1968, p. 71). In Innsbruck, which staged the Games of 1964 and 1976, the organizers were forced to build an Olympic Village for each event. That built for the Winter Games of 1964 was not available for the Games of 1976 as it had become a residential suburb of the town in the interim. The new Olympic Village was built on an adjacent site. The 1976 organizers later reported that having to build a Village was, perhaps, rather extravagant, as not all athletes wished to stay there, some preferring to be closer to event sites. In retrospect, they felt that accommodating athletes in hotels might have been preferable from cost, security and transport perspectives (HOOWI, 1967, p. 400).

Olympic-related investment in transport infrastructure was often central to the regional development objectives. Road construction accounted for 20 per cent of the total investment for the Grenoble Games of 1968 in the French Alps (COJO, 1968, p. 46), and was designed to decentralize the region and facilitate economic growth. The investment included a motorway link from Grenoble to Geneva, which acted as a catalyst for the regional economy and transformed the host town into a major conference and university centre (Chappelet, 2002, p. 11). The city's old airport at Grenoble-Eybens was closed to make way for the Olympic Village and was replaced by two new airports at Saint-Etienne-de-Saint-Geoirs and Versoud (COJO, 1968, p. 290). For the Sapporo Winter Olympics in 1972, transport investments included extensions to two airports, improvements to the main railway station, 41 new or improved roads (213 kilometres) and the construction of a rapid transit system (45 kilometres). This last project had already been started by the City of Sapporo, but was completed for the Winter Games using government funding.

With the increasing scale of the Winter Olympics, the risks associated with staging the Games became greater. First, the changing scale of the event affected the character and operation of the Games. One of the consequences of the Winter Olympics being staged in larger cities and across whole regions was that the focus and impact of the event became dissipated. Critics claimed that the size and dispersed geography of the Games had detracted from the camaraderie of the event and increased problems of transport. Secondly, warnings about the long-term limitations of the event as a tool of regional development began with the debt accumulated by the organizers of the Grenoble Games, together with the abandonment or demolition of some of its venues. It was also during this third phase that the award of the Winter Olympics of 1976 to Denver had to be reassigned, which is the only time in Olympic history that this has happened (Olson, 1974). The reason was local concern about the rising cost of the event and about how the organizers, led by business interests, were ignoring environmental considerations. An action group, 'Citizens for Colorado's Future' was successful in placing the issue on the State and City ballots in November 1972. The citizens then had a vote on whether the Games should be staged using state funding. The turnout was high (93.8 per cent) and 60 per cent voted against the Olympics, which meant that both state and federal funding for the event would not be forthcoming. Denver was therefore forced to withdraw its candidacy for the Winter Games of 1976, which were staged in Innsbruck at short notice.

There was also growing consideration of environmental factors elsewhere, though in different ways. For the 1972 Sapporo Games, the only mountain close to the host city and suitable for downhill ski events was Mount Eniwa, within the Shikotsu-Toya National Park. The National Park Council gave permission on condition that all related facilities were removed and the terrain in the affected area restored to its original state. Whether this condition was realistic or merely a compromise favouring the Olympic development is debatable. A comparable instance concerned the 1980 Games at Lake Placid, where the town itself lay within Adirondack Park, designated in 1971 and regulated by Adirondack Park Agency. The park's public lands were directly administered by the State Department of Environmental Conservation, which also operated bob-sled and luge runs, the biathlon and cross-country trails and the Whiteface Mountain Ski area (LPOOC, 1980, p. 18). The extensions of the ski jumps, originally built for the 1932 Games, had to comply with standards set by the Adirondack Park Agency and the Federal Environment Agency (*Ibid.*, p. 38).

Large-Scale Transformations (1984–2002)

The fourth phase (1984 onwards) is characterized by the most significant increase in participation in the Winter Games. By 1994, the ratio of support staff to athletes was 6.5 times bigger than in 1956. Numbers of athletes were also growing, with 2,400 athletes at Salt Lake City in 2002. The accommodation of athletes, media and spectators became a substantial infrastructural challenge in itself. After 1988, two or more Olympic Villages have become necessary to accommodate athletes closer to their event venues. Separate villages for the media were also necessary. These demands have favoured centres with larger populations. Perhaps more significantly, television revenue rose from $91.5 million in 1984 to $545 million in 2002, with the additional revenue partly funding ever more large-scale and ambitious urban redevelopment.

These various changes began more obviously to favour placing the Games in host centres with larger populations. Since 1984, the Games have been staged in centres with an average population of about 370,000, although two of the seven hosts have been substantially larger and two smaller. The role of the Winter Games as a means to secure major urban infrastructural change and modernization has intensified. The Games staged in Sarajevo in 1984, therefore, were taken as an opportunity to modernize the city by the government. The motivation for both the Calgary Games in Canada (1988) and the Lillehammer Games (Norway) in 1994 was to act as a stimulus to revive the local economy (e.g. COWGOC, 1988, p. 5). At Calgary, the Organizing Committee moved some venues originally selected by the Calgary Olympic Development Association to make them more viable after the Games (*Ibid.*) and the Games also caused some facilities to be provided much earlier than would otherwise have occurred. For example, the construction of the Olympic Saddledome (20,000 seats, C$7 million), home for a professional ice hockey team established in 1980, was fast-tracked to show the city's commitment to its bid (Hiller, 1989, p. 124). Large investments required to stage the 1992 Albertville Games appear, however, to have made more difficulties for other northern French Alpine resorts seeking finance for restructuring (Tuppen, 2000, p. 330). This shows that Olympic investment has 'opportunity costs' which may postpone or eliminate other forms of investment.

Given these changing circumstances, smaller hosts in this phase faced problems in justifying investment in permanent purpose-built Olympic Villages. Albertville 1992, which had a population of only 20,000 at the time, renovated a small spa at Brides-les-Bains as the Olympic Village rather than constructing a purpose-built facility. However, the village proved to be too far from the sports facilities, so seven smaller Olympic Villages were established in existing hotel accommodation closer to the event sites. After this experience, the IOC stated that it favoured the use of a single Olympic Village in future Games in order to promote contact between athletes from different countries (Charmetant, 1997, p. 115). At Lillehammer 1994, which had a population of 23,000, a temporary Olympic Village consisting of 200 wooden chalets, was constructed. These examples were significant departures from the trajectory of large-scale infrastructural investment.

The increasing scale of the event has also necessitated more formal recognition of environmental issues in the planning and development of related infrastructure (May, 1995). The intrusion of built structures into fragile environments, as well as the use of chemicals to create the appropriate conditions, has become a major issue in the preparations for the Winter Olympics. Most notably, the preparations for the Lillehammer Games of 1994 incorporated, for the first time, the principles of sustainable development. The proposed location of one of the main indoor arenas was moved to protect a bird sanctuary, while its heat circulation operated from excess heat from its refrigeration unit. Contracts with suppliers and contractors included environmental clauses. The approach influenced the IOC to add an environmental commitment to its Charter and inspired Sydney, the host of the Summer Games of 2000, to incorporate sustainable development as a core theme in its preparations (see chapter 14). The candidates for the Winter Games of 2002 were the first to be required to describe their environmental plans in their bid documents (IOC, 1999, p. 5). These attempts to incorporate environmental sustainability into the planning of Olympic events have, however, received criticism from some quarters as essentially shallow public-relations exercises (Lenskyj, 2000).

Discussion and Conclusions

The infrastructural implications of staging the Winter Olympic Games have grown in line with the increasing participation and interest in the event. The average number of athletes participating in the Games has increased from 325 in the first phase to 1,823 in the fourth. Television rights for the event now command about $600 million. As a consequence, the size of host centres has also increased to accommodate the infrastructural demands: from an average resident population of 3,122 in Phase I to 277,667 in Phase IV. The event has begun to emulate the Summer Olympics in its ability to modernize and stimulate urban regeneration. Nevertheless, the scale of investment can still represent a challenge to the hosts in ensuring that the post-Olympic legacy is positive and facilities are sustainable. Indeed, the increasing scale of the event has introduced new infrastructural demands, such as major improvements to transport systems. In some cases, the athletes' demand to be closer to competition venues has required accommodation to be fragmented into smaller units, although the IOC now demands a single Olympic Village.

Despite the emergence of more entrepreneurial approaches to the urban management of the Olympics, the role of the public sector appears to remain central to the organization and, to a certain extent, the funding of the event. The private sector does appear to be assuming more responsibility in urban governance, especially in terms of the initial motivation to stage the Winter Olympics emanating from business coalitions and the generation of income through corporate sponsorship and television revenue. However, public sector expenditure remains high and often pivotal to the success of the event. The French Government treated Grenoble 1968 as an *affaire nationale*, met 80 per cent of the basic sports installation costs and provided a subsidy of 20 million francs for operational expenses (COJO, 1968, p. 39). The Albertville Games of 1992 were originally conceived as a means of regional modernization by local businessmen, but it was the French government that funded the project. Similarly, the Norwegian government covered the huge costs and debts of Lillehammer 1994.

The debate about the increasing size of the Winter Olympics has been a long-running affair. Preparations for the Oslo Winter Games in 1952 included consideration of a proposal to reduce the number of events. It was feared that the increasing size of each Winter Games would detrimentally affect their character and make it impossible for any town to undertake the necessary arrangements.[5] There is no record of the response to this proposal but, in practice, the Games continued to grow. Avery Brundage, the IOC President from 1952 to 1972, criticized the huge expenditures at the Grenoble Games of 1968. He wrote: 'the French spent $240m in connection with these Grenoble Games and when you consider that this was for ten days of amateur sport, it seems to be somewhat out of proportion. With that kind of money involved there is bound to be commercialization of one kind or another' (quoted in Espy, 1979, p. 136). As a result of related controversies, Brundage hoped that the whole Winter Olympics would receive a 'decent burial' at Denver, the original host of the Winter Games of 1976 (*Ibid.*, 135).

Nonetheless, the Winter Games has survived and, in terms of its scope and size, it has continued its upward trajectory. Inevitably, it remains a much smaller event than its summer counterpart and, despite the trend towards larger centres, still has not produced equivalents to the urban transformations achieved, for example, by the Barcelona Games (see chapter 13). Although the Winter Olympics have received much less attention from both the media and from academics, they do have an interesting story to tell. Their inputs and legacies are on a smaller scale but, for the host centres and regions affected, can be no less profound and no less controversial.

Notes

1. The Nordic Games, founded in 1901, were organized by the Swedish Central Association for the Promotion of Sports. The Holmenkollen Week is a leading Norwegian winter sports event.

2. 'Skeleton' sees competitors drive a one-person sled in a prone, head-first position down an ice track. The availability of the run at St Moritz meant that the event was held there as part of the 1948 Winter Olympics, although it was generally referred to as 'toboganning'.

3. Olympic Museum Archive, Lake Placid General file 1928–1991. Letter, G. Dewey, Chairman of Lake Placid, to M. Le Comte, President of the International Federation of Bobsleigh and Tobogganing, Paris, 9 November 1929.

4. Olympic Museum Archive, Lake Placid General file 1928–1991. Letter from IOC, 29 March 1930.

5. Olympic Museum Archive, Oslo Correspondence COJO, 1947–1953. Undated draft of suggestion of the Special Committee regarding the reduction of the sports' programme of the Olympic Games, Jeux Olympiques de 1952 Oslo Correspondence COJO, 1947–1953.

Chapter 4

The Cultural Olympiads: Reviving the Panegyris

Margaret M. Gold and George Revill

The process of creating this project has been demanding, full of tension, creativeness and passion, just as when preparing for a sport competition. Our reward will be the emotions sketched on tourists' faces as they discover a land of many contrasting nuances, constantly poised between past and future, nostalgia and innovation.[1]

The Olympic revival in the nineteenth century incorporated a cultural dimension from inception. As noted in chapter 1, the modern Games were always intended by Pierre de Coubertin and his collaborators to be more than a collection of sporting competitions. Rather, they would take up the ethos of the *panegyris* from the classical festival – a festive assembly in which the entire people came together to participate in religious rites, sporting competitions and artistic performance. To recreate this characteristic in a modern idiom represented a considerable challenge, but Coubertin felt that much could be done, first, by adding ceremonies to dignify the Games and so provide some continuity with the past, secondly, by creating festivities to accompany the Games and, thirdly, by introducing artistic competitions as part of the Olympic programme.

This chapter examines this cultural dimension and its growth to embrace not just the Summer but also the Winter Games. It recognizes that while key Olympic rituals and the spectacle of the Opening and Closing Ceremonies are familiar from global media coverage, the other cultural components of the Games are much less well known. Indeed, even in the academic literature, the epithets 'neglected' or 'forgotten' are often used in relation to the cultural programme (Good, 1999; Stanton, 2000). After briefly discussing the nature of the classical heritage, this chapter explores why the founders of the modern Olympic movement gave prominence to the arts and how this was expressed in the Games between 1912 and 1948, with Olympic cities staging competitions in music, literature, painting, sculpture and architecture. Thereafter, as subsequent sections show, the cultural dimension has had a chequered history. The abandonment of artistic competitions in favour of exhibitions took place after 1948, with subsequent reinterpretations of the nature and duration of the associated festivals. The Olympic Charter limits the sporting festival to 16 days, but the only stipulation about the cultural festival is that it must run while the Olympic Village is open (IOC, 2004b, p. 80) – there are no specific limits about its maximum duration. This has permitted the Olympic Arts Festival to grow in scale, so that since 1992 the summer hosts have planned four-year Cultural Olympiads, with the cultural elements of the Olympics starting to mesh with the wider agendas that interest cities and governments. These agendas, as the above quotation from the organizers of the Turin 'Cultural Olympiad' in 2006 implies, suggest a legacy for cultural tourism, identity building or culture-based urban regeneration strategies.

Reviving the Classical Heritage

Knowledge of classical Greece pervaded Western European thought from the Renaissance onwards. Certainly scholars in the nineteenth century were fully conversant with the works of Homer, Herodotus, Euripides and Sophocles, all of whom explicitly alluded to the harmonious association of art and sport (Nikolaou, 1986, p. 78). There was familiarity with the representation of athletes in Greek art, who were held to embody ideals of beauty. In classical Greek culture there was also widespread appreciation of the importance of sporting competitions (*agones*), with sporting and artistic contests an integral part of religious ritual and ceremonial. The most important sporting events were the four festivals that had emerged as prestigious Pan-Hellenic gatherings by the sixth century BC, attracting Greeks from around the Mediterranean world. These were the Olympic Games at Olympia which honoured Zeus and Hera, the Pythian Games at the oracular shrine at Delphi (Apollo), the Isthmian Games in the Isthmus of Corinth (Poseidon) and the Nemean Games near Mycenae (Zeus). Of these, the Olympic and the Pythian took place every four years, while the Isthmian and Nemean took place biennially. These were *stephanitai* or crown games awarding symbolic prizes, normally wreaths, whereas the numerous other festivals were *chrematitai* or money games with valuable prizes (Golden, 1998, p. 33).

The Olympics were the oldest and most prominent of the four cycles of Games, with the first victors' list dating from 776 BC. They grew from a simple festival involving foot races to incorporate other athletic and equestrian events. By the fourth century BC, for example, they included running races, the pentathlon, wrestling, boxing, pancration (a form of wrestling), hoplites (a race in armour), chariot racing and horseracing with competitions for boys as well as men. Sport itself was encapsulated by ritual supervised by the religious authorities, with athletes and trainers bound by oaths and a truce to enable people to assemble freely at the appointed time. The festival spread over five days with a set programme of sporting competitions, prayers, parades, singing, music, orations, animal sacrifice, feasting, a ceremony on the final day for crowning victors, a final banquet and celebrations (Golden, 1998, p. 20; Toohey and Veal, 2000, p. 10).

In reality, the conditions at Olympia probably presented athletes and visitors alike with a 'notoriously squalid experience' (Spivey, 2004, p. 84), characterized by 'noise, congestion, smell, blood, slaughter, flies and heat'. However, historians favoured a romanticized vision; a picture of athletes, artists and scholars, coming together in an Arcadian setting surrounded by the glory of classical architecture embellished by great art. It was this vision that inspired Coubertin's ideas of beauty, harmony and the arts and their combination in the modern Games. In 1904 he announced that it was time 'to restore the Olympiads to their original beauty' and bring art and sport together (cited in Müller, 2000, p. 612).

The widespread circulation of these ideas, expressed in articles, speeches and memoirs over some 50 years, have ensured that the philosophy of the Games is seen very much as one man's vision – an impression that the IOC and related institutions have done much to perpetuate. Coubertin's writings, in particular, are treated with a reverential mystique, although frequent ambiguities in language mean that it is no straightforward matter to unpick his philosophy (Loland, 1995, p. 63). Moreover, there is a tendency to see Coubertin's views as a revivalist attempt to recreate ancient Olympia rather than to place the project firmly within the movement for social and moral reform or as part of aesthetic modernism, which sought through fusion of sport with genres of experimental performance to create 'new and homogeneous aesthetic spectacle' (Brown, 2001, pp. 96–97). Coubertin, for example, was one of many individuals engaged in creating open-air spectacle intended to unite performer and spectator in a shared experience. He also succeeded in getting figures from the peoples' theatre movement and modern dance to speak at meetings, write in the *Revue Olympique* and cooperate in arranging festivals to celebrate IOC events. They included Maurice Pottecher, founder of the People's theatre in Bussang, the writer Romain Rollard, the poet and playwright René Morax, and Jacques Delacroix pioneer of the system of movement known as eurhythmics (Brown, 1996a, 1996b). Collectively, their ideas had links to the Volkstheater movement in Germany (Bradby and McCormick, 1978, pp. 11–12) and the pageant movement in England (Readman, 2005). So while an alliance between 'athletes, artists and spectators' (Müller, 2000, p. 612) and attempts to create spectacle marrying together drama, music, physical movement and sport may strike an odd chord in the twenty-first century, they meshed squarely with the spirit of the times.

Coubertin encapsulated his concept of the renovated Games in terms of Olympism, which the Olympic Charter defines as:

> a philosophy of life, exalting and combining in a balanced whole the qualities of body, will and mind. Blending sport with culture and education, Olympism seeks to create a way of life based on the joy of effort, the educational value of good example and respect for universal fundamental ethical principles. (IOC, 2004b, p. 9)

'Olympism' mediated the cultural construction of the revived Games. Coubertin had realized that restoring the outward form of the Games was comparatively easy, since it only involved restarting the four-year cycle of Olympiads, but re-establishing their deeper meanings was more difficult (Müller, 2000, p. 569). For the ancient Greeks, these meanings centred on the power of religious observance and athleticism to honour the gods (*Ibid.*, p. 566). Coubertin had a utopian belief in the significance of athleticism,[2] but recognized that giving the modern Games a spiritual component was difficult in a world of competing religions. Instead, he suggested inculcating the idea of 'modern patriotism', symbolized by the national flag 'being raised on the pole of victory to honour the winning athlete … would keep the faith alive at the newly rekindled hearth' (*Ibid.*, p. 573).

Olympism would imbue the nascent Games with notions of beauty and harmony, a notion that Coubertin referred to as eurhythmy. This required suitable ceremonial expressions to communicate its essence both to spectators and participants. The diverse array of elements shown in table 4.1, intended to lend dignity to the Games, evolved over time with that objective in mind. Certain elements, like the release of pigeons or doves were part of the ceremonial from the outset; others, such as the judges' oath, did not appear until 1972. Some aspects, such as the Hymn or Anthem, were developed specifically for the Olympics; others, such as the Creed or competition motto, were assimilated from elsewhere.[3]

Classical precedent played an important part in shaping these practices, although more from inventive adaptation of ancient Greek custom than from direct attempts at replication. Perhaps the most revealing conflation of a classical precursor with invented tradition was the physical relaying of the torch to the host stadium and the lighting of the flame, probably the most evocative aspect of the Opening Ceremony. Certainly, the flame had an ancient forerunner that burned on the altar of Zeus at Olympia for the duration of the Games, and torch races,

Table 4.1. Key aspects of Olympic protocol.

Item	When introduced
Opening ceremony	1896
Motto: *Citius, Altius, Fortius*	
Pigeons (doves)	
Hymn (anthem)	
March of Nations	1906
Competitors' oath	1920
Olympic flag	
Closing Ceremony	
Olympic flame	1928
Olympic Creed	1932
Olympic torch relay and flame lighting	1936
Informal entry of athletes in closing ceremony	1956
Adoption of the 1896 Olympic Hymn adopted as the official Hymn	1960
Judges' oath	1972

staged at night with winners needing to complete the course with their torches still alight, were features of classical Greek sporting competitions (Harlan, 1931, p. 34). Yet although members of the IOC often referred to the 'Olympic flame', initially they used the expression metaphorically, as being akin to the Olympic spirit. It was only at Amsterdam 1928 that the practice of having a physical flame reappeared and the torch relay from Olympia was a wholly invented addition to the ritual, instigated at Berlin 1936 on the suggestion of Carl Diem, General Secretary of the German Olympic Committee.

In the 1960s and 1970s host cities (Tokyo, Mexico City, Munich and Montreal) began introducing folkloric elements into the Opening and Closing Ceremonies to soften the Western military tradition and add some local distinctiveness. The advent of live television transmission turned the ceremonies from a stadium event into global entertainment, providing a vehicle for cities quite literally to perform on a world stage. Moscow 1980 provided no less than an hour of artistic programming in their Opening Ceremony and a further 30 minutes in the Closing Ceremony to reflect the 'multi-faceted life and culture of the soviet people' (Organizing Committee, 1980, p. 280). Los Angeles responded with a show intended to make Moscow's efforts 'look like chopped liver' (Ueberroth, 1986, p. 301).[4] From this point, organizers employed an ever-increasing vocabulary of choreography, music, dance, aerial ballet, lights, lasers and pyrotechnic effects to create spectacle culminating, in the recent case of Athens 2004, in creating a lake in the centre of the stadium. Spectators were drawn into the performance by giving them cards, lights, masks, bells, pipes, whistles and even clothing to create special effects.

The idea of festivities beyond the stadium to accompany the Games was willingly adopted by the organizers of Athens 1896. The 'Receptions Committee', charged with accommodation and hospitality for athletes and visitors, initially came up with grandiose plans to recreate the ancient Panathenian festival. While lack of funds and fears over creating a 'parody of Antiquity' led to the abandonment of these schemes, the organizers provided music, theatre and torchlight processions (Georgiadis, 1996, pp. 83, 90). In that sense, the Greeks did not need Coubertin's advice about the value of festive accompaniments to the Games, since they already regarded such festivities as an integral part of how such events should be staged (*Ibid.*, p. 90). The same formula was repeated on a larger scale for the 1906 Intercalated Games (see chapter 2), with illuminations, processions, concerts, performances of 'Oedipus Rex' in the Panathenian stadium, a Venetian festival in Piraeus, and tours of the Acropolis.

The 1906 Congress

The idea of incorporating arts competitions into the Games required the approval of the IOC. To this end, Coubertin organized an Advisory Conference on the 'Incorporation of the Fine Arts in the Olympic Games and Everyday Life' at the Comédie-Française in Paris (23–25 May 1906). Its purpose was to complete the

Olympic project by discussing the development of art competitions as part of the programme. In particular, it sought to establish a dialogue between sports administrators and the arts world, with the aim of studying 'the extent to which and in what form the arts and literature could be called upon to participate in the modern Olympic Games and, in general, to be associated with the practice of sports in order to benefit from them and ennoble them' (Müller, 2000, p. 608). While only five IOC members attended,[5] the conference attracted around 60 participants mainly from France, of which half were artists, writers, architects, actors, arts managers and the rest sports administrators. The conference covered architecture, theatre, dance, decoration, literature, music, painting and sculpting, including the subject of music and literature competitions (see table 4.2). Its recommendations favoured establishing competitions in 'the pentathlon of the arts' – architecture, sculpture, painting, literature and musical composition – on an equal footing with the sporting events. The submitted works would need to have been created in the previous four years and inspired by the spirit of sport. They would be judged by an international jury with the winning works performed or exhibited during the Olympic Games (Müller, 1994, p. 74). The conference also agreed that the IOC should encourage artistic and literary performance at sporting events generally, including athletics meetings, automobile shows, horse races and regattas (Brown, 1996b, p. 3). Agreement was also reached over the aesthetic presentation of sports festivals including questions of building design, stadium decoration, ceremonies and parades. In his role as President of the IOC, Coubertin sent a circular conveying the wishes of the Conference to heads of universities, sports federations and clubs in October 1906 urging them to ensure that all major sports events:

> include a literary or artistic component through the addition of poetry competitions or appropriate drama productions, and above all outdoor choral music – stressing, moreover, the numerous advantages that sports clubs would enjoy by creating choral sections within them. (Quoted in Müller, 2000, p. 619)

Notably, however, the Congress did not follow the classical precursors in one respect. The ancient festivals contained competitions that involved performance in music, drama and recitation. At first glance, this would have seemed perfectly acceptable, since music competitions were long established by the early twentieth century (e.g. Vaubel, 2005), but this type of competition was not favoured by some of the Congress's participants. For delegates such as the French composer Louis Bourgault-Ducoudray, the aesthetic experience of singing in great choral ensembles was not just about the beauty of the music or the joy of participation but the 'disinterested' nature of the performance where great art alone was the reward. Writing in the *Revue Olympique* in July 1906, he expressed the view that this purity and beauty of purpose would be destroyed by choral competition as 'gold medals or sums of money' would generate 'rivalries and antagonism' – a wholly undesirable state of affairs (Brown, 1996b, p. 6).

Table 4.2. Programme for the Advisory conference circulated by Pierre de Coubertin, 2 April 1906.

	Conference Programme
Dramatic art	Outdoor productions; essential principles; recent writings; sports on stage.
Choreography	Processions; parades; group and coordinated movements; dances
Decoration	Stands and enclosures; mats, badges, garlands, draperies, clusters; night festivals; torchlight sports
Literature	Possibility of setting up Olympic literary competitions; conditions for these competitions; sporting emotion, source of inspiration for the man of letters
Music	Outdoor orchestras and choirs; repertoire; rhythms and alternation; fanfares; conditions for an Olympic music competition
Painting	Individual silhouettes and general views; possibility of and conditions for an Olympic painting competition; photography as an aid to the artist
Sculpture	Athletic poses and movements and their relationship with art; interpretation of effort; objects given as prizes; statuettes and medals

Source: Müller (2000, pp. 609–610)

Art Competitions and City-wide Festivities

The most celebrated legacy of the Advisory Conference were the art competitions. The Advisory Conference expected that the first art competitions would be introduced at the 1908 Games. The London Organizing Committee, with the help of the Royal Academy, formulated rules and subjects for two classes of painting, two of sculpture and an architecture competition (Cook, 1909, p. 179). The subjects were narrowly defined; for instance, for one of the painting and one of the sculpture categories there was a choice between a triumphal procession or the battle between Greeks and Amazons. For the other painting and sculpture categories, contestants had to select from a modern football match, classical discuss throwers, or Hercules and Antaeus. The architecture competition set three briefs: for a swimming bath of given dimensions; a town house containing a gallery for works of art and a private gymnasium; and a sports club for a small town of 20,000 inhabitants (Müller, 2000, p. 624). The intention was to display the entries to all the competitions in a 'gallery attached to the stadium during the games' but, despite this effort, the competitions were 'abandoned' when time ran out (Cook, 1909, pp. 179–181).

The first competition successfully staged by the IOC was for architecture and organized through the College of Architecture in Paris in 1910. The brief was to design a 'modern Olympia' to include 'buildings, porticos, arenas, tracks etc. required for athletic and artistic events included in the programme of the modern Olympic Games, the structures required for spectators, the buildings or spaces required for ceremonies associated with the Games and facilities for administration, athletes etc' (Müller, 2000, p. 625). The competition received nine entries and was won by the Swiss architects Eugéne-Edouard Monod and Alphonse Laverriére (Müller, 1994, p. 78; Lennartz, 2006a, p. 10). Their achievement is normally counted under the medal-winners for the Stockholm Games in 1912.

The remaining competitions were held in Stockholm, although not without difficulty. The challenge now facing Organizing Committees was how a group of sports administrators could organize art competitions, something deemed outside their expertise. This was invariably solved by involving the local arts establishment in the arrangement of the competitions but, in the case of Stockholm, there was little enthusiasm from the main arts institutions. The Royal Academy, in particular, objected in principle to the idea of competitions with such constricted subject matter, arguing that the results would be merely 'illustrations' rather than works of art (SOC, 1913, p. 807). Their opposition led the organizers to drop the art competitions from their Olympic Programme in February 1912 and allocate 5000 francs towards their organization should the IOC wish to organize the competition themselves. Coubertin assumed personal responsibility, collecting the competition entries and organizing the judging (although the basis on which this was done is unclear). After the carefully crafted topics of 1908 and 1910, the rules now simply stated that entries had to have some direct connection with sport and should not have been previously published, exhibited or performed (Mallon and Widland, 2002, p. 24; SOC, 1913, p. 808).[6] There were still relatively few entries: four in the painting competition, eight for sculpture and eight for literature (Lennartz, 2006a, p. 10; Masterson, 1986, p. 105). The winning entries went on display in Stockholm during the Games.

The festivities and cultural activities accompanying the games also slowly began to take shape. Given that the White City stadium was adjacent to the spectacular grounds of the Franco-British Exhibition, the organizers of London 1908 did relatively little to arrange entertainments other than plan receptions, balls and banquets for the Olympic family, excursions to places of interest in and around London and provide free tickets for theatres and concerts (Organizing Committee, 1908, pp. 394–398). By contrast, Stockholm 1912 created a substantial cultural programme. The main focus, as noted in chapter 2, was the multipurpose stadium, which featured cultural and sporting displays in the evenings. Elsewhere, the organizers encouraged institutions to offer attractions in the hope of developing Sweden as a tourist destination in the longer term (SOC, 1913, p. 283). The Royal Opera House, normally closed during the summer, was reopened for a programme of opera, music and dance, and the four principal theatres staged a varied season of plays, operettas and comedies (*Ibid.*, p. 827). Museums exhibited traditional Swedish handicrafts, with the open-air Museum of Skansen also hosting theatre productions for visitors during the Games. The Royal Library held an exhibition of manuscripts and books charting the development of sport in the region over five centuries – one of the first examples of a sport-related exhibition staged for the Games (*Ibid.*, p. 829).

The same formula of art competitions and associated city-wide festivities continued for the six summer Games between 1920 and 1948. During this period, the arts competitions attracted growing numbers of entrants to a steadily increasing number of art categories. The organizers of Antwerp 1920 actively promoted the art competitions, but the short time scale available for organizing the first post-war Games led to concern that there would be insufficient entries. They, therefore, organized two art exhibitions at the Royal Museum of Antwerp to run concurrently with the exhibition of competition entries: a retrospective of Belgian art since independence (1830); the other celebrating the emergence of Belgian art from the Great War and documenting the impact of war on contemporary art (Guillain, 2005, p. 27; Lennartz, 2006*b*).

Paris 1924 saw the arts competitions receive 189 entries from 23 countries, including a growing number of countries from outside Europe, including South Africa, Australia, Brazil, Egypt, the United States and Uruguay (Stanton, 2000, p. 78). The organizers publicized the competitions through foreign embassies in Paris, the international press and the personal efforts of the Marquis de Polignac, President of the Commission for Arts and External Relations. Large and eminent juries were assembled to judge the entries. The music competition, for example, had 43 judges, including Fauré, Ravel, Stravinski, Bartók and Honneger. These far outnumbered the seven entrants, to whom they declined to award any medals (Guillain, 2006, p. 23; Organizing Committee, 1924, p. 604). The artwork was displayed in the Grand Palace between May 16 and July 27. The organizers complimented the art exhibitions with an international festival of the performing arts, offering mass choirs and instrumental groups, music, folk ballets and plays (Guillain, 2006, p. 22).

Amsterdam 1928 saw 1,150 works submitted from 18 countries. The organizers re-divided the five art categories into thirteen new categories (three each for music, literature and painting; two each for sculpture and architecture) – the original plan being to display the art work in the planned Cité Olympique, with the complex catering for all the sporting competitions, integrated transport and visitor amenities. It was originally intended that this should include an exhibition hall and a sunken sculpture garden easily accessible from the main stadium (Organizing Committee, 1928, p. 179). For reasons of cost, this plan was abandoned and, instead, the exhibition was staged in the Municipal Museum of Amsterdam – a solution much preferred by the Art Committee who felt a 'well-equipped museum with quieter surroundings' was more suitable despite its distance from the sporting competitions (*Ibid.*, p. 180). Over 10,000 people visited the exhibition during the two months it was open (Bijkerk, 2006, p. 29).

Los Angeles 1932 offered nine competitions (three for painting; two each for sculpture and architecture; and one each for literature and music). Entries were received from 24 nations and exhibited in the Los Angeles Museum of History, Science and Art in Exposition Park, augmented by works of art from American Museums (Stanton, 2006, p. 41). Taken together, this produced a substantial exhibition occupying 15 galleries, the foyer, rotunda and main hall with over 1,100 items on display. Being easily accessible to athletes, officials and spectators, a record number of 384,000 visitors was recorded between 30 July and 31 August.

Berlin 1936 had 15 art competitions, the most ever held, despite political

LIVERPOOL JOHN MOORES UNIVERSITY
LEARNING & INFORMATION SERVICES

difficulties which meant that a number of countries, including Britain and France, refused to participate. The exhibition of the submitted work attracted 70,000 visitors (Organizing Committee, 1936, p. 1127). A major innovation was a performance of the medal-winning music compositions during the Games by the Berlin Philharmonic, conducted by the composers. This took place in the 20,000-seater Dietrich Eckart open-air theatre (see chapter 10). Berlin was also noteworthy for the extent of the auxiliary cultural programme. It was not the first Olympic city to stage exhibitions, live performance, folk culture or mass displays during the Games, but provided a new scale of offering. The extensive programme gave the regime an opportunity to express its cultural ideology in terms of the subject matter and art forms exhibited and to indulge in the spectacular mass displays and epic productions that were hallmarks of its propaganda. Classical music and theatre featured strongly. The German Opera House offered a Wagner Festival and the Dietrich Eckart staged large-scale productions such as Handel's 'Heracles', with 2500 performers, and a performance of Hamlet with the Prince of Denmark being accorded 'a first class Party funeral', with marching soldiers, trumpets and displays of weapons (Rürup, 1996). By contrast, the dance programme was curtailed on the instructions of Joseph Goebbels, who disapproved of Rudolf Laban's epic 'Von Tauwind under der neuen Freude'.[7]

The largest associated exhibition was 'Deutschland', a propaganda exercise aimed primarily at the 1.3 million German visitors who attended. This, in the words of Goebbels, was intended to show 'a reawakened, reborn nation, pulsating with the desire to create … the eternal Germany'. Besides this, the exhibition programme included two exhibitions with classical themes: 'Sport in Hellenic Times' and an exhibition of casts and reproductions of finds from German archaeological work at Olympia (Organizing Committee, 1936, p. 1132: see also chapter 2). Another exhibition, 'Great Germans in Contemporary Portraits' drew 63,700 visitors to a display of portraiture that featured the 'pioneers of German civilization in foreign countries' – including, ominously, countries soon to be incorporated into the Greater Germany (*Ibid.*, p. 1135).

The Reichssportfeld and particularly the Olympic stadium (see chapter 10) were the focus for the associated festive entertainments. The stadium staged spectacular performances during the period of the Games, including the Kraft durch Freude[8] movement's presentation 'Music and Dance of the Peoples', a military concert involving over 2,000 musicians and a festival play entitled 'Olympic Youth' (figure 4.1). This was conceived as 'an artistically constructed echo of the Opening Ceremony' and in many ways presaged the cultural content of contemporary Opening Ceremonies. Organized by Carl Diem, it was performed in the Olympic stadium after the Opening Ceremony and again two days later as a para-Olympic event. Diem used 10,000 performers, each of whom had signed a declaration claiming their Aryan descent, international celebrities, light, sound, and a musical score written by Carl Orff and Werner Egk to create an imposing spectacle. It presented a series of tableaux weaving Olympic, mediaeval and modern themes:

Figure 4.1. Berlin 1936.

'Children at play', 'Maidenly Grace', 'Youth at Play in a Serious Mood' and 'Heroic Struggle and Death Lament'. The last of these contained a celebration of sacrificial death for the fatherland, ending with the 'Ode to Joy' from Beethoven's Ninth Symphony, at which point searchlights created a dome of light above the arena and flames of fire leapt up around the edge of the stadium (Organizing Committee, 1936, p. 577).[9]

The Demise of the Art Competitions

After an interval of 12 years, London staged the Summer Games in 1948 and organized 14 art competitions with National Olympic Committees from the competing nations selecting three entries per class (Organizing Committee, 1948, p. 96). The painting, sculpture and crafts were displayed at the Victoria and Albert Museum in Kensington for a month, but plans for a concert featuring the musical entries were abandoned (Barker, 2006, p. 65). On the basis of this experience, the British Fine Arts Committee made recommendations for future Games, covering the categories of entries, subject matter, and marketing. It was not anticipated at this point that the 1948 arts competitions would be the last (Organizing Committee, 1948, pp. 197–198).

Numerous reasons have been given for the demise of the art competitions (Masterson, 1986; Bandy, 1988; Good, 1999; Guillain, 2005), including organizational problems, the poor quality of the entries, and fundamental conceptual opposition. Certainly the logistics of organizing truly global competitions in the time available had taxed many Organizing Committees, a problem compounded by the challenge of embracing different artistic traditions from around the world, different languages in the literature competitions, and a wide range of subject matter within categories. Olympic Organizing Committees could delegate the running of the competitions to arts administrators, but they still had to work through the National Olympic Committees with their memberships dominated by sports enthusiasts. The Olympic movement rarely succeeded in involving the worldwide artistic community and the number of participating nations remained low – never more than 25. The quality of the competitions, too, was of longstanding concern. They were shunned by the day's leading artists, resulting in incongruence between excellence in the sporting arena and the quality of the work in the artistic competitions. Tellingly, juries often refused to award medals. Over the seven Olympiads, only 145 of the possible 198 medals were awarded (73 per cent). In the case of music, awards were made of only 17 out of the possible 39 medals.

Two more fundamental factors were also at work. First, analysis by Stanton (2000) of the correspondence, minutes and memoranda produced by the IOC between 1949 and 1954 suggests that the specific reason for the IOC deciding to abandon the arts competitions was due to entrants being professional artists. The view was expressed that the professional status of artists went against the Olympic Charter and that artists would use success in the Olympics to promote their reputations and profit from the increased value of their work. Secondly, it was increasingly recognized that the basic concept was fatally flawed. On the one hand, twentieth-century Western art had moved away from the figurative work beloved by Coubertin and the philhellenes of the modern Olympic movement. On the other hand, it had become clear that there was no longer that engagement between artists and sport that was so central to classical Greek artistic culture. No amount of rhetoric on the union of body, mind and beauty could reverse that trend (Guillain, 2005, p. 29).

The first signs of change came at a small IOC sub-committee meeting in New Orleans in January 1949, called to revise the IOC Charter. It recommended that medals no longer be awarded for art competitions and that exhibitions of art be held instead. Although approved at the next full IOC meeting, the decision produced an outcry from those fiercely loyal to Coubertin's original vision for the arts and those convinced that exhibitions would fail without the incentive of medals to encourage participation. This, in turn, led to appointment of a committee to reconsider the matter. Its report led to the reinstatement of the arts competitions at the IOC meeting in May 1951.

This *volte-face* left the Helsinki Organizing Committee in an invidious position. They had earlier campaigned for the retention of the art competitions, but now had to request permission to continue organizing art exhibitions because there was insufficient time to revert back to organizing competitions (Stanton, 2000, pp. 234–236). In practice, however, there was little material difference since the exhibition model used at Helsinki 1952 was identical to the old competitions. The organizers requested that the National Olympic Committees collect contemporary work and submit it for display. Twenty-three countries responded and 181 works were submitted, but the resulting exhibition was deemed disappointing with only 5,000 visitors. The organizers awarded artists a diploma as a memento of their participation (Organizing Committee, 1952, p. 110).

The issue of the art competitions was raised at the next IOC meeting in April 1953. The IOC President Avery Brundage repeated his views on the evils of professionalism in the arts, but admitted that the exhibitions in Helsinki had met with 'relatively little success' (Stanton, 2000, p. 242). The meeting commissioned another inquiry into the art competitions but, before it reported, Brundage circulated a powerfully worded letter to IOC members in favour of exhibition programmes but suggesting a new model. These would be 'special exhibitions of outstanding works of art dealing with sport from the museums of the country where the games are being staged, or even borrowed from other countries' (*Ibid.*, p. 245). The IOC meeting in Athens in May 1954 supported this suggestion, which the commission of inquiry also recommended, although the link with sport was dropped. Brundage concluded the discussion by saying that this 'new formula' would ensure exhibitions of the highest standard and that if the Games went to Vienna there would be the best music in the world, in Russia the best ballet, in 'Italy or, when we add Greece, we have the possibility to see the most marvellous works of classical art in the world' (quoted in Stanton, 2000, p. 256). The Olympic Charter was then amended to read:

> The Organising Committee of the Olympic Games shall arrange exhibitions and demonstrations of the host country's art (architecture, literature, music, painting, sculpture, photography, and sport philately) and fix the dates during which these exhibitions and demonstrations shall take place. The programme may also include theatrical, ballet, opera, performances or symphony concerts.
>
> This section of the programme shall be of an equal standard and held concurrently and in the same vicinity as the sports events. It shall receive full recognition in the publicity released by the OCOG. (Cited by Masterson, 1986, p. 108)

Olympic Arts Festival, 1956–1988

The Olympic Charter now gave Organizing Committees greater flexibility in devising the artistic programme for the Games. There was no longer a requirement for the art content to have a specific sports connection – although this remained a recurrent theme over the years – but rather placed emphasis on the Olympic principle of excellence. Host cities and nations would put the best of their arts and artists on display, which in turn opened up a new role for the Olympic Arts Festival as a showcase for the host city and nation and as an event that meshed well with urban policy goals of host cities. In particular, the Olympic Arts Festivals contributed to urban and national agendas in four respects.

The first, present since the earliest Games, found Organizing Committees

LIVERPOOL JOHN MOORES UNIVERSITY
LEARNING & INFORMATION SERVICES

using the Olympics as an opportunity to show the cultivated nature of the host society. This invariably gave prominence to high art, with visitors offered a programme that included opera, symphony concerts, ballet and classical theatre. This expanded over time to incorporate programmes intended to show the vibrancy of the contemporary arts scene in music, visual arts, sculpture and new media. For non-Western countries with different artistic traditions, there was the added concern that their culture was undervalued, misunderstood or simply ignored by Western audiences. Therefore, for example, the Organizing Committee for Tokyo 1964 carefully crafted their Art Festival to introduce their culture to an international audience (Aso, 2002, pp. 18, 33). Tokyo also saw attempts to reinforce a 'particularistic Japanese national identity' and sense of community in the aftermath of war, occupation and economic change by means of a powerful portrayal of traditional arts and culture for the *domestic* audience (*Ibid.*, pp. 19, 33)

Secondly, the Olympic Arts Festival could also serve the goals of political ideology. Mexico City 1968, for example, sought to advance the interests of the developing world by making the cultural festival more inclusive, particularly embracing nations that did not traditionally perform well in the sporting competitions. This would, in the words of the Chairman of the Organizing Committee, 'promote mutual understanding and respect, brotherhood and friendship between nations and genuine international accord'. The IOC congratulated Mexico City 'for expanding the cultural programme … in such a significant manner' (Organizing Committee, 1968, p. 272). These aims were subsequently incorporated into the Olympic Charter (IOC, 2004b, p. 70) to encourage host nations to broaden the content away from the purely 'national' character stipulated in 1954. The new rule 44 stated:

> The OCOG must organise a programme of cultural events which shall be submitted to the IOC for approval.

> This programme must serve to promote harmonious relations, mutual understanding and friendship among the participants and others attending the Olympic Games. (IOC, 2004b, p. 70).

During the 1980s, a succession of Olympic Arts Festivals had openly ideological goals. The intent behind the Moscow Olympic Arts Festival in 1980 was to acquaint the visitor with 'the heritage and achievements of the Soviet multinational culture' (Organizing Committee, 1980, p. 402). The cultural festival at Los Angeles 1984 was accused of being 'part of a wider entertainment and tourist programme with strong profit-making elements' (Nikolaou, 1986, p. 17). Seoul 1988 saw South Korea use the Arts Festival as an exercise in cultural diplomacy by forging links with states that had previously refused them diplomatic recognition. The presence of the Moscow Philharmonic and Bolshoi Ballet, for instance, was of singular importance to the Koreans (Organizing Committee, 1989, p. 429).

Thirdly, the Arts Festivals could address economic development and urban regeneration. Chapter 1 noted the acceptance, by the 1980s, of the idea that the cultural sector had a role to play in the urban economy and could contribute to solving economic and social problems. The Olympic Art Festivals provided the catalyst to develop the cultural infrastructure by building or refurbishing exhibition and performance spaces, usually accompanied by measures to upgrade the urban environment to provide the basis for developing cultural and business tourism in the longer term. The first signs of this activity were witnessed in 1968 when both Mexico City and Grenoble gained new arts infrastructures, but by 1990s the expectation was that cities would make major investments in their arts sectors in preparing for the Games.

Finally, the Olympic Arts Festivals addressed the growing arts agenda that developed after the Second World War. From the 1950s, governments increasingly intervened in the arts sector with regard to audience development, access, and inclusion. These concerns, in turn, began to permeate the Olympic Arts Festivals. Moreover, policies to support traditional culture or intangible heritage could also be accommodated within these festivals. A re-evaluation of indigenous cultures, often previously denigrated and disregarded, can be seen developing within the Arts Festivals in Mexico (1968), Canada (1976, 1988 and 2010), and Australia (2000).[10] The Olympic Arts Festivals also offered opportunities to develop the cultural sectors within cities and nations through developing skills and expertise, consolidating art networks, developing partnerships – particularly with arts organizations in other Olympic cities – and establishing further arts festivals which could be continued after the Games. The results often left their mark not only in Olympic terms but in terms of museum and curatorial practice.[11]

Table 4.3 shows the considerable variation in the Olympic Arts Festivals between 1956 and 1988. They could run from a matter of weeks to a year. Content might be predominantly national (as at Melbourne 1956, Tokyo 1964 or Montreal 1976) or international, as with Mexico City 1968 or Seoul 1977 where 97 and 73 nations, respectively participated (Organizing Committee, 1968, p. 275; 1989, p. 429). The Festival might be confined to the Olympic City or spread to other locations, an idea that has gained ground since being pioneered at Mexico City 1968. The range of art forms included reflects the host nation's interests and agendas, with the ever-present content of elite art steadily being complemented by expressions of folk and popular culture. Open-air street entertainments have steadily become an important element in animating the city around the Olympic venues (as at Munich 1972, Montreal 1976 or Seoul 1988). Some cities have tried to retain the link between art and sports (including Rome 1960, Mexico City 1968 and Los Angeles 1984), while others ignored it (Tokyo 1964 and Montreal 1976). The one trend universally apparent was that the scale of the offering steadily increased in the period between 1956 and 1988. By the 1980s, the gigantism of the cultural festival had become established with the audience numbers being counted in their millions.

Table 4.3. Olympic Arts Festivals, Summer Games 1952–1988.

Olympiad	Length of Cultural Festival	Content and Themes	Highlights
Helsinki 1952	4 weeks	International exhibitions of architecture, painting, graphic arts, sculpture, literature, music	Submitted musical compositions performed in a concert
Melbourne 1956	4 weeks	National culture	Exhibition: *Showcase of Australian Art*
Rome 1960	6 months★ 3 weeks	National culture with an emphasis on history; sporting references in exhibition programme	Exhibition: *Sport in History and Art*; Medieval historical pageants
Tokyo 1964	7 weeks	Japanese high art and traditional culture.	Exhibition: *Ancient Japanese Art Treasures*
Mexico City 1968	1 year	International; high art and indigenous culture Nation-wide celebration of culture	World Folklore Festival Ballet of the Five Continents; *International Exhibition of Folk Art Exhibition of selected works of world art*; New Fire ritual at Teotihuacán
Munich 1972	3 months★ 6 weeks	*Olympic Summer* International; high art and folk culture	Exhibition: *World Cultures and Modern Art*; International folklore festival; Avenue of Entertainment: live performance in the Olympic Park
Montreal 1976	4 weeks	National – showcase for Canadian provincial culture	Exhibition: *Mosaicart* – Canadian visual arts *Artisanage* – craft demonstration; Canadian festival of popular arts; The Celebration – live outdoor performance
Moscow 1980	1 year★ 5 weeks	National, mass participation, high art and folk culture: national art of the peoples of the USSR	Exhibition: *One hundred masterpieces from the Hermitage Collection*; Exhibition: *Moscow in Russian and contemporary art*; Exhibition: *Sport – Ambassador of Peace* Opera and classical music
Los Angeles 1984	10 weeks	7 weeks: international festival for domestic consumption 3 weeks LA and US culture for international Olympic audience	Exhibition: *A day in the country: impressionists in the French landscape*; Performing arts programme; Art commissioning programme
Seoul 1988	7 weeks	Korean high culture and traditional culture for an international audience; international artists and companies; contemporary culture for domestic audience;	International festivals in folk culture, dance, theatre, music, song; The Olympiad of art – contemporary sculpture park; International modern art competition; Street festivals and Han River Festival

★ Length of cultural festival including exhibition runs and pre-Games programme
Source: Compiled from official reports of Organizing Committees

The Cultural Olympiads, 1992–2004

This era came to an end at Barcelona 1992, where the organizers changed the cultural agenda for the Summer Games by introducing a four-year Cultural Olympiad that culminated in an Olympic Arts Festival to coincide with the Games. For Barcelona, the official reason for the innovation was to develop the cultural infrastructure, demonstrate the richness of its cultural heritage and to make the city more attractive for visitors (COOB, 1992, I, p. 287). From this juncture, all the Summer Games staged Cultural Olympiads, although these longer festivals pose challenges for cities in terms of creative programming. The Cultural Olympiad starts well before the Olympic infrastructure is in place and only three years after the successful bidding process – a relative short time horizon by the standards of the cultural sector. Moreover, it is difficult to maintain the Olympic connection in the cultural events throughout the four-year period particularly in the light of perennially poor marketing (García, 2001, p. 198). Funding has also been problematic with Organizing Committees tempted to retrench by cutting the cultural budget, and art events have greater difficulty attracting sponsorship compared with the sports competitions. Barcelona 1992, Atlanta 1996 and Sydney 2000 suffered badly in this respect, with Atlanta having its cultural budget cut from $40 million to $25 million, offset only in part by $8 million from sponsorship

Table 4.4. Thematic annual programmes of the Cultural Olympiads: Barcelona 1992 to Athens 2004.

Barcelona 1992	Atlanta 1996	Sydney 2000	Athens 2004
1988 Cultural Gateway 1989 The year of culture and sport	1993 Olympic wonderland: encounters with Norwegian culture; Salute to Lausanne; Mexico! A cultural tapestry	1997 Festival of the Dreaming	2001 Man and space★
1990 The year of the arts	1994 Celebrate Africa 1994–1995 One hundred years of world cinema	1998 A Sea Change	2002 Man and the earth★
1991 The year of the future	1995 Nobel Literature Laureates gathering	1999 Reaching the World	2003 Man and the spirit★
1992 Olympic Arts Festival	1996 Southern Connections; International Connections	2000 The Harbour of Life: Olympic Arts Festival	2004 Man and man★ Olympic Arts Festival: ATHENS 2004-Culture:
Lasting 3 months	Lasting 9 weeks	Lasting 6 weeks	Lasting 7 months

★ Athens Bid Document, Vol III, p. 4.

Source: Compiled from Official Reports of Organizing Committees and Bid Documents.

(Good, 1999, p. 165; García, 2001, p. 156). The goals of the Olympiads tend to mix a strong domestic arts-related agenda of audience development and capacity-building in the arts sector with the desire to have an international dimension that promotes the city's Olympic and cultural role outside the host nation. The four-year format allows cities to take the Cultural Olympiad out to the participating nations with events and exhibitions staged abroad.

By and large, cities have tended to develop themed annual festivals (see table 4.4), although both Atlanta 1996 and Athens 2004 modified their programmes after the bidding process. In the case of Barcelona 1992, the series of annual festivals leading to the Olympic Arts Festival was said to have increased the local arts audience and introduced them to more challenging work (COOB, 1992, I, p. 323). The 1992 Olympic Arts Festival was designed for the Games' audience and had three main themes, mixing historical heritage, with contemporary and performing arts.[12]

Atlanta's four-year Cultural Olympiad had the twin aim of celebrating Southern culture while including a major initiative to develop a proper recognition of African American art. It presented both traditional and contemporary work and brought international artists to Atlanta from the five continents – symbolizing the Olympic rings. The organizers hoped that Atlanta would ultimately be 'recognized as an international centre for innovative arts, culture, and entertainment' (Organizing Committee, 1996, p. 146). In the years leading up to the Games, a series of multi-year projects and international festivals covering film, drama, and international culture under the title of 'Arts Atlanta: Preludes to the Centennial Olympic Arts Festival' were presented (*Ibid.*, p. 148). The Olympic Arts Festival itself, with its

Figure 4.2. Centennial Park, Atlanta 1996 – Olympic rings.

themes of Southern celebration and international connections, lasted 64 days and attracted over 2.6 million visitors: an attendance figure assisted by concentrating the programme in the Olympic Ring (where 37 of the 41 venues were located). In particular, two million visitors attended the 'Southern Crossroads Festival' in Centennial Park (figure 4.2), where 1,114 performers entertained the crowds on three stages and a demonstration area was provided for local artisan craftsmen (*Ibid*., p. 152).[13] Although the press grumbled that the cultural dimension had been neglected, seemingly confirmed by a leaked letter from a member of the Cultural Olympiad Advisory Board complaining of lack of support for his committee (Yarborough, 2000, p. 130), the festival's success in attracting visitors seemingly belied that view. The exhibition 'Five Rings of Passion' at the High Museum of Art remains a landmark in Olympic Arts Festival planning, despite only receiving approval to proceed nine months before the Games. Organized around five themes – the emotions of love, anguish, awe, triumph and joy – and with works from around the world, it managed to combine an Olympic theme with important artworks in a readily accessible location.

The Cultural Olympiad planned for Sydney 2000, as chapter 14 makes clear, was at pains to stress Australia's multicultural character. Four major festivals were staged whose themes ranged from considering Australia's place in the world at the Millennium, to showcasing the way that its environment has impacted on culture and the arts, to highlighting Australian artistic and cultural achievements and celebrating indigenous culture (SOCOG, 2000*b*, p. 303). The first of the festivals, 'The Festival of the Dreaming' was in many ways the most ground-breaking. Staged over six weeks in Sydney in the autumn of 1997, it was Australia's first major celebration of Aboriginal art and it involved more than 700 indigenous artists. These came principally from Australia, but contributions from other nations (New Zealand, Canada, Greenland, the United States, Korea and Oceania) made connections with indigenous experience. In the light of Australia's previous treatment of Aboriginal peoples, this opening festival of the Olympiad assumed great symbolic importance, particularly as it was held at the Sydney Opera House – a cathedral of Australian high art. By contrast, the subsequent annual festivals were hit by budget cuts and fell so far short of their desired impact that Cashman (2006, p. 82) considered them 'second or even third-tier'.

The six-week Olympic Arts Festival at Sydney 2000 presented a range of national, international and indigenous culture. It attempted to reconnect art with sport with, for example, the exhibition '1000 Years of Olympic Games' featuring artefacts loaned from Greece. Overall, the festival attracted criticism for its elite art emphasis in contrast to the *LiveSites!* programme of popular entertainment, run by Sydney City Council, that animated the city streets and Olympic venues and had a more immediate impact and appeal (see chapter 14).

Greece was anxious to leave a cultural legacy to the Olympic movement arguing that while for other host cities the Cultural Olympiads were secondary to the sport, for Greece it was 'part of its essence'. To this end, in 1988 an agreement between the IOC, UNESCO and the Hellenic Ministry of Culture established an International Foundation of the Cultural Olympiad with its headquarters at Olympia. This would promote understanding and respect between cultures and promote global values by developing links with participating nations. However, the subsequent absence of any substantial references to this organization either within the IOC or beyond shows that little has yet occurred that represents concrete outcome from this initiative.

The four-year Cultural Olympiad, which adopted the title of 'For a Culture of Civilizations', succeeded in commissioning new work, staging performances including classical drama in historic settings, exhibitions and conferences throughout Greece and internationally. This culminated in 'Athens 2004 – Culture' which ran from March to September 2004. The renovation of museums, the creation of new contemporary art spaces and the beautification of central Athens, including the restoration of classical heritage sites and a large-scale pedestrianization programme, have left Athens with a legacy on which to build cultural and convention tourism (see chapter 15).

Winter Games Olympic Arts Festivals, 1956–2006

As the previous chapter showed, the Winter Games started as relatively small sporting festivals in ski resorts where the emphasis was on sports facilities and accommodation. Organizing Committees routinely offered programmes of receptions, dinners and the occasional concert for the IOC and officials, but there were no expectations or requirements that competitions, exhibitions or arts festivals would be staged. The first winter host to provide an artistic programme was Cortina d'Ampezzo 1956 where lectures, concerts and exhibitions, including an exhibition on the history of winter sports, were held in the Circolo Artistico 'for those in search of more intellectual amusements of an artistic nature' (CONI, 1956, p. 255). Grenoble 1968, however, was the first occasion on which a Winter Olympic Arts Festival developed along the lines of the Summer Festivals and addressed a similar agenda. Here, the organizers offered a programme that embraced ballet, theatre, classical music, popular music and film during a 19-day festival and used the event as a catalyst to build a Civic Cultural Centre. Sapporo 1972 featured a 19-day festival concentrated on Japanese culture. Innsbruck 1976 staged a 'simple Games' in an effort to counteract the escalation of previous years, but the following Games at Lake Placid 1980 laid emphasis on the performing arts, particularly newly commissioned work. Sarajevo 1984 boasted the 'most versatile and richest programme of this kind that had ever accompanied the Winter Olympic Games' (Organizing Committee, 1984, p. 138).

Table 4.5 provides details of the Olympic Arts Festivals from Calgary 1988 to Turin 2006. Calgary was the largest city to host a Winter Games to that point and staged the most comprehensive programme using its wealth of theatres, concert halls, galleries and museums (CODA, 1988, p. 273). It covered all the

Table 4.5. Olympic Arts Festivals, Winter Games 1988–2006.

Olympiad	Length of Cultural Festival	Content and Themes	Highlights
Calgary 1988	5 weeks	Canadian high arts; Canadian artists; indigenous traditional and contemporary culture	Native participation programme; Exhibition: *The spirit sings: artistic traditions of Canadian First Peoples*; Dance; Literature; Wintershow'88 winter carnival; Rodeo
Albertville 1992	1988–1992 Youth of the World Festival 5 months	French cultural tradition: contemporary art; international artists; events held throughout Rhône-Alpes and Western Europe with the theme of breaking down international barriers	Performing arts; Contemporary dance; Music; Fringe theatre
Lillehammer 1994	2 years OAF 5 weeks	National and regional Norwegian culture and international culture; traditional and experimental art, high arts and informal Winterland festivals held in past Olympic cities;	Cultural programme surrounding the torch relay; Informal cultural programme; Sami cultural programme; Classical music; Popular music; Exhibition *Slowly we won the land*; Winterland; Exhibition: *Edvard Munch's monumental projects 1909–1930*
Nagano 1998	1 year OAF 3 months	*One heart – one world* Japanese traditional culture, high arts, Events taking place throughout Japan. International artists and repertoire	Classical music, orchestral, opera, traditional; Children's art and performance; Traditional drama
Salt Lake City 2002	5 weeks	*Light the Fire Within* National art and culture; the American West International artists	Newly commissioned Performing arts, new commissions e.g. *Here ... Now* tribute to Florence Griffith-Joyner; Exhibitions: *Declaration of Independence*; *Discover Navajo: people of the fourth world*; *Chihuly 2002*
Turin 2006	6 months	'Open to change and exchange'; Italian high art, traditional art and culture of the alps; international artists	Contemporary art and performance; Italian film; Museum collections; Exhibition: *Leonardo da Vinci masterpieces on show*; *Inuit and people from the ice*

Source: Compiled from Official Reports of Organizing Committees and TOROC (2005).

arts including literature and its Native Participation Programme was designed to involve Canada's Aboriginal peoples by presenting aspects of their traditional and contemporary culture (*Ibid.*, p. 271). By the 1990s it was the norm to have an international dimension in the programming so that even cities like Salt Lake City 2002, with its emphasis on American and Western culture, had international artists in its festival. The length of the festivals varied considerably from Calgary's five weeks to Lillehammer's two years. A number of hosts tried to make a wider geographical impact as in the case of Albertville 1992 with events throughout the Rhône-Alpes, and further afield including Paris, Barcelona, Lausanne and Antwerp (Organizing Committee, 1992, p. 476). Lillehammer 1994 staged Winterland Exhibitions in the Olympic cities of Atlanta, Tokyo, Barcelona and Munich presenting Norwegian music, theatre, literature, film and Sami culture. Nagano 1998 staged a year-long festival with events nationwide.

The Winter Games in Turin saw full convergence with the strategies adopted for the cultural programme by host cities of the Summer Games. With a population of over 850,000 and some two million in its urban region, Turin was the largest city yet to have hosted the Winter Games. It also staged the most dispersed Games given the distances between Turin and the snow sports venues in the mountains (60–80 kilometres). The city aimed to rebrand itself as the 'Capital of the Alps', an ambitious designation given the potential competition and its abiding reputation as an industrial city. It also sought to assert its role as a centre for culture, leisure, cultural tourism, business tourism, recreation and higher education, to capitalize on its existing cultural facilities, and to promote an urban regeneration agenda in the face of industrial restructuring of the car industry. The Cultural Festival – Italyart – fitted that agenda. Its organizers sought to 'promote, together with the historic heritage, the contemporary image of a territory open to experimentation, innovation and research' (TOROC, 2005, p. 3). The official programme (TOROC, 2005) listed 25 visual art exhibitions, seven dance and theatre productions, ten music productions, a festival of Italian cinema, a series of literary dinners and 11 historical and social events. In addition there were 126 events listed under the title 'Dedicated to Turin 2006', the result of an invitation to cultural organizations to contribute events and performances to the programme. These included exhibitions, performances, lectures, thematic tours and traditional culture. The sweep of the festival included Italian and international artists, the Occitan culture of the alpine valleys and the Inuit of the Arctic, life in ancient Egypt and masterpieces of Leonardo da Vinci, 'La Bohème', and Nordic myths.

Conclusion

This chapter has traced the circuitous path by which a cultural dimension has been incorporated into the modern Olympics. The Arts Festivals have absorbed the more haphazard festivities and cultural programmes of earlier times, and exhibitions have replaced the competitions. There has been a measure of convergence between the Summer Games and the Winter Games as winter hosts have taken on the organization of Olympic Arts Festivals and in some cases attempted longer festivals. Vancouver in its bid document for the 2010 Winter Games even promised the first four-year Olympiad. The Arts Festivals now extend past the Olympic Games to embrace the Paralympics, whose athletes, officials and spectators, can now benefit from the Olympic ambience of the host city as never before.

Yet despite this apparent success, the cultural dimension of the Games still struggles to gain significant international or even public recognition. For most people the Games remain essentially a sporting festival and they are unaware of the cultural aspect. The ideal of uniting art and sport has not been achieved and they remain separate entities. García (2002a, p. 13) blames this on the poor integration of the cultural programme in the overall organization of the Games and its consequent inability to attract the attention of Olympic sponsors who are naturally taken with the opportunities afforded by the ceremonies, torch relay and sporting events (*Ibid.*, p. 12). Yet research also suggests a deeper problem, as epitomized by the fact that journalists at the Main Press Centre and the International Broadcasting Centre in Sydney 2000 were either unaware or uninterested in the cultural information that these centres distributed (García, 2001b, p. 11; see also chapter 14). Sydney set up a Non-Accredited Media Centre that could more easily deal with non-sporting material but this simply reinforced the idea that the cultural programme was set apart from the sporting event (*Ibid.*, p. 12).

For the host cities themselves, the cultural Olympiad and Olympic Arts Festivals now take their place alongside other strategies in efforts to rebrand the Olympic city, create a platform for growth in cultural tourism and improve the quality of life for residents. Certainly many of the Games now leave a legacy of cultural venues and improved urban infrastructure that benefits residents and visitors alike but, in terms of rebranding, it is the Opening and Closing Ceremonies with their artistic segments that have far greater impact in projecting the image of city and nation to the world than the largely overlooked arts offering.

As far as the arts community is concerned, Cultural Olympiads have provided opportunities to stage high-quality exhibitions and performances, commission new work and develop partnerships. While the high art origins of the festivals are still much in evidence, there has been a broadening of the art forms on offer and the animation of city by means of live performance has created an atmosphere of inclusiveness. This has been achieved despite the fact that such festivals remain particularly vulnerable to budget cuts, when the inevitable escalation of expenditure on the Olympic infrastructure results in the need for cost savings elsewhere.

For arts organizations, these festivals can be a risky business. They bring visitors to town, but the competition for their time and money is intense. All benefit if cultural tourism is raised by the exposure of the city, region and nation in the long term but evidence of the short-term impact of the arts festivals on their operations is mixed. Scott (2004, p. 36) found some pessimism among arts managers in Australia and New Zealand about the impact of sporting mega-events on the arts sector prior to the Games. Against that, anecdotal evidence from Barcelona suggested that while local audiences stayed away from museums and galleries, this was compensated by a rise in the number of inbound visitors. The Atlanta's High Museum of Art exhibition 'Five Rings of Passion' attracted large numbers of visitors because it was located close to the Games venues, had a theme with an Olympic connection and operated a joint ticketing scheme with Olympic events. Scott's own study of two Sydney museums (Powerhouse and the National Maritime Museum) during the Games found similarly that proximity to the site of a sporting event, location on the transportation route to that site and a thematically linked exhibition programme raised attendances. Inevitably, the many venues that fail to combine these attributes fared less well.

As the cultural festivals have got bigger, the sport references have necessarily become relatively less important. The original concept of the Olympic celebration of the arts as an integral part of sporting culture was always a romantic notion borne of a particular reading of classical Greek culture and embodied in a number of the early classically-trained sportsmen at the end of the nineteenth century. The Olympic Movement has remained committed to a cultural festival that at best reinforces the idea of harmonious relations between the peoples of the world but, in reality, signally fails to demonstrate the connection between sports and the arts – for the simple reason that they inhabit separate spheres in the twenty-first century.

Notes

1. TOROC (2005, p. 3).

2. One of Coubertin's earliest surviving writings on the subject, dating from 1908 (cited in Müller, 2000, p. 543), talks about an ideal world where sport is so embedded within society that all young men practise physical exercise to perfect their health and increase their strength.

3. This dates back to the 1908 London Olympics where Coubertin was inspired by the sermon in St.Paul's Cathedral delivered by Ethelbert Talbot (Bishop of Central Pennsylvania) to participants in the Games: 'In these Olympiads, the important thing is not winning, but taking part'.

4. The Americans could not match Moscow's card stunts where 4,500 athletes manipulating cards, flags, shirt fronts and caps were able to create a backdrop of 174 giant images. Instead they used all spectators in the stadium to create 'one giant card trick' that would 'blow them away'. Each seat had a coloured card attached that, when held aloft, created the flags of all the competing nations (quoted by Ueberroth, 1986, p. 301).

5. The reasons for the poor IOC attendance was that Coubertin did not start to inform members about the Conference until the end of March and many of the members were attending the Intercalated Games in Athens (22 April–2 May 1906). Coubertin himself in his memoir of 1931 (Müller, 2000, p. 621) states that the timing of the Congress was deliberate on his part to give himself a reason not to travel to Athens to an event with which he profoundly disagreed.

6. Among the gold medal winners was Coubertin himself with 'Ode to Sport' submitted under the pseudonyms of Georges Hohrod and M. Eschbach.

7. After seeing the dress rehearsal with its 1,000 performers at the Dietrich Eckart Theatre in June, Goebbels cancelled the project and the professional dancers involved were sent on vacation for the duration of the Games. After the Games, Laban was sent to Franconia under

house arrest from which he escaped to Paris in early 1937, finally joining Dartington Hall in January 1938 (Green, 1986, pp. 111–112).

8. Literally meaning 'Strength through Joy', KdF was a state-controlled workers' leisure association, established in 1933.

9. This glorification of sacrificial death was echoed in the final months of the war when Diem addressed the Hitler Youth in March 1945. He lectured them on the men of Sparta and appealed to them not to shrink from sacrifice for the fatherland, even if they were conscious of possible defeat (Rürup, 1996, p. 219). Just over a month later many of these boys, and the Peoples Reserve Battalions troops fighting with them were killed trying to regain control of the Reichssportfeld from Russian troops.

10. See chapter 1 for discussion of the contrast between Melbourne 1956 and Sydney 2000.

11. Rome's 'blockbuster' exhibition 'Sport in History and Art', for example, ran for six months in the EUR Olympic complex. Spanning 3,000 years of Italian sport history with over 2,300 exhibits brought together from over a hundred collections and over thirty libraries across Italy, it represented a major achievement in exhibition planning and archival work that was four years in the planning (Organizing Committee, 1960, pp. 313–316).

12. These were: 'Two Thousand Years of Barcelona' which explored Barcelona's past from its Roman heritage to contemporary art; 'Art and Sport', which recalled the original purpose of the cultural dimension of the Olympic movement; and 'The Olympic Festival of the Arts' which included high art, street performance, modern work and incorporated the WOMAD (World of Music, Arts & Dance) festival.

13. Centennial Park, itself part of the transformation of central Atlanta, would provide the desired space for visitors, conventioneers and office workers that the city's business leaders had long wanted albeit, as chapter 2 showed, at the expense of the underclass.

Chapter 5

The Paralympic Games

John R. Gold and Margaret M. Gold

The Paralympics is becoming a truly worldwide event … we want it to be the same as the Olympic Games.

Tanni Grey-Thompson

Speaking to an academic audience, Dame Tanni Grey-Thompson (2006), the leading medal winner in the history of the Paralympic Games, noted the remarkable convergence of the Paralympic and Olympic movements. From pragmatic beginnings as part of the treatment of spine-injured ex-servicemen towards the end of the Second World War, disability sport has developed so rapidly that it now supports sport-specific national squads of elite athletes participating in international competition. As the summit of disability sport, the Paralympic Games have played a major part in changing social attitudes by emphasizing achievement rather than impairment and by accelerating the agenda of inclusion. They have also forced changes in official attitudes in countries where disability was ideologically problematic, if only to accommodate international opinion when bidding for the Olympics – given that Paralympics are now closely linked to that process (Gold and Gold, 2007).

This chapter considers the development of the Paralympics from small beginnings as a competition for disabled ex-servicemen and women in the grounds of Stoke Mandeville Hospital (England) to the present day ambulatory international festival held in Olympic cities immediately after the Summer or Winter Games. It traces their origins to the work of Dr (later Sir) Ludwig Guttmann at the National Spinal Injuries Unit at Stoke Mandeville Hospital in Buckinghamshire, who used sport as an integral part of the treatment of paraplegic patients. The sports competition held at the hospital to coincide with the Opening Ceremony of the London Games in July 1948 became an annual event attracting the first international participation in 1952, after which it became the International Stoke Mandeville Games. From 1960 onwards attempts were made to hold every fourth Games in the Olympic host city, although the path towards acceptance by host cities proved difficult. As will be seen, it was only from 1988 onwards that a process of convergence began that brought the Paralympics into the central arena of the Olympics, both literally and figuratively, leading to the host city being required to include a bid for the Paralympics as part of its bid for the Olympics.

The later parts of this chapter discuss the relatively modest ramifications of this requirement for prospective host cities, given that Paralympians make use of many of the same facilities as their Olympian counterparts. Although unlikely ever to drive major infrastructural or regeneration projects, the Paralympics have repercussions for the host city in the need to accommodate a group of athletes and officials with different requirements and in promoting the cause of a barrier-free urban environment. The implications of these provisions are discussed in relation to the Paralympics of the twenty-first century, particularly in relation to the emphasis placed on the disability agenda in the successful bid made by London for the 2012 Games.

Origins

The first stirrings of disability sport emerged in the late nineteenth century, primarily through the work of activists in the deaf community. The first Sports Club for the Deaf was founded in Berlin in 1888 and by 1924 national sports federations for the deaf had emerged in Belgium, Czechoslovakia, France, Great Britain, Holland and Poland. Collectively, these six federations sent 140 athletes to Paris in 1924 to participate in the First International Silent Games – the gathering that marked the birth of a four-yearly cycle of 'World Games for the Deaf' (Séguillon, 2002, p. 119). Subsequently divided into Summer and Winter festivals after the pattern of the Olympics, these were later recognized by the International Olympic Committee (IOC) as the Deaflympics.

The Deaflympics were important as an indicator of possibilities, but the deaf community retained a separate existence as a disability group rather than participating in the movement that would create the Paralympics. Instead, the latter stemmed from the treatment of severely injured servicemen at the end of the Second World War and particularly the work of Ludwig Guttmann – a figure whose role is comparable to that of Baron Pierre de Coubertin in reviving the modern Olympics (see chapter 2). Guttmann, a prominent Jewish neurosurgeon, had arrived in Britain as a refugee from Nazi Germany in 1939. After appointment to a research post at Oxford University's Department of Neurosurgery and then at the Wingfield-Morris Orthopaedic Hospital, he became director of what would become the National Spinal Injuries Centre at Stoke Mandeville Hospital (Aylesbury, Buckinghamshire). Guttmann later commented that paraplegia was the 'most depressing and neglected subject in all medicine' at this time (quoted in Goodman, 1986, p. 96), characterized by poor patient survival rates, low morale amongst nursing staff, and difficulty in recruiting specialist physiotherapists. His approach instituted a programme of 'total care', having patients turned physically every two hours day and night to prevent pressure sores and improving standards of bladder hygiene to help tackle problems of infection. Physiotherapy assisted limb flexibility and, for some patients, increased mobility. A pre-vocational work regime and various forms of recreation including concerts, visits and *competitive* sports, designed to keep patients busy and create a sense of purpose, complemented the medical regime.

In this context, therefore, sport transcended mere leisure. Not only was it 'the most natural form of remedial exercise' restoring physical fitness, strength, coordination, speed, endurance and overcoming fatigue, but also had the psychological impact of restoring pleasure in life and contributing to social reintegration (Guttmann, 1976, p. 12). Developing these ideas, Guttmann formulated the idea of a sports festival for the disabled that would promote contact with other patients and address attitudes about the capabilities of the disabled. On 28 July 1948, an archery competition took place on the front lawns of the hospital, involving 16 competitors arranged into two teams: one from Stoke Mandeville and the other from the Star and Garter Home for disabled ex-servicemen in Richmond-on-Thames. The event was consciously chosen as a demonstration of potential, symbolized by being held on the same day as the Opening Ceremony of the London Olympics, with archery seen as second only to swimming in its 'physiotherapeutic value … for the paralysed' (Special Correspondent, 1948). In 1949, Stoke Mandeville hosted a larger competition, involving 60 competitors from five hospitals participating in what became a steadily widening group of sports (table 5.1). During the meeting, Guttmann gave a speech in which he hoped that the event would become international and achieve 'world fame as the disabled men and women's equivalent of the Olympic Games' (Goodman, 1986, p. 150).

The Stoke Mandeville Games quickly acquired an international dimension, particularly by drawing on institutional connections that the Hospital had developed through training visiting staff, through staff moving to other hospitals and spreading Stoke Mandeville's characteristic approach to sport, and through ex-patients who pioneered paraplegic sport in their own countries. In 1952, another Olympic year, the involvement of a group of Dutch war veterans presaged wider European participation. In 1953, teams from Finland, France, Israel and the Netherlands appeared, along with a Canadian team. The Americans first participated in 1955, followed by the Australians in 1957 – by which time the Stoke Mandeville Games had commonly gained the nickname 'Paralympics' (Carisbroke *et al.*, 1956). The word 'Paralympics' at this stage was clearly a pun combining 'paraplegic' and 'Olympic' (IPC, 2006*a*), effectively confronting Olympian traditions of celebrating excellence and the perfectly formed body with the realities of disability. It was only over time that reinterpretation occurred. In part, this was driven by the Games embracing participants with forms of disability other than paraplegia. Equally, it resulted from a process of convergence that closely allied the Paralympics with the Olympic movement. With an ingenious revision of the etymology, the approved version of the term asserted that the first syllable of 'Paralympics' derived from the Greek preposition 'para', meaning 'beside' or 'alongside'. Viewed in this way, the Paralympics constitute a festival that

Table 5.1. Paralympic Sports.

Summer Games	Year included in the full Paralympic Programme
Archery	1960
Athletics	1960
Boccia	1984
Bowls	1968–1988, 1996
Cycling	1988
Equestrian	1996
Football 5-a-side	2004
Football 7-a-side	1984
Goalball	1976
Judo	2004
Powerlifting/Weightlifting	1964 men
Powerlifting/Weightlifting	2000 women
Rowing	2008
Sailing	2000
Shooting	1976
Swimming	1960
Table Tennis	1960
Volleyball – standing volleyball	1976–1996
Volleyball – sitting	1980
Wheelchair Basketball	1960
Wheelchair Fencing	1960
Wheelchair Rugby	2000
Wheelchair Tennis	1992
Winter Games	
Alpine Skiing	1976
Ice Sledge Hockey	1994
Nordic Skiing – Cross Country	1976
Nordic Skiing - Biathlon	1994
Wheelchair Curling	2006

Source: IPC (2006*a*).

exists alongside and operates in parallel with the Olympic Games, while retaining a separate identity (*Ibid.*).

Building Connections

As the Games grew, demands for greater professionalism towards the organization, funding and management of international sport for the disabled saw the establishment in 1959 of the International Stoke Mandeville Games Committee (later Foundation, hence ISMGF). This ran and developed the annual Stoke Mandeville Games and oversaw the organization of a parallel four-yearly 'Olympic' competition until 1972 (see table 5.2).

The process of building links with the Olympics, however, proved long and torturous despite highly promising beginnings. In 1956, during ceremonies at the Melbourne Olympics, the IOC had awarded the Fearnley Cup to Guttmann for 'outstanding achievement in the service of Olympic ideals' (Goodman, 1986,

Table 5.2. Summer Paralympic Games.

Year	Aegis	Location	Number of countries	Number of athletes	Number of sports for which medals awarded	Disability Groups
1952	Stoke Mandeville Hospital	Stoke Mandeville★	2	130	6	SI
1960	ISMGC	Rome	23	400	8	SI
1964	ISMGC	Tokyo	21	357	9	SI
1968	ISMGC	Tel Aviv, Israel★	29	750	10	SI
1972	ISMGF	Heidelberg, West Germany★	43	984	10	SI
1976	ISMGF ISOD	Toronto, Canada★	38	1657	13	SI, A, VI, LA
1980	ISMGF ISOD	Arnhem, Holland★	42	1973	12	SI, A, VI, LA, CP
1984	ISMGF	Stoke Mandeville★	41	1100	10	SI
	ISOD	New York★	45	1800	14	A, VI, LA, CP
1988	ICC	Seoul	61	3013	18	SI, A, VI. LA, CP
1992	ICC	Barcelona	82	3021	16	SI, A, VI.
		Madrid★	73	1400	5	ID
1996	IPC	Atlanta	103	3195	19	SI, A, VI, LA, CP, ID
2000	IPC	Sydney	122	3843	19	SI, A, VI, LA, CP, ID
2004	IPC	Athens	136	3806	19	SI, A, VI, LA, CP
2008	IPC	Beijing	150 expected	4000 expected	20	SI, A, VI, LA, CP
2012	IPC	London	150 expected	4200 expected	20	na

★ Years in which the Paralympic Games did not take place in the Olympic location.

Guide to abbreviations: *SI* Spinal Injury; *A* Amputee; *VI* Visually Impaired; *LA* Les Autres; *CP* Cerebral Palsy; *ID* Intellectual Impairment.

Sources: Compiled from IPC (2006a) and Scruton (1998).

p. 157), a remarkable degree of recognition less than a decade after the foundation of the Stoke Mandeville Games. The next stage was to take the Stoke Mandeville Games to the Olympic host city itself, and when the Games were held in Rome 1960 and Tokyo 1964 the convergence of the two sets of Games seemed assured. Such arrangements, however, depended on the goodwill of the host city, sponsorship and public funding to cover the cost. The Rome Games, for example, had the cooperation of the Spinal Unit at Ostia, gained sponsorship from INAIL (*Istituto nazionale per l'assicurazione contro gli infortuni sul lavoro* – the Italian National

Insurance Institute Against Accidents at Work), and had the support of the Italian Olympic Committee (CONI). The 400 disabled athletes used the Olympic Pool and Village, but last minute changes meant that those parts of the Village equipped with lifts were unavailable. Moreover, withdrawal of an offer to use nearby Olympic facilities meant that competitors were perforce bussed 40 minutes to the Tre Fontane sports ground (Scruton, 1998, p. 308). The Tokyo Games followed on from the Summer Olympics, accommodated competitors in the athletes' Village, and shared facilities recently used by the Olympic athletes. Its Opening Ceremony, with the Crown Prince and Princess acting as patrons, attracted 5,000 spectators.

From this point, problems with the host city seriously affected further progress. It was another 24 years before disabled athletes again competed in an Olympic host city (Seoul 1988), with a succession of cities refusing to host the Paralympics. The IOC, in its role of handling the bidding process for the Olympics, was only interested in the candidate cities' ability to meet the costs and needs of elite athletes. There was no stipulation that the Olympic city must host parallel games for athletes with disabilities. Admittedly, the Paralympics became a greater challenge to hosts as they grew in size (see table 5.1), especially with admission of a wider range of disability groups after 1976. The increasing scale of the Games, coupled with prevailing building standards that failed to accommodate the disabled, shortage of available funds and lack of any inclusive philosophy regarding athletes with disability proved obstacles for further collaboration with many Olympic cities.

For example, despite having sent three observers to Tokyo, Mexico City declined the Games in 1968 because of 'technical difficulties'. They were held instead at the sports centre of the Israel Foundation for Handicapped Children in Ramat Gan near Tel Aviv. In 1972, the University of Heidelberg staged the Games rather than Munich, as plans for the post-festival use of the Olympic Village had meant transferring the site to developers for conversion into private apartments immediately after the Olympic Closing Ceremony (Scruton, 1998, p. 320). Lack of suitable accommodation, real or claimed, plagued subsequent events. In 1976, Toronto acted as hosts rather than the Olympic city of Montreal, with the athletes housed at Toronto and York Universities. These two Paralympic Villages were located some distance from each other as well as from the competition venues. When the Moscow Olympic Organizing Committee failed even to respond to a request to stage the Games, the 1980 festival took place at Arnhem in the Netherlands. Here, too, the available accommodation (an army barracks) was inconveniently located for access to the sports venues. In 1984, the Americans agreed to host the Games for all disabilities, but not in the host Olympic city (Los Angeles). Instead, they were to be split between New York and the University of Illinois (Champaign); an arrangement that foundered when the latter withdrew, though funding problems, just four months before the Games. As a result, 1,800 amputee, cerebral palsy, visually impaired, and Les Autres[1] athletes competed at the Mitchel Park athletics complex in Uniondale, New York, with 1,200 athletes participating in the wheelchair events that were hurriedly rearranged at Stoke

Figure 5.1. Cauldron for the Paralympic flame, and the Village for the Paralympic Games, Stoke Mandeville, 1984.

Mandeville (*Ibid*., pp. 184, 202). Ironically, these were the first Games that the IOC officially recognized as the Paralympics (figure 5.1).

The early Winter Paralympic Games for the disabled fared little better (table 5.3). Established in 1976, initially they too did not take place in Olympic cities or even in the same countries. The first Winter Games took place in Örnsköldsvik (Sweden) rather than at Innsbruck (Austria). These were followed in 1980 by Games at Geilo (Norway) rather than Lake Placid, at Innsbruck in 1984 rather than Sarajevo (although an exhibition event was held in the Winter Games there), and Innsbruck again in 1988 rather than Calgary, which declined to hold the Paralympics.

This retreat from the positive pattern seemingly established in the early 1960s greatly disappointed the Paralympic movement. Guttmann (1976, p. 174) denounced the thinking that had prevented Mexico City or Munich holding the Games, commenting on 'the lamentable lack of appreciation of the place thousands of disabled sportsmen and women have earned for themselves in the field of international sport'. Chiefly as a result of this, a new complex of buildings was constructed at Stoke Mandeville (figure 5.2), comprising a Stadium for the Paralysed and Other Disabled (opened in 1969 and later renamed the Ludwig Guttmann Sports Stadium for the Disabled) and an 'Olympic' Village in 1981 (Goodman, 1986, p. 164). Thus the sporting facilities were finally separated from the hospital itself and from the notion of 'illness', reflecting the fact that disabled athletes were now achieving elite status with an emphasis on performance.

Table 5.3. Winter Paralympic Games.

Year	Aegis	Location	Participating countries	Number of athletes	Number of sports	Disability Groups
1976	ISOD	Örnsköldsvik Sweden★	17	250	2	VI, A
1980	ISOD ISMGF	Geilo Norway★	18	350	2	VI, A, SI, CP, LA
1984	ICC	Innsbruck Austria★	21	457	2	VI, A, SI CP, LA
1988	ICC	Innsbruck Austria★	22	397	2	VI, A, SI, CP, LA
1992	ICC	Albertville France	24	475	2	VI, A, SI, CP, LA
1994	IPC	Lillehammer Norway	31	492	3	VI, A, SI, CP, LA
1998	IPC	Nagano Japan	32	571	4	VI, A, SI, CP, LA
2002	IPC	Salt Lake City, USA	36	416	3	VI, A, SI, CP, LA
2006	IPC	Torino Italy	39	477	4	VI, A, SI, CP, LA
2010	IPC	Vancouver Canada	45 expected	650 expected	4	VI, A, SI, CP, LA

★ Years in which the Paralympic Games did not take place in the Olympic location.

Guide to abbreviations: *SI* Spinal Injury; *A* Amputee; *VI* Visually Impaired; *LA* Les Autres; *CP* Cerebral Palsy.

Sources: Compiled from IPC (2006a); Scruton (1998).

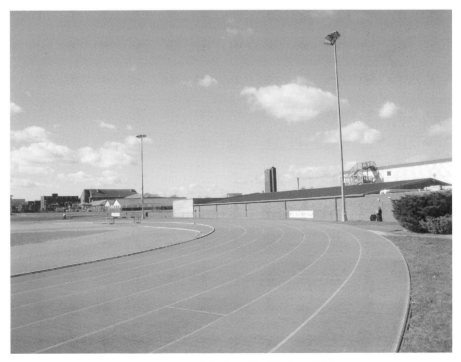

Figure 5.2. Stoke Mandeville stadium (Aylesbury, Buckinghamshire).

Institutional Convergence

The problem, however, was not simply the resistance of Olympic cities and their Organizing Committees, since the definition of disability and competing jurisdictions of relevant organizations also affected progress. The Stoke Mandeville Games originally confined entry to medically controlled paraplegics, but the organizers felt impelled to respond when other groups pressed for participation in internationally organized sports festivals. The foundation of the International Sports Organization for the Disabled (ISOD) in 1964 created opportunities for the blind, amputees and individuals with other locomotor disabilities (de Pauw and Gavron, 2005, p. 39). ISOD collaborated with ISMGF in broadening the scope of the 1976 Toronto Games to include amputees, visually impaired and Les Autres. Competitors with cerebral palsy joined the 1980 Games.

The expanding scope of disability sport quickly generated new international disability organizations. The need to coordinate their activities and eliminate duplication of events required further institutional arrangements, leading in particular to the foundation of the ICC (International Coordinating Committee of the World Sports Organizations) in 1982. This brought together nominated senior representatives from the four major International Sports Organizations: ISMWSF (the International Stoke Mandeville Wheelchair Sports Federation, previously the ISMGF), ISOD, IBSA (the International Blind Sports Federation), and the CP-ISRA (Cerebral Palsy International Sport and Recreation Association). These were later joined by CISS (International Committee of Sports for the Deaf) and INAS (International Sports Federation for Persons with Mental Handicap – later changed to Intellectual Disability). Thus constituted, the ICC gave the disabled sports movement a single voice for the first time. It also allowed greater clarity in developing relations with the IOC and Olympic Games Organizing Committees, which found immediate expression in the geographical convergence of the Summer Games at Seoul 1988 and the Winter Games at Albertville 1992.

The ICC oversaw the Games held in Olympic cities in 1988 and 1992, with the exception of the Winter Games in Calgary in 1988. The 1988 Seoul Olympics and Paralympics had separate Organizing Committees, but with sufficient coordination to allow the sharing of venues, equipment and key personnel. With the Olympic Village unavailable after the Olympics, a specially designed Village was constructed for the Paralympians. They also received the same spectacular Opening and Closing Ceremonies as the summer Games, watched by capacity crowds of 75,000.

Barcelona pioneered the organizational integration of the two sets of Games by giving overall responsibility to the Organizing Committee of the Barcelona Games (COOB), with a separate Division charged with overall responsibility to plan the Paralympics. This ensured explicit attention to the needs of disabled athletes and comparable treatment with Olympians. The Paralympic Games now had their custom-designed Opening and Closing ceremonial spectacles (Rognoni,

1996, p. 264). Free admission to Paralympic events ensured large numbers of spectators and there was substantial television coverage. At the same time, COOB imposed its own decisions, cutting the number of sports to 15 and refusing to allow the mentally impaired to participate in the Paralympics. Instead INAS held an officially recognized Paralympic Games in Madrid in which 1,400 athletes from 73 countries competed. This took place after the Barcelona Paralympic Games.

The final stage in the evolution of the institutional basis for the Games came with the establishment of the International Paralympic Committee (IPC) in 1989: an organization similar in structure to the IOC itself. Based in Bonn (Federal Republic of Germany), it serves as the umbrella organization for 162 National Paralympic Committees, five regional bodies, and four international disability-specific sports federations. It also acts as the international federation for 13 of the 24 Paralympic sports (IPC, 2006*b*, p. 6). Its vision is to enable 'Paralympic athletes to achieve sporting excellence and inspire and excite the world' and professes an eleven-point mission which includes sport development 'from initiation to elite level' (IPC, 2006*c*, p. 3). Crucially, since 1992 it is now the sole coordinating body for Paralympic sport recognized by the IOC.

As the IOC and IPC moved closer together, there was identification of areas that had produced conflict, notably, the use of the term 'Olympics' (which the IOC regard as their copyright), and the Paralympic Logo. The IPC Logo, originally introduced at the Seoul Games, comprised five traditional Korean decorative motifs (Tae-Geuks) in the Olympic colours (blue, black, red, yellow and green). Given that the IOC felt this was too close to their five-ring symbol, the IPC reduced the five Tae-Geuks to three in 1994 and replaced them completely as part of a rebranding exercise in 2003. The new logo, comprising three 'agitos' (from the Latin *agito* meaning 'I move'), was first used at the 2004 Athens Games, along with the new motto 'Spirit in Motion' (IPC, 2005, p. 6).

Four agreements between the IOC and IPC signed between 2000 and 2006 clarified the relationship between the two organizations, set out the principles for further cooperation and provided financial support for the IPC. An agreement in October 2000 brought the workings of the two organizations closer by co-opting the IPC President to the IOC and including an IPC representative on 11 of the IOC Commissions, including the Evaluation Commission – the body that examines the competing bids from cities seeking to host the Olympic Games. The IOC also undertook to pay an annual subvention towards IPC administration costs ($3 million per annum), annual sums for development projects, and specific assistance to help athletes from developing countries attend the Salt Lake City Winter Paralympic Games and the Athens Summer Paralympics (IOC, 2000*a*). An agreement in June 2001 elucidated the organization of the Paralympic Games, confirming that the location would always be the Olympic host city and would take place 'shortly after' the Olympic Games using the same facilities and venues. From the 2008 Summer Games and 2010 Winter Games onwards, there would be full integration of the two Organizing Committees (IOC, 2001). An agreement on revenues for broadcasting and marketing the Paralympics (August 2003) guaranteed IOC payments to the IPC of $9 million for the 2008 Games and $14 million for 2010 and 2012 (IOC, 2003a). The final agreement (June 2006) extended these arrangements through to 2014 and 2016, increased funding for the IPC and set out the respective roles of the IOC and IPC in the planning, organization and staging of the Paralympics, the use of technical manuals, the sports programme, and the number of accredited individuals (IOC, 2006a).

Accommodating the Disability Agenda

The move towards a 'one city, one bid' approach for selection of Olympic host cities was of vital importance to the IPC. It meant that the two festivals came into line as part of an overall package that prospective host cities would put together. Cities bidding for the 2008, 2010, 2012 and 2014 Games had to show total organization integration between the Olympic and Paralympic Games, with details of the Paralympic Games fully articulated in the bid documents. Indeed, the speed of integration was more rapid than these agreements stipulated, with both Salt Lake City and Athens establishing a single Organizing Committee (IOC, 2003a) and information on the Paralympic Games appearing in the official Reports of the Olympic Games since Sydney 2000 (e.g. SOCOG, 2000a, pp. 47–49).

This development, of course, needs to be set in proper perspective. On the one hand, it was never likely that this smaller festival, held in the wake of the main events, would assume the same significance as the Olympics or preoccupy the thinking of city planners to the same extent. For many cities, the right to stage the Olympics is a prize aggressively won, whereas 'they inherit the Paralympic Games as an obligation' (Cashman, 2006, 247). As such, the Paralympics tend to be fitted into the package offered for the Olympics – a pragmatic strategy given that they produce little demand for additional facilities, other than for a few sports such as boccia and goalball that have special requirements[2] and for modifications to transport and stadia to allow free access for competitors, officials and spectators. It is also scarcely conceivable that the Paralympics *per se* would ever act as a catalyst for major infrastructural investment or urban regeneration. Yet, on the other hand, their significance for the host city is far from negligible. A city's Olympic bid that features a lukewarm or ill-considered approach to the Paralympics may well suffer regardless of the strength of its proposals for the Olympics. In addition, the act of staging the Paralympics impacts on host cities through the way that they confront questions of disability, most notably with respect to creating a barrier-free environment.[3] Although, as noted, the requirement to integrate the two sets of Games only became binding with the 2008 Beijing Games, hosts with an established record of upholding disability rights and with legislation enshrining rights of access already in place have enjoyed an advantage in the bidding and preparation of the Games. Hence, cities such as Sydney, Turin and London could build on their existing practices which were already enshrined in legislation, whereas the Games in Athens and Beijing were the catalysts for initiating the disability agenda.

Sydney, for example, sought to address problems seen at Atlanta 1996, such as the lack of visibility of the Paralympic Games and poor coordination between them and the Olympics. As host for the Eleventh Paralympic Games, the city achieved a good working relationship between the bodies responsible for the two Games (SOCOG and the Sydney Paralympic Organizing Committee), which had shared departments, and with other Games-related organizations. The Games themselves took place in the Olympic Park, with the (Paralympic) Village home to 6,943 people, comprising 3,824 athletes, 2,315 team officials and 804 technical officials (BPA, 2007). The design of the Olympic Park also represented a drastic improvement in accessibility over previous Paralympics, with Australia able to capitalize on the country's longstanding active involvement in disability sport. The improved access provided in the Olympic Park, however, was 'only as good as the city and suburban network which fed into it' (Cashman, 2006, p. 254). For example, only 5 per cent of railway stations facilitated easy access for wheelchair disabled, and relatively few buses had low-floor access (*Ibid.*).

The Winter Games in Turin 2006 similarly sought to boost the visibility of the Paralympics. The Italians treated the staging of the Paralympic Games in Italy as a welcome reminder of history, given that Rome in 1960 had been the first Olympic city to welcome the Stoke Mandeville International Festival (BPA, 2007). Continuing the themes adopted by the Winter Olympics (e.g. as in figure 5.3), the Paralympics used the same accommodation and facilities (figure 5.4). The major

Figure 5.3. Welcoming slogan, Turin Airport, March 2006.

Figure 5.4. Turin Esposizione, venue for the sledge hockey, Paralympic Games, Turin, March 2006.

innovation was worldwide coverage of all sports of the Paralympic Winter Games, with over 100 hours of coverage provided through an internet television channel owned by the IPC (paralympicsport.tv), narrowcast free-to-air. Seen as a way of overcoming the resistance of the larger broadcasting networks, the webcasting experiment will be carried forward to future events.

By contrast, there was little tradition of disabled sport in Greece. This was addressed in the years leading up to the Athens Games in 2004 by developing an accessible sports infrastructure for athletes with disability that could be used in the preparation of Greek athletes and to permit training by other Paralympic teams (ATHOC, 2005, p. 178). Eighty-five per cent of the venues used were the same as for the Olympics, with additional ones for the Paralympic-specific sports. Nevertheless, while it was possible to plan for disabled access in new Olympic investment (including public transport, venues and the public spaces around venues), the wider environment posed challenges. The Official Report of the Games went so far as to call Athens 'unfriendly' to the disabled community and requiring 'drastic measures' to make the city accessible (*Ibid.*, p. 177). The Organizing Committee (ATHOC) produced design guidelines and accessibility information for the municipalities making up the Greater Athens area, where much of the Olympic infrastructure was located, to encourage them to upgrade their public spaces, particularly along key routes identified by ATHOC (see chapter 15). Furthermore, it urged private businesses to promote accessibility in their own premises and to raise awareness among their staff. To this end, ATHOC and the Chambers of Commerce of the four cities participating in the Olympics (Athens,

Thessaloniki, Heraklio and Volos) developed the Accessible Choice Programme (ERMIS). Businesses compliant with this programme earned the right to display a symbol indicating that they welcomed customers with disabilities and their details were included in a directory issued to all Paralympic delegations on arrival in Greece. Although attendances were less than at Sydney (850,000 compared with 1.1 million) and some venues were less than half-full, part of the value of the festival was considered to lie in its pedagogic impact. As in Australia, the organizers had developed an educational programme to promote greater understanding of the Paralympics and a large proportion of the audience were children. An accident that killed seven students while travelling to watch the Paralympics cast a shadow over this strategy, leading to cancellation of the artistic and entertainment sections of the Closing Ceremony out of respect. The ceremony continued, but with only the protocol elements required for the completion of the Games (*Ibid*, p. 511).

Beijing's plans for 2008 also reflect significant shifts in attitude. China's own participation in the Paralympic Movement is relatively recent. When invited to the Rome Games in 1960, the official statement declared there were no disabled in China (Lane, 2006). Relaxation of this ideological stance saw the establishment of the Chinese Sports Association for Disabled Athletes in 1983 (de Pauw and Gavron, 2005, pp. 127–128). Chinese athletes started to compete in international competition, with a small group entering the 1984 Games held in New York. No Chinese team participated in the Winter Paralympic Games until Salt Lake City in 2002. The increasing seriousness with which the Chinese then took sport for the disabled is reflected in the spectacular improvement in the performance of their athletes – rising from ninth in the medal table in 1996, to sixth in 2000 and first place in Athens 2004. This new priority reflects China's characteristic use of sporting investment as an adjunct of foreign policy (see chapter 16), as much as any root-and-branch change in prevailing attitudes. Nevertheless, the requirements of provision for 2008 have focused attention on the challenge of creating barrier-free Games in a city where access has only been on the agenda for a short time and where much of the infrastructure is anything but barrier-free. The Beijing Municipal People's Congress adopted the country's first local legislation relating to physical accessibility when passing the 'Beijing Regulation on Construction and Management of the Barrier-free Facilities' in April 2004. The regulations apply to public transport, hospitals, banks, public toilets and parks. As a result, for instance, underground stations are having ramps installed, disabled toilets, tactile paths for the visually impaired and public telephones for wheelchair users, with disabled seats available on trains (CIIC, 2004).

London 2012

There is no doubt that, perhaps for the first time, the quality of that portion of the Olympic bid which concerned the Paralympic Games was seen as constituting a major positive factor for the entire candidature. The location of Stoke Mandeville in London's Home Counties meant that there was a sense of the Paralympics 'coming home'. From the outset, Paralympians were part of the group responsible for organizing and drafting the bid and attended the vital IOC meeting in Singapore in July 2005, when the outcome was decided.

Under the new rules agreed in 2001, the candidate cities for the final phase of the Olympic selection procedure had to complete a questionnaire with 17 themes. Theme 9 related exclusively to the Paralympic Games and contained nine sets of questions covering the structural integration of the organization of the Paralympics within the Organizing Committee, the dates and the competition schedule, the venues, accommodation, transport operation, travel times, disability awareness (including staff and volunteer training), media facilities, vision for the Games, finance, and the Games' legacy (IOC, 2004*a*). In its bid, the London Committee capitalized on the heritage of disabled sport in the UK, a tradition of volunteering for Paralympic events, anti-disability discrimination in service provision dating back to the 1995 Disability Discrimination Act, and a good record in disability awareness training. The London Bid document set out three goals: to strengthen the Paralympic Movement; to deliver accessible and inclusive designs for all facilities; and to maximize media coverage (LOCOC, 2004, p. 173). The bid contained eight specific commitments for the Paralympics (*Ibid.*, p. 191):

- Creating an Olympic Village that is fully accessible to all from the outset;

- Maximizing media coverage and exposure, as pioneered by the BBC;

- Integrating Olympic Games and Paralympic Games planning;

- Training all Games workforce in the principles of inclusion;

- Establishing operational policies that encompass Paralympic values;

- Recruiting suitably qualified disabled people;

- Promoting the Paralympic Games nationwide;

- Creating a cultural programme featuring disabled artists.

London plans 11 Paralympic sports in the Olympic Park, seven in the 'River Zone' (ExCel in Docklands and Greenwich), road racing in Regents Park and sailing at Weymouth. Housing the athletes in the Olympic Village will mean that 95 per cent are accommodated within 15 minutes travel time from competition venues, linked by what are described as 'environmentally friendly and fully accessible' buses. Ticket holders for Paralympic events would travel free by public transport, with a Games Mobility Service for disabled spectators (*Ibid.*, p. 185).

In its assessment, the report of the IOC's Evaluation Committee was highly complimentary with regard to the bid's coverage of the Paralympics. There was praise for the degree of integration between the Olympic and Paralympic Games in terms of organization, management and physical planning. There was also acknowledgement of the rich history of Paralympic sport in the United Kingdom, the nation's reputation in television coverage and public support for disability sport, and recognition that capacities of UK Paralympic Sport were 'among the best in the world' (IOC, 2005a, p. 73). In particular, the report noted the proposal for a 'Paralympic legacy for all' including 'social, educational and sport legacies with a focus on improving society' (*Ibid.*).

Conclusion

The plans for London 2012 and the Evaluation Committee's buoyant assessment of them underline the extent of progress over the last half-century. The Paralympics have developed dramatically since the first competition between 130 British and Dutch athletes in 1952. Notwithstanding a chequered history and the characteristic dissonance between bid promises and final realities, the Paralympic Games have spread geographically, have moved into new sports, have encompassed a wider range of disabilities, and have helped give credence to the belief that access to sport is available to all. The growing scale of the Games provides relatively little challenge given that they primarily use facilities and accommodation provided for the rather larger sporting festivals that occur immediately before the Paralympics. Nevertheless, there are important qualitative changes. As the Games came progressively closer to the heart of the Olympic movement, they have ensured that the disabled community had to be accommodated, figuratively and literally, within the planning, design, cultural and educational programmes of Olympic cities. Cities could avoid those obligations in the 1970s and 1980s, but the bidding process now ensures that they must provide not only barrier-free Olympic facilities, but increasingly also a wider environment and society that welcome diversity. As such, attention to issues of access and discriminatory practices undertaken in relation to an Olympic host city at one point in time have a demonstration effect that may well have implications for that city, and the wider society, at all other times.

Notes

1. Les Autres athletes have 'locomotor conditions such as Arthrogryposis, Arthrosis, cerebral palsy (some types), spinal cord conditions (e.g. polio), multiple sclerosis and muscular dystrophy [and] are allowed to participate in events under the Les Autres classification. Les Autres also incorporates dwarf athletes under its classification. The locomotor conditions may be congenital or as a results of an injury or accident' (BALASA, 2007).

2. 'Boccia' is similar to petanque (French bowls) played individually or as a team game by people with cerebral palsy and other locomotor disabilities. 'Goalball' is a three-a-side gymnasium team game for the blind or visually impaired played on a special court of the same size as that used for volleyball. It involves trying to propel a heavy sound-enhanced ball past the backline of the opponents' half of the court.

3. For more general thinking on planning and disability, see Imrie (1996), Gleeson (2001) and McCann (2005).

Part II

Planning and Management

Chapter 6

Financing the Games

Paul Kitchin

Eight years can be an eternity in the history of the Olympics. In 1976, the Eighteenth Summer Olympics at Montreal failed to generate enough Games-related income to cover the costs incurred in hosting the event, with a shortfall of some $1.2 billion. At a time of economic recession in North America the Games were seen as costly and of inconsequential benefit to host cities. The 1976 Games themselves were affected by a sub-Saharan boycott and were still mired by the terrorist atrocity of the previous Munich Games. The future of the International Olympic Committee itself was at stake. In 1984, the Los Angeles Organizing Committee for the Olympic Games embraced and refined the commercial forces surrounding the Games. Labelled at the time the 'Burger Games', due to the close involvement of corporate sponsors including McDonalds, the event produced an operating profit of between $215 and $225 million (Magdalinski and Nauright, 2004), and created a tangible legacy for the Amateur Athletic Federation of Los Angeles (AAFLA). The key to this success was the minimal outlay of expenditure by using existing venues and tying sponsors into providing in-kind services as well as pure finance. A variant of the financing model used is now current IOC practice and a viable and successful Olympic movement is the result.

This contrast between Montreal 1976 and Los Angeles 1984 is instructive. It pinpoints the time when the financing of the modern Olympics changed rapidly and decisively. The driver of the modern Olympics has been the ability of the Olympic movement to generate economic value from its intellectual property through establishing the biggest sporting and cultural festival on the planet. The 'Olympic movement' here is taken to incorporate the IOC, the International Sporting Federations, and the National Olympic Committees, which each have a significant stake in ensuring the Games' financial health. As such, their main products are not solely the Summer and Winter Olympics but also their complex Olympic ideology, with its associated themes and symbols that are licensed for commercial purposes.

That ideology, of course, is expressed in the philosophy of Olympism (see chapter 4). Established through the Olympic Charter, its principles determine the manner in which the movement uses its media and commercial partners to distribute theme-laden messages across the globe. That the Olympics focuses on the drive for excellence is a desirable theme for most commercial organizations, hence its value in creating appeal. The main symbol of the IOC, the five-ring logo, constitutes one of the most valuable revenue accumulation devices as it is recognized throughout the world. In addition to the symbol, other valuable intangible assets such as the motto *Citius, Altius, Fortius* (Swifter, Higher, Stronger) and the Olympic Hymn are carefully manipulated to support Olympism. Simply put, the communication of Olympism and its associated themes materially assist the financing of the Games, although the heart of Olympic finances lies with the city that successfully bids for the Games. The host city establishes the Organizing Committee for the Olympic Games (OCOG) and stages the event. The IOC carefully controls the parameters of what is to be delivered through the Olympic Charter, but the IOC does not, and has never, managed the event. Operationally, the OCOG has the responsibility for tailoring the IOC's premier product to the characteristics of the host city. During the bid process, the OCOG sets the parameters of the financing model used to stage the event.

The purpose of this chapter is to provide an overview of the finances of the Games, from a business-historical perspective, to complement the more detailed discussions of the experiences of individual Olympic cities in later chapters. As such, it indicates the past growth and potential trends in direct revenue sources acquired and the major sources of expenditure, although it does not provide detailed economic analysis of underlying economic models and processes.[1] In addition, it reviews the increasingly important sources of revenue creation from indirect means.

Revenue Sources

The ideals of Olympism place those staging the Games under considerable pressure. As public attitudes have eased regarding the involvement of commercial interests in sport, the current situation looks relatively ideal (Shank, 2005), but progress to the present financial model has a turbulent history. The direct revenue streams of television broadcast rights, sponsorship, ticketing and licensing have evolved through periods of consumer reluctance to accept commercial involvement in sport. Throughout the history of the modern Olympics, criticism has occurred at various stages lamenting the growing commercialization of the event (Guttmann, 2002). The current staging of the modern Games is due to a symbiotic relationship between the providers of capital, the commercial stakeholders, and the Games organizers, the cities who seek the capital. Direct revenues are those that accrue to the IOC and OCOG from commercial interest in the Games. This section considers the development of fees for broadcasting rights and how these have financed not only the Games but also the IOC itself. It also examines the rise of commercial involvement and its current form of tiered sponsorship deals, born from the application of sound marketing communications theory and carefully managed exclusivity to create effective partnership for all parties involved. It also considers revenue derived from other commercial sources, such as ticketing, licensing and other financial options.

Broadcasting Rights

The technological development of the broadcast of sound and image has occurred alongside the evolution of the modern Olympics and, indeed, no other single factor has had such a significant impact on the management of the Olympic movement. Much scrutiny and commentary is now devoted to the sums available to the IOC from broadcasting rights deals, which are distributed to all of the stakeholders involved in running the Games. Nevertheless, the history of this revenue source caused much contention within the Olympic movement, especially between the various OCOGs and the IOC.

The emergence of radio and television broadcasting created issues regarding access to a number of sporting events. Debates on the rights of the public to news and broadcasters access to events of national and international significance arose in the 1920s and continued through to the 1950s (Haynes, 1999; Barney et al., 2004). Even at this early stage, the available wealth spawned divisions and controversies both within the Olympic movement and between the IOC and the broadcast networks. Restricted access to the Games sites for television news-crews created tension, as the newscasters believed they should have similar access to the Games as that of the traditional print media. This meant that the major television networks boycotted the broadcast of Melbourne 1956 (Wenn, 1993; Barney et al., 2004). Once the major networks did reach agreement with the IOC, the broadcasters gained access to the Games sites and the right to broadcast the events in return for the levying of a broadcasting rights fee. As the Olympics have progressed, the broadcasting rights fees progressively became an integral part of IOC finance (IOC, 2006b), although it can be argued that this development increasingly placed the Olympic Games in the hands of American broadcasters (Bernstein, 2000).

Figure 6.1 highlights the rise in broadcast rights fees through each Olympiad. The period from 1960 to 1980 was characterized by the increasing pressure of commercialism on the Olympic movement. At this time, the IOC faced the dilemma of attempting to maintain its amateur ideals while examining revenue sources to support its existence (Barney et al., 2004). For the television networks, obtaining the Games was an effective source of programming content that fostered the sale of advertising space. The IOC then contained few members with business executive experience compared with the present day. It is important to remember that these decision-makers were, until relatively recently, ex-athletes or senior sporting officials, implying that the internal capabilities and resources of the organization were not optimally suited to commercial negotiations. This meant that negotiations for the broadcast rights fee were characterized by tensions and one-sided dealings with the more commercially aware television

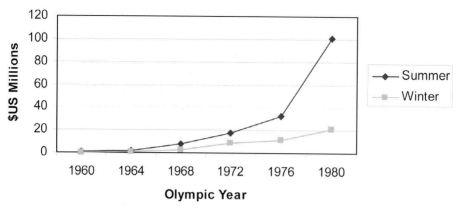

Figure 6.1. Olympic broadcast revenues (1960–1980).

networks. Negotiations often favoured these parties over the IOC. Nevertheless, at the beginning of the 1970s, the IOC received up to 98 per cent of its operating revenues from broadcast fee income (Barney *et al.*, 2004). Understandably, the over-reliance on this one source placed the IOC in a high-risk position.

The second period of note is the dramatic increase in broadcast revenues that occurred between 1984 and 2004 (figure 6.2). One reason for this growth was not just the increased utility of sport programming for television but also the competitive nature of the North American television market. This increased state of competition effectively bid up the value of the television rights, providing artificially high revenues to the IOC. The competitive nature of television rights negotiations within the United States increased these fees even further (Bernstein, 2000). A second significant reason for the growth in revenues was the development of greater professionalism within the IOC and the host cities, with their increasing commercial acumen allowing them to negotiate greater value for the Olympic movement from these Olympiads.

The increases in broadcast revenues apply to both the Winter and Summer Games, but the greater global appeal of the sports represented in the latter, and its

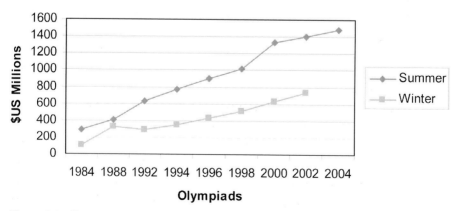

Figure 6.2. Olympic broadcast revenues (1984–2004.)

proportionately higher value as a resource for commercial television stations, mean that the fees gained from broadcasting the Summer Olympics are substantially higher (figure 6.2). Commercial stations not only generate income from the sale of advertising space during the event but also acquire greater control over access to valuable event images for news and information services. To demonstrate the potential value of the Olympics as a programming source, the National Broadcasting Corporation (NBC) of the United States paid $793 million for Athens 2004, $705 million for Sydney 2000, and $545 million for the 2002 Salt Lake City Winter Olympics just for the rights to broadcast in the United States (IOC, 1997).

Until Athens 2004, the rights fee was distributed between the OCOG and the Olympic movement through a 60:40 split. The IOC changed the distribution percentage before the Athens Olympics to a 49:51 split, arguing for a larger portion of the proceeds in order to fund the Olympic movement. The justification for giving the OCOG a smaller percentage was that, with increased television rights fees, the real value remains on an upward curve. Hence, despite the lower percentage, the OCOG is still likely to receive increasing revenue. This enables it to guarantee a certain level of income well in advance of the staging of the event which, in turn, provides leverage to meet Games-related expenditure.

Commercial Involvement and Sponsorship

There is little new about concerns regarding the over-commercialization of the Olympic movement. A report into Los Angeles 1932 indicated that there were issues over the over-commercialization and the money-orientation of the Olympic Games (IOC, 2006b). It is clear that an initially amateur organization founded to promote the intrinsic benefits of sport on an international scale would always face allegations of too much influence from commercial sources. Regardless, commercial involvement stems back to the first of the modern Summer Olympics in 1896 where revenue was generated through the sale of space in the official programme. The next three Games saw revenue (and cost) sharing arrangements with International Expositions, but thereafter a viable event required dependable commercial revenues. The Olympics in Stockholm 1912 first used local sponsors in an official capacity to help finance the Games. In the interwar period, there was a pressing need to investigate commercial avenues to enable the Olympic movement to grow.

These considerations proceeded against a background of concern that the increased reliance on commercial revenues would influence the ideals and quality of the Games and decrease their appeal. The amateur sporting ideal initiated through Coubertin's reign remained strongly ingrained throughout the Olympic movement. This feeling, coupled with a lack of internal expertise in financial matters and distaste in some quarters for anything that seemingly compromised amateur status, meant that the IOC did not initially capitalize on this growing commercial interest. During the 1970s, however, the Olympic movement suffered significant financial problems that required a change of approach (Magdalinksi and Nauright, 2004). To overcome the lack of specialist skills within the IOC, the organization employed an external sports marketing agency, International Sports Leisure Marketing AG (ISL), to assist in the creation of a special marketing programme that would reduce the IOC's dependence on television rights fees by spreading the income base and reducing the organization's overall risk position.

Returning to the contrast between the marketing of Montreal 1976 and Los Angeles 1984, one can note that a major difference between the two events was the management and activation of commercial sponsorships. Marketing communications theory suggests that the most effective method of ensuring sponsorship effectiveness is to create a clear message between the commercial brand[2] and the consumer (Shank, 2005). The greater the total number of different brands communicated to a given number of spectators, the greater the risk of mixed messages – as was the case in Montreal. Hence, the reduction of total sponsors and the creation of exclusive brand categories by the organizers of the 1984 Olympics allowed the OCOG to raise higher revenues simply by offering an environment that was more effective for communication between brands and customers.

At a similar stage to the development of Los Angeles's commercial system the IOC, with the support of ISL, developed The Olympic Partners (TOP) programme. This scheme formalized the use of commercial partners to assist in the funding of the Olympic movement and focused on agreements lasting for each Olympiad. This ensured that the sponsors were involved in both the Summer and the less globally attractive Winter Olympics. The initial value of these deals was on average $11 million, which included value-in-kind services. These services are beneficial to the OCOG, as valuable knowledge and expertise held by the partner can be accessed and contribute to more effective event operations.

TOP consists of a tiered structure to ensure brand exclusivity and clear communication. Eleven worldwide TOP sponsors occupy the highest level, each contributing an average of $78 million per Olympiad (IOC, 2006b). One of the key aspects of this plan is the creation of categories that protect the investment made by the sponsors in ensuring that their intended associations and messages are undiluted by the presence of competitors.[3] The next level down is the domestic sponsorship programme, targeted at national level sponsors of the host city. The value of these sponsorships varies depending on the domestic conditions of the host city but, importantly, the revenues flow directly to the OCOG. Even the domestic programme, managed by the OCOG, is structured into hierarchies. During Sydney 2000, the national sponsors were termed Team Millennium Olympic *Partners*, and below them were categories of *Suppliers* and *Providers*. Once again, a key feature is the provision of in-kind services. The fact that the OCOG is able to capitalize on this assistance by allowing potential suppliers to gain benefit over rivals works to the advantage of both the OCOG and the Olympic movement.

Atlanta 1996 experienced problems due to a lack of coordination between the OCOG, the US National Olympic Committee (USOC), and the IOC. Uncoordinated commercial activities and ambush marketing[4] led to problems with over-commercialization. One of Sydney 2000's strengths came from the State adopting anti-ambush marketing legislation and maintaining a no advertising policy at stadia; not even for TOP partners (Haynes, 2001). Today, the Olympic movement uses these carefully crafted commercial programmes, including even the torch relay, to manage the aspects of sponsorship (global and domestic), ticketing and licensing related deals. The success of TOP's design, and its strict protection by the IOC, is that it associates the commercial sponsor with all aspects of the Olympic Games.

Ticketing

Gate revenues are one of professional sports' oldest forms of revenue. Admission charges have been present in every Olympics since 1896 and are the most traditional of all the direct revenue sources. The complexity of ticketing arrangements derives maximum benefit for the OCOG, which has sole rights to the revenue raised through this method. Los Angeles 1984 demonstrated the potential to capitalize on ticket sales generating between $90 million and $150 million,[5] which equated to 45 per cent of all facility costs, or even the equivalent amount that the OCOG donated to the AAFLA as a legacy payment (Hill, 1992; IOC, 2006b). Atlanta 1996 derived one-quarter of its total revenue from ticket sales from only 82 per cent of the tickets sold. At Salt Lake City 2002, organizers managed to sell 95 per cent of all tickets, which at the time of writing, remains a record. Nevertheless, the overall contribution of ticket sales to total revenue is declining, from 17 per cent for 1993–1996 to 14.2 per cent for 2001–2004 (IOC, 2006b). There are numerous reasons for this decline. The less-than-planned ticket sales in Athens might have contributed, but ticketing is a complicated event management issue that can leave lasting impressions in the host city after the Games have moved on.

Managing ticketing involves the OCOG in the challenging task of balancing the needs of the Olympic family,[6] the corporate interests and the citizens of the host country, and Games tourists. For example, despite the post-event accolades (Barney et al., 2004; Haynes, 2001), the Sydney 2000 organizers faced harsh criticism for their role in managing the allocations of tickets to specific events (Thamnopoulos and Gargalianos, 2002). The most watched individual sporting event in Australia in the year 2000 was the 400 metres final won by Cathy Freeman. Although over 10 million people within Australia (half of the total population) watched the event on television, the tickets on sale at the 90,000-seater stadium were only available to select groups of individuals. After the euphoria of the win subsided, the accusations that the organizers 'sold-out' to commercial interests caused a significant public relations issue (Haynes, 2001).

Within any given stadium, there is a limit to the number of the tickets available

for spectators; hence the ticket prices are determined to a considerable degree by the demand for any given event. Generally, the Opening and Closing Ceremonies and the 100 metres finals are the premier events on the athletics programme and the tickets sold for those sessions can command higher prices. By contrast, the qualifying rounds for other lesser-profile sports have lower public demand and attract lower ticket prices. Each event within the Olympic programme has its own level of demand, which, if interpreted properly, can yield a ticketing strategy designed to maximize possible revenue streams. Provisions to make tickets accessible for all socio-economic groups are included in the policy, but whether or not there is significant appeal to these groups is a matter of debate.

Comparisons between OCOGs on ticketing policies are difficult to achieve since a wide variety of strategies is available to organizers.[7] In the first place, the options available to them are more than just one price for all. The use of differential pricing allows tickets to be sold at inflated levels where there is excess demand; for instance, seats at the finishing line of track or swimming events can command higher prices than those at the back of the stadium. Even with events low in demand, the use of differential pricing to attract children, seniors or other groups that have different price elasticity[8] is useful. A second strategy available to event organizers is the use of corporate hospitality areas that offer exclusive service and benefits. Due to the importance of the sponsorship funds in the staging of the Olympics, these value-added tickets are usually included in a bundled deal. This form of ticketing enables the OCOG to receive higher revenues for the seats within the stadium, although problems can occur if organizers fail to estimate demand correctly. The Sydney 2000 organizers made headlines for overestimating consumer demand, with the launch of an Olympic Club scheme designed to tap into the perceived pre-Olympic demand for access to the Games sites and allow consumers to purchase a Stadium Australia Gold Pass that secured a seat at the stadium for the entire Games. This scheme proved a failure, with the 72,000 tickets allocated though this method being significantly below expectations. Other initiatives such as the Premium Packages designed to allow consumers to purchase a package of category 'A' tickets (for the best seats) was ineffective, illustrating the point that special ticket categories need specialized planning and promotion in order to be effective (Thamnopoulos and Gargalianos, 2002).

Previous experience on such issues as ticketing policies and differential pricing is available to OCOGs from the Transfer of Olympic Knowledge (TOK), the document passed from host city to host city. This document which provides information on costs for the Opening and Closing Ceremonies, for example, can help in the calculation of costs and ticket prices, particularly for popular events. However, a variety of other considerations means that previous experience can only be a rough guide for forecasting demand and determining ticketing price. These include the venue capacity, session times, competing sessions, and the importance of the session – largely determined by whether or not medals are at stake (Preuss, 2000). Moreover, the popularity of specific sports in the host

country brings unique qualities to the local market. For instance, swimming is an important part of Australian culture and one of the best opportunities for the Australian team to win gold. The sheer size of the Sydney International Aquatic Centre (20,000 seats) as prepared for the Olympics in 2000 was testament to the likely demand for tickets for the swimming events.

As consumer demand for high-quality event experiences increases, OCOGs continue to develop complex ticketing strategies to enable optimal return on sales. Understandably, this is a contentious and high-profile aspect of the staging of the Olympics but, given previous experience, sound operational procedures are necessary to create important, and dependable, financial sources for financing the Games.

Licensing and Other Financing Options

The marketing function of licensing involves owners of intellectual property passing over the right to use trademarks, logos and symbols to a third party as a revenue generation tool. Licensing is a practice used in many industries and has been adopted by sporting organizations since the 1970s. Its importance for the Olympics cannot be overstated. The organizers of Sydney 2000 raised $52 million from the sale of licensed goods, while the Salt Lake City Winter Games in 2002 produced $25 million from this source – equivalent to 10 per cent of total revenues for the Games. The emotional value of merchandize is strong for event consumers as it provides them with tangible evidence of the intangible experiences of the event (Shank, 2005). The greater the emotional value of the event, the greater consumer demand for event-related merchandize.

Licensing deals are also intended to reflect the host city's cultural and symbolic characteristics. The use of mascots linked with the host city is one of the primary communication tools at the OCOG's disposal. The introduction of Waldi, for the 1972 Munich Olympics, as the first official mascot, was a key feature of the IOC marketing programme for children. A further driver of license and merchandize is the 'collect-ability' of Olympic mementos. Pin collecting has been a pastime of many Olympic enthusiasts around the world and is an activity in which the athletes and the spectators can both engage. The growth of online auction houses has made it possible for collectors in many parts of the world to continue this practice between Olympic events. Perhaps due to the high level of criticism about the over-commercialization issues after the Atlanta Games, the IOC took steps to control the number of licence agreements. These have now decreased since a Summer Olympics peak of 125 at Atlanta 1996 and a Winter peak of 190 at Nagano 1998.

A further manifestation of licensing programmes for the Games is the existence of philatelic and numismatic programmes, which are longstanding revenue sources for the Olympic movement (IOC, 2006b). Although the sale of stamps has a history as long as the modern Olympics, it was not until the 1960s that stamps started to raise significant revenues. Originally, the sale of stamps by national postal

authorities was carried out in an *ad hoc* manner rather than coordinated through Olympic planning. A tightening of the IOC licensing policy and strengthening of agreements between the local OCOGs and their national postal authorities have created revenue sharing deals (Preuss, 2000). The revenue from stamp sales comes from adding a surcharge on the face value of the stamp. Preuss goes further to state that, during this time, the next host city began to levy its surcharge as soon as the previous Games were finished, thereby increasing the sale time and maximizing the capture of revenue.

The numismatic programme was established at Helsinki 1952. At this stage in Olympic history, the range of licensing deals was limited, so any additional income for the OCOG was beneficial. Coins cast in Olympic editions contribute directly to the OCOGs' revenues. Similar to the stamps, there is a surcharge on each coin that is minted that goes to the OCOG (Preuss, 2000). Although not of the same magnitude as other sources of finance, the numismatic programme can provide useful revenues for the host city. An example of this is the A\$12 million made by the Sydney Organizing Committee (SOCOG) from the sale of Olympic Commemorative coins in 2000. When placed in perspective, this income equated to half of the initial bid costs to win the Games.

The use of lottery and other gaming techniques to raise revenues for governments has been a key feature of general economic policy for the past 15–20 years. In Australia and the United Kingdom, lotteries have proved one of the main sources of finance for the establishment of new sporting facilities. The IOC itself has encouraged host cities to use special lotteries as financing tools for Olympics. Moscow 1980 and Seoul 1988 adapted existing lotteries for Olympic financing, whereas Montreal used a lottery to help reduce the debt burden incurred by the 1976 Games. Lotteries, however, have the socially regressive habit of redistributing income from lower classes, attracted by the large prizes and undeterred by the small chances of winning, into projects that generally advantage the middle class. Moreover, the creation of an Olympic lottery may take funds away from other worthy lottery-funded causes, which can include non-Olympic sport. For London 2012, the establishment of an Olympic lottery is a major contributor to the finance model employed.[9] Careful examination of this proposal, though, reveals that the existing lottery funds for sport will be diverted into Olympic channels, favouring the elite end of sport to the possible detriment of sports with wider participation. Taking these factors together with increased competition from the establishment of new lotteries means that overall estimates may be optimistic, leaving a potential shortfall in revenues.

In summary, a number of sources of revenue assist in financing the Games. The rises in broadcasting rights and commercial sponsorship revenues have spread the Olympic movement's revenue base allowing it to become less dependent on one source. New ticketing packages and better licensing agreements present further ways of increasing revenue for host cities. An indication of the revenues that accrued to the Sydney 2000 Games can be seen in figure 6.3, which

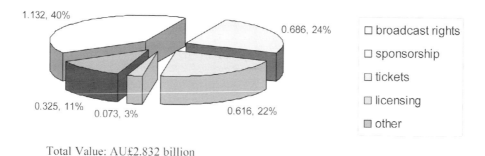

Total Value: AU£2.832 billion

Figure 6.3. Value of finance sources – Sydney 2000 (AUS$ billion).

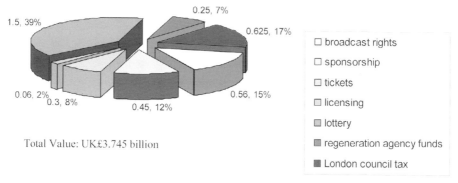

Total Value: UK£3.745 billion

Figure 6.4. Value of finance sources – London 2012 (£ billion).

highlights the range and contribution of sources available and shows that no one source contributes over 50 per cent of total revenues. The London Organizing Committee for the 2012 Games will draw income from a slightly broader base than that employed at Sydney 2000 (*Anon.*, 2005). The addition of regeneration agency funds and local council taxes, highlighted in figure 6.4, provides further sources for income diversification and additions to the revenue options for the IOC and OCOG.

Expenditure

Turning to expenditure, the steady increase in the costs needed to stage an event such as the Olympics needs little emphasis. There have been fluctuations in Games-related expenditure incurred through the building and refurbishment of venues and facilities. Generally, host cities employ at least some refurbished and existing facilities, which are generally more cost effective than new purpose-built facilities. Over the past 40 years, however, there has been a general rise in the total expenditure related to the Games for two main reasons. First, the process of bidding for the Games naturally increases the level of complexity and associated operational costs. As each candidate city vies for selection, ever-more challenging designs have been used to woo IOC and International Sporting Federation

members. Secondly, organizers have chosen to use the Olympics as a catalyst for other economic development, which can add enormously to costs (see chapter 9).

Expenditure falls into three main categories, the first of which concerns the sports venues. For the Summer Olympics, the main expenditure items for the host city are sporting facilities, including the main stadium, the aquatics centre, velodrome and other stadia. For the Winter Games, the construction of venues for the seven Olympic disciplines is not obligatory for all events. For the skiing and the biathlon, for example, the existing natural terrain can be used, although manipulation of these environments creates environmental concerns and can increase expenditure dramatically. Developments in Banff National Park, for example, meant the costs of the 1988 Calgary Winter Olympics increased above initial budgets. The second category includes expenditure items that enable the support activities associated with staging the event. The construction of an Olympic Village, a broadcast centre and Games-related additions to the host city's transportation system can lead to large outlays in expenditure. The final category relates to the operational costs of staging the event itself, which can be as much again as the costs of the facilities.

The main stadium, the centrepiece of every Olympic Games, stages the Opening and Closing ceremonies, and holds the Olympic flame throughout the event. It has been the focal point of every Games since 1896 but, as seen in table 6.1, the construction of the stadium has not always been solely for Olympic use. The use of a refurbished or existing stadium can keep costs down dramatically, as shown by contrasting Montreal 1976, which spent $2 billion on new sporting facilities, against the $242 million expended on refurbished venues at Los Angeles 1984.[10] Traditionally, the host city has relied on public funding to cover these expenditure items. After the debt created from Montreal, the involvement of private funding sources was required in order to gain public support for the event. The use of private funds enabled the Los Angeles and Atlanta organizers to keep sporting facility costs lower than the more publicly-funded Games at Sydney and Athens.

Legacy strategies that can ensure the use of the facility after completion of

Table 6.1. Summer Olympic stadia: construction history.

Existing and used for Games	*Refurbished*	*Constructed for Olympic Use*	
Paris (1900)	Paris (1924),	Athens (1896)	Munich (1972)
Los Angeles (1922)	Moscow (1980),	St Louis (1904)	Montreal (1976)
London (1923)	Los Angeles (1984)	London (1908)	Seoul (1988)
Melbourne (circa 1850s)	Barcelona (1992)	Stockholm (1912)	Atlanta (1996)
Rome (1952)		Antwerp (1924)	Sydney (2000)
Japan (1958)		Amsterdam (1928)	Athens (2004+)
Mexico (1952)		Berlin (1936★)	Beijing (2008)
		Helsinki (1952★)	London (2012)

★ Created for an Olympics cancelled by World War.

+ Constructed on site of previous stadium.

the Games are becoming increasingly important in Olympic planning, although the recent experiences from Sydney 2000 and Athens 2004 point to continuing difficulties. Although created with a mixture of private and public funds, Stadium Australia, for example, has experienced financial trouble since the end of the 2000 Games (see chapter 2). One of the major reasons was the lack of legacy planning for the stadium, which has to compete with other stadia in Sydney for sporting events. Limited booking for the stadium generates continuing losses, running at A$38 million per annum six years after the event (Glendinning, 2006). Whatever criticism Atlanta received over the over-commercialization of the 1996 Games, turning the main stadium over to a private sporting franchise effectively restricted the level of subsidy from public funds.

The main stadium, arguably, can be used for a multitude of activities during and after the event, but other venues are often sport-specific. In addition, existing facilities in such sports are rarely of sufficient standard to be upgraded to cater for Olympic specifications. Hence, it is normal for aquatics, cycling, luge and bobsleigh venues to be constructed for the Olympics. Although hosting an attendance roughly equivalent to 20–25 per cent of the main stadium, the aquatics centre required for the Games is a major cost consideration. In Sydney, the aquatics centre was roughly one-third of the cost of Stadium Australia (Auditor General, 2002), with costs inflated by technological advances, such as ozone pool hygiene systems to improve water quality. The development of numerous sporting facilities in Sydney provided the state of New South Wales with a significant level of sporting infrastructure after the Games, but the designers of these constructions failed to capitalize on the use of multi-purpose, temporary, or existing venues that assist OCOGs in obtaining greater value from expenditure and creating positive legacies for the host city.

Besides the sporting facilities, the traditional pattern for housing the Olympic athletes and officials was to use makeshift facilities or locations across the host city. For London 1948, the Olympic Village comprised old airbases and educational accommodation in London's suburban fringes. In 1956, the Village built at Heidelberg, in the suburbs to the north of Melbourne, was a considerable distance from the main Olympic competition site. The OCOGs concerned used these existing sources in an attempt to keep costs down. As the needs of athletes have increased, so have the services and facilities on offer at the athlete's Village. It is now common practice for the OCOG to construct the Village for the Games to enable it to be serviced by up-to-date technology. From this, it is possible to derive a positive legacy by converting the newly constructed apartments into public and private housing after the event. In Barcelona and Sydney, the former Villages now provide a mixture of housing that contributes to the cities' housing stock and adds a valuable source of revenue to cover Games-related expenditure.

Media centres represent another major source of expenditure. Given the importance of the broadcasting revenues, the resources ploughed into media centres reflect both the growing significance of broadcasting and press stakeholders

and acknowledgement of the power of the media in promoting the Olympic themes across the globe. The construction of an efficient and comprehensive International Broadcast Centre (IBC) is a key aspect of the bidding process for prospective cities.[11] From the IBC, the regional broadcasters can distribute the 'feed' of sound and visual images to their own markets, tailored for greater appeal. This system has been running since Munich 1972. This arrangement means not only control of images, but also ensures that the stadia are not cluttered with the infrastructure of numerous broadcasting networks. The main feed for the Athens 2004 Summer Olympics culminated in a total of 3,800 hours for 220 countries, which was considerably higher than Salt Lake City Winter Olympics coming in at 900 hours for 160 countries (IOC, 2006b).

The final considerations for Games-related expenditure are the event operations costs. Aspects such as sport and media operations, security, and site management require careful planning. Due to the high profile nature of the event and the risks of failure for a city's reputation, it is natural to see the use of well-tried systems and experienced human resources. The expenses of coordinating all the various agencies and organizations responsible for delivering the many aspects of a mega-event are considerable. In this regard Sydney spent A$586 million, the private cost of Stadium Australia, simply to coordinate the other government agencies (e.g. those responsible for transport, health, water and security) during the event (Auditor General, 2002). Changes in external circumstances can increase operational costs in dramatic circumstances for Olympic planning budgets; for example Sydney 2000 paid only a fraction of the security costs spent at Athens just four years later (see chapter 9). Operational costs can be largely met by the OCOG and, compared to facility and infrastructure costs, have relied less on public funds. Combined with the generation of economic activity for government departments and agencies and subsequent tax revenue accumulation, the level of economic activity generated by the event can assist in justifying the expenditure.

Indirect Revenue: Economic Impact

Apart from Los Angeles and Atlanta, few Games have balanced their direct costs with revenues. To a greater or lesser extent, that equation is tempered by the fact that staging the Olympic Games is not solely for profit reasons. Since the Second World War, many countries and cities have desired the Games because of their unique ability to address such objectives as place promotion, employment creation, urban regeneration, and attracting tourists and general investment. These non-sporting goals require public funds in order to come to fruition, but the *indirect* benefits generated may be seen as sufficiently desirable to compensate for some operational losses. Such arguments have invariably aroused controversy but, without acceptance of the principle that associated indirect revenue flows to the host city from this initial expenditure, it might well be difficult to gain public support for this scale of project.

This applies particularly to arguments surrounding regeneration. The use of sporting mega-events as a means of regenerating large parts of urban areas has been a matter of public policy since the 1980s (Gratton *et al.*, 2005) and has become steadily more important for both the bidding process and in justifying the final accounts for the Games. The arguments derive from the changes in the economic environment that forced many manufacturing centres into recession as job losses and plant closures led to the decline and dereliction of large swathes of the inner city (see chapter 9; also Paddison, 1993; Hiller, 2000; Andranovich *et al.*, 2001). Allying the Olympics to urban regeneration, of course, greatly changed the nature of financing the sporting festival and altered the way that bid committees set about their task of convincing their own publics and the IOC alike.

The key stakeholders in the bidding process, for example, will commission reports to investigate the potential economic impact of the Games in order to influence public opinion. Baade and Matheson (2002) observed that a key consideration is whether an economic impact study is prospective (*ex ante*) or after the fact (*ex post*). Games proponents often use economic impact studies carried out *ex ante* to assist in highlighting the benefits that can be obtained through the staging of the event. This serves their purpose but is not always as rigorous as those carried out *ex post*. Unfortunately however, there have been few *ex post* studies to measure the final economic impact of the Olympics. To complicate matters further, Kasimati (2003) noted that there are three different types of multipliers that can be used to assess economic impact. Multiplier effects can be measured in terms of sales created, employment or household income change, with the one chosen often reflecting whichever best suits the purpose of the organization undertaking the study. Furthermore, each multiplier can be used with different modelling approaches creating numerous potential impacts, each producing different figures. This complexity allows proponents of bids to use the most attractive potential impacts (sales and employment) to justify a bid for the Games, even if other more reliable multipliers (household income) show less attractive benefits.

The question of employment generation from hosting mega-events provides a focus around which to demonstrate the over-simplifications throughout the economic impact process. The overall employment impact of a mega-event is of three types. The first is direct employment, which occurs from the preparation and staging of the Games. Next is indirect employment that occurs in the support activities for the preparation and staging of the Games in industries such as hotels, construction, and wholesaling. Finally, expenditure within the local economy that has arisen due to the Games creates induced employment.

The bid stage of the event normally cites full-time equivalent (FTE) jobs in support of the case being made, but these are open to question. David Green (2003), for example, took proponents of the Winter Olympics at Vancouver in 2010 to task over their use of FTE employment statistics. He argued that their figures of 244,000 new jobs were overestimated by up to 400–500 per cent on what is likely to occur. Figures like those used to support Vancouver's successful

bid often fail to take account of the fact that host city workers may already be employed and that employment migration will occur, which could take jobs away from local residents. Hiller (2000) had similar issues with proponents for Cape Town's unsuccessful 2004 bid. In that instance, the supporters of the Olympics projected 90,000 permanent jobs. Although this figure was intended to indicate the three types of employment impact mentioned above, proponents of the bid seized upon the figure as referring to local jobs in the Cape Town area – which was manifestly untrue. Variation in how well employment multipliers are used is reinforced by findings from Baade and Matheson (2002), which show that the total employment gains created in the case of Atlanta 1996 can vary between 3,500 and 42,500 depending on the basis used. The major factor here is that even these figures have taken into account all the economic factors from an *ex post* situation. The significance of this argument is that the authors are able to determine exactly how much money is being spent to create one job, thereby allowing consideration of issues of opportunity cost, which 'corresponds to what we give up by doing a project – the value of the best alternative we could proceed with if we were not to do the project' (Green, 2003, p. 6).

Opportunity cost, however, is rarely considered by those proposing to stage the Olympics. With all the focus currently on indirect revenue creation through the Olympics, little thought is devoted to accounting for what other benefits could accrue to host cities by spending the money in other ways. Whether it be job creation, urban regeneration, city marketing or any other of the numerous indirect benefits of the Games, some sense of opportunity cost is essential in order to increase public accountability if and when problems arise in the staging of the Olympics.

Notes

1. For these aspects, the reader should look, *inter alia*, to authors such as Gratton and Taylor (2000) and Preuss (2000). A range of political, economic and socio-cultural factors within the host nation determines finances chosen, therefore meaning that comparisons between host cities are difficult to achieve.

2.. A brand is a consumer-focused, non-sport organization that enters into a sponsorship agreement for a range of different business objectives – one of the most important of these is communication with a desired target market.

3. Nevertheless, the inclusion of Panasonic and Samsung who sponsor separate categories but compete outside the Olympics in many similar areas is a confusing proposition when looking to support the argument of clear communication.

4. 'Ambush marketing' is a situation in which a brand that pays to become an official sponsor of an event discovers a competing brand finding ways to link itself to that event without paying the sponsorship fee. Although rarely illegal, it erodes the potential value of the event if the organizers cannot guarantee exclusivity.

5. This figure varies between sources, but for the point of discussion it is generally regarded as significantly higher than for any previous Olympics.

6. Rule 66 from the Olympic Charter requires OCOGs to allocate sections of seats for members of the Olympic Family.

7. This section draws on Preuss (2002).

8. Price elasticity is the degree to which consumers respond to price changes.

9. See figure 6.4.

10. Figures at 1995 prices; source Preuss (2000).

11. The IBC is where 'the feed' (sounds and images) from the venues are collected and stored.

Chapter 7

Promoting the Olympic City

Stephen V. Ward

We will never know the true significance of French President Jacques Chirac's widely reported casual denigration of Finnish cooking in securing the 2012 Summer Olympic Games for London instead of the longstanding favourite, Paris. According to a secretly taped restaurant conversation with the German Chancellor and the Russian President, he said of the London bid that, '[y]ou can't trust people who cook as badly as that. After Finland, it's the country with the worst food' (Barkham, 2005*a*). The following day the story appeared in the French newspaper, *Libération* and was widely picked up by international news media. It was variously presented as a huge insult to British and Finnish cookery, a sign of French arrogance or, simply a colossal error of judgement. Two days later the IOC met in Singapore to make its decision (Campbell, 2005). When successive rounds of voting had eliminated all other candidate cities, only Paris and London remained, with London winning by just four votes. Finland had two of these, so its delegates' choices (which remain entirely anonymous, of course) could well have swung the result in London's favour.

Whatever actual truth may lie within it, the real importance of this anecdote is the insight it gives on the world's most extraordinary process of competitive city marketing. In one incident it captures the unique mixture of high politics, the expectation of good living, intense media interest and moments of complete farce that descend on the process of trying to win the Olympic prize. Many commentators have noted the rivalry between cities across the world for all kinds of mobile investment and consumption (e.g. Hall and Hubbard, 1998; S.V. Ward, 1998). They have also observed that this competition has become ever more intense in recent years, as traditional city economies have faltered and capital has become more mobile. In turn, this has put growing pressure on city leaders to engage in place marketing and promotion, which serves as a means both to achieve tangible physical and economic change by attracting new investment and activity and, in a deeper sense, to facilitate symbolic reconstruction.

The tangible prizes for the city marketers are no longer the manufacturing plants that were once the economic bedrock of cities. Nor has this traditional imperative simply shifted into the producer services that have replaced manufacturing in a

post-industrial age. The process now goes much further, as cities compete to be centres of cultural and leisure consumption. To this end, many cities have invested heavily in new or extended cultural and other leisure facilities such as museums, galleries, performance venues and sports facilities (Bianchini and Parkinson, 1993). Part of this move into the cultural marketing of cities also embraces major events and spectacles that can animate the new cultural investments and intensify the process of cultural consumption. In a crude sense, all these changes attract more tourists and increase consumption. In a longer term fashion, however, the investments and the activities they contain contribute to raising the quality of urban life which, it is thought, will make cities into magnets for the new movers and shakers of the global economy – the entrepreneurs and the creative people from whom new innovations will flow.

These changes in the physical character and economic activities of cities also play an important part in the process of symbolic reconstruction. New buildings, structures and places, particularly those with iconic potential, play an important part in the re-branding of cities. So too, albeit in a more transitory fashion, do the major events and spectacles staged by cities (Gold and Gold, 2005; Smith, n.d.). New physical icons and transitory spectacles provide images that can be deployed to point to a changing city. As well as being a way of attracting new investment and consumption, city marketing is also a way of manipulating the signs, real and promised, of change and integrating them into a new brand identity for the city. This is self-evidently important in promoting the idea of a changing city to investors and consumers. It is also extremely important as a way of selling the idea of change to those who actually live in the city and have to bear many of the costs of that change, financial and otherwise.

At the pinnacle of this most recent phase of city marketing is that associated with the Olympics. This applies particularly to the Summer Games which are a truly global affair (D. Miller, 2003); somewhat less so to the Winter Games, although they have the compensatory marketing benefit of reaching the majority of the world's most affluent countries. Given their scale, it is perhaps surprising that these mega-events continue to be awarded to just one city, rather than to a country as, for example, with major soccer events such as the FIFA World Cup. For their part, despite the often questioned financial and other benefits, many cities remain eager to compete for the Olympic prize. As of the early twenty-first century, the chosen city gets a large injection of funds from the IOC ($1.1 billion in the case of Sydney 2000), paid for from world broadcast rights, sponsorship and merchandizing deals (Lee, 2005). It also receives a huge boost to tourism and other consumption, substantial new investment (funded from multiple but usually government sources) and an enduring boost to property values (Halifax plc, 2004). Staging these Games signals to outsiders and citizens alike that the host city really is a world city, well placed in other respects to become, or remain, a key hub in the global economy. Even being a serious contender confers real marketing benefits, showing that a city is ambitious for international attention (Hiller, 2000).

The result is that no other variant of city boosterism even approaches the extraordinary series of events now associated with the bidding for these events. This begins at the national level as candidate cities are chosen and proceeds through a shortlist as the IOC decides which cities' bids should go forward to the final selection. The city eventually chosen as host is then presented with a colossal media opportunity to show itself to the world, to market its brand to anyone, anywhere. This builds up as the Games approach, culminating with the event itself. By 2001 it was calculated that 3.7 billion viewers in 220 countries had watched the 1998 Nagano Winter and 2000 Sydney Summer Olympics in the four-year period that ended in 2000.[1] All this media exposure, provided it is reasonably positive, influences many tourist decisions at the time of the Games. This tourism impact will focus on but extend beyond the city to the country and the wider region. More importantly, there is also huge long-term potential for both tourism and investment (Kasimati, 2003).

No other city marketing opportunity achieves this global exposure. At the same time, provided it is carefully managed at the local level, it also gives a tremendous opportunity to heighten and mobilize the commitment of citizens to their own city. The competitive nature of sport and its unrivalled capacity to be enjoyed as a mass cultural activity gives it many advantages from the marketing point of view (S.V. Ward, 1998, pp. 231–232). In a more subtle way, it also becomes a metaphor for the notion of cities having to compete in a global marketplace, a way of reconciling citizens and local institutions to the wider economic realities of the world. The notion of competition *in* sport can be elided, fairly smoothly, to embrace competing *for* sporting events, to the idea of cities having to compete with each other more generally.

Who Promotes the Olympic City?

It follows from the foregoing discussion that marketing the Olympic city in the later stages itself becomes a mass activity. Seemingly, everyone from heads of government downwards takes part. Particularly important are the media, especially television, radio and newspapers, which play a key part in widening the commitment. They may also play a questioning or critical role but usually, at least for cities whose Olympic bid aspirations progress to the short-list and the final play-off, the net effect will be positive. Yet this mass media involvement normally only becomes critical after the bandwagon has begun to roll, reaching a peak during the Games themselves. More important therefore is the question of who actually starts the more difficult process of getting it moving in the first instance.

The detailed answer has of course varied but one or a small group of individuals have normally been involved (Hill, 1992, pp. 90–238). The national sporting and Olympic organizations are in evidence, but these are rarely powerful enough on their own to provide the primary leadership for such a complex undertaking that cuts across so many aspects of city and national life. In some cases, the key actors

have, not surprisingly, operated mainly within the sphere of government, whether at city or a wider level. It is not difficult to appreciate why this has been so in cities within nations with Communist regimes at the time of the Games. Although only one, Moscow 1980, has actually hosted the Summer Games with Beijing set to stage the 2008 Games, other communist cities – Budapest, Belgrade, Tashkent and Havana – have entered short-listed bids (Gold and Gold, 2005, 179–180).

The government role has also been central in the promotion of Olympic cities under other authoritarian regimes, notably Seoul 1988 – awarded in very controversial circumstances in 1981 (Hill, 1992, pp. 189–217). The best known Games staged by a totalitarian state, Berlin 1936, were not primarily instigated by government (Hart Davis, 1986), although here the special circumstances of interwar Germany apply (see chapter 10). Awarded to the city in 1931, before the Nazi state was created, their initiator had to persuade a suspicious Hitler (who saw them as promoting dangerously internationalist sentiments) that they were worth backing. Once he had been persuaded however, the Führer's Games set new standards in Olympic marketing, albeit with overtly propagandist motives that transcended the city itself to promote the Nazi regime.

Yet the centrally-planned, totalitarian and authoritarian examples have been the exceptions. The most typical Olympic bidders have been cities within capitalist and more or less democratic countries. Even in these nations, though, there are very notable examples of key actors being essentially political figures holding some kind of governmental office. Most typically in such cases, though, the impetus has usually been more genuinely city-based, with Mayors or their nominees often playing a critical part. A very notable example was Montreal, which bid for the 1972 Summer Games and staged the 1976 Games, thanks to the drive of its Mayor Jean Drapeau (Organizing Committee, 1976). More recently, successive Mayors of Barcelona, Narcis Serra and Pasqual Maragall, were directly responsible for Barcelona's successful bid for the 1992 Summer Games (COOB, 1992, I). In 2005 the bids of both New York and Moscow for the 2012 Summer Games were led by their cities' Deputy Mayors.

Even where city government leaders have been the driving force, this does not mean that Olympic bidding and marketing simply become a special department of the municipal administration. The most common feature amongst the individuals or small groups, who have promoted most of the recent successful city bids to stage the Olympics, has been the prevalence of what has recently come to be termed 'regime politics' (Stone, 1993; Painter, 1998). This kind of urban action involves relatively few key figures who might well include city government leaders but would be likely also to involve local and regional business leaders, national government appointees or relevant Ministers. The resultant partnership thus has an unusual status, in which the limits of governmental and private action become difficult to define.

The exact composition of these interests has not been the same in all aspiring Olympic cities. However, most differences in the source of promotional effort

are ones of degree. The usual pattern of recent years, certainly for successful bids, has involved a mix of national and city government and entrepreneurial effort and there has not even necessarily been a consistent pattern in the same countries. Birmingham's 1986 bid for the 1992 Games and Manchester's first (1990 for the 1996 Games) bid were advanced by city and local entrepreneurial effort without any effective central government backing (Hill, 1992, pp. 90–119). Yet Manchester's second bid (1993 for the 2000 Games) had significant material and symbolic central government backing (Law, 1994). Finally, for London's successful 2005 bid for the 2012 Games, central government support of all kinds was very substantial. In part, these differences reflected the changing political character of national government, under successive Prime Ministers Thatcher, Major and Blair. It is also highly likely that national government, whatever its complexion, had little inclination to back bids that had only a small chance of success. All politicians prefer to associate themselves with winners.

While most of the original push has come from the middle ground between the public and private sectors, there have been cases where the impetus has been predominantly private. This has been especially so in the United States where national government has not involved itself to any great extent in Olympic bidding (Andranovich et al., 2001). Partly because of this, there have been few of the constraints on city boosterist ambitions that have operated in other countries. Just as they have explored every other conceivable way of promoting themselves, American city business-led coalitions were remarkably quick to see the city marketing potential of the Olympic Games. The result is that an astonishing number and variety of American cities have advanced short-listed bids for both Summer and Winter Games (Gold and Gold, 2005, pp. 141, 179–180; Essex and Chalkley, 2004). In part this was possible because, until 1955 when the host city for the 1960 Summer Games was decided, the United States Olympic Committee allowed multiple American cities to bid against each other for the same Games. Thus four US cities were candidates in 1946 (for the 1948 Games), and five in each of the 1947 and 1949 decisions for the 1952 and 1956 Games. This somewhat farcical process meant that the competition to stage the Olympics was to a considerable extent just another means for American cities to assert themselves over their domestic rivals.

Los Angeles, the history of which has been built more completely than that of any other large American metropolitan city on promotional puff, appropriately holds the record with two hostings (1932 and 1984) and seven other short-listed bids (Andranovich et al., 2001). Had the domestic bidding rules not changed in 1955, it would have notched up an extra four bids. Behind all its post-1945 bids was a private business organization, the Southern California Committee for the Olympic Games. This had been formed in 1939 by a Los Angeles group of businessmen with the intention of bringing the Games back to the city after its earlier hosting of them. Eventually, in 1978, with Jean Drapeau's financially ruinous Montreal Games fresh in everyone's mind, they were successful in

regaining the 1984 Games against only one other, very half-hearted, contender (Teheran). To both the IOC, on the one hand, and local and state interests, on the other, the promotional language and the eventual reality of the Games were the same – frugality and commercialism (Hill, 1992, pp. 156–162). Existing facilities and infrastructure were to be used, commercial sponsorship aggressively sought.

Although the 1984 Games had many perceived weaknesses that reflected this ethos, the approach proved highly profitable (especially so for Los Angeles and the United States) with the result that it both saved and changed the Games. The Los Angeles experience paved the way for the resurgence in competition to stage the both Summer and Winter Games since the 1990s. However no subsequent Games have been quite as completely privatized in their approach. It was, predictably, another American city with a long record of boosterism which most consciously modelled its own bid on Los Angeles (Andranovich *et al.*, 2001; Whitelegg, 2000). Atlanta's bid for the 1996 Games was led by a local lawyer, Billy Payne, who played the central role in advancing the city's bid. Once again the model was highly privatized though a key difference was that, unlike Los Angeles, city government soon sought active involvement once the Games had been secured. This added regeneration and wider city objectives, causing some confusion about the promotional message. Not surprisingly the Games, whose organization remained private throughout, failed to deliver these muddled objectives. It was the widespread criticisms of Atlanta that have drawn subsequent bids back in the direction of public initiative, albeit without neglecting the methodologies of private business. These, embracing the full range of marketing and branding arts, remain absolutely central to the Olympic story.

How is the Olympic City marketed?

In a very formal sense the key marketing material produced by would-be Olympic cities is the so-called candidature file. This is the official bid document, in recent years running to several volumes, submitted by short-listed candidate cities to the IOC. It is prepared by the bidding organization to set out the case for their particular city. The file will first be assessed by technical adjudicators (who may weed out unsatisfactory bids) and then forms the basis for the final voting by IOC members. At its core are technical details about the projected budget and how the various sports events and participants are to be accommodated in an effective and secure fashion. Although much of the file is thus very specific, it also has to display the wider city's capacity to host a large international event successfully. Thus the need to deal with logistical considerations, about how the movement of people associated with the Games will be handled, involves broader scale matters such as transport. The report will also include a general volume or section that markets the city and its wider setting. This part of the submission tends to showcase the city's attractiveness and openness in a way that also tries to communicate a more general sense of a wide and deep local commitment to sports and to hosting a successful Olympics.

Central it may be, but a city's candidature file is generally reckoned to be less a vote winner than a vote loser if it reveals any significant deficiencies relative to other cities. The bidding team of an aspirant Olympic city cannot rely on it to any major extent once it has passed the original test of technical competence and general credibility. Therefore a very wide range of marketing approaches and methods is deployed around this central element, many of which have to come into play long before the IOC becomes involved (e.g. McGeoch and Koporaal, 1994). Building the wide and deep commitment within the city and beyond is itself a major task. It involves a great deal of public and media relations work by the group initiating the bid to win support first within newspapers, television and radio. Media executives, editors and journalists all need to be briefed and persuaded. Business leaders, politicians and other prominent figures will similarly be schmoozed and convinced of the benefits of making a strong bid (and of contributing to it in money or other material ways to raise awareness). A typical wider marketing output at this stage would be a special issue or supplement of the local newspaper that would also carry considerable amounts of advertising expressing business and public agency backing.

Provided they can be convinced that the candidature will be competently advanced, many companies associated with a bidding city are likely to see benefits in the wider exposure that will result. The experience of Atlanta suggests that bidding for the Olympics (and, once awarded, the preparation period for the Games themselves) can shift business contributions away from more routine city marketing campaigns (S.V. Ward, 1998, p. 207). Overall, however, the total amount of business contributions to city marketing tends to increase. If, of course, the bid should eventually prove successful, then the benefits of early support in gaining an inside placing for any business opportunities during the Games themselves will be even more palpable. Yet this perception of benefits seems often to hold true even if the bid eventually turns out to be unsuccessful. Thus, despite their city's ignominious defeat in consecutive final IOC voting to decide the locations of the 1996 and 2000 Games, much of Manchester's business community would certainly have been happy to see a third bid to host the Summer Olympics. It was this support which also underpinned what became the city's successful bid to host the 2002 Commonwealth Games.

Alongside all this wooing of business, there will be an increasing engagement with the community, locally and more widely, to win the backing of key individuals and gain at least the semblance of widespread popular support. Any local organizations or individuals with sporting links, especially Olympic sporting links, are almost certain to be harnessed in some way to the bid. Typically the bidding organization will sponsor local sports and cultural events that will raise awareness and often involve the distribution of personal marketing items such as tee shirts, flags, balloons, pens and key-rings that bear its logo. Sale of these and the fees to enter mass events are often a way of raising funds for the campaign. Sydney's bidding team, for example, organized a mass community walk across

the Harbour Bridge, charging two Australian dollars per participant and thereby raising A$300,000 (SOCOG, 2000*b*, pp. 15–17). These approaches have the added benefit of enabling mass voluntary identification with the city's bid. In recent years, bid teams have become more adept at marshalling this, recruiting volunteers at an early stage to help spread the word and provide a tangible sign of the level of popular support. Barcelona, for example, had an army of over 100,000 volunteers to call upon by the time the bid campaign was transformed into the Games Organizing Committee (COOB, 1992, I, pp. 207–208).

The logo itself forms a key identifier for the bidding campaign. This would usually embrace a combination of Olympic imagery and various signifiers of the bidding city. In cases such as Sydney, these would be iconic buildings or structures, in others more symbolic associations (McGeoch and Korporaal, 1994, pp. 67–70). A key requirement, however, is that it has to be capable of being reproduced in many different media. The publicity officers of the bidding organization would typically try to ensure that this appeared around the city and beyond, and especially in major media and at airports. Another promotional device that has occasionally been used at this stage has been the Olympic mascot. In most cases mascots have appeared after the award of the Games, the best known being Moscow's 1980 bear cub mascot, Misha. An exception was Barcelona's bid team who launched a competition to design a mascot to build youth involvement (COOB, 1992, I, pp. 299–300).

These and other marketing devices form part of a widening promotional campaign. Business and community commitment provides marketing assets which can actually be used in the successive encounters with the IOC and National Olympic Committee (especially so if there are other bidding cities from the same country). Governments will be similarly aware that overwhelming local support is fundamental for a credible bid. Manifestations of this support will appear in the formal bid. Commonly, for example, the more general sections of the candidature files include portraits and brief statements of support from key individuals from business and the community, along with figures from politics and government and those with an international profile. In their bids, Atlanta, for example, secured the endorsement of film star Kim Basinger. Sydney, which borrowed many of Atlanta's marketing tactics, had the support of Nicole Kidman and her then husband, Tom Cruise (Burroughs, 1999; ACOG, 1990; McGeoch and Korporaal, 1994, pp. 141, 286). Although Cruise was American, there would usually be some local connection between the star and the place. Occasionally though, some bidders make serious mistakes in this direction. Berlin's generally rather mishap-prone bid for the 2000 Summer Games suffered when they claimed the endorsement of tennis stars Steffi Graf and Boris Becker without actually asking them (McGeoch and Korporaal, 1994, p. 108).

From the beginning the bidding organization needs to ensure that it can meet, and impress its case on, anyone likely to be able to advance the bid and affect its success. Any possibility of encountering IOC delegates, such as in meetings

of other sports organizations, is seized upon and often planned in great detail (SOCOG, 2000*b*, pp. 17–18). Similarly, IOC gatherings ostensibly unrelated to the Games for which bidding is taking place become major opportunities to promote would-be Olympic cities. Thus meetings to decide the location of Winter Olympics are also significant marketing occasions for later Summer Games. Still more important are the Olympic Games which precede the fateful decision. The festival atmosphere which prevails at these times is particularly helpful to the bidding teams of intending future Olympic cities.

Yet the potential demands on bidding teams' time and effort are huge. Successful bidding cities appear to be those which can field a larger number on such occasions, especially of very senior individuals. London's recent bid certainly benefited by having both Lord Sebastian Coe and Keith Mills who were able to share the burden (Campbell, 2005). As well as following the course of the sporting event itself, the bidding teams will be drawing lessons from how the Games are staged. They will need to be attuned to perceived successes and failures to which they can respond in their own bid. Stamina is essential for the many events (including those hosted by opponents) that provide multiple opportunities for persuasion (McGeoch and Kaporaal, 1994, 148-168).

The official hotels occupied by delegates usually become the key arenas for this activity. While bidding organizations will have their own hotel suites, the more open meeting places of the hotels are highly significant locations because of their public nature. Here they literally have the opportunity to lobby any passing IOC delegates. Members of bidding teams will often try to station themselves in strategic positions in lobby areas where they can engineer 'chance' encounters, spy on opponents and generally see who is talking to whom. Some bid teams have tried to use more novel settings for these occasions. At the Barcelona Games of 1992, for example, the Milan team, bidding for the 2000 Games, moored a large yacht in the harbour, until it was ordered out by a senior IOC official.

Until 2002, a key marketing episode was when IOC delegates exercised their rights to inspect would-be host cities. Not all IOC delegates would visit all places, though those that did would usually come in several waves, amounting to another extraordinarily demanding period for bidding teams. In preparation, the bidding teams prepared very detailed dossiers on the individual delegates, listing their various interests and personal details. This information was sometimes traded by members of previous bidding teams and cities which themselves had bid several times were able to draw on their own previous experiences. Invariably delegates were very well looked after, in a fashion that approached the care lavished on official visits by leading heads of state. Sydney, for example, ensured that all traffic lights encountered by visiting IOC groups were changed to green on their approach, to avoid delays or any sense of traffic congestion (McGeoch and Korporaal, 1994, p. 196).

The ostensible purpose of these visits was to show delegates the city, its sporting credentials and its capacity to stage the world's biggest sporting event.

supporting Paris at Singapore, delivered shortly after his arrival, was generally judged to be unfocused (Campbell, 2005). Nor were the political rivalries between the Gaullist French President and the Socialist Mayor of Paris sufficiently subordinated to the overall objective. By contrast, Barcelona's 1986 handling of the highly combustible mix of competing Spanish, Catalonian and city affiliations and sensitivities at the Rome IOC meeting showed consummate political dexterity (Hill, 1992, pp. 218–230). Australian city, state and national politics might have been less genuinely explosive but Paul Keating's prime ministerial intervention in 1993 on behalf of Sydney was nonetheless a powerful and meticulously prepared contribution (McGeoch and Korporaal, 1994, pp. 276–278).

Leading sportsmen and sportswomen, preferably Olympic medallists, with some charisma or star quality are common elements in these final set-pieces. In a hand that turned out to be full of aces, not the least effective in London's final presentation for 2012 was the globally known footballer, David Beckham. There has also been a growing tendency to exploit the winsome potential of children and young people in the final presentations, either *en masse* in flag-waving or similar roles or as individual speakers. Atlanta had its 'dream team' of 58 youngsters and Sydney used an 11 year old school girl as one of its individual speakers (Organizing Committee, 1996, pp. 13–14; SOCOG, 2000b, p. 20). The latter is a particularly risky tactic, given the greater possibility of a child being either overawed by the occasion or conversely so nauseatingly self-possessed as to irritate the audience.

Yet, alongside such strong presences, the key figure in the final presentation will always be the leader of the bidding team. The necessary qualities of conviction, persuasion and self confidence that will have been well tested in the earlier stages of the bidding process now have to face their ultimate test. Before the world's and, perhaps more searchingly, their own country's and city's media, these figures have to capture in their words and body language the essence of their city's case. They also have to make it look easy, which it is certainly not. However effective and relaxed these people may have been in making off the cuff speeches or in lobbying conversations over the bid's course, the final speech is on a different level. Like the rest of the presentations, these final speeches are normally honed and rehearsed over a long period, every word and nuance carefully judged. Rod McGeoch reckoned to have rehearsed his speech for Sydney at least sixty times so it was deeply imprinted on his memory (McGeoch and Korporaal, 1994, p. 277). It seems unlikely that his was an unusual experience.

The Promotional Message

Marketing methods and presentational style are very important in promoting aspiring Olympic cities. So too are the technical details and the sense of strong backing from business, governments and communities. Yet even taken together, these are not enough. There has to be an overarching marketing proposition around which the bid can cohere in an intellectual sense. To be successful, this will first

this stage. Nevertheless, the presentation can certainly make a difference. For this reason, they are very carefully constructed and rehearsed, often over a long period. Every word and inflection are carefully judged. Sydney's successful bid, for example, was planned by a TV producer with speeches written by a former Prime Minister's speechwriter (McGeoch and Korporaal, 1994, pp. 277–278). All those making speeches were trained and coached by a communications consultant.

For all this attention to detail, however, there are some common pitfalls. The videos are often a weak point, usually because they try to say too much. Explicit details of a city's infrastructure, cultural assets, love of sport or visual charms are important to get across but not necessarily very engaging unless done with imagination. There is also a temptation to use video clips to present too many talking heads. As well as subtly reminding delegates of the important people who were not able (could not be bothered?) to make it to the presentation, this can have the effect of making the presentation disjointed. Nor are there very many people, important or otherwise, who have a sufficiently strong screen presence to engage an audience.

This is not to say that the videos are not made to the highest professional standards and aspire to a celebrity quality of their own (Barkham, 2005*b*; BBC News 24, 2006). There has been a recent tendency to use well known film-makers to create them. Thus in the 2005 IOC selection meeting for the 2012 Summer Games, Steven Spielberg prepared the New York video and Luc Besson that for Paris. Even so, neither escaped the 'travelogue' and 'talking heads' tendencies already noted. Besson's film, for example, showed an extraordinary technical virtuosity in its opening animated scenes with the Olympic Rings dancing happily through the landmarks of Paris. A truly beautiful city was presented at its most engaging. Within a few minutes, however, Parisian charm and Besson's virtuosity were squandered. There followed an essentially dreary succession of middle-aged men (including, for example, several trades union leaders) expressing their support to camera. It mirrored the style of Paris's overall presentation.

By contrast, London's effort had no celebrity film-maker to direct it. Instead two comparative unknowns with almost no feature film experience, Daryl Goodrich and Caroline Rowland, directed and produced its short and, in the circumstances, rather low-budget video (Johnston, 2005). Moreover it was not shown as a whole but split into two sections. It contained no talking heads or touristic scenes. It focused instead on four children from different parts of the world seeing the Olympics and being inspired by a particular moment of sporting achievement. In time, they grew up to become world class sportsmen and women themselves. Yet the children were from Nigeria, Mexico, Russia and China, rather than the United Kingdom. Absolutely nothing that was place-specific about London appeared in the film. The idea was instead to associate it with deep rooted Olympian ideals.

Another source of weakness can sometimes be in the very senior government figures that now normally play a part in these presentations. The problem is often a result of only fleeting engagement with the campaign. Chirac's 2005 speech

medical treatment and other favours. When these allegations (from a Swiss IOC member) came to light there was an IOC investigation that saw three delegates resign, ten replaced, ten warned and only two exonerated. Following this scandal, the IOC decided to ban delegate visits. Instead it has strengthened the demands for technical and financial information from bidding cities, to provide a more evidence-based rationale for decisions. (Though, to judge from the final choice of the 2012 Summer Games, this still has not given primacy to the candidature file.)

Another consequence has been that the final IOC selection meeting has taken on even more importance because this is now the most significant opportunity for bidding organizations to meet rank and file delegates. Despite the new strictures, there remain differences of opinion as to how much lobbying is proper. Bidding teams constantly strive to find new ways to do some last minute promotion. On the eve of the 1990 IOC decision in Tokyo, Atlanta's bid team somehow managed to recruit chambermaids at the hotel where the IOC delegates were staying (McGeoch and Korporaal, 1994, p. 292). The latter thus went to bed to find their pillow cases had been changed to bear a message urging them to sleep 'with Georgia on their minds', a timely linking of Hoagie Carmichael's famous song with Atlanta's home state. Sydney's campaign took a flavour of the city to Monte Carlo where the IOC held its selection session in 1993. Celebrity lunches of the glitterati, sporting and otherwise, were familiar enough fare to Monaco's super rich but the street theatre, koala and kangaroo costumes struck a more exotic note (McGeoch and Korporaal, 1994, p. 285). Despite meticulous planning and securing of permits, however, some of their efforts were reined in by the city authorities.

Lobbying tactics were also a sore point following the 2005 IOC meeting in Singapore where the 2012 Summer Games venue was determined (Campbell, 2005). In contrast to the tactics of the Paris bid team, which deployed the already gaffe-prone President Chirac in the main presentation, London used the British Prime Minister and his wife in person only in the pre-presentation lobbying. Over a quarter of the IOC delegates were individually subjected to a full Blairist charm offensive in a two-day series of brief interviews that went on far into the night. It is difficult to believe that a good proportion of the delegates did not leave these encounters starry-eyed at having each just had, within the confines of a relatively small room, the full and undivided attentions of a major world statesman and his almost equally well-known spouse. At any rate, these Anglo-Saxon tactics profoundly annoyed the French, a fact lovingly recorded in the British media.

The final selection event itself is the great marketing set piece of the competition. Depending on the number of final bids, each presentation might last thirty or more minutes. In recent years, successful bids have combined charismatic individuals, technical wizardry and pure theatricality. Each candidate city uses individual speeches, not usually of any length, promotional videos, computer-generated simulations of intended Olympic venues, elements of cultural display and political campaigning. In theory, all the work ought to have been done by

In reality, however, they were very much more than this and the technicalities were only a small part of these occasions. Lavish entertainment was usual, along with expensive and carefully selected gifts for all the visiting delegates. In case this luxury might appear too shallow, many bidding cities also tried to introduce a more personal dimension, involving parties in the homes of leading members of the bidding team or other prominent citizens of the host city. Great care would be taken to ensure that language and cultural affinities, so far as possible, matched upon these occasions, thereby underlining the openness of the city to visitors from all parts of the world.

Such visits were not without their risks. Few bids to host the Olympics are entirely without a local opposition. All successful bids have managed this process effectively, so that opposition was from an early stage marginalized. Yet there have certainly been cases where the IOC visits presented local opponents to the bid with a prime opportunity to market their own viewpoint. Unsuccessful bids by Toronto for the 1996 Summer Games and by Berlin for 2000 both suffered in this way (McGeoch and Korporaal, 1994, p. 107; Kasimati, 2003). Their rivals were quick to exploit any such public expressions of opposition in their own marketing efforts. Bidders from more authoritarian countries were naturally at an advantage, though action outside the country by dissidents could have the same effect. It was used, for example, to damage Beijing's first bid (for the 2000 Games), when memories of the crushing of the democracy movement in Tiananmen Square were still fresh (McGeoch and Korporaal, 1994, pp. 225–227).

Yet there were altogether more serious problems beneath the surface of this part of the choice process. As the competition to host both Summer and Winter Games intensified in the 1990s, it is clear that the proper limits of legitimate marketing and promotional activity during these encounters were becoming very blurred. In part this may have reflected genuine cultural differences in expectations about how promotional activity should be conducted (Booth, 1999). Gifts such as alcohol, tobacco, perfume, luxury products associated with the bidding cities or other personal gifts to delegates were routine (Jennings and Sambrook, 2000, pp. 115–130). There had been growing unease for many years, with allegations of improper favours granted in response to outright or coded demands from delegates in the desire to obtain precious votes. Moreover, since votes in the final selection process remained secret, delegates could not be called upon to justify their voting decisions by their National Committees.

The Olympic movement began to prohibit the most extravagant forms of hospitality by bidding cities in 1991–1992. It was not, however, until 1998 that sufficient evidence emerged to cause the practice to be comprehensively changed (Jennings and Sambrook, 2000, pp. 115–130; D. Miller, 2003, pp. 321–329). The occasion was the IOC delegate visit prior to the selection of the location for the 2002 Winter Olympics, which were hosted by Salt Lake City. The Utah city's Mormon heritage had scarcely endowed it with a reputation for venality. Yet during the visit several delegates and their families were allegedly bribed with holidays,

involve a simple and easily grasped idea of the intended event as it will be delivered at that particular time and in that particular city. In addition, and very importantly, it must also demonstrate that the event will be a historically momentous realization of the internationalism and altruism of the Olympian ideal.

One might reasonably question how far the contemporary Olympic movement itself, with its extraordinary commercialism and luxury hotel lifestyle, may be squared with this lofty ideal (Simson and Jennings, 1992; Barney *et al.*, 2004). The record of IOC delegates in choosing the locations of Summer and, increasingly, Winter Games certainly suggests a strong preference for highly sophisticated cities. This is a material reality that certainly needs to be addressed in the marketing message. So too do elements that relate very directly to competitive sports and, in a more subtle way, to the higher purposes of the Olympian ideal.

The result is that there are many common features in the marketing messages of Olympic candidate cities. Almost all will have spoken to the internationalism of the movement by portraying themselves in some sense as cities of the world. A good example of this is Barcelona's bid which stressed its international connectedness, and the amount and quality of its hotel accommodation and visitor attractions, and its cultural sophistication (COOB, 1992, I, p. 303). Culture has been a theme of increasing importance in the Olympic movement. Barcelona, for example, was able to stress its own high cultural reputation, mentioning legendary figures with strong associations such as Gaudí, Miro and Picasso (COOB, 1992, I, p. 303). Living testimony was provided by the Catalonian opera singer, Monserrat Caballé, a powerful ambassador for the city's Olympic hopes.

Another way of signifying culture was to stress the multi-culturalism of the city, a feature especially of Atlanta, Sydney and London's successful candidatures (ACOG, 1990; SOCOG, 2000b, pp. 15–17; LOCOC, 2004). Another important theme was a general openness and welcoming attitude, a theme first emphasized by Melbourne's 'Friendly Games' in 1956 and which Sydney sought to revive in its 1993 bid (McGeoch and Korporaal, 1994, p. 138). Cities that were less obviously multi-cultural, such as Barcelona (at least in 1986) or Beijing, tended to portray themselves as conduits through which a major cultural group might be claimed for the Olympic movement. Barcelona thus linked itself to its wider linguistic community in Latin America (COOB, 1992, I, p. 312; BOBICO, 2001, I, p. 3). For Beijing, the vastness of the world's Chinese population scarcely needed any labouring of the point.

Alongside these elements of the message that emphasized the city, there were others that focused more specifically on sports. Candidate cities, certainly those in the most highly developed parts of the world, are virtually obliged to argue that their populations are keen participants in and spectators of all types of sport. They will also try to show that their climate will be particularly conducive to sporting attainment when the Games are held. In keeping with all claims of this type ever made by city promoters, considerable scepticism must be exercised (S.V. Ward, 1998). Atlanta, for example, averaged its night and day temperatures to reach the

claimed figure. Similarly Barcelona's claimed mild climate proved stiflingly hot during the actual Games.

In recent years, several campaigns have also sought to claim that theirs will be an 'Athletes' Games', most explicitly by Sydney which used these exact words (SOCOG, 2000*b*, p. 20). By this, cities usually mean that they do not want to allow commercial considerations to swamp sporting ideals. Close proximity of proposed athletes' accommodation and sports venues is often associated with this claim. In part this emphasis has emerged as a reaction to the most highly commercialized Games, notably those of Los Angeles and Atlanta. There may also be a specific need for the marketing message to rebut potential criticisms of the bidding city. For example, the 1963 Mexico City team that successfully bid for the 1968 Summer Games devoted much attention to countering its own, rather serious, weak points, namely, that its altitude and poor air quality would prejudice a successful sports occasion (Organizing Committee, 1968, II, pp. 11–13).

Normally this kind of operation would be done in a less overt manner that stresses positives rather than overtly acknowledging negatives, at least in presentational set-pieces. Thus all post-Munich Olympic candidates have stressed the safeness of their cities, sometimes against compelling counter-evidence. Even Barcelona's confident campaign experienced a serious wobble when the Basque terror group ETA launched an attack and murdered a policeman in the centre of the city on the eve of the critical IOC meeting in 1986 (COOB, 1992, I, p. 310). Almost two decades later, London's team did not have to face the far more serious atrocities until the day *after* it had secured the 2012 Olympics. Had these events been transposed that would surely have been a terrible testing of even the most well-conceived promotional campaign.

It would be possible to go further with these widely occurring aspects of the Olympic city promotional message. The examples used have been drawn from those that won their bids to host the Games. However, it would be possible equally to document the same elements of the marketing message from those that lost. In 2005, unsuccessful New York and Paris stressed their cultural qualities, their accessibility and their attractiveness to visitors every bit as much as London. This tendency to a generic message begs the question: does the marketing *message* itself really make a difference? Perhaps the role of marketing and promotion is simply to prove commitment, a matter more of method and persistence than of what is actually said?

If the message is important, we can be sure it is not because a city says the same thing as everywhere else. The decisive aspect and, it can be argued, the thing that does sometimes differentiate the winners from the losers, is the presence in the marketing message of a compelling 'big idea'. As Tony Blair recently remarked in a reflection on London's success in winning the 2012 Games, it was not simply a case of saying that yours was the sleekest, smartest city.[2] To work, the 'big idea' in the marketing message has to connect to the Olympic ideal in more than a superficial sense. The rhetorical ambition of the ideal itself, based on an altruism and purity

of purpose that transcends the ordinary selfishness of humanity, is important here. So too is the associated vanity that lies within the Olympic movement's self image, that it is a portentous and positive force that anticipates the tides of global history. Candidate cities, if they really want to succeed, do well to flatter this vanity in their promotional rhetoric.

In this vein, we can note how many successful bids have sought to position themselves and their message, sometimes almost subliminally, as part of a momentous transition or movement. Barcelona's bid, for example, was portrayed by Pasqual Maragall as part both of 'plucky little Catalonia' and the 'great Spain which is awakening' (COOB, 1992, I, p. 312). In this view Spain was finally moving beyond the sterile centralist Franco dictatorship to become a fully democratic and culturally diverse entity, a progressive influence on its neighbours and its linguistic realm. The significance of this proposition was acknowledged when the IOC President Juan Antonio Samaranch, himself Barcelona-born, pointedly chose to pronounce its winning name not in Castilian Spanish but in the long suppressed but lately reborn regional language of Catalan.

The 'big idea' within Beijing's successful bid in 2001 for the 2008 Summer Games was that it represented a China that was now ready to emerge from its own economic and political isolation, '… to speed up its modernization and integration into the international community' (BOBICO, 2001, I, p. 1). The references were highly coded, so much so as to be almost invisible in the case of moving towards democracy and better standards on human rights. Yet after the city's rebuff largely because of this issue in 1993, helped by some subtle negative campaigning by Sydney and other cities, it definitely had to be addressed if the city's candidature were to succeed (McGeoch and Korporaal, 1994, pp. 226–227). Interestingly though, in 2001, Paris's attempt to use human rights arguments against Beijing rebounded, damaging the French rather than the Chinese bid (D. Miller, 2003, pp. 340–341).

Other cities have appealed to different aspects of the Olympic ideal. The language of Atlanta's Black civil rights martyr, Martin Luther King, permeated its message of a brave city that was realizing his integrationist vision and would use the 1996 Olympics to show this to the world (ACOG, 1990). A key word throughout all Atlanta's promotion was 'dream', a direct reference to King's most powerful speech. The prominence in the bid campaign of a Black former Atlanta Mayor and Ambassador to the United Nations, Andrew Young, also provided vigorous testimony to the reality, playing a key role in swaying African IOC members. Sydney linked its bid to environmental sustainability, setting a new benchmark for the Olympic movement (SOCOG, 2000b, p. 19). It used the Executive Director of Greenpeace International, himself Australian, to substantiate the claim (McGeoch and Korporaal, 1994, pp. 139–141).

We have noted how many cities make use of youth in their message. London was unusual in making youth its big idea. It spoke of the city as 'a beacon for world youth' with a 'voice that talks to young people' (LOCOC, 2004; BBC News 24,

2006). A London Games would inspire the young people of the world to become involved in sport and grasp the opportunities for self-improvement and social betterment that it offered. It was a theme that was consciously echoed throughout its presentation, most obviously in the video mentioned above. The team's leader, the double Olympic gold medallist Lord (Sebastian) Coe, told what was essentially the same story, of how as a boy he too had been inspired by Olympians of an earlier generation (Campbell, 2005). David Beckham brought in the theme of childhood, referring to his boyhood home in the heart of the area where London's Olympics were to be located. His presence, despite then being one of Real Madrid's *galacticos*, also underlined his 'real' loyalty, to his birthplace rather than his adopted city, which in 2005 was London's strongest rival after Paris for the 2012 Games. London also used large numbers of real children on the stage, living testimony to the city's multi-ethnic, multi-cultural character. Most commentators, including many in France, agreed that London's final presentation did make a difference.

Conclusion

Marketing is then a key part of the Olympic selection process. While it is no substitute for a competent bid that is technically and financially convincing, it can make a difference. For those centrally involved in that promotional process, it may well be the pinnacle of their careers. If they win, they are likely to be fated by an ecstatic city and a grateful nation. They will be the new gods, literally Olympians, of the marketing profession, likely to command, if they so choose, high fees to address business gatherings throughout the world. They may well become advisers to subsequent bidding cities or find lucrative roles in the Olympic movement. The intelligence they collect about IOC delegates and the mechanics of the bidding process will be a tradeable commodity. Even the runners up will be able to cash in on some of the bidding assets they have accumulated.

Yet, paradoxically, winning the right to be an Olympic city is only a prelude to the real marketing event, the actual Games themselves (Barney *et al.*, 2004; Lee, 2005). Once the host city has been selected, the promotional devices invented to advance the bid immediately become commodities that can henceforth be sold to enhance the products of sponsors. The symbols that originated as an image to disseminate a speculative proposition now become the basis for a carefully controlled market brand. Branding is essentially about the ownership of an idea that is then transferred to an actual product, which is quite literally what happens. The big idea of the successful city's vision of its Games is now expressed in an increasingly tangible product. Naturally a burgeoning brand marketing department is needed within the organizing body to police the use of such images and symbols. All this will have been carefully planned and forms a mandatory part of the candidature file. To ensure this plan is properly implemented, cities will find powerful and experienced allies in the IOC, anxious to extract every last scintilla of monetary value from the Games. In the end, therefore, many of the great Olympic

ideals resolve themselves into material matters. For all the lofty ambitions of Olympianism, it is perhaps appropriate that it falls to the marketers to compete in what has become the greatest Olympic challenge of all.

Notes

1. *Marketing Matters: The Olympic Marketing Newsletter*, 'Olympic Marketing 1980–2001', issue 19, July 2001.
2. BBC News 24, item on London's Olympic victory, broadcast 1 January 2006,

Chapter 8

Accommodating
the Spectacle

Jon Coaffee and Lorraine Johnston

Britain's Olympic bid is something else, or ought to be; and good luck to it. The problem here, and it is a big one, is that British politicians, lobbyists, developers, planners and architects have the unerring habit of confusing big events such as the long-forgotten millennium, or the future Olympic Games, with an opportunity for instant redevelopment. Mix bricks, mortar, a dash of the passion contemporary politicians always have for such headline-grabbing ploys, a sprinkle of public relations razzmatazz; then, stir in a spoon of hubris and, hey presto, our cities are lumbered with yet another … scheme that, a year after the big event, is nothing more than a damp squib.

Jonathan Glancey (2004)

Spectacle, as noted in chapter 2, is an integral feature of the Olympic festivals. In this respect, the modern Olympics are events that go far beyond the customs and practices of normal sporting competitions. They embody numerous symbolic elements and quasi-religious rituals believed to have connection with the ancient Olympics, along with newly invented traditions such as the torch relay, the five rings, the flag and the Opening Ceremony oath. Increasing incursion of media considerations have led to even more dramatic displays, ceremonies and urban design, with MacAloon (1981, cited in Cashman, 1999, p. 5) noting that the modern Olympics are 'an immense playground, marketplace, theatre, battlefield, church, arena, festival and Broadway of cultural images, symbols and meaning'. This trend is not without its critics. For many observers, there is a tension between the practices adopted in the modern Olympics and the ideals of those that revived the Games in the late nineteenth century. From this perspective, the Games have become 'an overhyped commercial extravaganza and a gross mass spectacle in which corruption and nationalism are more prominent than high-minded idealism' (*Ibid.*, p. 8).

This chapter discusses attempts by selected cities to respond to the demands of supplying spectacle that is now intrinsic to hosting the modern Summer Olympics. Spectacle here is regarded as 'any form of public display put on for the guidance and edification of a large audience of spectators … created by consciously

manipulating space, landscape or objects to produce displays that draw a powerful emotional response from spectators whose participation is part of the experience of spectacle' (Gold and Revill, 2003, p. 38). In examining this subject, this chapter deals less with the content of spectacle – a topic that arises at numerous points in this text – than with the problems that cities encounter in *accommodating* the spectacle. We argue that the search for spectacle embarked upon by bidding and host cities also has potential pitfalls linked to democratic governance, city and regional economic debt, and security and safety concerns – which, only recently, have emerged as themes of central concern for the media.

As such, the early parts of this chapter argue that this type of critique is not restricted to the Olympic Games. Rather, it can be directed against any form of mega-planning project that suffers from what Peter Hall (1980, p. 3) termed the 'pathology of the planning process' by which, once started, many projects are either abandoned or proceed with massive cost overruns. Other recent planning theorists have also questioned why such large-scale planning projects continue to be commissioned when there is a strong possibility that they will be economically unprofitable, environmentally damaging and undemocratically accountable. Flyvbjerg *et al.* (2003), for instance, have introduced the concept of the 'megaproject paradox' to highlight situations where mega-planning strategies are increasingly adopted against a background of opaque costing and governance processes. After unpacking the Summer Olympics' experiences of spectacle from this standpoint, the latter parts of the chapter reflect on the presence and implications of enhanced security in the organization of Olympic spectacle. In particular, they take the metaphor of the 'Games-as-target' to draw attention to the increased threat faced by host cities from international terrorism and the problems of creating a secure environment for Olympic spectacle.

The Megaproject Paradox

In recent years, the notion of the urban or planning megaproject has generated much attention amongst academics and policy-makers alike. The idea meshes with prevailing philosophies of urban development, whereby city leaders have enthusiastically followed entrepreneurial strategies in the course of their efforts to develop and promote their cities. Increasingly though, there have been conflicts arising from the predicted and actual cost of such projects, with questions asked about the transparency of related planning decision-making processes and, ultimately, about the appropriateness of risk management protocol employed by those in charge of such spectacular projects.

Great Planning Disasters by Peter Hall (1980) was perhaps the first text that explicitly charted the ways in which large planning projects turn out to be disasters. Hall attributed this tendency to two key variables – overestimation of demand and underestimation of cost. He drew attention to the fact that cost escalation for such planning projects typically amounts to around 50 per cent, further arguing that

what he refers to as 'the art of imaginative judgement' will only be alleviated once more effective and transparent forecasting of projected trends is undertaken (*Ibid.*, p. 250). The most dramatic example given was that of the Sydney Opera House, which opened in 1973 with construction costs amounting to fifteen times the figure specified in the initial budget.

Subsequent studies of the costs and benefits of planning megaprojects have taken Hall's basic premises and expanded them to take account of differing social, economic and political contexts, as well as emphasizing the different spatial aims and outcomes of such projects. For example, some analyses have focused on projects directed at specific 'urban islands' or at gaining sub-regional and regional infrastructural benefits (see, for example, Swyngedouw *et al.*, 2002), whilst others have emphasized the 'place promotional' benefits of projects in the form of conventions and major cultural and sporting events (e.g. Roche, 2000). American policy-oriented research provides further examples. For instance, Altshular and Luberoff (2003) in *The Changing Politics of Urban Mega-Projects* identified the shifts in American urban policy that have led to the recent boom in megaprojects, paralleling this trend with similar impulses in the 1950s and 1960s that were linked to ideas of urban 'boosterism' and local 'growth machines' (Molotch, 1976; Logan and Molotch, 1987). In so doing, they have pinpointed the large-scale cost escalation that many projects in both eras endured, having serious implications for local taxpayers and often leading to community-based resistance and protest – a state of affairs that they term 'negative pluralism'.

From their work identifying the conceptual basis of the planning of megaprojects, Flyvbjerg *et al.* (2003) provided a detailed exposé of a selection of large-scale infrastructural projects and how the concept of 'risk' and its acceptance by the public and private sector (and society at large) have been central to megaproject development. On one hand, they pointed to the emergence of the megaproject as a 'new political and physical animal', that such projects have 'witnessed a steep increase around the world in … magnitude, frequency and geographical spread' (*Ibid.*, p. 136), and have been financed by 'a mixture of national and supranational government, private capital and development banks' (*Ibid.*, p. 3). On the other hand, they also drew attention to the fact that such projects commonly have a calamitous history of cost overruns, largely arising as a result of what Huber (2003, p. 595) described as 'a combination of intentional ignorance, megalomania, and in the later stages of such projects – blame shifting'.

In this context, Flyvbjerg *et al.*'s (2003, p. 3) central pillar of enquiry was the ironic megaproject paradox:

At the same time as many more and larger infrastructure projects are being proposed and built around the world, it is becoming clear that many such projects have strikingly poor performance records in terms of economy, environment and public support.

They maintained that the main cause of that paradox was 'inadequate

deliberation about risk and the lack of accountability in the project decision making process' (*Ibid.*, p. 6). In short, as Talbot (2003, p. 173) commented, the central idea was to 'debunk the utopian thinking behind many large scale public infrastructure projects' and to set out a schema as to how to improve the management of such complex undertakings.

Taken together, this body of work identifies four key themes relevant to the staging of a megaproject that emerge as being central to the planning of a modern Olympic Games. First, it is commonly asserted that the impacts of such projects are, within reason, priceless and that 'some may argue that in the long term cost overruns do not really matter and that most monumental projects that excite the world imagination had large overruns' (Flyvbjerg *et al.*, 2003, p. 4). This, of course, fails to take into account the significant risk of municipal bankruptcy and the large-scale and long-term local government debts – often leading to higher local taxes – that can accrue.

Secondly, for decades megaprojects have been the subject of dubious costing procedures that lack realism, underestimate financial contingency and, significantly, undervalue safety and environmental costs (Merrow, 1988). In short, 'megaprojects often come draped in the politics of mistrust' (Flyvbjerg *et al.*, 2003, p. 5) with tendered estimates systematically and deceptively hiding the real costs of construction – at least, until the project is under way.

Thirdly, initiators and managers often present their projects to the public in terms of supposed benefits to the environment and society, as well as with regard to citywide and regional economic and employment growth. These 'benefits', however, are routinely exaggerated. In similar vein, there are widespread and recurrent accusations that such projects have been partially funded or had their cost overruns met by massaging 'mainstream' public service budgets. In this sense, megaprojects can be seen to exacerbate social disadvantage and inequality.

Finally, the governance of massive public expenditure on megaprojects often lacks financial and democratic accountability, with such projects associated with the development of so-called 'pro-growth regimes' and the closure of local politics to local citizens. In the course of scrutinizing urban megaprojects and associated governance structures, many commentators have argued that the focus by city leaders on growth, competition and development has necessitated a recasting of the way in which we view the dynamics of urban governance. For example, work on 'urban regime theory' (e.g. Stone, 1989) has stressed the importance of understanding local political contingency. It has also pointed to the impact of elite groups, principally motivated by economic considerations, in constructing self-serving urban governance practices that serve narrowly-defined interests within both the public and private sectors.

Subsequently, other writers, drawing on neo-Gramscian theory, maintain that a more 'strategic relational approach' to understanding urban governance is required (Jessop 1997; Macleod and Goodwin, 1999). They argue that by using such an approach 'urban governance – its policy paradigms, institutional form, and regime of political representation – can be understood as part of the creation and maintenance of hegemonic projects' (McGuirk, 2004, p. 1024). This can be viewed as inculcating strategies that selectively favour elite capital interests, mobilize their resources to realize state capacity via partnerships, and do so through interventions aligned with their policy preferences at the urban scale (*Ibid.*, p. 1028). In short, these new institutional arrangements or governance regimes often only involve the 'the usual suspects, namely government experts, administrators and politicians' (*Ibid.*, p. 1026) who, between them, dominate the mainly autonomous webs of power relations in a particular place. As Swyngedouw *et al.* (2002, p. 34) remarked, less democratic and more elite priorities characterize these new governing forms. However, such regimes have become increasingly skilled at conveying the impression that their activities are democratic, and hence legitimate, even where decision-making processes occur well in advance of any tokenistic consultation with wider communities of interest. As such, theoretical approaches to stakeholder involvement and risk assessment involving deliberative, communicative and collaborative approaches will rarely be successful for megaprojects due to the strong influence of powerful actors in the planning process. Degrees of participation by outsiders to the regime appear to be achieved, more often than not, through invitation or co-option.

Olympic Megaprojects as Spectacle

The foregoing analysis highlights the characteristics that have plagued the development of mega-projects. Their proliferation, therefore, may seem surprising, but they have undoubted value as spectacle – as display that captures, or at least is intended to capture, the imagination of those that experience the spectacle. This property undoubtedly helps to explain why the number of cities seeking to develop such projects has expanded greatly in recent years. After all, as already indicated (see chapter 1), the Olympics, especially the Summer Games, are now considered as perhaps the quintessential mega-events, in which the processes of globalization of both economy and culture are played out in specific localities. As Dunn and McGuirk (1999, pp. 23–24) point out:

> Hosting an Olympic Games represents the opportunity to attract enormous investment and consumption spending both during and after the Games. It can also generate significant ongoing local development, particularly in tourism and retail sectors… A locality's capture of the jewel in the crown of hallmark events becomes a mechanism for driving material land symbolic transformations of place and have profound implications for governance at a local and regional scale.

The interlinkage between the Olympics and spectacle is now fundamental to the representation and understanding of the event, especially due to the global reach of television. The Games, as John MacAloon (e.g. 1981, 1984, 1989) has consistently argued, represent a hybrid cultural form that contains elements of 'festival', 'ritual', 'spectacle', and 'game', but television has helped to prioritise the element of spectacle over the others. For his part, Roche (2000, p. 165) also indicated the importance of 'the logic of "spectacle", whereby the awe experienced by the spectators in the stadium and watching on television takes precedence over the Olympic meanings and values associated with the other dimensions'. Events such as the Opening and Closing Ceremonies attract some of the largest audiences of any Games and are vital for generating the television revenues that now account for over half of Olympic income and constitute 'the engine that has driven the growth of the Olympic Movement' (IOC, 2005b; see also chapter 6).

Yet whatever the allure of the large-scale spectacle now associated with the Olympics, the task of accommodating that spectacle cannot mask the geographies of difference that can occur in a host city. The planning rhetoric of recent Olympic cities draws particular attention to the elements that would represent the positive 'legacy' of the event. These specifically centre on regeneration, inward investment, place promotion and tourism, and are articulated at the expense of more critical voices that have questioned the very logic and justification for such mega-event-led urban renaissance. Various examples since the 1970s of attempts by urban authorities to use Olympics to stimulate urban development and growth illustrate the 'darker side' of accommodating the spectacle in the shape of unethical governance and dubious financial management (Yiftachel, 1994).

In this context, it is worth noting that even Barcelona 1992, often eulogized as the most successful Games in recent decades, has also been accused of having its 'dark side'. For example, in the short term, the Barcelona Games only made $3 million from $10 billion invested. As noted in chapter 9, the 1992 Barcelona Olympics was a celebrated exemplar of urban rejuvenation linked to major sporting events, from which a 'Barcelona Model' or 'cult of Catalonia' has emerged that other urban policy-makers slavishly follow in the hope of similar gains. However, as Garcia-Ramon and Albert (2000) observed, there were 'shadows in the process' surrounding the 1992 Games. These led to the privileging of physical and design-led intervention, at the behest of pro-growth coalitions, and saw benefits aimed at a global political-economic audience at the expense of locally-specific social needs of the most disadvantaged areas of Barcelona (see also chapter 13).

Analyses of Sydney 2000 and Athens 2004 similarly stress the overestimation of projected benefits and downplaying of concerns about financial mismanagement amidst attempts to create the Olympic spectacle. The National Government, for instance, needed to step in and rescue the finances for Sydney 2000 in order that the full construction programme might take place, while the predicted long-term 'Barcelona style' tourist boom failed to materialize. Indeed as Gardiner (2005, p. 19) commented: 'Australia spent A$1.6 billion (£900 million) on infrastructure for the Games, but generated just a one per cent increase in Sydney's Gross Domestic Product. Indeed, many of the sporting facilities are still under-utilized creating a burden on the taxpayer estimated at A$46 million (£19.6 million) per year' (see also Vigor et al., 2004).

Despite the IOC President Juan Antonio Samaranch hailing the Sydney Olympics as 'the best Olympics ever', other observers pointed to the accompanying negative consequences of hosting the Games, especially for the city's local communities. As Lenskyj (2002, pp. 227–228) commented:

> In the real world – in the street, low income neighbourhoods, homeless refuges, and indigenous communities – there was indisputable evidence that the staging of the Olympics served the interests of global capitalism first and foremost while exacerbating existing social problems. From this perspective, the best ever label was clearly misplaced.

Lenskyj went on to assert that Sydney 2000 had suffered a series of 'serious shortcomings'. These included lack of community involvement and democratic decision-making; by-passing planning legislation; lack of transparency and financial accountability, with indirect costs quietly omitted from the budget while indirect benefits were showcased; extra public subsides given by National Government; issues of social equity; and a lack of detailed environmental audits. She concluded that there was:

> extensive secrecy and obfuscation on the part of Olympic and government officials. In the absence of thorough and accurate financial, social and environmental impact assessment – and in the general euphoria surrounding the 'best ever Olympics' – they are unlikely to engage in any serious post game initiatives that will benefit all … residents. (*Ibid.*, p, 231)

Similar pronouncements were also made after Athens 2004, which saw costs spiral from an estimated $4 billion to nearer $8 billion.

Overall, the negative side of accommodating spectacle sees Olympic venues derided as costly 'white elephants', creating 'islands of gentrification' (Garrido, 2003, p. 9) and 'rich ghettos' funded by the private sector (Woodman, 2004). Commentators have also drawn attention to the short-term nature of employment prospects and the balance between pursuing growth strategies over destruction of urban green spaces (Marrs, 2003). Other assessments have also revealed the ever-present risk of a post-Olympic economic downturn once the special circumstances that accompanied the Games have evaporated (PriceWaterhouseCoopers, 2004). Moreover, from the perspective of local governance, researchers have also investigated how planning an Olympic Games bid, or hosting the actual event, is initiated and pursued almost exclusively by a selective coalition of public and private sector elites. Some have argued that this leads to the formation of a pro-growth regime, which is vital to an Olympic bid by helping, first, to coordinate and manage resource flows and, secondly, to respond to the action and policies of external actors, most notably the IOC, multinational investors and the nation state (Andranovich *et al.*, 2001; Burbank *et al.*, 2001; Emery, 2002). For instance, Searle and Bounds (1999) showed how, following Sydney's success in winning the rights to stage the 2000 Olympics, the Organizing Committee developed a business-led and pro-growth approach with little consultation outside elite political and business networks. This was despite concerns raised about the sustainability of planned facilities, which would be built at the expense of other developments, and placing other areas of Sydney under special legislative planning powers designed to speed up the construction process.

The inevitable tendency when this type of elite regime appears is that the voice of the average citizen becomes marginalized in the Olympic decision-making processes. As Burbank *et al.* (2001, p. 164) reported in their study of bids made by American Olympic cities:

> A common element (in these bids) was that citizens were largely left out of the policy making process (and that) ... in general citizen participation in the process of bidding for organizing an Olympics is minimal.[1]

They also indicated that typically 'piecemeal resistance' focusing on specific development linked to environment destruction and simple 'Nimbyism' are recurrent themes in Olympic bids. For example, protest arising from Toronto's bid for the 2008 Games was organized primarily through the symbolically named 'Bread not Circuses' coalition, which argued for what they called 'socially responsible games'.[2] This protest partly drew on Lenskyj's (2002) analysis of Sydney, which maintained that the bid organizers were likely to suppress the real costs and impacts of the Olympics and that success in the bidding process would reduce funding to non-Olympic projects. These impacts, they claimed, might well persist long after the immediate task of accommodating Olympic spectacle had faded from the city's immediate agenda.

Securing Spectacle

The chance to create spectacle goes beyond the official programme of the Olympics and the activities of a host city's planners and architects. Given the media prominence of the Games, particularly the Summer Olympics, it is not surprising that they provide a tempting forum for public protest by those seeking significant exposure for their cause. The result is that the Games have become an iconic target, which imposes a burden of security on host cities well beyond what they would otherwise face. In light of these circumstances, the scrutinizing committees and delegates of the IOC carefully examine bids to ensure that host cities provide the necessary safety and security for the smooth running of the Games.

This requirement came to the fore after the so-called 'Munich Massacre' in 1972 when members of the Israeli Olympic team were killed after being taken hostage by the Palestinian terrorist organization Black September. The need to address the phenomenon of international terrorism saw the security bill for future Games soar (Reeve, 2001). According to the *Wall Street Journal* (*Anon*, 2004), the average cost of security at the Olympics Games rose from approximately $80 million to $1.5 billion over the 20 years between Los Angeles 1984 and Athens 2004. When viewed on the basis of cost per athlete, this equates to rise from $11,627 per capita to $142,857 per capita (see table 8.1). It is a requirement that has also changed the character of the Games. For most organizers, their preparations for the Games must now necessarily include attempts to equate spectacle with safety and to design out terrorism, often by relying on highly militarised tactics and expensive, detailed contingency planning (Coaffee and Wood, 2006).

Security for Los Angeles 1984 created an important prototype in this field. The Games' security was organized by the private sector, but successfully launched a relationship between the numerous public safety agencies and the Organizing Committee replicated in subsequent Games. At Los Angeles, the arguments to spend large amounts of finance on security were largely premised on heightened tensions emanating from the Cold War. Notably, less than three months before the Opening Ceremony, the Soviet Union announced that it was boycotting the Games, blaming not only the overt commercialization of the Olympic spectacle, but also a lack of adequate security measures. This, they argued, amounted to a violation of the Olympic Charter.

By contrast, Seoul 1988 witnessed the South Koreans engage in an extensive security operation, with their major concern being the entry into the country of 'terrorists' from North Korea. This involved over 100,000 personnel drawn from the police, the military and private security organizations – then the largest such force assembled to secure the Games. The organizers also drafted in thousands of volunteers to help the security effort. The Korean question became further enmeshed in Olympic security when riot police were sent in to break up demonstrations by student protestors seeking unification of the two countries. For many observers, the security operation captured the headlines of the news media rather than the sporting spectacle.

Barcelona 1992 saw the deployment of over 25,000 security personal due to fears expressed over reprisal terror attacks linked to the recently finished 1991 Gulf War, coupled with the threat of possible action by the Basque separatist movement ETA. Although this operation used fewer personnel than in Seoul, defensive measures at certain sites were highly militaristic. The security forces, for instance, constructed large-scale bunkers around the perimeter of the main

Table 8.1. Security costs of Olympic Games, 1984–2004.

Games	Total security cost ($ million)	Cost per Athlete ($)
Los Angeles 1984	79.4	11627
Seoul 1988	111.7	13312
Barcelona 1992	66.2	7072
Atlanta 1996	108.2	10486
Sydney 2000	179.6	16062
Athens 2004	1500.0	142857

Source: Adapted from the Wall Street Journal, 22 August 2004.

Olympic Village, with tanks situated at strategic locations. This complemented secure fencing and numerous closed circuit television cameras within the village, as well as a highly visible police presence at the sporting locations.

Prior to Atlanta 1996, the US authorities did not consider terrorism a major risk to the Games, despite the serious terrorist attacks on American soil at the World Trade Centre (1993) and the Oklahoma City Federal Building (1995). As the *Wall Street Journal* emphasized, terrorism ranked behind heat-related illness and the possibility of soccer violence on the official lists of 'potential worries' (Editor, 2004). That said, law enforcement agencies assigned more than 20,000 military and law enforcement personnel to monitor security measures, supplemented by 5,000 unarmed volunteers, in an operation that some saw as the most hi-tech and measured in Olympic history. On the eve of the Games, for example, Macko (1996) argued that:

> When it comes to the security of these Games, nothing has been left to chance in Atlanta and the other venues that will be used by the athletes. An army of law enforcement officers will outnumber the athletes themselves. The security for the 1996 Games is said to be the tightest ever in history. Security planners for the Olympic Games have tried to cover every angle possible – from cops on patrol to scuba divers and helicopters and high-tech devices such as ID badges with computer chips.

He continued:

> The two things that constantly weigh on the minds of the people in charge of the security are the bombings of the World Trade Centre in New York City and the federal building in Oklahoma City. Strategies to combat any possible terrorist attack have been planned and then have been re-planned. Security planners have spent more than two years in their planning.

Despite these intensive preparations, the small-scale bomb blast that occurred at an unsecured public space designed for the Olympics, killing one person and injuring over a hundred, reawakened fears of further attacks.

Persistent fears of the spectre of violence led to even tighter measures to protect the official Olympic spectacle at Sydney 2000. The cost and sophistication of security rose steeply from that incurred in Atlanta and involved nearly all Australia's Special Forces plus 30,000 personnel drawn from the police, private security and volunteers. Immediately before the Games, Browning (2000) observed that: 'Sydney in September will be under siege'. Even though the national government considered, in public at least, that the risk of attack was unlikely, the media began drawing connections between Osama Bin Laden, the most wanted person on the CIA's list of international terrorists, and Australia.

Although no major incident took place during the Sydney Games, the issue of terrorist violence took on an unprecedented significance for Athens 2004, particularly in view of the security situation in both Greece and internationally (see chapter 1). The cost of security for the Games consequently increased dramatically. As table 8.1 reveals, the Greek authorities spent well over five times more than the amount spent by the Sydney organizers, with the Olympics forcing the Greek state to speed up the modernization of its state security system. The authorities deployed over 70,000 specially trained police and soldiers at the Games' venues as well as a further 35,000 personnel patrolling the streets. Military hardware used for security was the most expensive yet used for the Olympics. It included a network of 13,000 surveillance cameras, mobile surveillance vans, chemical detectors, a number of Patriot anti-aircraft missile sites, NATO troops specializing in weapons of mass destruction, AWAC early warning surveillance planes, police helicopters, fighter jets, minesweepers, and monitoring airships (see Smith, 2004). The airships themselves became icons of the Games and attracted much media interest. Indeed, the dirigible that broadcast images for US television networks and gave spectacular aerial footage of the Games shared the skies with a second airship that patrolled the airspace above the Olympic sites on behalf of the Security Forces.

The Olympic stadium in Athens, always likely to be the site that constituted the most spectacular target, received the heaviest fortification. According to Peek (2004, p. 6), Athens was 'supposed to be one of the most secure places on earth, impenetrable to terrorists plotting a possible attack on this summer's Olympics'. For the duration of the Games, the city became a 'panoptic fortress' to give assurances to the rest of the world that the city was safe to host the world's greatest sporting spectacle (Samatas, 2004, p. 115). However, the retrofitting of such security systems is envisioned as a long-term project that will be maintained after the Olympics and which critics have argued will be become a menace to privacy, freedom of speech and civil liberties (*Ibid.*, p. 117; see also chapter 1).

Securing Olympic spectacle and protecting against the spectacle of terrorist violence will remain an overriding concern for Olympic organizers. This has become increasingly stark in the United Kingdom as London gears up to hosting the 2012 Games. Security concerns and responses not only played a critical part in the bidding process, but have also dominated media discussion after the host city was announced, especially after the series of terrorist bomb attacks on the London Transport network on 7 July 2005 – the day after London was confirmed as host city. These attacks have led to a massive increase in perceived security needs and prompted organizers to draw up ever more detailed plans. This could lead to the initial security bill quadrupling from £224 million to over £1 billion, the adoption of advanced biometric security systems to monitor crowds, officials and athletes, and to special measures to track suspects across the city (Coaffee and Wood, 2006).

Conclusion

The creation of spectacle is an inherent part of the Olympic Games, as manifested in systems of historic ritual, architectural innovation and grand projects, supreme athletic performance, and, more recently, the creation of eye-catching ceremonies to accommodate the demands of global television. At the same time, the history of the Games suggests that the experience of accommodating Olympic spectacle places the event in the same bracket as other types of megaproject; embracing a similarly risky and uncertain strategy in terms of financial liability and possible regenerative gains for the host city. Indeed, in November 2006, a little over a year after being awarded the 2012 Games, both the Organizing Committee in London and the British government had to concede that massive cost increases were fuelling concerns that the Games might ultimately be a large 'white elephant' project, embodying many of the principles of the megaproject paradox. As one commentator (Jenkins, 2006, p. 37) noted:

> Within 17 months of winning the bid the cost of building (not even running or taking part in) the Games has risen by 40 per cent to £3.3 billion, plus a further £4 billion for 'regeneration and contingency'. Last July, apparently, nobody had thought of 'inflation' or 'transport costs', let alone 'site decontamination' or 'increased security'. They had not thought the project would need an extra £400 million for delivery fees. For the elephant of course, all this is just canapés. The real meal is yet to come. (Jenkins, 2006, p. 37)

Much recent work has also drawn attention to the trend whereby Olympic host cities develop pro-growth regimes to organize and fund the Games, which often close off the decision-making process to particular sections of society.

In terms of the relationship between security and Olympic spectacle, the IOC regulations and guidance for host cities make clear that there is a responsibility to provide a safe environment for the 'Olympic Family' (competitors, officials and dignitaries), while ensuring that such securitization does not get in the way of the sporting activities or spirit of the Games. As Thompson (1999, p. 106) observed, 'the IOC has made clear that the Olympics are an international sporting event, not an international security event, and while Olympic security must be comprehensive it must also be unobtrusive'. This, increasingly, is a difficult scenario for host cities to achieve. Certainly if the risk of terrorism remains at its present critical level, there is the possibility of seeing core notions of Olympic spectacle to some extent replaced by dystopian images of cities under siege as organizers, security personnel and the media attempt to deliver an Olympics, in maximum safety and with minimum disruption, to the global television schedule.

Notes

1. For a good example of community involvement in Olympic bids, see Hiller's (2000) account of Cape Town's bid for the 2004 Games.
2. See http://www.breadnotcircuses.org.

Chapter 9

Urban Regeneration and Renewal

Jon Coaffee

Increasingly, the Olympic Games are being viewed as a once-in-a-lifetime opportunity for the host city (and sometimes country) to embark on a series of major development or redevelopment projects that have the potential to change the way in which the city operates, the feeling local citizens have for their city, and the perception of the rest of the world toward the host city and country.

Chernushenko (2004)

Since the 1960s notions of what have been termed 'urban regeneration' or 'urban renewal' have become increasingly prominent within public policy circles as a result of the attempts made at restructuring of cities and their economies in the face of deindustrialization. At the outset, it is important to stress that there is no single agreed definition of the terms 'urban regeneration' or 'urban renewal'. The former, however, might be seen as 'a comprehensive integrated vision and action which leads to the resolution of urban problems and which seeks to bring about lasting change in the economic, social, physical and environmental condition of an area that has been the subject of change' (Roberts and Sykes, 2000, p. 17). The latter, for its part, is a more limited term, essentially concerned with the physical replacement of worn-out or dilapidated areas of the city.

In recent years, the relationship between sport and strategic urban regeneration has gripped the imagination of policy-makers. This is largely due to the perceived economic and social benefits of hosting major sporting events and developing sporting infrastructure, which offer perceptions that have increasingly permeated policy-making agendas linked, *inter alia*, to economic revitalization and the development of sustainable communities (Coaffee and Shaw, 2005). In this context, much has been written about the potential for cities to improve and develop urban infrastructure and to stimulate widespread urban regeneration by hosting the Summer Games (Essex and Chalkley, 1998; Olds, 1998; Tufts, 2001; and Searle, 2002) or their Winter counterparts (Teigland, 1999; Richie, 2000; and Essex and Chalkley 2004). Similarly, much has appeared with regard to a closely-related issue, namely, the impact of hosting the Olympics on the marketability of place. Although most often associated with the broader activity of boosterism, by which towns and cities seek to promote themselves in relation to national or international rivals (e.g. see chapter 7), place marketing has an important relationship with urban regeneration.

Acting as an Olympic city presents planners with a period in which the city has the advantage of an unparalleled shop window by which to represent itself to the world. This, in turn, provides opportunities to attract the inward investment and encourage private-sector land development that are now so important to the activity of urban regeneration. Indeed, given the continuing effect of economic globalization and associated socio-cultural flows, it has become increasingly difficult to isolate the opportunity that planners gain to regenerate their local economies from the simultaneous activity of presenting the city's credentials on the global stage.

Any discussion of such matters necessarily recognizes that there has been a general re-conceptualization of what planners and other built environment professionals view as 'regeneration' and their assessment of the current value of sporting and cultural events to achieve this end. At the beginning of the modern Olympic movement, the urban impact of the Games was minimal. Over time, as the Olympics grew in scale and complexity, their impact on the city grew, but mainly involved the direct consequences and multiplier effects of building stadia and directly related facilities and services. It was only more recently that policy-makers viewed regeneration as a holistic intervention. As such, it targeted a variety of interrelated physical, social, environmental and economic problems in a coordinated fashion largely mediated through redesign of the built environment and infrastructure. In the last decade, city planners have again reconceptualized notions of regeneration by linking its various components to environmentalist ideas about sustainability. Olympic-led regeneration, therefore, is now associated with programmes and projects which target health, education, employment, local economic development, community cohesion, housing needs, crime reduction and environmental improvement, as well as large-scale physical development schemes.

This chapter, which contains four parts, provides an overview of the association between urban regeneration opportunities and the modern Olympics, in particular the Summer Games. The first presents an historical perspective that briefly highlights the impact of Summer Olympics on host cities between 1896 and 1980. The second part considers the growth of more economically rational and private sector-led models of Olympic regeneration management during the 1980s. The third section considers the development of holistic and citywide models of regeneration, which were initially adopted in relation to the 1992 Summer Games at Barcelona. The final part considers the attempts that have been made since 1992 to adopt the normative Barcelona model for Olympic city regeneration whilst paying attention to the environmental implications of hosting the Games.

Olympics and the Urban Impact

Relatively little need be said about the earliest Olympics of the modern era (1896–1906), in which Organizing Committees essentially fitted the Games either into the existing city (Athens 1896, 1906) or into the temporary built environment of more prestigious International Expositions (Paris 1900 and St Louis 1904) in which they were run as mere 'side-shows' (Matthews, 1980). Whatever impacts the International Expositions might have had (Gold and Gold, 2005), the urban impact of the Olympics *per se* was negligible. The period from 1908 to 1932 saw the Games better organized, larger in scale, and using facilities constructed specifically for the Olympics. London 1908 set the pattern. Although still associated with a Fair (the Franco-British Exhibition), the London organizers supplied a purpose-built venue and facilities as well as greatly improving the organization and planning of the Games (Organizing Committee, 1908; Mallon and Buchanan, 2000). In particular, they persuaded the Exhibition organizers to build the required stadium (the White City) in return for three-quarters of the gate receipts. Transport improvements were introduced specifically to cope with the crowds attending the Exhibition and Olympics, with a new underground railway station added to the network at Wood Street (see chapter 2). The stadium was considered the finest in the world at that time and provided a partial blueprint for future Olympic venues, although opinions differ as to its legacy for London. While its management found it difficult to find alternative uses for a stadium of this scale (see chapter 2), other commentators regarded it as a useful venue that adapted itself to changing needs. For example, Levin (2001; see also Grose, 2001) argued that:

> the fair grounds, and Olympic stadium, remained and served as the site for future exhibitions and events. White City became a pleasure/amusement park, and the stadium's functions ranged from training Olympic athletes to the site for greyhound dog races until the stadium was demolished.

The practices pioneered at London 1908 supplied new approaches to the development of sport facilities, which were adopted four years later at Stockholm 1912, and in subsequent Games at Antwerp 1920, Paris 1924 and Amsterdam 1928. Los Angeles 1932 similarly developed purpose-built sports facilities for the Games, but for the first time also constructed a purpose-built Village that was auctioned for housing needs after staging the Games. The Berlin Games of 1936 provided a watershed as far as expenditure on the Games was concerned, although the specific question of the impact on Berlin was secondary to the incumbent Nazi regime's desire to present positive imagery of the Third Reich to the outside world.

In stark contrast to Berlin, the Games immediately after the Second World War gave organizers less opportunity to carry out major works. London 1948, held with Britain in the grip of Austerity, required considerable improvisation to provide the necessary facilities, with Helsinki 1952 and Melbourne 1956 concentrating their activities on sporting facilities and associated athletes' Villages. It was from Rome 1960 onwards that urban renewal became a significant factor in Olympic planning. The Roman authorities channelled substantial investment into new infrastructure, particularly transport, which began to be planned hand-in-hand with new sporting facilities. Chalkley and Essex (1999, p. 379), for example, noted that in addition to the sporting facilities, the city of Rome:

> developed a new municipal water supply system, new airport facilities, improved public transport, street lighting and the illumination of monuments and numerous decorative improvements to the city. Interestingly, the changes produced by the Olympics Games led to calls for the next Games to be cancelled because of the scale and complexity of the related urban developments.

The opposite, however, occurred. Rome 1960 had changed the way in which municipal authorities perceived the task of hosting the Summer Olympics. Tokyo took the scale of sporting facilities and the extent of associated urban change to new levels in 1964, although the approach was still characterized more by renewal than regeneration. While motivated by a political agenda connected with proclaiming the country's re-emergence on the international stage after the Second World War, the Japanese government saw the Games as much an opportunity to invest in public transport and utility infrastructures designed to modernize Tokyo as to provide sporting facilities. The city authorities developed many new highways, metro-lines, monorail, airport and port facilities, along with improvements in the city's water supply and waste management systems. The areas immediately adjacent to the main stadium (see figure 9.1) were also rejuvenated, with landscaping and the addition of new metro stations. Subsequently, this newly accessible district became a centre of commerce.

Figure 9.1. The main Olympic Stadium for the 1964 Games in Tokyo.

Entrepreneurialism and Short-Term Urban Upgrading

The strategy adopted at Rome and Tokyo would presage the future, although the trend beyond renewal towards a regenerative approach was by no means a linear path. Although both Munich 1972 and Montreal 1976 invested in both sporting facilities and associated urban and infrastructure elements, neither competed with Tokyo in terms of the scale of investment in urban development projects. Moscow 1980 also saw little effort to invest in facilities not directly related to sport, other than a new airport terminal, media centres and hotels.

Los Angeles 1984, as noted in chapter 6, provided a defining moment in the financing of the Summer Olympics but its approach to issues of general urban development was to limit costs while still maintaining spectacle. The prevailing strategy reflected the fact that the Organizing Committee ran the Games as a commercial enterprise along private sector lines, given the refusal of local taxpayers to foot the bill. The approach was to update and reuse existing sporting and utility infrastructure. The campuses of the University of Southern California and the University of California at Los Angeles, for instance, provided accommodation to serve as the Olympic Village, which then passed back to the universities after the Games. The International Airport was also hurriedly upgraded (Burbank *et al.*, 2001). Although not necessarily obvious at the time, the Olympics also stimulated the development of a regional fibre-optic telecommunications system in Southern California. This provided an advanced regional communications infrastructure that helped to boost the burgeoning information technology sector of the Los Angeles area at a crucial moment in the evolution of the industry (Moss, 1985). Equally significant were the attempts by the organizers to integrate a community regeneration element into their plans although, cynically, this might also be inter-preted as a way of 'encouraging' volunteering. For example, programmes such as the 'Olympic neighbour programme' run in 1983 introduced youths in south-central Los Angeles to Olympic athletes and served as an impromptu orientation session for those working, or thinking of volunteering to work, at the Games. Overall despite being heralded – or in some quarters derided – as the 'capitalist' Olympics, Los Angeles 1984 was seen as 'great for the city' and 'contributed to a sense that (Los Angeles) was the place to get things done' (Burbank *et al.*, 2001, p. 80).

The organizers of Seoul 1988 similarly exploited the notion of the Olympics as a catalyst for improving urban infrastructure (particularly transport). The Games provided an opportunity to revalorize and refurbish the city, undertake reconstruction of water systems, improve parks and open space through pollution abatement programmes, and introduce air pollution controls. For example, the Official Report drew attention to various aspects of 'government support and people's participation' such as environmental beautification programmes, improvements in health and hygiene standards, realignment of traffic systems, promotion of tourism, and the expansion of cultural facilities (Organizing

Committee, 1989, p. 798). The Report also laid great emphasis on identifying the future legacy of the Games, but expressed this in promotional terms rather than urban regeneration:

> The successful staging of the Seoul Olympic Games provided a momentum to bring Korea close to the ranks of advanced countries on the strength of bolstered national development and the enhancement of general level of awareness among the people. The economic growth and enhancement of sprit of the public bolstered Korea's stature in the international community. (*Ibid.*)

Many analysts, however, expressed concern that the Korean authorities had focused upon spatial form rather than social process. As Gold and Gold (2005, p. 203) noted:

> the methods chosen to improve the city's built environment and infrastructure ... attracted international criticism for paying greater attention to urban form than to social cost. Ideas of improvement centred on the removal of slums and the creation of modernistic, often high-rise, development for high income residential or commercial use.

The Barcelona Model

The key moment for thinking about the regenerative impacts of hosting the Summer Olympics was undoubtedly Barcelona 1992 (see also chapter 14). Indeed, the 'Barcelona Model' for regenerating the urban environment through staging the Olympics now provides the blueprint for other cities bidding for Summer Games, as well as offering the conviction that Olympic legacies can be positive in terms of urban planning and regeneration rather than simply making short-term profits for organizers (Monclús, 2003; see also Marshall, 1996; DETR, 1999).

For some observers, the Olympic Games were more about bringing about an urban rejuvenation and associated tourist boom to Barcelona than about the sporting event, with the sports almost seeming a convenient pretext. Infrastructural projects accounted for 83 per cent of the total budget, with significant investment required due to the demands of a growing population, high levels of unemployment and severe deprivation in particular neighbourhoods. Projects related to Barcelona 1992 fundamentally changed the look and appearance of the city, with the regenerated Barcelona Seafront and the Torre Calatrava communication mast becoming instantly recognizable symbols of the new Barcelona (see figures 9.2 and 9.3). Clusa (2000) identified the wide array of projects developed, which included renewal of the stadia, the construction of a Sports Palace, building a ring road and approximately 35 kilometres of other major highways, 4,500 new flats derived from the Olympic Villages, the two communication towers, five new 'centrality areas' (offices), enlargement of the airport, general improvement of sports and leisure facilities, investment in the cultural sector (especially in the city's museums), 5,000 new hotel rooms and public access to 5 kilometres of new beaches, with Barcelona opening itself to the sea.

Figure 9.2. The newly regenerated Barcelona seafront.

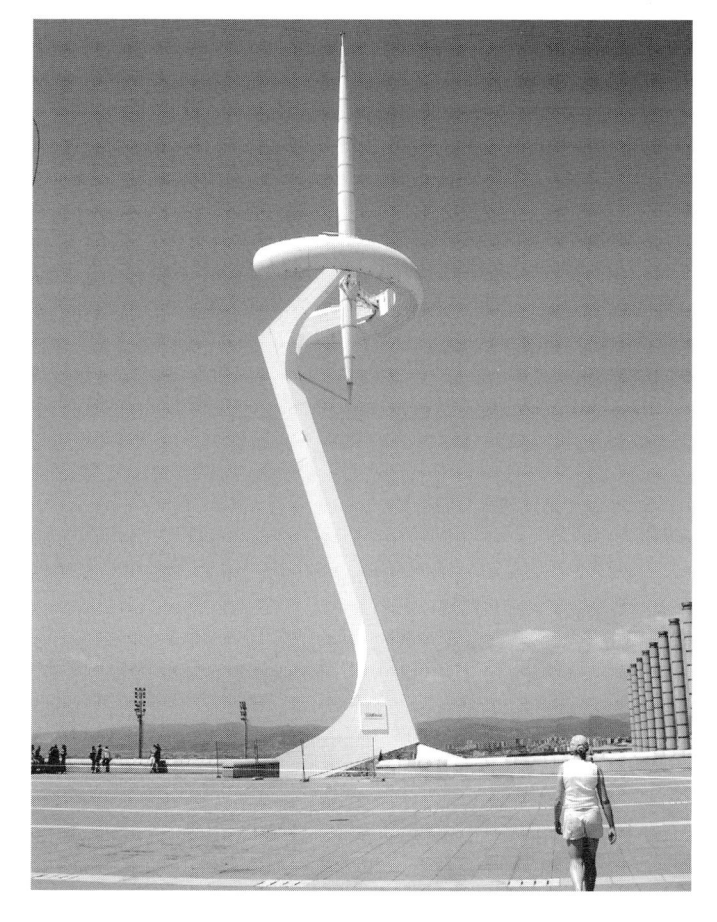

Figure 9.3.
Torre Calatrava
communication
mast: a potent
symbol of the
newly regenerated
Barcelona,

The underlying model has not been without its critics, as chapter 8 clearly showed, but this extensive list of improvements instantly recommended itself to city planners in other countries keen to replicate the major features of the Barcelona experience. In this regard, the most important element was to emphasize the need for long-term and strategic planning rather than the piecemeal and area-specific interventions that had been associated with many of the previous Summer Games. The Olympic planning process envisioned Barcelona positively as an accumulation of its distinct neighbourhoods rather than simply a number of different districts. The aim was to construct a sense of shared identity and ownership of the proposed urban restructuring effort – as such, interventions were linked to local priorities as well as overall city aims. The planners chose, for example, to locate new public buildings specifically to stimulate or 'pump prime' regeneration in adjoining areas, dispersed retail development around the city rather than large-scale centres, and encouraged mixed function land uses. Underpinning this strategic vision was the strong political and local leadership required to drive the process forward and to develop a flexible approach to regeneration programme management, which allowed the infusion of significant private finance to help fund the renewal projects and alleviate some of the financial risk that Olympic cities faced.

The municipal authorities in Barcelona also sought good quality architecture and urban design. They introduced schemes to refurbish and conserve important historic buildings and monuments, with tax incentives given for high quality refurbishments, but also encouraged innovative architectural thinking. Attention given to green and open space concentrated as much on maximizing the opportunity for social mixing as on issues of density or addressing narrow functional needs. The pre-Olympic preparations focused on to social programmes as well as morphological change. The authorities employed holistic approaches to tackling the problems of poorer neighbourhoods, recognizing as interrelated problems poor education, high crime rates, poor health, unemployment and poor leisure facilities, and the lack of social mixing in disadvantaged neighbourhoods.

Barcelona's success in linking wide-scale and strategically oriented urban regeneration with the hosting of the Olympics has had profound implications for urban planners throughout the world, but particular significance in the United Kingdom, where the rhetoric surrounding contemporary *urban renaissance* draws strongly on the Barcelona experience. This 'driver' of urban policy owes much to the architect Lord Richard Rogers who master-planned the Barcelona sea-front and was largely responsible for the influential British policy document *Towards an Urban Renaissance* (DETR, 1999). For instance, this work used the example of Barcelona and its Olympic experience to promote the virtues of a particular style of regeneration design and management. Pasqual Maragall, the Mayor of Barcelona at the time of the Games, wrote the Foreword to the *Urban Renaissance* report. In it, he laid emphasis on improvements in urban quality and the 'marriage between City Hall and the School of Architecture and alliances made with the public and private sectors' (Maragall, 1999b, p. 5). He further noted:

The 1992 Olympics were not the cause of Barcelona's design fame. For example, the prestigious Harvard University Prize was specifically given for the quality of urban design up to 1987. A commitment to develop networks of new plaza, parks and buildings was the cause of our success. The Olympics helped multiply the good works. (*Ibid.*)

Towards an Urban Renaissance supported this assertion by highlighting the long-term re-imaging attempts undertaken in Barcelona, which the Olympic megaproject consolidated and showcased:

The Catalonian capital re-invented itself throughout the 1980s and 1990s with a series of urban design initiatives that improved the quality of the public space in the city and radically enhanced its infrastructure. Under Mayor Pasqual and architect Oriol Bohigas, the city created 150 new public squares at the heart of urban communities. The city succeeded in winning its bid for the 1992 Olympics and coupled this with a strategy of urban regeneration that has paid long term dividends to the citizens of Barcelona, rather than making a short term profit for event organizers. (DETR, 1999, p. 72)

In contrast to the profound transformations in Barcelona, Atlanta 1996 returned to the model of Los Angeles 1984 and focused investment into sporting facilities. Lack of public funding and primary reliance on private finance resulted in a lack of lasting and strategic regeneration. As Burbank *et al.* (2001, p. 118) observed, the underlying vision quickly turned sour:

Mayor Jackson's dream was to scale the twin peaks of Mount Olympus by staging the best Games ever and uplifting the people of Atlanta. In the end, however, the politics of image building and downtown revitalization displaced neighbourhood redevelopment, as well as the needs and dreams of central city residents.

That said, there is evidence that as a result of the Olympics significant investment for infrastructure improvements flowed into Atlanta, with the Federal government supplying $371 million for housing projects and road, transit and sewer construction. The airport received an additional runway capable of accommodating international flights at a cost of around $450 million.

Environmental Sustainability vs Commercialization

After Atlanta, policy towards hosting the Olympics has embraced three separate sets of factors that have influenced regeneration policies. First, both Sydney 2000 and Athens 2004 drew on relevant aspects of the experience of Los Angeles 1984 and Atlanta 1996, most notably the concept of developing public-private partnerships to organize the Games. Secondly, both host cities provided evidence of trying to follow the model of regeneration through Olympic hosting that was successful in Barcelona, while concurrently projecting themselves to the world as vibrant global cities. Thirdly, Organizing Committees have had to meet the IOC's requirement that host cities adopt more environmentally and socially responsible approaches to planning, which, in turn, have influenced how commentators view and evaluate the regenerative legacy of the Olympics.

For example, the organizers promised that Sydney 2000 would be 'the sustainable Games'. The rhetoric employed in the media leading up to the event was deeply imbued with optimism that the Games would leave a lasting and sustainable legacy. Large areas of disused industrial and military land at Parramatta in Western Sydney underwent significant transformation to provide the main location for the sporting venues, showgrounds and Olympic Village. As Dunn and McGuirk (1999, p. 25) commented:

> This part of western Sydney has been undergoing a profound and symbolic restructuring. The prior land use … can be fairly be described as noxious industrial. The area was dominated by an industrial complex of chemical manufactures, brickworks and abattoirs. The Olympic village will be sited over what were a landfill garbage tip and an Australian Navy ammunition dump. The area was, and still is badly contaminated by industrial, chemical and household wastes.

They continued by noting the importance of the regeneration as being 'clean and green' (*Ibid*., p. 27). As Weirick (1999, p. 77) further noted, 'Sydney decided to promote an environmental image, and the idea of the "Green Games" captured the imagination of the world'. This included a series of innovative designs for the Olympic Village, although many of these ideas were dropped from the preparations after the bid was won:

> A consortium of young designers developed the concept of an eco-village which was incorporated into the bid books. The eco-village was to be aligned so as to maximize solar energy. Water would be recycled through the wetlands so as not to create pollution, and the Village would be linked to public transport. (*Ibid.*)

Although the eco-village was never built, other commentators emphasized the changes in building design, with the introduction of 'green criteria' for individual construction projects (Prasad, 1999). That said, observers argued that a significant part of the investment in air, road and rail infrastructure had little direct relevance to facilitating travel for the Olympics. They also suggested that Sydney's planners had pressed ahead in pursuit of commercial gain and with the aim of opening up new sites for commerce rather than attempting to address the inherent problems of environmental pollution and transport congestion faced by the city (Weirick, 1999, p. 74). The rhetoric of the 'Green Games' that had preceded the Olympics had long since faded away. The Olympic Park, designed to be Sydney's showcase venue after the Games and the heart of significant and lasting urban transformation, closely resembled a 'ghost town' (Mahne, 2004). Searle (2002) noted how post-

Games analyses showed the lack of profitability of the Sydney Olympic stadia and related facilities and argued that, during their construction, the true extent of the associated financial risks was kept from the public eye.

In a similar manner to Sydney, Athens 2004 was seen as an opportunity for the city's authorities to display the Greek capital to the world, to modernize its substandard transport systems, and to leave a tangible legacy of regeneration for the city. Here, too, environmentalist rhetoric suffused the initial plans for the Games. The organizers claimed that: 'Athens 2004 would be the first Olympiad using 100% green energy' and that 'all projects will be realized with the use of environmentally friendly technologies and materials, and this will be a prerequisite in all relevant tenders' (cited in Videl, 2004).

Certainly, the 2004 Olympics heralded a construction boom and offered a model for urban regeneration that contrasted with the fragmented approach that typified previous attempts at regeneration in Athens. Planners, architects and urban designers were forced to think citywide not just in terms of the development of new and expanded transport services and impressive sporting facilities, but also with regard to the construction of large-scale residential communities. The Olympic Village here comprised three large, separate athletes' villages, which after the Games were transferred for use as private residences. The lower densities, greenery, open spaces, safety considerations, and appropriate car parking and access marked out these neighbourhoods as quite distinct from the traditional Athenian residential landscapes.

More problematically, the potential of Athens for regeneration was badly affected by delays in construction, which dogged the schedules of work before the Games and led to a familiar scenario of builders working around the clock to complete the venues as intended. The apparently 'green' construction technologies that, it was claimed, would be employed were largely absent. An environmental audit of the Games that Greenpeace carried out argued that, in construction of the Olympic villages, nearly all environmental recommendations were ignored and energy conservation, product recycling, the use of solar energy and natural cooling systems were all dropped from final plans (see also chapter 15). As a spokesperson argued:

> Instead of moving forward, the Athens 2004 Games have gone way back as far as environmental issues are concerned. The International Olympic Committee has called the environment the third pillar of the Olympics, behind sport and culture. Right now, it seems all but invisible. (Cited in Videl, 2004)

There are, of course, firm grounds for arguing that the city has been able to promote a regenerative agenda through staging the Olympics. The widening of existing highways and the addition of two extra metro-lines have contributed to lessening the city's atmospheric pollution as well as providing greater accessibility to the revamped beaches. However, the substantial costs of maintaining the 30

Olympic venues and the lack of concrete plans for post-festival use of those facilities indicate yet again that there is no guarantee that an unequivocally positive legacy will automatically follow staging the Games.

Holistic Regeneration

When looking ahead towards Beijing 2008 and London 2012, it is clear that the stated agendas of host cities must now include the combination of lasting regeneration and sustainability – at least at the bid stage. Central and municipal governments aim to transform Beijing into a truly global city through major regeneration programmes that tackle the city's inherent environmental and infrastructural problems and leave a lasting legacy (Ness, 2002, p. 1). As Chernushenko (2004) observed:

> Sydney took a huge step toward building for and hosting a 'greener Games'. Beijing has now committed to doing so. But in order to host the Olympics in a cleaner, greener city, Beijing must find solutions to some significant and unique challenges, notably in such areas as air and water quality, wastewater and solid waste management and transportation. With these challenges come tremendous opportunities: for the city and country, and for domestic and international suppliers of innovative technology, as well as planning and management skills.

These challenges take their place alongside other perceived needs that the Organizing Committee seeks to balance. *Inter alia*, these include showcase architecture and property development in order to create a 'modern high tech metropolis' (RICS, 2004). The plans envisage spectacular stadia in the north of the city and elsewhere with the aim of stimulating further regeneration of the adjoining areas, aided by significant upgrades in existing transport systems including new underground and surface railway lines and a new international airport terminal (see chapter 17). The argument is that 'the commercial, residential and infrastructure developments that will accompany the Games will effectively act as a catalyst to change the entire physical structure and planning of the city' (Van de Berg, cited in RICS, 2004).

The organizers of London 2012 seek to combine the environmental achievements of the 2000 Games in Sydney with the holistic approach to physical regeneration associated with Barcelona 1992 (see Weaver, 2005). When launching London's bid in January 2004, the British Prime Minister readily appropriated the urban change mantra, stressing that 'as well as being a wonderful sporting and cultural festival, the Games would drive the environmentally friendly regeneration and rejuvenation of East London' (Blair, 2004, p. 1). The bid organizers (LOCOC, 2004) claimed that: 'the key catalyst would be the development of the 500 acre Olympic Park … containing the main sporting facilities, would be set in 1,500 landscaped acres – one of the biggest new city centre parks in Europe for 200 years'. Moreover:

London 2012 … would form part of the most extensive transformation of the city for generations … and its legacy would transform one of the most underdeveloped areas of the country… All development would form part of an enormous and tangible legacy, ranging from sport and venues through to infrastructure and environment. London 2012 would change the face of the capital forever. (*Ibid.*)

The London team also pledged to make 2012 'the greenest Games in history' (Townsend and Campbell, 2005). The city's Mayor, Ken Livingstone, reiterated that commitment in September 2005 after London was officially awarded the Games when launching a set of design rules for developers and contractors to follow. Issued in the hope of avoiding 'white elephant facilities', the guidelines represented clear recognition that sustainable regeneration will not accrue automatically and requires proper planning.

Conclusion

This chapter has shown that urban regeneration, as either a limited exercise in physical renewal or as part of dramatic transformations of the host city, has for many years been a key element of the Olympics and central to the decision of municipal authorities and national governments keen to bid for the right to host future Games. The Summer Games in particular continue to offer an unrivalled opportunity for a host city to propose, plan and deliver major regeneration work over a 5–7 year period. Whereas, in previous decades, urban impact meant little more than that which emanated from physical development, latterly the emphasis on regenerative impacts has shifted away from constructional or renovative activities towards more holistic notions of regeneration. Approaches that embody these notions focus on the economic, social, cultural and environmental benefits of hosting the Olympics and the legacy that this brings to cities and surrounding regions. Such is the attention now given to these considerations by the IOC that bidding cities routinely treat the regeneration legacy as an important, perhaps the most important criterion by which they develop their proposals. Whether the actual impacts ever meet those promised, of course, remains open to conjecture.

City Portraits

Part III

Chapter 10

Berlin 1936

Monika Meyer-Künzel

The sports venues of the 1936 Olympic Games left Berlin a significant but difficult legacy. The grounds of the former Reichssportfeld, especially the Olympic Stadium, are important reminders of the history of the city of Berlin and the German state. They show us that sport cannot be non-political. In a staged spectacle the image of a tolerant and open regime was played to the world, but behind the illusion Jews and political dissidents were persecuted systematically and preparations were made for the Second World War, with its devastating effects on Europe and beyond.

This chapter analyses the construction history of the Berlin Olympic Stadium and its surroundings up to the present. Observations on aspects of National Socialism (Nazism), with which the 1936 Games are always associated, are touched upon and presented only to the extent that they are significant to the topic. Nevertheless, the focus would be too narrow if the history of the Olympic facilities concentrated only on the period around 1936. The history of the sports facilities began at the start of the twentieth century during the formation of the German Olympic movement. The various phases of stadia and sports field development were closely tied to Germany's efforts to host the Olympic Games, with the movement first becoming successful during Germany's Weimar Republic. Since 1946 the stadium and other former Olympic facilities have repeatedly been the setting for great national and international events. Especially noteworthy are the games of the 1974 FIFA World Cup that presented the opportunity for the first fundamental renovations. Berlin's renewed bid for the 2000 Olympic Games was controversial both in the city and nationwide, and provoked a lengthy discussion about the future of the stadium: should it be torn down on the basis of cost or kept as a historical building complex? The final decision favoured the Olympic Stadium, which was adapted for contemporary sport in preparation for the 2006 FIFA World Cup.

Becoming an Olympic City

Since the founding of the IOC in 1894, German sports officials had argued seriously about whether holding an international sports competition would comply with the

Olympic tradition of ancient Greece and whether German participation would be sensible. This discussion remained active in Germany into the Nazi period. Between 1896 and 1904, independent committees were formed for Germany's participation in the Olympic Games, and each time they had to discuss this issue with the public, sports associations and government authorities. In 1904 the first successful German National Committee for the Olympic Games was formed out of the committee for the Games in St Louis: the Deutscher Reichsausschuss für die Olympische Spiele (DRAfOS). The goals of the DRAfOS were to organize national games, to have German teams participate in international games, and to bring German sports clubs together in a unified association for physical fitness.

Efforts to bring the Games to Berlin in 1908 and 1912 failed because there was no suitable stadium available. After financing had been secured in 1911 and the start of stadium construction had been set for September 1912, the IOC at their meeting in Stockholm in July of 1912 decided to grant Berlin the Games for 1916. In 1913 Carl Diem[1] became the general secretary of the Organizing Committee for the Berlin Games. The Deutsches Stadion (German Stadium) was inaugurated that same year.

Due to the outbreak of the First World War in 1914, the 1916 Olympic Games were cancelled without an official declaration by Germany or the IOC.[2] In the period following the First World War, sports officials, notably from France, pressed for the exclusion of German athletes from the international arena. This prevented German participation in the 1920 Games in Antwerp and the 1924 Games in Chamonix and Paris, with the IOC no longer including German members in its lists.[3] However, Pierre de Coubertin and Carl Diem made efforts to find ways to lead Germany back into the Olympic movement. In 1924, German members were again appointed to the IOC and Germany received an invitation to the 1928 Games in Amsterdam.

The thought of a renewed candidacy of Berlin seemed logical and so, at their meeting on 29 January 1927, the DOA (the German Olympic Committee – Deutscher Olympischer Ausschuss)[4] decided that Berlin should bid for the 1936 Games. The official bid was announced at the 29th IOC meeting held in Berlin in May 1930. A year later Berlin was chosen at the 1931 session in Barcelona. On 24 January 1933, the Organizing Committee held their founding meeting. Theodor Lewald,[5] who was voted President, presented the committee's goals: conversion of the Deutsches Stadion, the composition of an Olympic anthem, the organization of an art exhibit and the presentation of an Olympic festival. Six days later on 30 January 1933, Adolf Hitler was appointed Reichskanzler and the National Socialist dictatorship began in Germany.

Sport during the Third Reich

The position of the Nationalsozialistische Deutsche Arbeiterpartei (NSDAP) was strengthened again in March by the elections for parliament (the Reichstag). The streamlining of sport by the regime began when the Interior Minister appointed SA-Gruppenführer Hans von Tschammer und Osten as Reichssportkommisar and Reichssportführer. The National Socialists quickly liquidated the Deutscher Reichsausschuss für Leibesübung (DRAfL). The guidelines passed on 24 May 1933 for creating the Deutscher Reichsbund für Leibesübungen established a sports organization according to the Führerprinzip. The Reichssportführer was also the head of the DOA and a member of the leadership of the Organizing Committee of the Olympic Games.

For a long time the Nazis had mounted anti-Olympic campaigns. During the period of the Weimar Republic, these efforts were generally unsuccessful but, after Hitler became Reichskanzler, many in the NSDAP saw a chance to prevent the Olympic Games from being an international event and to hold a Germanic or German combat games instead. The Kampfring gegen die Olympischen Spiele, an organization of National Socialist student groups, demanded on 6 February 1933 that 'the 1936 Olympic Games must not be held in Germany' (Schmidt, 1992, p. 219). Just six days after winning the Reichstag election, however, Hitler received Lewald, with Joseph Goebbels[6] also present, and declared that he would support the Games (*Ibid.*, p. 220). Hitler and Goebbels had recognized very early on the opportunities for Nazi propaganda in hosting the Olympic Games in Germany with its international presentation and the appropriation of the Olympic ideal. On 15 January 1934, Goebbels founded a propaganda committee within the Organizing Committee and thereby created an instrument to manipulate the Games to his liking (see Hoffmann, 1993, pp. 13ff).

After Hitler's appointment as Reichskanzler, the world, and especially the United States, raised concerns that the Games could be misused by the new German rulers. On 3 May 1933, IOC President Count Henri de Baillet-Latour wrote to the German IOC members, saying that 'they must bring proof to the upcoming session in Vienna that the government of the Reich does not oppose the Olympic rules' (quoted in Schmidt, 1992, p. 222). The misgivings continued and there were repeated attempts during the preparation period of the Games to create an international boycott (Hoffmann, 1993, p. 12). These efforts increased further as the Nazi system was consolidated and the persecution of Jews became more and more obvious from actions such as the 'Nuremberg Laws' of 1935. In June 1936, after many failed attempts to come to an international decision, the congress of the 'International Committee for the Defence of Olympic ideals' in Paris called for a boycott of the Games. The same congress proclaimed an 'Olympiad of the People' in Barcelona for 19–26 July 1936. Due to Franco's coup which started on 17 July 1936, however, these games could not begin and the boycott did not occur.

Olympic Facilities

The location of the Olympic Stadium and the sports facilities is in the western part of Berlin in a hilly and wooded area. This area had been used for military purposes since the early nineteenth century and was accessed from an army road leading west. At the beginning of the twentieth century, the Kaiser indicated his intention to turn this site over to the public for recreation and leisure. In 1906 the Prussian Federation of Horse-Breeding and Horseracing Sports was able to lease a plot of land for a racecourse and for general sporting purposes. Between 1907 and 1909, the Rennbahn Grunewald was built there according to the plans of Otto March[7] and Albert Brodersen while taking the utmost care to preserve the existing Grunewald pines on site. The area was peripheral, but always had well-developed access to transport. Two roads, two commuter train lines (S-Bahn), built at the beginning of the twentieth century, and an underground train (U-Bahn) line connected the sports grounds with the centre of Berlin.

After the unsuccessful bid in Rome to host the 1908 Olympic Games, DRAfOS and committed athletes attempted to secure financing for an Olympic stadium from 1906 to 1911. In February 1906 the first stadium proposal by Otto March was published in the press and commentaries were printed even then with regard to future Olympic Games. As the discussions on the financing were drawn out, the stadium was not opened until 1913 after nine months of construction:

> The stadium [was] in a dug-out hollow in the interior space of the horse racecourse in Grunewald. In order to not block the view of the back straight, only low stands [could] be built [for 50,000 spectators]. In the otherwise large interior space there [was] a 600m-long track and a 666 2/3 m-long bicycle course... The spectator seating across from the stand side [was] left out as space for a 100m-long swimming pool. Under the swimming pool stands there [were] rooms for a stadium laboratory. (Borges *et al.*, 1995, p. 122)

At the prompting of Carl Diem, further expansion took place after the founding of the Deutsche Hochschule für Leibesübungen in 1919. As a result, the Deutsches Stadion was expanded according to the plans of architect Johannes Seiffert. The Hochschule opened on 15 May 1920, and Diem commissioned Seiffert in 1924 to propose sites for its enlargement. Seiffert chose a 20 hectare area north of the racecourse, where the Deutsches Sportforum was built in three phases between 1926 and 1936. It was designed by Seiffert as well as by Werner and Walter March, with the Nazis beginning to influence matters in 1933. Up to then, Werner March had designed open, interconnected spaces and had pursued a modest, but prominent effect. Instead, the map of the area in 1936 revealed a monumental site – 300 metres long and 220 metres wide – with an interior field of honour referring to an oversized hall of pillars. The college became an academy, the Reichsakademie für Leibesübung.

Meanwhile, plans for changes to the stadium were under way. In 1925 the DRAfL began considering modernization of the stadium and commissioned Werner March[8] to create a draft proposal in 1927. This proposed expanding the stadium and adapting it to meet the latest hygienic standards. The design proposed by March was presented to the IOC at the 1930 Berlin session. It called for deepening the stadium and expanding the stands to hold 70,000 spectators. The swimming pool would also be relocated to the narrow eastern end of the stadium where it would be accessed from a prominent plaza. March displayed a model for the conversion of the stadium at the Deutsche Bauausstellung in 1931. A few months later, he presented his proposals for developing it to the DOA. When the approval was given for hosting the 1936 Olympic Games, March was commissioned to plan the stadium.

On the day the Olympic Organizing Committee was founded, one week before Hitler was appointed Reichskanzler, the committee decided to avoid costly new construction and to expand the existing stadium instead. The scheme, however, did not meet the approval of the National Socialists. Their influences on the Olympic planning designs led to a complete change of the plans and therefore to a new stadium. In the spring of 1934 the Deutsches Stadion was torn down to make way for the construction of the Olympic Stadium.

From the earliest conceptions, the Deutsches Stadion was intended to be the central sports venue of the Olympic Games. Until October 1933, attention centred on to the modernization of the stadium, when Hitler decided that the core of the events would be the Reichssportfeld,[9] with an Olympic stadium built on the site of the Deutsches Stadion itself.[10] A tour of the construction site on 5 October 1933 by Hitler accompanied by Frick, the Interior Minister, and Lewald marked the beginning of a phase in which Werner March's construction and urban planning design were broadly overhauled in line with the Nazis' demands for symbolic presence. Hitler ordered the abandonment and demolition of the racecourse and the generous expansion of the sports sites. He wanted the 'largest stadium, the largest assembly field, the largest open-air theatre' (Schmidt, 1992, p. 30). He also intended to relocate the traditional May festival from the field in Tempelhof to the Reichssportfeld.

In the newspaper *Vossische Zeitung* on 6 October 1933, Hitler explained that 'German sport needs something gigantic' (Schäche, 1991, n.p.; also Schäche, 2001). After DRAfL was disbanded and the racecourse was acquired, the German Reich was the sole owner of the land and developer of the sports facilities. By 9 October 1933, March[11] had revised his designs, but they did not yet contain the large assembly field that Hitler wanted. Therefore, the meeting on 10 October 1933 at Hitler's offices with Frick and Goebbels as well as Lewald and Diem did not lead to the desired approval but instead to further planning decisions by Hitler on the construction and layout of the stadium. He demanded an assembly field for 500,000 people (Maifeld) and an open-air theatre for 200,000 spectators (called the Dietrich-Eckart-Bühne).

By December 1933, March had created three variants that differed particularly in their layout and size of the assembly grounds. All designs assumed that the racecourse would be abandoned, but the existing buildings and the surrounding park-like facilities would remain intact. Furthermore, March maintained the development of the Sportforum, the Graditzer Allee, the Schwarzbergallee (as the main entrance to the grounds), and the S-Bahn train line as the southern boundary of the grounds in all his alternative designs. Invariably, the assembly field was west of the stadium and the open-air theatre was in the Murellen ravine (Murellenschlucht).

At another meeting with Hitler on 14 December 1933, Werner March presented a solution using modified plans and a scale model. They showed the double-axis plan that was finally implemented: an east-west axis which emerged from the Schwarzbergallee containing the sequence of Olympic Plaza (Olympischer Platz), the stadium, the Maifeld and the Führer Tower (Führerturm); and a north-south axis that integrated the street Rennbahnstrasse and led to the central stadium (see figure 10.1). This proposal had an assembly field of 107,000 square metres and was estimated to hold 150,000 people.[12] Werner March received the approval to start construction according to this solution. The estimated costs had since increased from 2.6 million Reichsmark to more than 36 million.[13]

The Reichssportfeld was opened on 23 and 24 May 1936 with the central complex of the Olympic Stadium, Maifeld (figure 10.2) and swimming stadium (figure 10.3), as well as the riding arena, the hockey stadium, the Sportforum with a number of sports and training areas, the open-air theatre, a tennis stadium with various tennis courts, a dance space, a firing range, residence halls, parking lots and areas for small businesses. With the Reichssportfeld, March had designed the first Olympic park complex (Wimmer, 1976, p. 192).[14] He included the spatial design and the landscaping considerations of earlier developments, the existing usable facilities, optimal transport access for the entire facility and for individual sports

Figure 10.1. Reichssportfeld, map of the area, 1937.

venues, and the 'construction plan elevated to a gigantic level by the developer' (Eckert and Schäche, 1992, n.p.). Moreover:

> March's overall design presents a clear arrangement of space and a dominant east-west axis that the broad spaces and expansiveness of the facilities are arranged along. The grounds are differentiated by the staggered height contours of the accompanying sports facilities that are adapted to the available situation on site. The integration of the Reichssportfeld into the landscape is accomplished on one hand with the natural effects of plants on the scarce areas available between the sports sites and on the other hand with the expansion of the green belt leading around the grounds to achieve the desired bridging effect into the adjacent wooded areas. (*Ibid.*)

Instructed to abandon the planned renovation of the German Stadium in favour of building a new Olympic stadium, Werner March looked for inspiration to the historical models of Antiquity, such as the Coliseum in Rome, and to contemporary stadium structures, such as the Olympic stadium in Amsterdam. In addition, the basis for his design was also formed by considerations of the spectators' view and of organizing how to empty the stadium.[15] March proposed an oval stadium, the

Figure 10.2. Maifeld, 1936.

Figure 10.3. Swimming pool, 2005.

longitudinal axis of which would run along an east-west line. As in the Deutsches Stadion, the interior space would be a sunken area. This made it possible to place the middle level of the stadium at the level of the surrounding terrain, which significantly improved the development. The tiers of seating towards the west were non-continuous so that the marathon gate opened to a view of the bell tower on the Maifeld and created a monumental entry into the stadium.

Though the stadium's shape was never presented for debate, there were serious arguments about the exterior between Hitler and Speer[16] on one side and Werner March on the other. After Hitler toured the stadium grounds and viewed a test section of the façade on 31 October 1934, he expressed his irritation about the thin abutments and the missing stone coverings. The contrasts between March's contemporary architectural conception and Speer's powerful and forceful views could no longer be bridged, and so in February 1935 March was relieved of his decision-making responsibilities for the styling of the stadium.[17] Despite this interference in his designs, Werner March received the gold medal for the Reichssportfeld and the silver medal for the stadium in architectural competitions in 1936; the 'Grand Prix' of the Paris World Exhibition in 1937; and honours and medals abroad.

The Maifeld was west of the Olympic Stadium and was laid out as an assembly field, 395 by 295 metres, for 180,000 people. A set of stairs separated the lower-lying field from the level of the stadium. Four towers and four large sculptures emphasized the spatial differentiation. Banks of earth formed the boundaries on the north and south sides of the field. On the west side, the monumental east-west axis of the Reichssportfeld reached its end point at the stands with the Führer and speaker stand and the bell tower. In the middle of the stands, the bell tower rose over the three-storey structure that contains the access to the field and the tower as well as the Langemarckhalle on the middle storey. Construction of this 50 by 10 metres hall of honour for athletes who died in the First World War is attributed to Carl Diem who himself participated in the battle at Langemarck as a soldier and brought soil from the German soldiers' cemetery back to Berlin.

The open-air Dietrich-Eckart-Bühne theatre,[18] which Goebbels demanded, represented for him an 'important instrument for fulfilling cultural duties of the people and mental and political promotion to the nation' (Schmidt, 1992, p. 60). He wanted 'to fill the German people … with a national will in the sense of National Socialism' (Ibid.). As in many other locations in Germany, a large theatre was to be created here for Germanic festivals of song and dedication and other political events. Goebbels wanted the theatre to hold 500,000 to 1,000,000 people. However, March never proposed a structure that even approached that number of spectators. His first draft proposed an arena for 35,000; in the end, it was built for 20,000 people. In the 30 metre deep natural basin of the Murellenschlucht, Werner March created an open-air theatre in the image of the Theatre of Epidauros from Antiquity.

In the final designs for the Reichssportfeld, the swimming stadium was along the cross axis on the north side of the stadium. Two grandstands, facing one another with a total capacity of 17,000, were fitted with two watchtower-like staircases and framed the pool for swimming and diving. In contrast to the Olympic stadium, the design for the swimming stadium remained largely free from interference by Hitler and Speer.[19] Noticeably, there was no Führer or speaker podium in this stadium. Elsewhere, Werner also integrated a hockey stadium for 18,000 spectators into the sports sites of the Sportforum.

Among the other sports venues in Berlin, the Deutschlandhalle (Germany Hall) on the Berlin trade fair grounds (Messegelände) near the Eichkamp S-Bahn station are worth mentioning. The Deutschlandhalle was built for 20,000 spectators and was the first hall ever built for Olympic Games. For the rowing competitions, the existing facility on the lake Langer See in Berlin-Grünau was expanded and a stage was added. At the Avus automobile racecourse, architect Clemens Schürmann from Münster built a velodrome.

The Olympic Village

During the first discussions of the spatial organization of the Olympics, Werner March had intended that the military grounds in Döberitz, about 15 kilometres west of the Olympic Stadium, should become the site of the Olympic Village. This giant area was located between Spandau and Wustermark, Falkensee and Potsdam. There were large barracks on the avenue Hamburger Chaussee and a manoeuvring field further south. On 28 March 1933, the Organizing Committee asked Reichsminister General Field Marshal von Blomberg to make the Döberitz Barracks available for use as the Olympic Village. There were 280 rooms available in the officers' barracks. However, the head of the Wehrmacht Office, General von Reichenau, who was himself interested in sport and the Olympic Games, made the further suggestion to use part of the training area north of the Hamburger Chaussee to build a separate Olympic Village. This suggestion was accepted at the site tour that took place on 7 November 1933.

On 26 April 1934, the Organizing Committee gave the Reichswehr the public memorandum entitled 'Olympic Village' with the request to begin the necessary measures. From that point, the Reichswehr acted as the developer of the Olympic Village. It commissioned Werner March to propose a draft scheme for building the facility. He then founded a consortium of architects including Dr Georg Steinmetz, who was responsible for the residential buildings, Walter March, in charge of the common facilities, and Heinrich Wiepking-Jürgensmann, responsible for landscaping. The implemented design had an organic urban quality (figure 10.4). There was an entry plaza along the Hamburger Chaussee that enabled traffic to flow freely underneath the freeway. The reception halls that formed almost a quarter-circle bordered the area on the northwest. The Village extended from this entry area along streets that followed the edges of a valley floor. The individual residential buildings followed the natural contour lines and enclosed green 'village

Figure 10.4. Olympic Village, Döberitz, general layout 1936.

commons'. At the end of the valley, the businesses and dining halls were housed in the Haus der Nationen (House of Nations). The grounds were marked by the existing trees, as well as a hilly topography, brooks and a small lake. Additionally, the Village had a swim hall and a sports hall, as well as a Finnish sauna at the lake. The scattered settlement of one-storey bungalows in an almost idyllic and attractively set landscape met with general approval and appreciation.[20] In February 1936 the Village had to be expanded to the neighbouring Flak barracks in order to house the surprisingly high number of registered athletes. On 10 April 1936, the Olympic Village was handed over.

Ceremonial Aspects

The Berlin Olympic Games were characterized by an unprecedented level of ritualization. This change originated not only with the Nazi rulers but also with the German sports officials who were in contact and agreement with the IOC during their preparations. In this spirit Carl Diem had the idea in 1931 of a torch relay from ancient Olympia to each location of the Games – a ritual that has been a permanent part of the Opening Ceremony of the Olympics since Berlin 1936. In 1932 there was a competition for an Olympic anthem. On 31 July 1933, Pierre de Coubertin met Carl Diem and determined that Beethoven's chorus on Schiller's ode 'An die Freude' would be an element of the opening ceremony. The performance of the 'Olympic Youth' festival written by Carl Diem and the torch relay were planned (see also chapter 4). On 20 October 1934, Richard Strauss finished composing his Olympic anthem with lyrics by Robert Lubahn. This was presented to Hitler on 29 March 1935.

The opening day of the Games was designed as a day-long stage production about Adolf Hitler, Nazi Germany and the Olympic Games. The day began with a reveille concert for the IOC in front of the Hotel Adlon, on the avenue Unter den Linden. After a celebration by the National Socialist Youth in the Lustgarten park the arrival of the Olympic flame was celebrated by 28,000 members of the Hitler Youth, participants of the international youth camp and a group of student athletes. At the same time, there were school sports events at 70 playgrounds and sports facilities throughout Berlin. Hitler held a reception for the IOC in the Reichskanzler-Palais and rode from there with members of the IOC, the Organizing Committee and representatives of the government and the NSDAP party to the Reichssportfeld. In an unprecedented ceremony, this group entered the Olympic Stadium through the marathon staircase, proceeded together and took their places in the honorary box to the sounds of Richard Wagner's 'Huldigungsmarsch'. As noted in the *Deutsche Olympiade Kalender*: 'In this way Hitler held the attention of the spectators for several minutes. He also benefited from the form of entry into the stadium for officials and honoured guests that was already used at previous Games' (quoted in Borges *et al.*, 1995, p. 273).

Subsequent Usage

The fate of the Olympic complex at Berlin makes a fascinating story in light of current interest in legacy, with its fate inextricably interwoven with the advent and aftermath of war, the partition of the city and its eventual reunification. In the plans for 'Berlin, the City of Colleges', the Reichssportfeld represented the central assembly and sports grounds. The urban area on both sides of the Heerstrasse was to have a complete re-configuration with large ring roads and spokes, but these plans were never implemented (see also Matzerath, 1984, pp. 308–311). In 1938, parts of the tunnel system were converted to bunkers and a manufacturing facility for anti-aircraft weapon fuses. In the period before and during the war, various large athletic and political events were held on the grounds and in the Olympic Stadium. The International Olympic Institute under the direction of Carl Diem moved into the buildings of the Deutsches Sportforum. Most of its activities ended after it was severely damaged by bombing in 1943.

On 26 June 1945, Diem composed a public memorandum in Berlin for the continued use of the Reichssportfeld. He described it as a 'People's park, symbolic German sports site, central German place of learning, practice grounds for greater Berlin and a central seat of administration of sport'. Essentially, it should continue to be used as it had been previously, but the administrative area was reduced and the settlement of the Friedrich-Wilhelm-Universität was suggested (Schmidt, 1992, p. 331). In June 1945, the stadium was again being used for practical purposes, with the swimming stadium in operation and available for the general population. This short phase of opening the grounds ended in July 1945 when the British Army requisitioned the Reichssportfeld. Henceforth, the facility was made accessible to the public only partially and in phases, transferring the Olympic Stadium, the swimming stadium with the Frauenplatz, the riding grounds and the hockey area to the Magistrat (city council) of Greater Berlin on 22 June 1949. From 1963 onwards, the stadia came under the administration of the Land (region) of Berlin.

The main facilities of the Reichssportfeld have been registered landmarks since 1966, but there have been numerous changes to meet changing needs. The Olympic Stadium has undergone a series of renovations and conversions since 1949; the most extensive being its partial covering by architect Friedrich Wilhelm Krahe, for the 1974 FIFA World Cup. The swimming stadium also underwent a series of modernizations and structural changes. The most comprehensive were the measures for the 1978 World Swimming Championships when more pools were built in the surrounding green spaces. The theatre, known today as the Waldbühne, saw the installation of an open-air movie theatre in 1951, with the war-destroyed stage area rebuilt in 1961. In 1982 a tent roof structure designed by Wolfgang Noack was built over the stage, making it a venue for large concerts. Public access to the Maifeld, as well as the eastern entry zone of the stadium, was only granted for specific events. Initially after 1945 the shrine to the fallen soldiers and the bell tower lay in ruins, with the remains of the bell tower blown up for safety reasons in 1947. Both were rebuilt between 1960 and 1962, again under the direction of Werner March, although a lively debate broke out about the use of the Langemarckhalle. From 1988 to 1990, a sports centre (Horst-Korber-Sportzentrum) was built along the Glockenturmstrasse according to plans devised by the architectural firm of Langhof, Hänni and Meerstein. It contains a regional performance centre for various types of sport such as handball, hockey and volleyball.

The British Forces installed their Berlin headquarters in all other areas, covering the entire Sportforum and the tennis stadium. These areas were inaccessible to the public and were not under the authority of any German planning body. In 1956, the Haus des Deutschen Sports, the Friesenhaus and the gymnastics hall were rebuilt. The rebuilding preserved the outward appearance, but adapted the buildings' interiors to meet the needs of the British administration. Various buildings of the British Army, unconnected with sports, were also erected on the grounds.

Berlin's Bid for the 2000 Olympic Games

In 1990, German reunification, the unification of the two halves of Berlin, and the treaty among the Allies, the German Democratic Republic and the Federal Republic of Germany opened the opportunity for the first time for a comprehensive use of the former Reichssportfeld. In reunified Berlin, support quickly grew among the public for the idea of celebrating the beginning of a new epoch in world history by hosting the 2000 Olympic Games. They also recognized the opportunity of renovating the stadium with the financial means that likely would be made available for hosting the Games.

For the Olympic bid, the FPB (Freie Planungsgruppe) – was commissioned to draft a spatial design. By October 1990, the Berlin Senate had defined the basic principles of the plan. These included the idea that the Reichssportfeld and the Olympic Stadium would be the location for the Opening and Closing Ceremonies and the competitions in track and field, football, baseball, hockey, modern pentathlon and water polo. The Olympic Village would be built in a neighbouring wooded area in Ruhleben. The unique feature of these plans was their inclusion of other existing sports facilities in the western and eastern parts of the city. In its bid, the FPB linked its proposed expansion of the northern line of the S-Bahn ring into an Olympic Express with its scheme for modernizing the sports venues near the northern line for the Olympic Games. This scheme would have been the first time in the history of the Olympics that a decentralized layout for the Games would be tied effectively to the building of a public transport system usable after the Games. These plans, however, were shelved in 1993 when the IOC awarded the 2000 Olympic Games to Sydney.

From 1993 onwards, the situation for the Land of Berlin, which held the rights of use of the Reichssportfeld, and for the German state, the landowner, was completely changed. By losing the bid for the Games, they also lost the opportunity to finance at least part of the significant renovation tasks with a profitable event. After the British forces left Berlin according to the Treaty of 1994, Berlin had the additional burden of having the Haus des Deutschen Sports and the Sportforum again available for other uses.

The essential aspect of all thinking about using the Reichssportfeld and the stadia was the restoration and conversion costs as well as the historical significance of the facilities. The costs of renovating the Reichssportfeld were estimated at about €5,000 million, but the financial situation of the City of Berlin and the German state was extremely strained. From that perspective, restoration without financing from revenues was hardly imaginable. Possible plans for public facilities included a recreational area, a historical park or a sports facility, but none of these could be financed. Officials and politicians then considered how commercial uses might improve returns. Basic uses under consideration, such as an amusement park, hotel, shopping centre, residential area or office space, would increase the frequency of visitors, but additional music events were complicated due to the noise problems. As almost all the buildings and a large part of the open spaces were registered landmarks, it would be more difficult to promote the grounds to private investors.

The Olympic Stadium posed particular problems. International sports associations complained about its shabby and insufficient facilities and its structural condition meant that its long-term use could no longer be guaranteed. The award to the German national football association in 1998 of a different mega-event, the 2006 FIFA World Cup, provided an opportunity for a full review given that the Olympic Stadium in Berlin would be its most important venue. On the basis of various appraisals and an architectural competition, Berlin and the German

Figure 10.5. Olympic Stadium, view from Olympischer Platz, 2005.

Federal government decided to renovate the Olympic Stadium according to the plans of the Hamburg-based practice gmp (Architekten von Gerkan, Marg und Partner). Construction work was completed in 2004 at a cost of €242 million, of which Berlin funded €46 million (figure 10.5).

With regard to other major installations, the Deutsches Sportforum was again placed under the administration of the Federal government in September 1994, and was open on a limited basis for sports clubs. Today, the fields and facilities of the Sportforum are used for professional and amateur sports alike, and the diverse activities of a wide variety of clubs define the grounds. For its part, the Olympic Village was shaped by its long association with military purposes. As originally intended, the Wehrmacht used the Olympic Village after the Olympic Games. The Soviet Red Army possessed the facilities from 1945 to 1991 and used them to house Soviet soldiers and their families. Very few of the athletes' residences remained. Instead, a large number of concrete tower blocks of up to five storeys were built, although integration into the landscape remained largely intact. The community building, the Hindenburghaus, the sports and swim halls and the original buildings intended for athletes from Switzerland, Turkey and the USA were all still maintained and used. When the Russian troops left in 1991, the Village was empty and succumbed to disrepair, looting and vandalism. The swimming hall was destroyed by arson in 1993.

Since 1994, the regional development society of the Land Brandenburg has attempted to develop the entire 120-hectare barracks area into a residential neighbourhood, albeit with little success. There was discussion of using the Haus der Nationen as a hotel or office space, but no definite use is in sight for the Hindenburghaus, which was the cultural centre of the Olympic Village. The lake also has mostly been filled in, although plans exist for its re-creation if circumstances allow.

Conclusion

The facilities in Berlin remain some of the most impressive structures of the Olympic Games of the modern era, although the area had only a limited effect on the development of the City of Berlin.[21] The choice of location for the Games was determined by personal relationships and financial problems, not urban design or overall considerations of city interests. The chosen site, however, was satisfactory in many ways for implementing a sufficient area, quality of development and uniquely designed sports venue for the political symbolic intentions at the time. The Reichssportfeld was designed as a venue for mass events in such a way that different events could be held separately and simultaneously at different points on the grounds.

The implemented designs of Werner March possessed significant urban and landscaping qualities. It is an urban planning accomplishment still recognized today that he integrated a facility capable of holding almost 400,000 people at one time into the pastoral landscape of Grunewald between the Havel and Spree rivers while overcoming issues concerning travel by large numbers of people to and from the site. The extension of the plans into monumental proportions has its basis in Hitler's intention to create the prototype of a National Socialist assembly venue. Such abuse of the Games, the athletes, the spectators and the Olympic ideal for the propagandistic goals of the Nazi government was indissolubly linked to this kind of forceful architecture.

The Olympic Village is also unique in the history of the Olympic Games, as it was built by the military and was intended for military purposes after the Games. The layout and use of the Village are contradictory. The almost idyllic setting is still recognizable today, with the Haus der Nationen strongly resembling the organic architecture of Alvar Aalto. This is in direct contrast to the monumental architecture of the Olympic grounds and the intentional use of the Village after the Games as barracks. It is distressing in retrospect to see the similarities when comparing the Village entrance and the Olympians' housing with the barracks at Dachau, Auschwitz and Majdane. Just as unsettling is the knowledge that the peaceful co-existence of nations took place in barracks.

The thought of again holding the Olympic Games for 2000 at the former Reichssportfeld seemed logical but still provoked widespread protest. Issues of dealing with and re-using the architectural legacy of Nazism proved to be a significant problem for the public. There was also the concern that the necessary investment for both parts of Berlin to grow together again would instead be used for symbolic building projects. However, part of the bid's designs was completed. The northern line of the S-Bahn ring was made operational again which significantly improved the infrastructure and traffic connections for the northern part of Berlin. Individual sports facilities were modernized or rebuilt. And the planned Olympic Village on the inlet in Rummelsburg (Rummelsburger Bucht) was partially completed as a waterfront housing development with a mixture of residences and services.

Notes

1. Carl Diem (1882–1962) was organizer and patron of German athletics from 1903 onwards. He was the General Secretary for the 1916 Olympic Games; a co-founder of the German College of Physical Education (Deutsche Hochschule für Leibesübungen) in 1929; the General Secretary of the Organizing Committee for the 1936 Olympic Games from 1933 to 1937; the director of the Reichssportfeld in 1936; director of the International Olympic Institute in Berlin from 1938 to 1945; founder of the German College of Physical Education (Deutsche Hochschule für Leibesübungen) in Cologne in 1947; and secretary of the newly founded German National Olympic Committee from 1950 to 1952. Starting in 1906 Diem composed reports and wrote books about the Olympic Games. At the end of July 1912 Carl Diem's book *Die Olympischen Spiele 1912* was published as the first Olympic book in German (Diem, 1912). In 1942 his three-volume work *Olympische Flamme* was published (Diem, 1942).

2. A winter sports festival which had been planned for February 1916 in the Black Forest and Berlin was not held. As a substitute for these games, there were national Olympic Games in Amsterdam from 24 June to 3 September 1916, and an international sports festival was opened in Stockholm on 8 July 1916 for Scandinavian athletes.

3. During this time the idea of holding national Olympic Games was formed. Such games were held in Berlin in 1922, in Cologne in 1926, in Breslau in 1930, in Nuremberg in 1934, and in Breslau again in 1938. The Breslau games in 1938 were also the first German gymnastics and sports festival (Deutsches Turn- und Sportfest).

4. The German Olympic Committee (DOA) was constituted in February 1926 as a sub-committee of the national committee for physical fitness (DRAfL – Deutscher Reichsausschuss für Leibesübungen), which originated in the DRAfOS .

5. Theodor Lewald (1860–1947) was the Secretary of State in the Interior Ministry and was the acting National Commissioner (Reichskommissar) in 1903 for the 1904 World's Fair in St. Louis. Starting in 1919, he was the president of the DRAfL and by 1933 he was the president of the Organizing Committee for the 1936 Olympic Games. In 1924 Lewald was appointed to the IOC at the wish of Coubertin and, in 1925, he was appointed to the Executive Board of the IOC. In 1938 he resigned from the IOC. Lewald was publicly reviled by the Nazis as a 'half-Jew' and was forced in 1933 to give up the presidency of the DRAfL.

6. Director of the newly created Ministry for 'People's Enlightenment and Propaganda' (Reichsministerium für Volksaufklärung und Propaganda).

7. Otto March (1845–1913) lived and worked in Berlin. After his studies at the Berlin academy for construction (Berliner Bauakademie) he began a career as an independent architect in addition to his job in the public service sector. His proposals influenced his contemporaries and later architects such as Ernst May, Walter Hegemann and his son, Werner March.

8. Werner March (1894–1976), son of architect Otto March, became well-known due to his proposals for the Reichssportfeld in Berlin for the 1936 Olympic Games. After his studies in

architecture in Dresden and Berlin he worked as an independent architect starting in 1925. In 1936 March became director of the Technical Institute for the Construction of Practice Venues (Technisches Institut für Übungsstättenbau) at the National Academy for Physical Fitness (Reichsakademie für Leibesübungen). In Germany, he performed various tasks of urban planning and construction of large structures until he volunteered for military service in 1940. In 1946, March worked as a planner for urban history in Minden. In 1953, he became Ordinarius of the professorship for urban planning and housing at the Technische Universität Berlin. In the 1950s and 1960s he received international contracts for the construction of stadiums in places such as Egypt and Greece.

9.   March's plans for the Reichssportfeld and especially the influence of Hitler, Goebbels and Speer are described comprehensively in Schmidt (1992). Wolfgang Schäche (1991) holds a significantly different opinion regarding the disagreements between Hitler and Speer on one side and March on the other. 'To that extent, the almost bizarre thesis of interpreting the Olympic Stadium with its architectural contradictions as documentation of rivalling ideologies (contemporary architect versus regressive position of Hitler and Speer) is therefore to be approached with extreme scepticism' (*Ibid.*, n.p.).

10.   Other event sites for the Olympic Games were dispersed throughout the city, such as the Germany Hall (Deutschlandhalle) at the trade fair grounds (Messegelände), various stadia, and the Avus automobile racecourse. The sailing competitions were held in Kiel.

11.   As the architect, Werner March was responsible for the urban planning and the architecture of the grounds; Heinrich Wiepking-Jürgensmann was responsible for the landscape architecture.

12.   It is worth noting that despite the enormous pressure placed on him, March knew how to create the dimensions of the Reichssportfeld facilities so that they still maintained a human scale. This is partially due to his designing the Maifeld for only 150,000 people instead of the 500,000 requested, and the open-air theatre for only 35,000 instead of 200,000. The Dietrich-Eckart-Bühne in the end was actually built for only a 20,000 audience.

13.   On 15 December 1933, Hitler was quoted in the newspaper *Völkischer Beobachter* as saying: 'On this day I have given my final approval for the start and the completion of the structures on the stadium grounds. Germany will thereby have a sports venue unequalled by any other in the world'. Quoted in Hoffmann (1993, p. 17).

14.   Eckert and Schäche (1992, n.p.) on this topic wrote: 'The Reichssportfeld facility in this design presents a sports complex designed by function and purpose that already was developed in the 1920s. In this context, note the following path-breaking facilities: the Müngersdorf sports complex in Cologne by Fritz Encke (1920–1923), the Zentralsportpark in Frankfurt am Main by Max Bromme (1921–1925), the Volkspark with the 'Rote Erde' stadium in Dortmund by city planning commissioner (Stadtbaurat) Strobel (1925–1927) or the Sportpark Tempelhof by Ottokar Wagler in Berlin'.

15.   See also the text by Werner March as published in Schmidt (1992, pp. 42 ff and 64 ff).

16.   Architect Albert Speer (1905–1981) was one of Hitler's closest confidants which placed him in an exceptional position. The dictator appreciated Speer's unconditional loyalty and the ability with which he created large construction projects in short amounts of time. Hitler saw Speer as the artist and visionary that he himself would like to have been. Beginning in 1932 Speer received construction contracts from the Nazis and in 1934 became the most influential architect in the Third Reich. In 1938 he was appointed as the general building inspector (Generalbauinspekteur) for the capital city of the Reich, Berlin. Among his most important projects are the monumental structures and productions for the Reich party conventions in Nuremberg, the chancellery (Reichskanzlei), the German pavilion for the Paris World Exposition in 1937 and the plans for the conversion of Berlin into 'Germania', capital city of the world, with numerous monumental structures. In 1942 Hitler appointed him to be the Minister for Weapons and Ammunition (Reichsminister für Bewaffnung und Munition), and in 1943 he became the Minister for armament and war production (Reichsminister für Rüstung und Kriegsproduktion). Speer's organizing of the war economy was based on using forced labour and prisoners from concentration camps. In the

Nuremberg Trials in 1946 he was sentenced for war crimes and crimes against humanity. After his release he published his memoirs (Speer, 1969), in which he attempted to portray himself as a 'respectable Nazi' and 'misled citizen'. However, more recent publications reveal his role as one of the most brutal leaders of the regime.

17.   Schmidt (1992, p. 46) continued: 'The overall contemporary architectural design for the Olympic Stadium is no longer recognizable today. The stylistic adjustments made by architect Albert Speer during the realization planning continued to alter the outward appearance of the stadium. Almost all of March's intended construction elements and wall surfaces made of nidged concrete were covered with shell limestone. The natural stone material was intended to express the values of simplicity, durability, hardiness, being down-to-earth, greatness and power that were propagated by the National Socialists'.

18.   Naming the theatre after the founder of the anti-Semitic newspaper *Auf gut deutsch* and the first editor of the *Völkischer Beobachter* was an indication of its Nazi orientation. See also Schmidt (1992).

19.   Hitler admitted in 1935 that: 'He was certainly not satisfied with everything happening at the Reichssportfeld, but he did not have enough time that year to attend to such matters' (quoted in Schmidt, 1992, p. 62).

20.   From today's perspective, the history of the Village's origins and its intended use after the Olympic Games as a military facility are irreconcilable with the Olympic mentality of peace. The entrance buildings of the facilities and athletes' barracks are macabre, as they appear in a slightly adapted form in the Nazi concentration camps.

21.   A comparative evaluation of the urban planning effects of large events on the locations where they are held is explored by the author in her work *Der planbare Nutzen – Stadtentwicklung durch Weltausstellungen und Olympische Spiele* (see Meyer-Künzel, 2002). The urban planning for events is documented and evaluated in the context of each political, social and cultural situation. The work therefore compiles a cross section of the planning goals of large events, their realization and their long-term use after the Games and explains them with extensive pictures and planning materials.

Chapter 11

Mexico City 1968

Michael Barke

The torch for the 1968 Games was lit at Olympia in mid-August 1968. It then began a journey that moved from Greece and circulated to European sites with Olympic and Mexican connections. These included Genoa (Italy), the birthplace of Christopher Columbus, Palos (Spain), where Columbus' expedition started in 1492, and Barcelona, a major seat of the Spanish empire. From Europe, the relay conveyed the torch by sea to San Salvador, the site of Columbus's first landing in the Americas, then on to Vera Cruz where four additional torches were lit. The five torches, echoing the five Olympic rings, then made their way to Mexico City by different routes. On 11 October, they arrived at the pyramid of the Moon at Teotihuacán to the north of Mexico City, where a ceremony imitating the Aztec ritual of New Fire – celebrating the resurgence of life and the triumph of light over darkness – was enacted. On the evening of 12 October, Norma Enriqueta Basilio, a 20 year old 400 metre runner from Baja California, lit the Olympic flame; the first woman in Olympic history to be given the honour.

There were thus strong resonances of Mexico's history in the main public ceremony leading up to the Games, but the intention to engage fully with the present was symbolized in the choice of a young female to light the flame. She 'represented a new kind of Mexican, tall, thin and beautiful, contrasting the older generation that she called short and fat' (quoted in Witherspoon, 2003, p. 113). Although Mexico's rich cultural history was not ignored during the Nineteenth Olympiad, it was reinterpreted in ways that emphasized national unity rather than diversity. More than anything, from the Mexican perspective, the project was about modernity. Despite the efforts of the political elite from the late nineteenth century onwards (Tenorio-Trillo, 1996), the organizers of Mexico City 1968 were well aware that much of the rest of the world saw the country in Third World terms and their response was driven by the need to counter such stereotypes at almost every turn. Thus, issues of international prestige were never very far from the minds of the chief protagonists.

Indeed, Mexico City 1968 remains one of the most memorable Olympics of the twentieth century – perhaps more because of non-sporting events than some undeniably spectacular sporting achievements. Along with Berlin 1936 and

Moscow 1980, the Mexico City Games demonstrated overtly the political context of the modern Olympics. Whereas the politicisation of the Berlin Games could easily be dismissed as an aberration of Nazi Germany, Mexico City was more significant in that no single ideology could be held responsible for events and that the manifestations of that politicisation were apparent in many different ways. Some were obvious; others more subtle. Some were internal to the host country; many others were products of issues and pressures external to Mexico. After 1968, it became impossible to deny that sport and politics were inextricably linked.

The Mexico City Games were also highly significant in terms of the development of the relationship between the Olympics and television (Wenn, 1995). From this juncture, the way that the Games were 'packaged' and 'sold' would be as important as the actual Games events themselves. Equally, the selective framing of events was foreshadowed at the Opening Ceremony of the Mexico City Olympics where the cameras studiously avoided the massed ranks of heavily armed security forces surrounding the stadium.

Another notable feature of the 1968 Games was that they were the first held within Latin America or, more significantly, in a 'developing' or 'Third World' country. This, in itself, was a remarkable choice that requires explanation. How did Mexico manage to win the contest to stage the 1968 Olympics? Having done so, how did a relatively poor developing country set about staging the Games in infrastructural terms? This process, itself inevitably immensely complicated and expensive to accomplish, has acted as a deterrent to many cities and countries from even entering the competition to host the Games. In that light, how then did Mexico and its capital city accomplish this feat and at what cost? Part of the answer to the latter question raises further questions about how the Games were promoted, not least to the Mexican people and citizens of Mexico City. Questions of how the country and city presented itself to the outside world are also important here. Finally, with the benefit of hindsight and nearly four decades of reflection we can ask what the 1968 Olympics really meant in their wider context, that is, beyond the sports fields and arenas. This series of issues is still debated in the historiography of modern Mexico, but it is perhaps insufficiently recognized that the answers may be very different from an 'internal' perspective than from an 'external' one.

Winning the Games

Answers to these questions begin by noting that the Mexican elite had, from the late nineteenth century, sought to portray their country in modern terms and to engage with international cosmopolitanism (Tenorio-Trillo, 1996). Participation in World's Fairs, in the Olympic Games and, eventually, presenting a bid to host those Games represented a natural progression in nation building and representation. Adolfo López Mateos, President of Mexico from 1959 to 1964, took the decision to compete for the Olympic Games of 1968. He continued to be involved after retiring as President, serving on the Committee that organized the Games. Remarkably, López Mateos managed the feat of staying on good terms with the United States whilst refusing to break ties with Cuba's new revolutionary government. Significantly, he was also the first Mexican President to engage in substantial travel abroad (Riding, 1987) in a determined attempt to establish Mexico's international prestige. There is little doubt that he saw hosting the Olympic Games as a major step forward in establishing Mexico as a modern nation on the international stage (Krauze, 1997). Although a very different President and with considerably less charisma, his successor from 1964 to 1970, Gustavo Díaz Ordaz, eventually became no less determined that Mexico should host the Games and in a way that would enhance Mexico's international prestige. His inherent authoritarianism and inflexible perspective led him to interpret the student movement of 1968 as a communist-inspired plot to disrupt the Olympics, an interpretation that was almost certainly inaccurate (Zolov, 1999). Nevertheless, it is clear that, in competing to host the 1968 Olympics, national boosterism was placed on the agenda very early in the process.

There were three important components to this strategy. The first was to establish international legitimacy for what was still a single party state. The second was to generate a stronger sense of nationalism while, third, demonstrating the modernity of Mexico. We shall return to these issues later, but what must concern us first is the international scale and the factors operative at this level that led to what remains the only successful Olympic bid made by a Third World country.

Ostensibly, there were considerable objections to Mexico, with doubts being expressed about the country's ability to organize the Olympic Games (Arbena, 1996) and, especially, about the altitude issue. Mexico went to great lengths to counter both these objections, having sponsored numerous scientific studies on the effects of altitude, offering to defray the expenses of athletes whilst acclimatizing to conditions in Mexico City and hosting a 'mini-Olympics' in 1967 (Wrynn, 2004). Support on the altitude issue eventually came from a somewhat unexpected quarter in the form of Avery Brundage, president of the IOC who observed 'The Olympic Games belong to all the world, not the part of it at sea level' (quoted in Guttmann, 1984, p. 123).

One important factor was that the competition to hold the Games, although initially apparently formidable, eventually turned out to be not particularly strong. While the bid comes from the potential host city, Mexico City's bid could scarcely be described as emanating solely from the metropolis itself and was about much more. Three other cities competed to host the 1968 Olympics – Detroit, Buenos Aires and Lyons. Detroit had also attempted to host the Games in 1952, 1956, 1960, and 1964 and was to try again – unsuccessfully – in 1972. Despite its long involvement in the bidding process, Detroit's bid in 1968 was lacklustre and revealed weaknesses in the shape of lack of hotel space, failure to mobilize significant local enthusiasm, and shortcomings in financial arrangements (Zimmerman, 1963). Detroit's bid was not helped by the fact that Los Angeles, only six months before the final vote, had challenged Detroit's bid to represent the United States at the IOC decision-making meeting in Baden-Baden in October 1963 (*Anon*, 1963). The rival and mutually-damaging campaigns of Los Angeles and Detroit undoubtedly harmed Detroit's ultimate bid in the eyes of the IOC adjudicators, particularly through Los Angeles pointing out previous Detroit failures and publicly airing its continuing weaknesses (Witherspoon, 2003). The bid from Buenos Aires was widely recognized as weak, lacking in detail or any real sense of enthusiasm and, in the event, only received two votes. Lyons probably represented a greater threat with advantages of governmental support, France's record in hosting previous Olympics, the city's accessibility from Africa and the Middle East, and promises to enlarge the airport and expand an existing stadium from a capacity of 60,000 to 95,000 (Daley, 1963). The fact that Lyons was a much smaller place, however, probably counted against it. The Mexican strategy was skilful, determined and enthusiastic and struck many of the right notes with the voting panel, including dealing effectively with the altitude issue (Wrynn, 2004).

Whether by fortune or subtle appreciation of the international mood, the Mexican bid caught the imagination of the times and presented a distinctive and appealing image, albeit one with a specific national agenda. Thus, in their presentations , Senator Carillo presented the Mexican people as:

> simple, humble, hard-working and honest. They were a determined people who had transformed their nation after the Mexican Revolution, and the Olympics would symbolize the success of that transformation. (Cited in Witherspoon, 2003, p. 41)

and Dr. Eduardo Hay, concluded with:

> We seek the Games not for us, not for our business, but for our youth. That is why we are asking for this. Not to have another title. You can be sure that the Mexican public will be with you with the best of them.

Having said this, the Mexican delegation also exploited Cold War political allegiances to the full with intensive lobbying of Soviet and related members of the IOC and, of course, its natural allies in the Third World representatives. Through this means, Mexico won support from Latin American, African and Soviet-bloc representatives in order to defeat the main opponents from North America and Europe. An effective bid from a developing country that could demonstrate its capacity to put on the Games was therefore always going to appeal to a large number of the voters in this new international environment. López Mateos and the Mexican delegation understood this well. Avery Brundage, who had voted for Detroit, commented:

> What helped Mexico was that it is one of the smaller-scale countries, and some members felt they could do more for the Olympic movement by giving encouragement to such a country. (Cited in Witherspoon, 2003, p. 44)

Hence, its campaign was highly effective and skilfully managed, and in the final analysis Mexico City won the right to stage the 1968 Games because of geopolitical alignments and the prevalent international atmosphere of the 1960s. This atmosphere worked in favour of a country such as Mexico in a manner not previously seen and probably unlikely to be repeated.

Yet there was more to Mexico City's bid than politics. Unlike Detroit, Lyons and Buenos Aires, Mexico City could draw on the country's impressive record of accomplishment in hosting major international events, with the capacity to meet most of their accompanying demands. The country had staged the 1926 and 1954 Central American and Caribbean Games, the Pan American Games of 1955 when over 2,000 athletes from 22 countries attended, the Modern World Pentathlon Championships of 1962 and the National Children and Junior Sports Games of 1961 and 1962. Mexico City itself had numerous and impressive sports facilities and arenas, many of them built recently and publicly funded (Arbena, 1991; Brewster, 2005), a large number of hotels and other visitor facilities, and an apparently dynamic growth-oriented philosophy, albeit one that had yet to engage with contemporary ideas of city region planning (Campbell and Wilk, 1986).

The development of these facilities reflected the profound belief of many of the protagonists of the Mexican Revolution that a process of nation-building was necessary and that sport could be one of the main instruments through which this could be achieved. Although initially reluctant (McGehee, 1993), the Mexican government gradually came to understand the wider significance of sport and participation in international events, especially after the Central American Games of 1926 when 'Mexicans had held what they considered to be their own Olympics' (*Ibid.*, p. 326). Symbolic events, most notably associated with November 20, 'Revolution Day', celebrating Francisco Madero's call to arms in 1910 against the 34-year rule of Porfirio Díaz , were celebrated with parades at which athletes took a prominent place (over 50,000 in 1934) and 'sports that were perceived as modern and western led the way' (Lorey, 1997, p. 51). 'Gradually Mexican cities and towns began to create a nation by acting it out in countless local and regional exhibitions, parades and gatherings' (Tenorio-Trillo, 1996, p. 245). From 1930 onwards the annual 'Revolutionary Games' were also inaugurated. Sport, and especially international sport, became not only an opportunity to promote the image of the country abroad but also to provide a unifying focus around which, hopefully, different regions, peoples, and sections of society could rally (Brewster, 2005). 'By the late 1920s regional integration became one of the featured themes of sports displays on November 20' (Lorey, 1997, p. 55) and the subservience of the regions to the centre was symbolized by the ritual relay race from Puebla to Mexico City.[1]

Perhaps the first major physical manifestation of this desire to use sport as a means of national unification after the chaos of the Mexican revolution of 1910–1919 and its aftermath, was the construction of a National Stadium in May 1924 (McGehee, 1993). In the same year Mexico sent its first group of athletes to the Paris Olympics, although they were privately funded. This participation led directly to Mexico hosting the 1926 Central American Games which, although modest, were an important catalyst for interest in sport more generally. However, it was not until 1932 that the Party of the Mexican Revolution (PRM) established the national sport confederation with the specific objective of creating 'an integrated nation [composed] of healthy, virile and dynamic men' (quoted in Arbena, 1991, p. 355).

Interest in sport grew rapidly during the 1930s and especially in the post-war years, although one issue that surfaced at this time was the extent to which Mexico was importing and imitating developed, Western, and especially US sporting activities rather than enhancing or developing an indigenous sporting culture. Inevitably, the former was the preserve – at least initially – of the mainly white middle classes and the meaning of such activities for the *mestizo* and Indian populations was highly contested.

A major boost was provided by the 1955 Pan-American Games, in support of which the government built an athletes' Village, numerous sporting facilities and distributed over one and a half million free tickets to the public. Indeed, on an earlier visit to Mexico City, Avery Brundage (1951) had observed 'the second Pan-American Games will be held in Mexico City in 1955 and new facilities of Olympic calibre are already under construction'. The event was a great success in terms of the facilities and organization and it also led to the creation of a generation of athletics fans in Mexico. The combination of popular support and government ideology which '… interpreted participation in the Games as an opportunity to express national identification' (Espy, 1979, p. viii), meant that the momentum was now firmly behind any bid to host the world's major sporting events.

Producing the Games

It has been argued above that the process of bidding for, and winning, the right to stage the 1968 Olympic Games was integral to a much larger project on the part of the Mexican government. It was part of a campaign to establish international recognition, to create a stronger sense of nationhood and also to modernize the nation. The Olympic bid and that for the 1970 FIFA World Cup only make sense within this wider context and it is no coincidence that this agenda was driven forward by one of Mexico's most outward looking Presidents. Not surprisingly, therefore, major investments were made in transport and tourism, but these served to reinforce the position of Mexico City as the centralized hub of the country (Nolan and Nolan, 1988; Clancy, 1999). Indeed despite various attempts to achieve the opposite (Barkin and King, 1970), with some recent checking of urban population growth rates (P.M. Ward, 1998), most political, social and economic processes since the mid twentieth century have served to highlight the concentration of economic and political power in Mexico City.

The Olympic Games supported this trend. All the sporting events were held within the city apart from sailing, which took place at the Acapulco yacht club (Arbena, 1996). In winning the bid, the Mexican delegation had made much of the fact that, in contrast to their competitor cities, considerable infrastructure was already in place. Nonetheless, much more needed to be done. The basic budget amounted to $84 million of federal spending and $75 million from private sources for projects directly related to the Games, especially the building of the Olympic Village with 29 structures varying from six to ten storeys (Witherspoon, 2003, p. 108). However, this excluded other infrastructures deemed to be necessary, such as a new six-lane motorway linking the main facilities, improved water supply and sewage disposal systems and, controversially, the new subway system. Although it was supposed to be open for the 1968 Olympics the latter did not start until 1967 and only partially opened by 1969. Thus, whilst the Olympics and the 'modernization' project were instrumental in promoting this massive investment, the principal catalyst had passed before a significant component of the infrastructure was even partially open.

Ward (1990, p. 217) has argued that in Mexico City, 'the purpose of monuments constructed since the 1960s appears to be one of reinforcement: of the modern, of the abstract, and of the international'. If not precisely beginning with the Olympic Games, this process was boosted by that event and laid Mexico City's cultural environment firmly open to international scrutiny. If an important component of the ideological background to the Nineteenth Olympic Games was to demonstrate Mexico's engagement with modernity, this was probably best demonstrated in the 'audacious plan for decentralized facilities that turned the whole city into a temporary festival ground' (Gordon, 1983, p. 99). No thoughts of regeneration or emphasizing the core areas of the city played any part in the relationship between the sporting events and urban structure. The overall philosophy was expansionist. This was also the period of considerable faith in large-scale transport planning, of freeway building and catering for motor vehicles, trends that inevitably privileged an advance to the periphery rather than a focus on the core. New peripheral freeways were built and the city's public transport system was increased by an additional 1,500 special vehicles to provide access to the new and existing facilities, scattered widely over Mexico City, in an 'unprecedented dispersion' (Muñoz, 1997, p. 35), some being over 30 kilometres apart. Olympic routes were colour coded and marked by streamers, whilst enormous balloons or fibreglass figures indicated the sites themselves.

The main focus was in the south of the city at the Olympic Village, known as the Miguel Hidalgo Village, which contained 5,000 units in several tower blocks – 'more than previous Olympic Villages, it was a city' (Gordon, 1983, p. 101). It was the intention after the Games that they would be sold as condominium apartments. A second Olympic Village, the Narciso Mendoza Village, also known as Villa Coapa, was built for the Cultural Olympics with 686 houses and flats, the latter in four-storey blocks (Muñoz, 1997). Both Villages were inspired by the features of mass social housing prevalent in Europe in the 1960s and reflected the *grandes ensembles* tradition (*Ibid.*). The new 25,000-seat Sports Palace for indoor sports, costing $8 million was 9 miles (more than 14 kilometres) to the north-east of the Olympic Village at the Magdalena Mixhuca Sports Park where the velodrome was also located, whilst the new Olympic Pool and Gymnasium was built in the smart southern suburb of Coyoacan. The rowing basin was located still further south at Xochimilco. Although not built with Olympic funds, the Aztec stadium (designed by Pedro Ramírez Vázquez in 1966) was used for Olympic football in 1968 and later for soccer's World Cup Finals in 1970 and 1986. Among the other renovated buildings was the 12,800 capacity National Auditorium at Chapultepec, used mainly for gymnastics. The main sporting location for the athletic events, however, was also not new, being the renovated University City Stadium built in 1953 but expanded to a capacity of 80,000. Inevitably, there was much scepticism from the 'First World' about whether this entire infrastructure would be ready in time (for example, see Giniger, 1968*a* and *b*).

The main axis for the Games was the so-called Route of Friendship in the southern periphery of the city, a newly-built freeway connecting most of the main Olympic locations. This urban motorway became famous for one of the most high-profile cultural events associated with the Olympics, with the distinguished architect Pedro Ramírez Vázquez (President of the Organizing Committee of the Mexico Olympics) and the architect and sculptor Mathias Goeritz promoting its iconic status.[2] In 1966, Goeritz proposed to Ramírez Vázquez that the Olympics should be marked with an invitation to sculptors from around the world to create a sequence of abstract sculptures in concrete, which would be sited along the Route of Friendship (Wendl, 1998, p. 115). Goeritz's ideology was clear in his speech of welcome to the international sculptors, where he asserted his belief that:

> An art integrated from the very inception of the urban plan is of fundamental importance in our age. This means that artistic work will have to leave its environment of art for art's sake and establish contact with the masses by means of total planning.

In the event, 19 sculptures were executed along a 17 kilometre stretch of the motorway with the Olympic Village at its centre. The sculptures were initially well signed and illuminated at night and critical reception was generally favourable but, as we shall see, the subsequent fate of the sculptures has been less fortunate.

Another dimension of contemporary modernity reflected in the Games was the design of the logo, the creation of an American and an Englishman (see below), deliberately psychedelic in inspiration, but also reflecting the Pacific Coast Huichol Indian designs that used stark black and white lines. The number '68' was generated from the geometry of the five Olympic rings with MEXICO set in the middle of a series of concentric swirls and the whole logo was claimed to be a fusion of Mexican indigenous culture with the Op Art movement then spreading over the globe (Brewster, 2005).

The infrastructure of the 1968 Olympics was clearly intended to demonstrate to the world Mexico's advance as a modern nation, but this message was reinforced in other ways. Technological and organizational accomplishments were not the only medium for this message, since there was also a clear understanding that a cultural impression had also to be made. However, just as the new buildings were not echoes or celebrations of Mexico's rich pre-Columbian cultural heritage but 'reflect[ed] a technology of rapidly rising sophistication in an economy where labour was still cheap ... they were designed by architects and engineers of international outlook – citizens of architecture's world state' (Gordon, 1983, p. 107), so too did the Cultural Festival accompanying the Olympics play down indigenous cultural forms. Instead they sought to celebrate internationalism. The chief protagonists were emphatic in their desire to break away from the value-laden stereotype of Mexico as 'the land of *mañana*' as Avery Brundage had remarked to the Mexican president Díaz Ordaz at an IOC meeting in 1966 (quoted in Zolov, 2004, p. 168). This intention was clear to the two foreign artists appointed to design the Olympic logo, Peter Murdoch from Britain and Lance Wyman from the United States, whose only instruction was that 'the sleeping man with the sombrero did not properly represent Mexico' (*Ibid.*, p. 173).

After the excesses of Tokyo 1964, the Mexico City Olympics were perceived as comparatively low cost, but in the context of a developing country this is, of course, a relative concept. Overall, the total cost of building and organization was $175.8 million, of which $53.6 million (30 per cent) was spent on new or remodelled sports facilities, $16.5 million on municipal improvements, $16 million on the Olympic Village and $12.7 million on the Cultural Village. The remaining $77 million was spent on direct outlays by the Organizing Committee, the vast majority of which was spent in Mexico. Nevertheless, there were numerous other, Olympic-related expenditures which never entered the official calculations, not least the wages of the security forces massed outside the key locations. To offset this expenditure, $20 million revenue was received in ticket sales, television rights, and the profits from Olympic souvenirs. In total, the 'official' Mexican government subsidy was about $56.8 million (Gordon, 1983, p. 108). At the peak of the Games, some 14,000 people were employed directly, but the majority only on a temporary basis. Hardly surprisingly, 1968 was a good year for economic growth in Mexico – net tourism receipts increased by 15.5 per cent to $510 million and GNP increased by 7.1 per cent (Hofstadter, 1974).

For the first time, the sporting Olympics were accompanied by a Cultural Festival that went on throughout the entire Olympic year, with the participation of 97 countries (Arbena, 1996). International figures were invited, including Robert Graves, Arthur Miller, Eugene Ionesco, Martha Graham, Evgeny Evtushenko, John Cage, Dave Brubeck, Duke Ellington, and Alexander Calder (who designed the 80-foot high sculpture *El Sol Rojo* outside the re-opened Aztec stadium). Many of the cultural events took place in the Olympic Village and in the extensive Chapultepec Park on the western side of the city, although museums and auditoria throughout the city were also used. Overall, there were 1,500 events throughout the Olympic year of which 550 were dispersed through the country (Zolov, 2004).

That the Cultural Festival was conceived as an integral part of the whole Olympic experience is indicated by the fact that it was organized by the architect Pedro Ramírez Vázquez who had been a member of the delegation to Baden-Baden in 1963 and became Chairman of the Mexican Olympic Committee in 1966 in succession to López Mateos. It has been argued that the main driving force for this was to 're-energize Mexican domestic support for the Olympics following nearly three years of divisions and doubts' (Zolov, 2004, p. 168). If this were the case, there was no obvious attempt to appeal to a broad spectrum of Mexican society. Although Mexican folk culture (especially dance) played some part in the Cultural Olympics, each participating nation was asked to bring 'jointly with their athletic delegations two works of art: one representative of any of its brilliant cultural stages of the past; the other the best of its contemporary art' (*Ibid.*, p. 175). In other words, the celebration was international and it seems difficult to imagine how inviting numerous foreigners to come and display their folk heritage could actually enthuse a population as large, diverse and geographically distinctive as that of Mexico.

Assessing the Games

While it is true to say that the efficiency of organization for the 1968 Olympics took many international observers by surprise it was not an opportunity for unqualified self-congratulation. Rodríguez Kuri (2003) argued that the background to the organization of the Cultural Olympics in particular demonstrated a 'matured modernity' within Mexico. In other words, it was a 'natural' outcome of the stage of development that Mexico had reached. Yet the preceding discussion has demonstrated that the primary engine driving forward the Mexican Olympic project of 1968 was the need to convince the outside world of its capabilities and, as part of that project, no opposition could be tolerated.

The official announcement that Mexico City had been awarded the 1968 Olympic Games was met with almost universal joy within Mexico. For example, as a Mexican student argued in 1968:

the very fact that this country has been chosen as the theatre for the Olympic games signifies that it has reached a high degree of development and equipment. One can see other signs in the intensity of foreign investment and the level of productivity we have attained here. (Quoted in Calvert, 1973, p. 316)

Within a short space of time, this optimistic view was challenged. The government had certainly hoped that the excitement of preparing for the Olympics would generate an atmosphere of popular support. Although sport was demonstrably being used as an instrument of unity, it has been claimed that Mexicans evidenced an ability to resist such cultural impositions (Brewster, 2005).

In this context, the events immediately preceding the Olympics in the summer of 1968 are often cited. For example, Essex and Chalkley (1998, p. 192) observed:

> the costs of the Games were such that many ordinary Mexicans questioned whether the money might not have been better spent on dealing with poverty and alleviating the city's severe social problems. This opposition resulted in violent protests which police and army units quelled with force.

However, this is to recycle a common misunderstanding about the student movement of 1968, which was about much more than the cost of the Olympics. Although many Mexicans did question the cost of the Games, most informed views now agree that this was not the primary basis of the civil unrest of 1968. Although the savage repression and massacre at the Tlatelolco rally on 2 October was undoubtedly exacerbated by the fact that Mexico was about to stage the Opening Ceremony (Preston and Dillon, 2004), the student movement was intent on reminding the world that Mexico was a one-party state with a history of corruption and police repression (Zolov, 1999). The Olympics provided the opportunity for higher profile protest but it was not the object of that protest.

Any sympathy and good feeling that the Mexican government may have won through its difficulties in the summer of 1968 was quickly eroded by its subsequent behaviour. According to official figures, the death toll at Tlatelolco was 49. Foreign journalists estimated the figure at well over 200, later adjusted upwards to 260 deaths and over 1,200 injured (Toohey and Veal, 2000). An Italian journalist, Oriana Fallaci, had attended the rally and was wounded. Instead of receiving help

Figure 11.1. Security Forces facing demonstration in Mexico City, October 1968.

Figure 11.2. Detainees being strip-searched, Mexico City, October 1968.

from the state security guards, her watch was stolen from her wrist (Preston and Dillon, 2004). Injured students were indiscriminately tortured in an attempt to uncover the names of organizers and ringleaders of their movement (Witherspoon, 2003). The government quickly took steps to lay the blame firmly at the door of the usual suspects – Communists and other foreign agitators – whilst sentencing over 100 'ringleaders' to heavy terms in jail, some for 25 years. The Olympic Games continued but the image of Mexico, so carefully prepared and massaged in the years leading up to October 1968, was now something much darker than the planned official representation. Whatever the roots of the student protest of 1968, most of the benefits of hosting the Olympics – the modern image, the enhanced presence on the international stage and the attempt to create the sense of one nation – were eroded by the repression and the evident lack of political harmony, despite all the effort to present such an image (Zolov, 2004).

Turning from the political repercussions of the events surrounding the Games, one of the main alleged benefits of hosting the Olympic Games is the prospect of an enhanced city image both nationally and especially internationally. Undoubtedly, the level of awareness of a city is bound to increase when its name is repeatedly mentioned in the national and international media. However, increased awareness is not the same as enhanced image and in the case of Mexico City the latter proved to be problematic. The Games themselves passed off remarkably well and the organization and staging were generally judged to be good. Yet the dominant and lasting images were of the 'Black Power' demonstration of the American sprinters Tommy Smith and John Carlos during the 200 metre medal ceremony, the police repression of Tlatelolco, and the fact that the Games were on the point of cancellation at least twice – once through the potential boycott of countries objecting to the invitation to participate sent to South Africa (Hill, 1996) and once through the security fears following the 12 October massacre.

The Games also served to highlight some of Mexico City's problems of urban infrastructure, especially those to do with transport. The concept of a decentralized Games with events widespread across the city proved to have many practical difficulties, especially as some aspects of the transport infrastructure had not been completed on time. Contemporary accounts also pointed to the cosmetic nature of some of the alleged urban improvements. The gaudiness of displays and liberal use of colour in street decoration could not wipe out the reality, for example on the walls of neighbouring slums, which were painted in shocking pink, purple and yellow, temporarily hiding the deprivation within (Salázar, 1968).

Although seen as an integral part of the modern image of the 1968 Olympics, the sculptures on the Route of Friendship were quickly usurped from their original purpose, adorned with graffiti and used to convey entirely different messages. Today, many of them are damaged, stained concrete structures often partially hidden by roadside weeds and disregarded by motorists speeding by. Other elements of the Olympic iconography were also usurped and used as part of the protest campaign. For example, the symbolic white doves of peace used widely in the graphic arts programme in association with the official motto for the Olympics, (*Todo es possible en la paz*: Everything is Possible in Peace), were ironically spattered with red paint after the October massacre.

If the fate of the sculptures on the Route of Friendship was considerably less than their authors would have wished, the same is true of the Olympic Village. The intention had been to sell the 904 four-room apartments in the private market but two years after the Games the Village was still half empty with no-one on the waiting list (Schmitt, 1971). The city centre is 15 kilometres to the north, there are no shops or supermarkets and no significant places of employment adjacent to the site, so a car is essential. A major deterrent to early rapid sales was that the apartments were severely vandalized by the athletes themselves (*Ibid.*, p. 261). Subsequently, the two Olympic Villages have ended up as dormitory commuter areas entirely dependent on private transport (Muñoz, 1997).

One final and possibly significant epitaph on the 1968 Olympics relates to the historiography of Mexico City. In the main English language monograph on Mexico City (Ward, 1990), the Olympic Games warrant only a brief mention (*Ibid.*, p. 217) and in its equivalent by two French authors published in 1979, none at all (Bataillon and Rivière d'Arc, 1979). In the context of the evolution of the modern urban structure of Mexico City, the Olympic Games of 1968 are little more than a footnote. Consequently it is difficult to argue a case for any underlying change in city structure emanating from the Olympics. Nevertheless, it was important and symbolic at the time and, in the broader context of the city, its relationship to Mexican governance and the perception of the nation on the global stage, the events of 1968 are of fundamental significance, albeit profoundly different from those originally intended.

Notes

1. Although Spanish is, of course, the official language of Mexico, there are at least 90 indigenous languages, mostly with a regional ethnic basis.

2. Ramírez Vázquez built the National Museum of Anthropology and the Aztec Stadium in Mexico City and went on to design the administrative buildings of the IOC and the Olympic Museum in Lausanne, Switzerland. Mathias Goeritz had designed a group of high-rise concrete towers in Mexico City called the Torres de Satelite in the suburb of Ciudad Satelite, planned in direct relationship to a super-highway.

Chapter 12

Montreal 1976

Daniel Latouche

The Montreal Summer Olympics were to be a modest affair, remembered for the harmony they would bring back to the Games and for demonstrating that even a medium-sized city could stage a successful world event. These were to be the Olympics with a human face. In this chapter,[1] we take stock of the fact that three decades later a different legacy has taken hold and the 1976 Olympics are best known for their extravagant cost overrun ($700 million on an inflated $1.2 billion price tag), for the boycott of 26 African nations, and for coming close to an abrupt cancellation.[2] Although Montrealers still retain a rather positive image of those three weeks in July, they remain convinced that in the short run the Games proved a catastrophe for the city's economy and its reputation, with very little to show except an over-sized and under-used stadium.

Is this vision of the 1976 Montreal Olympic legacy an unfair one, dictated only by the size of its abysmal deficit, a distortion which prevents us from realizing that the cat is already very flat indeed?[3] Can things be that bad? Is there no silver lining running through this sad script? How are we to judge an event which took place in a context which although only 30 years old seems to resonate from another era? In 1976, the Olympics were still a young affair with the majority of Games having taken place before the Second World War. In Montreal, athletes from the first modern Olympiads were still alive and regularly interviewed. The dominant political perspective was that of 1945 with political divisions inherited from the Yalta Conference. Nuclear deterrence was a household concept and the Cold War a permanent political fixture. In 1976, the Internet did not exist, PCs were unknown, Urban Studies had not discovered consumption-based economic development and Cultural Studies were still years away from deconstructing the tourist gaze.

While the debate still goes on in specialized circles as to whether the Munich, Montreal or Moscow Games should be awarded the prize for the worst-ever Olympics, there is no doubt that the Montreal Games have their place in the triangle of Disappointment Games. Such failures, exaggerated or not, are there to remind us that the worst is always possible and that with each 'successful' Games, the chances increase of seeing the next ones falter, often on the most innocuous detail. There is, however, failure and failure. While it can be argued that both and Moscow were the victims of political circumstances over which they .le control, the failure of Montreal was entirely self-induced.

or is the disappointment limited to the financial side of the operation. If one is to look at the 1976 Olympics as the birth of a new elite 'sport', the *Urban Triathlon*, the initial performance of a city which had just come out of a successful World Exhibition (Expo 67), a sort of Pre-Olympic Trial, was far from *éblouissante*. In all three disciplines of this new highly competitive sport, (1) City marketing and promotion, (2) Urban development and mega-event economics, and (3) Local planning and governance, Montreal did not do very well. How could things go that wrong?

City Marketing and Promotion

Marketing and promotion are important components of both a winning candidature and the successful completion of the Games themselves. The tools, techniques and objectives vary depending on the message the organizers want to put forward and successful marketing campaigns make certain not to mix the messages or confuse the audiences. During the bidding war, the sole objective is to convince a majority of IOC voters to support your bid. Contrary to the regular electoral process, this first audience is almost totally irrelevant for the second phase of the operation as the IOC Grand Electors play no significant role during the preparation phase. Nevertheless, what you say and what you do – and not do – to win the minds and hearts of the IOC will come back to haunt you during the preparation phase of the Games.

How Not to Win the Candidature Competition

Until 1976, the fight to hold the Games was principally a national affair pitching country against country, political system against political system. The choice of Tokyo 1964 or Mexico City 1968 can be understood only against a background of 'national' calculus having to do more with the need to move the Games outside of their European-North American confines, confirm the rehabilitation of former enemies or choose a country acceptable both to the West and the USSR rather than the technical and marketing quality of one bid versus the others (Augustin and Gillon, 2004).

The choice of Montreal marked a first in the sense that the IOC, following its own rules, chose a city and only secondarily a country or a continent, a tendency which persisted with the selection of Los Angeles, Barcelona, Atlanta and Sydney. This is not to say that national and geopolitical considerations no longer play any role in the competition to be selected as the 'national' champion or in the final selection process. In fact, in the cases of Beijing and later London, decisions appeared to have been determined by non-city related factors (Martins, 2004). Even in Montreal, these 'outside' considerations were never too far from the surface, although they rapidly became instrumentalized by a single individual,

Mayor Jean Drapeau. As told on previous occasions (and certainly embellished with each new version), the idea of having the Olympics Games in Montreal first came to Drapeau during an impromptu visit to Lausanne in 1963 (Auf der Maur, 1976). Following the last-minute withdrawal of Moscow from arranging a Class A International Exposition in 1967, Montreal gained the nomination from the Bureau International des Expositions in its place. Desperate for fresh ideas, Drapeau visited the team organizing the Swiss National Exhibition, Expo '64 (part of a series held every 25 years). For the practical reason that the headquarters of Expo '64 were located in the same building as the Olympic Museum, the Mayor was 'introduced' first-hand to the Olympic movement and told of the benefits that both Tokyo and Mexico expected to receive as host cities.

Jean Drapeau not only brought back a number of ideas for his exhibition – including its name, Expo 67 – but also the conviction that the Olympics represented the long-awaited solution to a more pressing problem, the need for Montreal to get a decent sports stadium. In 1961, the newly-elected Mayor had surprised everyone by applying for a franchise from the National League, one of the two professional baseball leagues then operating solely within the territory of the United States. For Drapeau, Montreal's future as a tourist destination and economic centre lay in obtaining a professional sports franchise in order to reassure Americans as to the normalcy of this Francophone and somewhat peripheral city. At the time, the answer of the Baseball Commissioner had been a well-publicized: 'First get yourself a stadium and then we will see'.

Two years later, in 1966, Montreal made a bid to the IOC, arguing that the city was simply the best place to stage the 1972 Games. By this time, it was in the final throes of organizing its very successful World's Fair and would soon inherit a large-scale stadium as a result of having obtained an American baseball franchise. In the event, Montreal did not get the 1972 Olympics, in part because it became clear that a reverse promise had been made to the baseball authorities who had been told that a baseball franchise could safely be awarded to Montreal since an Olympic-size stadium was just around the corner.[4] Apparently, the message was better received at the baseball end, as the Montreal Expos began their operation in April 1969.

With the Montreal baseball team operating in a temporary stadium, the pressures on the city to build the much-promised world-class stadium mounted. Following Mexico City 1968, it was decided that Montreal would try again to win the right to stage a Summer Games. Between 1966 and 1970, the Mayor travelled the world and met at least once with each national Olympic Committee to make sure that Montreal was the second-choice of all those whose support had been promised to either Los Angeles and Moscow. Needless to say, IOC delegates from countries whose vote were considered crucial were personally invited and given VIP treatment during Expo 67, with a promise to all those involved that since their Pavilion, although a temporary structure like all Expo exhibits, was among the most significant on the site, everything would be done to preserve it for future generations.

Nevertheless, the Mayor's major problem did not so much lie with the other candidates as with the negative campaigning staged by Vancouver, already hustling to get the 1978 Winter Olympics. Another major obstacle was the lukewarm support of the Canadian government and the Canadian Olympic Association (COA). At the time of the final IOC selection meeting, COA remained unreconciled to the fact that Drapeau had forgotten to consult them before going public with Montreal's campaign. They had always assumed that Toronto, which had no World's Fair and no baseball team to show for its efforts, and not Montreal was the 'natural' Canadian candidate. As for the federal government, it emphatically did not want to appear to support a Montreal initiative to the detriment of Vancouver or Toronto, where its electoral base was in urgent need of reinforcement if it was to be re-elected in the coming 1972 election. In order not to put the federal government on the spot and run the risk of an official rebuff, Mayor Drapeau agreed not to force Ottawa to declare a firm financial commitment.

Following allegations from Vancouver officials which resurfaced during the showdown meeting in Amsterdam as to the absence of any serious financial planning on the part of Montreal, each candidate city was asked to provide financial guarantees and make a detailed presentation.[5] While both Los Angeles and Moscow managed satisfactorily, Drapeau chose to turn the tables and insisted in his presentation that all such talk of money was demeaning to the Olympic ideals and that the entire financial issue was out-of-order and rather insulting in light of Montreal's reputation and since the city had every intention of presenting a 'modest' Games.

This mixture of bluff, shrewd calculus, self-promotion and hard sell would never again produce similar results,[6] but it gained Montreal the maximum return for a very limited investment. In 1972, no major company chose to associate itself with the Montreal bid, nor were they asked to do so; no doubt a wise decision considering the negative fallout from the Nike controversy at the Mexico Games. There was no significant engagement of the local community and no attempt by the Bidding Committee to sponsor events in order to raise awareness and monies for the project. In fact, there was simply no Committee in the first place. No army of volunteers and spokespersons was recruited and none was required as there was little opposition to the whole enterprise. The Olympic Mascot, Amik the Beaver, made only a brief and late appearance on one of the official posters. Instead the Mayor relied on an elaborate intelligence system which allowed him to know everything that could be known on each delegate so as to be able to fine-tune his argument, a task made somewhat easier since there was only one line.

On all issues which were raised as to the city's capacity to host such a large and intense international event, the candidature file and the Mayor had the same answer: Expo 67, the immensely successful World Exhibition organized by Montreal on three artificial islands in the middle of the Saint-Lawrence River. To the question: 'Would people come to Montreal in the middle of summer?', the answer was inevitably 'They will. As a matter of fact many of the 50 million visitors of 1967 have been looking for an excuse to come back to Montreal'. 'What about security?' 'Montreal is the safest metropolis in North America. In 1967, even the Queen of England and Lyndon B. Johnson could visit the city'.[7] 'What about transportation?' 'Montreal already has the world's most efficient metro system, one which will be expanded. And a brand new airport will also be built'.

Promoting an Olympic City in a Worst Case Scenario

Present in Munich, Drapeau saw at first-hand the devastating effect of the terrorist attack on the unfolding of the 1972 Games. In subsequent working visits, Montreal officials were told of a 30 per cent drop in the number of tourists visiting or planning to visit the Bavarian capital. Having gone through what he considered the De Gaulle ordeal of 1967 – when the French President made use of the ceremonial balcony at City Hall to proclaim his support for Quebec sovereignty – and subsequently the FLQ crisis of 1970, the Mayor came back from Munich determined that nobody, especially not the Quebec sovereignty movement, was going to derail 'his' Games. Eventually, he would face the reverse problem as nobody wanted to be associated with such a colossal failure.

Although unforeseen at the time, Munich 1972 had a direct impact on both the planning and the promotional model used to prepare for the Montreal Games. Not inclined by nature to delegate or to share authority, Drapeau made clear from the beginning that all decisions concerning the Games were to be taken by his office. Until very late in the process, he effectively resisted all attempts to have the Official Organizing Committee run the operations. His suspicion was directed at all those who did not recognize his absolute leadership and did not agree to act as grateful foot soldiers in his Grand Project. This group included the labour movement, suspected of working hard to destabilize his Administration, and even the Federal and Provincial governments, the latter being suspected of being both too nationalist and too soft in its dealings with community and progressive groups.

As the months passed, the increasingly paranoid Mayor made sure that no one even closely associated with the intellectual and cultural effervescence prevalent in the Quebec of the 1970s was even indirectly associated with the promotional and marketing efforts necessary to stage such an endeavour. Only one person was found to be acceptable, French architect Roger Taillibert, who was given a free hand to propose a concept for a new 'revolutionary' stadium. As doubts rose as to whether or not the facilities could be built in time, not to mention their cost, the promotion campaign turned into a 'public relations' one, whose sole purpose was 'damage control'. On occasion, the obsession with details was pushed to extremes as when the Mayor insisted that all documents and materials made extensive use of the colour red, a colour associated with Canada, the Federal government and generally 'les Anglais' and as little as possible of blue, considered too French and too nationalist.

The transfer of the flame from Greece to the host city is usually the occasion of a symbolic appropriation of the Olympic ideal by the population and much thought usually goes in figuring out the itinerary as well as choosing the 'correct' runners. In 1976, for the first time the transmission of the Olympic flame from Greece to Montreal came by way of an electronic signal which landed not in Montreal but in Ottawa, the Federal capital. A Montreal official objected to this technological hijacking but, for the Federal government, it was imperative that the flame travelled electronically so as to show off Canadian telecommunication *savoir-faire* (Canada was then desperately trying to sell a communications satellite to Greece). For a moment, it was suggested that the 'flame' could land electronically at the tip of the Gaspé Peninsula and then travel along the banks of the Saint-Lawrence, following in the footsteps of the early French explorers. In the end, this itinerary was considered too risky politically as it was pointed out that a similar path had been followed in Mexico and only served to reanimate long subdued ethno-cultural tensions. Instead, it was decided that the flame would bypass Quebec as much as possible and arrive in Montreal from the west and not the east, a decision tantamount to bringing the Olympic flame to Cairo through the Libyan Desert, in order not to cross the Nile.

More was still to come on the saga of the flame. Located 200 kilometres west of Montreal, in the neighbouring Province of Ontario, the Federal capital is linked to Montreal by the Ottawa River (Rivière des Outaouais) which also separates the two Provinces. Thus the flame could have arrived at Montreal using the waterway or the Quebec side of the river. As later recalled, the reaction of Federal authorities at the idea of a Quebec-only itinerary bordered on hysteria, no doubt because of the vivid memory from 1967 when General De Gaulle travelled from village to village along the old Chemin du Roy and then reached Montreal just in time for his controversial 'Vive le Québec libre' speech.

Instead the flame would follow a 'safe' itinerary crossing only occasionally into Quebec and then coming back on the Ontario side, definitively entering Quebec at the last moment and then reaching the centre of Montreal (Montreal is an island) after going through rich Anglophone suburbs west of the island. It rained for most of the day and especially for the final leg of the Olympic Run through the city of Westmount, the symbol of past Anglo-Saxon domination in Quebec, and where the Olympic flame spent its first night on Quebec soil. At no time did the Olympic flame travel through central Montreal as the Mayor had made sure that the relay did not use Sherbrooke Street where, just days before, he had unilaterally ordered the demolition of the 'Urban Art' exhibition which he disliked so much. Even 30 years later, it is easy to imagine how the local press played such grand manoeuvres.

Three series of posters were produced for the 1976 Games, often after acrimonious and somewhat esoteric debates. For example, the main poster presented a schematic view of the Olympic stadium but ran immediately into controversy as it served to remind all participants of the unfinished status of the central infrastructure. The poster representing Montreal was certainly the least inspiring one. Unable to agree on a pictorial representation of the city and unwilling to use its best known trademarks, the small mountain in the middle of the city or the Saint-Lawrence River, designers came to rely on a sculptured head of a Greek athlete superimposed on part of the Montreal coat of arms. So much for civic identity and pride.

The end-product of this constant political interference was a surreal promotional campaign with no central message except to emphasize that everything was indeed under control, an obsession with protocol and the requirement that Montreal be presented as a city with no conflict, no history, and no tensions of any kind. The results were nothing short of catastrophic with probably the most insipid Opening and Closing Ceremonies in the history of the Games, certainly a paradox in the land of Céline Dion and the Cirque du Soleil. One came out from the ceremonies with the image of a city drowning in political correctness and good intentions, a city made up of a multitude of ethnic, religious and linguistic groups coexisting peacefully because of their shared love for gymnastics and folk-dancing.

Tensions with the cultural community, already high from when the Mayor ordered city employees to tear down the 'Corridart' exhibition, evolved into full-scale artistic war around the orientation to be given to the Arts and Culture Programme. Again posters became the centre of attention as their design pitted Quebec and Canadian artists against one another, mainstream versus *avant-garde* clans, and stage against music performers. As the Quebec cultural community became more and more involved in the definition of the arts programme, artists from other Provinces insisted that their presence should be equal to that of Quebec. This created interminable discussion as to who would pay for what and for whom, with the Federal government agreeing to pay for English-Canadian artists and even, under certain conditions, for the controversial arts posters.[8] The requirement that artists from all ten Canadian provinces, as well as from First nations, share equally in the Arts Festival only produced a cacophony of voices and performances, translating into a box-office nightmare and a full-blown cultural war.

Urban Development

Any assessment of Olympic-induced urban development includes the economic spill-over from the Games, especially in terms of tourism, the multiplication of sport and leisure facilities, the post-Games quality of urban design and architecture, the physical infrastructure left behind and the new housing facilities inherited by the city. On all five counts, the performance of the Montreal Olympics, although not as bad as could have been expected under the circumstances, provided numerous lessons for subsequent Games.

The Montreal Games and Urban Economics

The first formal cost-benefit analysis of any Olympiad was prepared for the

Montreal Games (Iton, 1977). The fact that it has received so little attention is in part due to the enormity of the financial burden imposed by the Games, which made it impossible for even the most complacent cost-benefit analysis to hide. In addition, the study was but an afterthought to the Games and played no role during the bidding phase of the exercise. Yet the value of the study, *The Economic Impact of the 1976 Olympic Games*, goes beyond what it tells us about the 1976 Games. It also illustrates how imaginative economists can be in order to make a point. For example, rather than using the official Quebec input-output econometric model, researchers preferred the less disaggregated Canada-wide model in order to argue that all of Canada and not just Quebec benefited from the Games.

Equally imaginative was the attempt to provide the Games with a progressive image. In order to counter the frequently heard argument that public monies spent on the Olympics, including those coming out of the Olympic Lottery, could have served better purposes, the study makes a valiant attempt to assess the health consequences of the Olympics, going as far as calculating morbidity and premature death rates in and around the Olympic installations. Of course, they were unable to arrive at a precise figure for health savings, but nevertheless concluded that a sizable portion of $129 million annually lost because of premature deaths in this underprivileged part of town could be recuperated if only a fraction of Montrealers made use of their new sport facilities.

Compared to more recent documents, the Montreal cost-benefit analysis is a rather primitive affair with few equations and much approximation.[9] One advantage of producing an *ex post facto* cost-benefit analysis – in 1977 – rather than before the preparation phase is the possibility for its authors to confirm some unpleasant facts, such as the small impact of the Games on tourist flows. For example, the number of American tourists who visited Quebec in the months prior to the Games was actually lower than normally expected, as visitors simply postponed their visit to coincide with the Games. In the following months, the number of visitors also dropped, although this is probably as much due to the economic situation as to the negative image left by the Games.

The study also highlighted some unexpected findings, mostly regarding the economic impact of the Games; findings which would have been more difficult to obtain in any pre-Olympic study. For example, one could have expected that with a final price-tag of more than a billion dollars, spent almost entirely on construction costs, the Montreal economy would have received a lasting boost. Apparently, this was not the case and if there were a boost, it left little trace. For example, in order to prove that inflated labour demands were not the major reason for the ever-ballooning deficit, John Iton, the McGill economist in charge of the study, confirmed that during the year prior to the Games, unit labour costs did not rise more significantly in Montreal than in Toronto. This was for the simple reason that the $1.2 billion investment had very little spill-over in the local economy.

The 1976 Olympic Facilities and the Creation of a Sports Space

Although rarely mentioned, the Antwerp Games of 1920 were nevertheless important inasmuch as for the first time the local business elite, sports enthusiasts for the most part, promoted the candidacy of their city by insisting on the sport facilities which Antwerp would inherit.[10] Since then, cities have always put forward the legacy of Olympic installations as an argument for holding the Games, while juggling their act in order to find the correct mix between existing and new facilities, specialized or multifunctional ones, on a centralized or decentralized site.

Clearly, the functionality of the infrastructure for the events for which they were designed is one major element of any analysis. Their contribution to the city's sport and recreational offering provides a second. Third, the total and marginal costs of the enterprise must also be taken into account, as well as the financing schemes required to pay for them. A fourth set of criteria relates to the image of the city and involves, among other things, the architectural quality of the facilities. Finally, the overall contribution of the sport infrastructure to the urban development and planning process should also be considered.

How well did the Montreal infrastructure perform on these five counts? Having advertised a 'modest' Games, the Montreal bid to the IOC made clear its intention to use existing facilities for most competitions. The only explicit commitment was for a new 70,000 spectator stadium. The stadium was to become the centrepiece of what rapidly became known as the Olympic Park where new facilities for cycling and swimming were also constructed. All in all, 35 per cent of all finals were held within the Park. From a strictly functional perspective, the installations proved a success with all those involved: the athletes, the organizers, the IOC, the spectators and journalists. The proximity of the Olympic Village to the main installations – athletes could walk to their events – and the concentration of events within the Olympic Park was particularly appreciated. All installations directly related to the competition were finished in time and no serious glitches developed following the lack of 'break-in' time for most of the newly built installations.

There was some attempt to relax some of Coubertin's most sacred rules, like the necessity of holding the Finals of the equestrian Olympics in the Olympic Stadium. All other equestrian competitions were held 80 kilometres south of Montreal in what would eventually become a high-class resort community. The promoters of this residential development-in-the-making insisted on having all equestrian events in their town, but eventually failed since one of the Mayor's original arguments had been that temporary stables could be built to accommodate horses and training in a park just north of the Stadium. Nevertheless, the city of Bromont managed to stage the equestrian competition effectively and to this day continues to promote itself as the equestrian capital of Quebec and even Canada, a fact which contributed decisively to IBM's decision to establish one of its major Canadian installations there.

Seven Olympics later the debate as to the final costs of the Montreal Games still goes on, this time centring on the pertinence of spending an additional $500 million to tear down the Olympic Stadium in order to make room for an 'urban forest' more in tune with the objectives of sustainable development and healthy cities. As for two professional sport teams (football and baseball) scheduled to use the stadium, they adamantly refused to play in what is generally considered a gloomy and very permeable concrete cavern.[11] Potential users of the motocross racing or commercial fairs variety are still waiting for a permanent roof to replace the retractable one which did not survive even its first Montreal winter. Finally, no one has formulated a plausible use for the Stadium's Leaning Tower – the tallest such tower in the world – while the Velodrome has been transformed into a biological reserve. As for the swimming and diving installations, they aged so rapidly that when Montreal was awarded the 2005 International Water Competition, the city had to lease temporary swimming pools. Only one set of infrastructure passed the test of time, the Claude-Robillard Centre, built for the handball and water-polo competitions and which was used as the major training facility for track-and-field athletes. With all the elegance of a blockhouse, the Claude-Robillard Sport Complex is also home of the Montreal Impact, the much-adored Montreal soccer team. It would seem that in his obsession to make Montreal into a baseball town, Mayor Drapeau had been blind to the multicultural transformation of the city, today more in tune with the *ballon rond* than with its oval counterpart.[12]

Urban Design and Architecture after the 1976 Olympics

The architectural legacy of the Montreal Olympics is difficult to assess with even a minimal degree of 'objectivity'.[13] The fact that the Olympics followed two decades of highly positive architectural (Place-Ville-Marie, Place Bonaventure) and urbanistic achievements (Expo 67, the Metro, the Underground City) in Montreal complicates matters even further. Visually the 56,549 capacity stadium with its fluid and elliptical forms is truly a work of art. Those who see the stadium and the adjacent Velodrome and Swimming Hall as artistic contributions like to point out that in Montreal only one major functional building dared to escape the tyranny of the modular approach dominant since the Renaissance. For Luc Noppen, a well-known architectural critic, temporary difficulties in finding a proper use for such a monument should not obscure the fact that for once an architect had had the Kennedy-like vision to challenge the technological community to achieve what everyone said could not be done. Nonetheless, as Jean-Claude Marsan (1994), later Dean of the Architecture School at the University of Montreal, pointed out, it is difficult to make a lasting contribution and become a famous architect, if the technological innovations on which your future reputation rests fail to ever materialize.

Nothing much is known about the architectural vision of Jean Drapeau who in this case acted very much like the Prince in selecting *his* architect, *his* project, even *his* material (cement). He is known to have profoundly disliked the Buckminster Fuller designed dome built for Expo 67, while being enthusiastic about the French Pavilion which he worked hard to preserve first as a Civilization Museum and later as the site of the Montreal Casino. His only well-known architectural aspiration was to give Montreal a 'Tower-like' signature, much along the lines of the Eiffel Tower which he briefly envisaged asking the French to move to Montreal at the time of Expo 67. When defending the choice of a French architect, he never ceased to praise the non-American quality of this choice and repeatedly mentioned the need for Montreal to inscribe itself in a European monumental tradition where buildings mean something. In the eyes of the Mayor and of an architect more than ready to oblige, the stadium was not to be a simple object for mass consumption, a strictly functional construction like the ones in Mexico City and Munich. The Stadium was to be a statement, not of Québécois identity but the local incarnation of a cosmopolitan world culture where the superior values of the intellect and of human fraternity would prevail. As Drapeau frequently reminded perplexed visitors, Montreal's destiny was to be the Athens of North America, nothing less.

Urban Infrastructures

Montreal 1976 is often considered as standing in the middle between those Olympics where nothing much happened on the urban redevelopment level (Los Angeles, Moscow, Mexico) and those where redevelopment was a central element of a city-boostering strategy (Barcelona, Sydney). The reality, however, is a far cry for even such a moderate assessment. Except for the extension of a metro line to reach the Olympic Park located 7 kilometres from downtown, Montrealers would be hard-pressed to identify any urban infrastructures which could be considered an Olympic inheritance. In at least one case, however, the legacy is certainly there but few are willing to lay a claim to it. To elaborate, in 1969 the Federal government had decided to build a new International Airport, 50 kilometres north-west of Montreal. Having expropriated 80,000 acres (32,375 hectares) of highly productive agricultural land, although the airport only needed 14,000 acres (5,665 hectares) the government rapidly found itself in a middle of a Kafkaesque situation. The Provincial government, which had preferred a site to the south-east, adamantly refused to pay for the high-speed link as well as numerous highways which such a location called for. The successful Olympic bid put an end to all discussion and the airport was built according to the Federal government specifications. In 2002, Mirabel Airport was closed and all flights, domestic and international, were transferred back to Dorval Airport, now renamed Pierre Trudeau Airport, in 'honour' of the Canadian Prime-Minister who single-handedly imposed the Mirabel choice. The cost of the entire operation has reached more than $600 million, not including the $300 million needed to rehabilitate the older airport.

Although not directly called for by the Olympics, the Federal government also used the occasion of the Olympics to push through an urban renewal project which meant tearing down 600 housing units in order to build a massive Television Tower in the eastern part of Montreal. One project that, fortunately, did not materialize was the completion of the east-west expressway which would have cut Montreal in two. The expressway was to provide a rapid link to the Olympic Stadium, but was deemed redundant once the metro extension was approved. Except for this indirect, although valuable contribution, the new metro line had little impact on attendance at the many large-scale events since held in the stadium or on future urban and housing development in the eastern part of town. With a 3,000 space underground parking lot, the comparative advantages of taking public transportation are at best minimal.

Housing

To study the evolution of Olympic Villages, according to Francesc Muñoz (1997, p. 28), is to study 'the history of ideas about how to develop the city, how to plan it and how to manage it'. If this is the case, what then can we learn by looking at the Montreal Village?

While the Olympic Villages of the 1960s can be considered as examples of Fordist functionalism and those of the 1990s as personification of the post-modern search for eclecticism, the two Villages of the 1970s (Munich and Montreal) are clearly post-1968 affairs with an emphasis on leisure, autonomy and integration of different functions within the same building. This is clearly the case with the two large-scale pyramids of Montreal where the first floors are entirely occupied by services, convenience stores, cafeterias, medical clinics and pools, serving 980 apartments capable of housing 11,000 athletes and trainers. Like the rest of the Olympic facilities, the construction of the Village went ahead under increasing difficulties, a complete lack of planning and control, much hesitation and considerable costs overrun. Confronted with rising scepticism as to the estimated costs of the Games, the Organizing Committee (*Comité Organisateur des Jeux Olympiques* – COJO) first floated the proposal of a temporary Village (like Los Angeles 1932). When this idea was rejected, it was then proposed to build not one but five different Olympic Villages, located within a 3–10 kilometre radius from the Stadium. That idea, first proposed by a group of students and faculty from the Urban Planning Department of the University of Montreal, was uninspiringly defended by the Mayor before the IOC with the result that it was also rejected. For their part, the IOC made it clear that it wanted a full-blown permanent Village, close to the major sites and built, at least, to a specified minimum standard quality.

Within months of this second refusal, the Mayor and the COJO had a new proposal which was officially unveiled in June 1974, with construction beginning the following November. There was no architectural competition, nor even a discussion of possible options as Drapeau simply imposed his own idea, with the result that the Montreal Pyramids closely resemble – some even mention the possibility of plagiarism – those of the Baie des Anges in Southern France. At the press conference unveiling the plans for the Village, he proudly announced the name of the contractor for the project, but failed to mention that there had been no costs estimates and that the financing was still undecided. Unable to produce such estimates, the Mayor simply forced the project upon the COJO in October 1974, not even bothering to inform them that the contractor in charge of realizing the Village had already withdrawn from the project. The Village was officially completed in June 1976 three weeks before the opening of the Games and a bare eight days before the first contingent of 197 athletes was registered. The overall costs went from $22 million in February 1975, the first such estimate, to $43 million in mid-July, and to $80 million in August 1976.

The difficulties encountered throughout the planning and construction phases of the Montreal Olympic Village overshadowed all discussions as to what to do with the Village after the Olympics. The original idea of spreading out the Village in five neighbourhoods was in line with Montreal's long standing tradition of not conforming to the American or French policy of massive 'Public Projects' or 'Barres', but instead of spreading low-cost housing throughout the urban fabric. In order to placate rising criticisms, the Mayor came out with the idea of turning the Pyramids into middle-income apartments for retired people. The suggestion proved impracticable as all internal corridors in the Pyramids are in fact located outside and open to the weather, not a genial situation considering the severity of Montreal's winters. Despite this, both buildings have since been fully privatized and are considered a choice location.

Urban Planning and Governance

Olympics are large-scale events which require specialized infrastructures, often spread-out through the city and beyond, and the capacity to handle a large and temporary influx of visitors. These infrastructures have to be put somewhere, not an easy task considering that this locational choice may have little to do with the future use of the facilities. During the hectic two weeks of the Games, the activities of the city must go on and the need to accommodate visitors and participants must not interfere with the daily lives of citizens.

As can easily be deduced from the difficulties encountered, Montreal did not fare particularly well on either the planning or the governance side of the exercise. In fact, the Olympic saga contributed more than it benefited from an effective planning and governance system as it showed that a more transparent and rational urban regime was not a luxury for a city with such ambitions.

City Planning in Pre- and Post-Olympic Montreal

Much of the blame for the organizational and financial difficulties encountered by the Montreal Games has been put on the overall planning process (or lack of it), with enough blame available to cover all those involved and not just the Montreal COJO. For example, the COJO is often singled out for having waited until 1973 to present its first global *proforma* budget and for the fact that no cost constraints were ever put on Monsieur Taillibert who was never asked to submit anything more than sketches for the realization of his future masterwork.

Published in late 1980, the detailed report of the Quebec Government Commission of Inquiry on the costs of the Twenty-First Olympics apparently was of some use to the Los Angeles and subsequent COJOs (OCOGs) which have managed to forgo some of the most astonishing excesses of the Montreal managerial experience. Yet there is another aspect to the planning story of the Montreal Olympics, that of the urban and city planning *per se*. If Barcelona is to be considered as the best example of an Olympic city benefiting from a strong urban planning tradition, Montreal 1976 was city planning's worst nightmare. It is not so much that the city planning process was ill-adapted (as in the case of Moscow), too centrally-decided (as in Seoul) or purely elite-oriented (Atlanta), rather that it simply did not exist. In the truly entrepreneurial and 'visionary' style which was his own, Mayor Drapeau had always strongly rejected even the idea of city planning arguing that all his great 'accomplishments' – the Metro, the new downtown, Expo 67 – had been conducted outside any formal planning process. Under no circumstances, he argued, would Montreal limit its own development in order to follow technocratic and bureaucratic constraints.

No one at the IOC complained of the lack of a formal City Plan for Montreal, much less of the lack of a democratic input in this plan or in the entire Olympic process. In fact, the absence of a City Plan and a City Planning Board came in handy when it was time to decide on the location of core infrastructure or the reassignment of city facilities. In fact, the *Plan Général des Installations Olympiques* came to be presented by the Mayor as *the* Plan for the Montreal of the future. On a few occasions, when asked to detail his vision of the future of Montreal, the Mayor allowed himself to speculate on the idea of transforming Montreal into a permanent Olympic city by integrating the Olympic ideals, as defined by Pierre de Coubertin, into both the form and the fabric of the city. When a few heroic city-councillors – no doubt avid golfers – objected to the elimination of the Municipal Golf Course and its transformation into an Olympic site (north of the Olympic Stadium) the Mayor simply replied that he did not play golf and that it was not an Olympic sport and did not figure in the future plans of the city.

Clearly, the absence of a Comprehensive City Plan had a detrimental impact on the Olympic planning process itself and, by extension, on the entire Olympic operation. It meant that the COJO faced no constraint of any sort and that all city installations were there for the taking. As is often the case in similar situations, since the COJO could do anything, it ended up doing nothing and, in the end, doing anything to catch up for lost time.

Very rapidly, it became clear to many inside and outside the City Administration that this was indeed not the way to prepare for an Olympics and certainly not the way to run a city. Unfortunately, the Mayor, especially during the first few years after Montreal's successful bid (roughly from 1970 to 1974), could count on the blind support of both the Federal and Provincial governments since both levels of government had actively supported the Mayor during the pseudo-terrorist events of 1970. For Pierre Trudeau, the Liberal Prime Minister of Canada and Robert Bourassa, the Liberal Premier of Quebec, Mayor Drapeau, although somewhat difficult to manage, was a staunch ally who had shown strength in his campaign to eradicate the 'separatist' and 'leftist' threat. Since the first criticisms of the Mayor's way of doing things came from the Parti Québécois and associated left wing groups, they carried precious little weight, especially since the Mayor was particularly adept at dividing the two groups. He enjoyed pointing out to the French-speaking population that any criticism of the Olympics and of his stewardship was but an English plot against Quebec while reminding Anglophone citizens that to criticise the Games would contribute to a victory of the 'Séparatistes'. After the Munich incidents, the anti-terrorist argument of the Mayor became particularly convincing following the Parti Québécois traditional pro-Palestinian and leftist stand.

Very rapidly, however, the Olympic debacle reached Olympian proportions and in the 1974 municipal election, the local opposition party gained its first seats and began successfully to harass the Mayor on his almost dictatorial conduct of civic affairs. The absence of a Comprehensive Plan reached almost mythical proportion as the Opposition came to blame all problems, from the most structural – the pre-eminence of Toronto – to the most daily ones – potholes and snow removal – on the absence of a Comprehensive Urban Plan. Montreal, they argued, was apparently the only city in the World without one.[14]

An unexpected aspect of the fallout from the Montreal Olympic experience has been the almost obsessive attention given to citizen involvement in the bids of other Canadian cities for Olympic status. In fact, the preoccupation with community involvement in the planning and staging of Olympic Games originated with the 1988 Winter Games in Calgary whose success was attributed to the 95 per cent rate of satisfaction expressed by citizens, a level of support which translated itself in an unprecedented number of volunteers and the festive atmosphere which characterized the Games (Hiller, 1990). Probably the real impact of the Montreal experience came with Toronto's attempt to stage the 1996 Olympics and the almost perfect scores of that city on both the community involvement and democratic participation level. As celebrated by observers, Toronto's democratic performance was above any reproach and only the fact that other cities were not forced to show the same track record has been said to explain the failure of Toronto. If only this high level of undemocratic attitudes among its rivals could have been detected in time, Toronto it was argued, would have won over Atlanta. According to Lenskyj (1992), even the decision to award the Games to Sydney was unfair since that country's performance on the aboriginal issue and the quality of the Sydney community involvement was far behind that of Toronto.[15]

All major hurdles in the Olympic drama have an important impact on local governance, that is, on the ways local governments and authorities operate.[16] The impact is compounded in the case of federations (Canada, Australia, Switzerland, and Germany) or quasi-federal systems (Spain) by the multiplicity and the intricacies of the constitutional architecture. The decision to present a city's candidacy and obtain the official support of the national Olympic Committee, selection by the IOC, organizing and holding the Games and, to a lesser extent, organizing the post-Games management of the infrastructure involve complex negotiations between local actors themselves and central authorities, civil society, and interest groups.

As a rule, the ability to work together and to bring everyone aboard the Olympic coalition is an important ingredient in getting selected by both the national and international Olympic structures, probably more so in the latter case since the national selection process is more influenced by political considerations at the national and sub-national levels. In their comparative analysis of the mega-event strategy of three recent American Olympic Cities (Los Angeles, Atlanta and Salt Lake City), Greg Andranovitch and his colleagues provide us with insightful understanding of how the three local governance regimes help shape the candidacy of each respective city and of the management model used by each to organize the Olympics (Andranovich *et al.*, 2001). According to the authors, all three bids were the product of regime politics with the city's business elite in the driving seat but nevertheless seeking the endorsement of elected officials to provide public legitimacy. In all three cases, this business group was successful in incorporating the visions of city leaders and the specific agendas of local stakeholders who felt they had little choice but to go along in order to share in the benefits. Without the active backing of local officials, support from local groups would have been difficult to achieve and in both Salt Lake City and Atlanta this support made the difference when referenda were held. Although they were not entirely successful in imitating the purely private entrepreneurial model put forward by Los Angeles in running the Games, both Atlanta and Salt Lake City came close to it.

By looking at the Olympics through the prism of the urban regime which contributed in shaping its bid and organization, we can move past the usual clichés on the 'capitalist' nature of the Los Angeles Games or the public-private-partnership prevalent in Salt Lake City. The question then becomes: what kind of impact did the local governance regime have on the Games themselves and, indirectly, on the Games' contribution to local development? Clearly, the model used for Los Angeles pushed in the direction of ever-more spartan Games. Paradoxically, the fact that the Games did not benefit from any public funding also made it difficult for the local authorities to obtain satisfaction on certain elements deemed to be politically sensitive as when Mayor Tom Bradley insisted that the Los Angeles Organizing Committee set aside the objections of local residents and install a rowing basin in the San Fernando Valley. Such a decision, which the Mayor had sought to obtain long before the Olympics, would have allowed the city to apply for grants from existing federal programmes and help redevelop part of the area. Since neither the city nor the Federal government was willing to provide additional financial support, the Organizing Committee had little choice but to find a different site and the Mayor was forced to concede defeat.

Yet, what of the other way around: what impact did the Olympics have on these three urban regimes and indirectly on the way Los Angeles, Atlanta and Salt Lake City govern themselves? Los Angeles went smoothly and even turned a sizable profit, a majority of which was returned to the development of local youth sport programmes. Four new facilities were built, all privately financed and approximately $145 million went directly to local and state authorities. The construction of the airport was speeded up and the Games are said to have contributed $9.6 billions to the Southern California economy. By contrast, the political fallouts were less impressive. In the very short run, Mayor Bradley benefited from the successful and 'profitable' Games. Unfortunately he had very little to show for his involvement. It takes a substantial amount of 'pork' for 'pork barrel' politics to operate.

Against that background, we can note that, except for a brief interval (1957–1960), Jean Drapeau served as Montreal's Mayor from 1954 until 1986. Up to the end, his urban vision was exclusively made up of large-scale projects of which the Olympics were to be the final step before the 'mother of all projects', moving the United Nations to Montreal, had a chance to materialize. Throughout this period, the tireless Mayor was hard at work to realize his dream of 'One Island, One City' and thus replace the 28 municipal administrations now coexisting on the Island into one powerful city government, capable of standing up to the Quebec government which has full responsibility for municipal administration. Fearful of his autocratic manners and strongly attached to their respective local identity, suburban Mayors always thwarted attempts at amalgamation and prevented Drapeau from realizing his dream. The best that he could achieve was the establishment of the Montreal Urban Community (MUC), where Montreal had a majority of seats (including on its Executive Council) and whose unelected President represented no challenge to Montreal. Responsibilities for territorial planning, the police, food inspection and evaluation were given to the new structure (borrowed from a singular concept in France). The MUC came on line in 1970 and, although clearly a set-back for the Mayor, was used by him as a supporting argument to boost the candidacy of Montreal against those of Los Angeles and Moscow. As Mayor Drapeau carefully argued – not always with total respect for the facts – the MUC formula provided Montreal with the best of both worlds, a less decentralized governance structure than in Los Angeles and a less centralized one than in Moscow.

Apparently the argument worked as Montreal's candidacy suffered no local dissenting voice. Worried that Montreal could try and pass along to them some of the spiralling costs of staging the Olympics, suburban Mayors set up the

Conference of Suburban Mayors in order to present a united front against the central city. In fact, the Olympic fiasco, by increasing animosity between local municipalities prevented the emergence of any intra-island grouping or even region to settle on the North or South Shore. In short, Montreal came out weaker not stronger from the Olympic exercise.

One important set of collateral damage concerned relationships between Francophone and Anglophone in Montreal and for that matter throughout Quebec. The 1976 Games were regarded as a strictly Montreal affair, a largely French-speaking city, and for many Anglophones the financial fiasco simply confirmed their image of Francophones and heralded of what would happen if they were ever put in charge of a country of their own. The fact that the Parti Québécois gained power on 15 November 1976 was considered by many a by-product of the Olympic fiasco. Thirty years later most of the issues which came to the surface at the time of the 1976 Olympics are still there to be solved, be they those of Anglo-Franco relationships, public housing or the best way to organize local governance of the island of Montreal.

Conclusion

If staging the Olympics were the equivalent of a Triathlon, it is doubtful if Montreal would have accumulated the required number of points in the city marketing, urban development and local governance competition to make it to the finals. In this sense the Montreal experience serves to remind us that some of the clichés regarding human behaviour often have a solid base in reality. It does indeed happen that if something can go wrong, it will and that some cities, like individuals, are known to reach their level of incompetence more rapidly than others.[17]

On a less philosophical level, one lesson from the Montreal Games stands above all others and that is the importance of the strategic campaign orchestrated by cities to win the bidding war. This was a battle of the 'winner takes all' variety and where the 'good guys' do not always win. Nevertheless, the way the war is conducted and the victory achieved often come back to haunt, with a vengeance in the case of Montreal, the organizers of the Games. The Montreal bid was a one-man affair conducted with the secrecy appropriate for a military operation. There were no campaigns to mobilize the local population, no army of spokespersons ready to testify, no business interests willing to lend their know-how in return for 'future considerations'. Montreal was, above all these commercial and often populist considerations, probably closer to the ideal of the Coubertin Olympic than any other set of Games, but when the going got a bit rougher, none of these allies from the first hour could be counted upon. Worst still, having worked hard to make sure that artists, intellectuals and associated progressive forces be arrested at the times of the FLQ crisis of 1970, Drapeau was left with very little support among the very people with whom his appeal for more humanist and universal Games could resonate. Apparently the lesson as to the importance of the Pre-

Games manoeuvring has tended to be lost in recent years. For example, one could have imagined the open warfare between Mayor Delanoe and President Chirac if Paris had succeeded in overcoming the respective *faux-pas* of the two leaders and been awarded the Games over London and Madrid.

A second lesson concerns the very idea of an Olympic urban legacy and some of its unintended effects. As expected, there has always been some disagreement as to the 'real' (as opposed to 'imaginary') legacy of specific Olympics. For example, Atlanta is considered by many a good example of low-impact Games (in the same league as the Los Angeles one) with little impact on the city, while others insist that the city performed extremely well in terms of sports facilities and urban amenities (Essex and Chalkey, 1998), while still a third group concludes that the new facilities only serve to deepen the divide between rich and poor as they tended to stay away from the poorest areas of town (French and Disher, 1997). In Sydney and Athens, both Olympic Committees went all out in making sure the urban legacy of 'their' Olympics went unrivalled and that the public everywhere be informed about it. So successful was Sydney that the IOC itself recognized that this issue of legacy was a determining factor in the exponential growth in the number of countries, athletes, journalists and officials participating in the Games and in the willingness of National Committees to submit bids for future Games. However, as recognized by the Pound Committee (Pound, 1994), set up to study the exponential growth of Olympic budgeting, aspiring cities are in a bind inasmuch as competing cities are increasingly judged by the quality of the investments they are willing to make in sport and urban infrastructure, a criterion which not only pushes Olympics up the financial pole but also increases the risk of going overboard. To insist on environmental-friendly Games and even sustainable infrastructures will unlikely put an end to a spiral which began in Montreal.

One would have expected the difficulties around the Montreal Olympic Stadium to have prompted an intense debate as to what kind of stadium Olympic cities need. Until Sydney, the stadium question remained a non-issue as all contestants made sure to mention that their own proposal would avoid all the mistakes of Montreal. The Atlanta case is an interesting one inasmuch as it was decided that an entirely new facility was to be constructed while satisfying the requirements of its future use as a baseball stadium.[18] Sydney was awarded the 2000 Games in 1994 and it was decided that what urban planning had done for the success of the 1992 Games, high-quality 'ecological' architecture could do for Sydney. In the end, the success of the Sydney Games seems to have been more favourable to an open debate about the future of sport and Olympic Architecture than the experience of Montreal had proven.[19] Unfortunately that debate came too late for the Athens Games, which again went in for a 'monumental' Olympic Stadium of the 'grand statement' variety.

Finally, there is the uncomfortable question: 'so what?'. True, the Montreal Games were an urban catastrophe which few other cities have had to endure, but apparently, the city survived without too much difficulty. Mayor Drapeau has gone and so have the baseball team and Mirabel airport, but the city's cultural, economic, social and even political scene is thriving and, with four major universities, Montreal has become one of the leading academic and research centres in North America, while the downtown area would be unrecognizable to the 1976 visitors. Anglos and Francos still do not mix much, but are happy to have two cultural scenes to choose from. In fact, none of the positive things now associated with Montreal – its multicultural flavour, its four-month all-out festival period, a vibrant and cosmopolitan artistic scene – can in any way be associated with the 1976 Olympics.

Notes

1.   This chapter is part of an on-going research project on 'Architecture and Politics in the New Glocal Age'. Financial support from the Social Sciences Research Council of Canada is gratefully acknowledged.

2.   Not to mention that in 1976 Canada attained the dubious achievement of being the first host country not to win a gold medal at its own Games, a feat repeated at the Calgary 1988 Winter Olympics.

3.   In fact most of the 1900 'laws' found on the 'Murphy's Laws and Corollaries' site (http://rooso.epfl.ch/dm/murphy.html) can be said to apply to the Montreal Olympics – a telling fact in itself – including the less known 'Enough Already Law' which postulates that the more you run over a dead cat, the flatter it gets.

4.   The competition included Madrid, Detroit, Montreal and Munich which was selected in the first round. Later on the Mayor was to acknowledge one serious mistake in his first Olympic campaign, his last minute promise to provide free meals and lodging for all athletes, a promise which was judged 'so shocking' and contrary to the spirit of the Olympics.

5.   Bad memories rarely die. In May 2006, much of the role of Vancouver in the years before the 1976 Olympics resurfaced in Montreal newspapers when it was revealed that Vancouver had asked both the Federal and Provincial government for a minimum additional grant of $90 million to stage the 'modest' and 'self-financing' Winter Games of 2010.

6.   In the end, the Mayor's calculus proved correct. In the first round Moscow obtained 28 votes, Los Angeles 17 and Montreal 25. In the second round, Montreal managed to attract all 17 LA votes (Purcell and McKenna, 1980).

7.   Luck and timing are also important ingredients in any successful bid. In May 1970, it was still possible to argue that Montreal was free from the political and social tensions which affected the rest of the world. Six months later, an improvised commando unit belonging to the so-called *Front de Libération du Quebec* kidnapped James Cross, a British diplomat stationed in Montréal, and murdered Pierre Laporte, Minister of Labour in the Quebec government.

8.   The posters were finally produced by a group known as the 'Artists Athletes Coalition' set up precisely to counter the overwhelming Québécois overtone of the arts programme. As reported by Bruce Kidd, a Canadian runner turned academic, the Canada Council director had only one condition: 'We love your proposal and we're prepared to give you twice as much money as you've asked for, as long as you agree to one condition – Canada and not Montreal has got to go on top' (Kidd, 1992a, p. 161.)

9.   The most recent 'update' of the economic impact analysis of the Vancouver Winter and Paralympic Games (Intervistas, 2002) is an 85 page document complete with graphs, figures, tables and matrices.

10.   See Renson and den Hollander (1977). The Antwerp games initiated numerous other

traditions including arguments as to who should pay for the infrastructure upkeep and the overall deficit.

11. In 2004, the baseball team, the Montreal Expos, folded and moved to Washington, DC.

12. This rather austere complex is named after Claude Robillard, the first Director of City Planning of Montreal, who died in 1968 and was known to stand up to Mayor Drapeau.

13. For a spirited defence of this 'unfinished cathedral', see Morin (1997). For a more technical attack on the Stadium, see COCO (1980). The rebuttal from the architect in charge of the project is to be found in his memoirs (Taillibert, 1977).

14. A Development Plan was finally adopted in 1992, 4 years after the Municipal Opposition had finally replaced Mayor Drapeau and his Civic Party.

15. If Mayor Drapeau were still alive, he would surely point out that good guys often finish second and that too much democracy does not always carry the day. Competition for mega-events has now become so intense and of the 'winner takes all' variety – a very un-Coubertin attitude – that cities that 'lose' are quick to suggest that they are also 'winners'. On the Toronto, Manchester and Cape Town 'failed' bids, see Kidd (1992b), Hiller (2000) and Cochrane et al. (1996).

16. This section will not consider what was perhaps the most dramatic and direct governance impact of the 1976 Olympic Games, the election in November 1976, of the Parti Québécois.

17. See note 3.

18. Times are changing. In Atlanta the main controversy has not been the stadium which was entirely built with private support, but whether or not the baseball team should abandon its name of 'Atlanta Braves', a reference to American Indians, in favour of a more politically-correct one.

19. Even the Sydney Stadium has come under some scrutiny, although in a subdued and polite manner – not particularly Australian qualities. See, among others, Searle (2002).

Chapter 13

Barcelona 1992

Francisco-Javier Monclús

The trick in Barcelona was quality first, quantity after…

Pasqual Maragall[1]

The profound urban transformation experienced by Barcelona over the last 20 years is linked, to a large extent, to the 1992 Olympic Games. The case of Barcelona has been the focus of international attention and has been specifically analysed from different perspectives by economists, geographers or town planners. On many occasions, its 'exemplary' nature has been referred to as the 'Barcelona model', which 'for urban transformation … has been a reference for other cities since the mid-'80s – the outstanding example of a certain way of improving cities' (Marshall, 2004, p. 1). It must be said that this has been a common theme in most of the existing literature, particularly that originating locally and prepared by the leading figures of the Olympic experience (Barcelona City Council, 1983, 1987*a*, 1987*b*, 1996, 1999*a*, 1999*b*). To these viewpoints are added those of international critics, who have interpreted this unique experience as one of the most successful in the history of the Olympic Games (e.g. Chalkley and Essex, 1999). The 'Barcelona model', a much discussed and indiscriminately used expression, has been characterized in several ways, depending on the period and the aspect which is considered to be most representative of town planning in Barcelona (Monclús, 2003). For some, it would be a way of acting in accordance with the proliferation of specific interventions in public areas, which were undertaken from the beginning of the 1980s. For others, the most outstanding element would be the rebirth of the city with the implementation of a series of strategic urban projects linked to the 1992 Olympic Games.

The reclassification of public spaces and the new urban architecture of Barcelona have attracted the attention of many international critics. Different authors have highlighted the formal dimension of these transformations and the high quality of the public spaces (Buchanan, 1984, 1992; Rowe, 1991, 1997; Sokoloff, 1999; Gehl and Gemzoe, 2001, 2004). From a more strategic perspective, linked to the rebirth of cities and to the significance of events in a growing context of deindustrialization and 'spectacularization' of urban politics, the ability to administer an extraordinary event such as the 1992 Olympic Games, of turning it into a 'lever' and a strategic instrument of urban renewal and recovery, has been highlighted (Borja, 1995; Marshall, 1996; Portas, 1998; Ward, 2002). In any case, the opinion appears to be widespread that the true success of the Barcelona Olympic Games was the transformation experienced by the city, through a series of actions that would normally have taken decades and which were introduced in just 6 years. In these perceptions, the enterprise of the political class, as well as the 'creative planning' of the experts and the spirit of citizen cooperation, is particularly noteworthy.

In this chapter, Barcelona's Olympic experience will be looked at from a perspective associated with the debate on the impact of major events. The first part refers to the background, origins and criteria that were the basis of the candidature from the 1970s; the second, the development of the Olympic programme and the associated urban actions during the 1980s; and the third, its subsequent impact in the urban sphere and the catalysing effects in other urban projects. The final section considers the benefits and limitations of the Olympic operation, as 14 years after the Games it is possible to have a historical perspective, although it is not easy to assess an urban strategy which still represents the foundations of present actions in the city.

From *Reconstruction* to Urban *Marketing*

An important question is that of continuity and change in urban strategies. According to some interpretations of the Olympic Games, the methods of 'progressive' intervention, of the first years of democratic recovery (in the first half of the 1980s), would have continued. Other more 'continuist' viewpoints regard the Olympic Games as a period in which many of the plans and projects designed in the 1960s and 1970s took shape. What is important to point out is that the profound modification of the urban structure of Barcelona associated with the Olympic Games is not just a result of the new proposals arising in the preparatory process of the Games.

The '92 programme' can be understood as a bid to re-launch the city in the context of economic and political crisis which Barcelona experienced from the mid-1970s until the mid-1980s; a context in which strategies adopted by other European cities, affected to a different degree by deindustrialization and economic globalization processes, were also placed. Some interpretations recognize two differentiated stages: prior to and following the Olympic nomination in 1986. In the first period (1979–1986), the 'progressive' nature of 'recovery' planning of a city with large urban deficits is stressed. In the second (1986–1992), 'strategic' urban planning would have been imposed with greater emphasis on determining factors of returns and less interest in urban improvement actions (Montaner, 1990; Montaner and Muxí, 2002).

Although to a certain degree these stages correspond to a change in the economic and urban cycle affecting many European cities, in the case of Barcelona – as in many other Spanish cities – the recovery of democracy must also be taken into consideration, particularly following the municipal elections in 1979. In any case, the debate on these stages and the different versions of the so-called 'Barcelona model' is not merely a formal debate, but expresses different interpretations of its profound nature. Compared with those who associate the experience with changes induced by globalization and covering a longer period of history, some see a greater continuity between the different historical stages. For example, the anthropologist Manuel Delgado (2005) suggests that 'the vision of Barcelona as a stage', as characterized particularly by the Olympic Games, began with the first Universal Exhibition of 1888. To some extent, it seems clear that the Olympic Games initiative can also be recognized as part of a long tradition in the pragmatic use of major events: the Universal Exhibition of 1888 (García-Espuche et al., 1991), the International Exhibition of 1929 and, possibly, the failed Exhibition project for 1982.

Without going back too far in time, it is possible to find some continuity with previous projects. The attempt to hold an International Exhibition in 1982 is particularly noteworthy (presented in 1973). To a certain extent, this would be the case of the Greater Barcelona Project which was defined in the 'Barcelona 2000 Project' led by Josep Porcioles, the mayor who determined the destiny of the city for more than 15 years during the Franco regime (from 1957 to 1973)[2] and who

Figure 13.1. Plan de la Ribera 1964 (COAC).

launched a strategy aimed at obtaining state investment for Barcelona (Barcelona City Council, 1971). The proposal had been approved in 1970 by the Council of Ministers and was developed during the following three years with the support of Juan Antonio Samaranch (then a lawyer but later the influential president of the IOC). The intense criticism of the Expo 82 project, 'Porcioles' favourite municipal project in the final stage of his mandate', condemned what was seen as its speculative nature, compared with the central argument and 'leitmotiv' put forward by its defenders: 'that the Expo will be a driving force in the resolution of our urban development problems' (Alibés et al., 1975). Although the proposal for this International Exhibition never came to fruition – among other reasons, because of its origins in the period of political conflict at the end of the Franco regime – 'it gave way to important urban transformation proposals and the design of important road networks' (*Ibid.*). Therefore, it is not unreasonable to relate this strategy to the different attempts to promote key projects through international events, even going back to the Greater Barcelona discourse, formulated at the beginning of the twentieth century (Monclús, 2000) and redrafted at the beginning of the 1970s (Moreno and Vazquez-Montalbán, 1991).

Without considering the profound differences of this 'pre-democratic' project for an Exhibition in 1982 with that of hosting the Olympics of 1992, it is important to stress that in the 1970s diverse hypotheses of urban transformation were formulated that would later be key parts of the 1992 programme. This not only affected infrastructure improvements that would contribute to the modernization of the road network but also more aesthetic urban projects, such as those aimed at 'opening the city to the sea'. Among the latter, the so-called 'Riverside Plan', devised in 1966 with the objective of revaluing the waterfront, stands out. It was frustrated due to powerful opposition from the citizens of Barcelona (although designed by Antonio Bonet Castellana, a prestigious modern architect with works in Barcelona and Argentina).[3] The fact that it was decided 20 years later to locate the Olympic Village in this area is at the heart of the debate presented here: to what extent was it these plans rather than other, very different plans that became a reality in the democratic period during the 1980s (Moreno and Vazquez-Montalbán, 1991, p. 101)?

It must be remembered that Barcelona has experienced a profound crisis in its urban growth model since the 1970s. The failure of the Greater Barcelona idea is relative, although it is true that an agreement between different visions and interests was imposed. This agreement was translated into the new urban development plan for the city, the PGM (Pla General Metropolità – General Metropolitan Plan) of 1974–1976. The situation in Barcelona in the mid-1970s matched the explosive urban growth and 'modernization' experienced in Spain during the years of Franco's dictatorship and 'economic development policy'. The industrial city. which in 1930 had one million inhabitants. had become a metropolitan region of more than four million, in which extensive industrialization experienced a profound crisis. This was the period of 'Grey Barcelona' – the city of 'development

Figure 13.2. Barcelona Harbour, 1965 (M. Guárdia, 2002).

policy', of 'informal' growth, of 'peripheral' developments, and shortfalls in urban facilities, all set against a background of growing of speculation (Guardia *et al.*, 1994).

With the return to municipal democracy, but in direct response to these circumstances, the city councils began to consider solutions to the problems created by the absence of strict urban development policies, with overcrowding and shortage of land for infrastructure and facilities in the city. It is important to point out that the profound political and social transformation following the death of Franco in 1975 coincided with an economic crisis that seriously affected the industrial foundations of Barcelona. The fact that many of the technicians who had been working in public institutions since the 1960s were assuming key positions was also influential. In short, the superimposition of the economic, political and urban development crisis enabled the PGM to be approved in 1976.

This Plan was the framework on which actions for the recuperation of public spaces and facilities were defined over the following years. At this time, there was a conflict of interests centred on two aspects: reclaiming land for green areas and amenities; and proposals for changing road layouts. With the approval of the PGM, an important land reserve was obtained (critical for the 1992 Olympic operations) and more than 56 hectares, freed by former industries, were acquired. In fact the change in the PGM enabled areas dedicated to Olympic projects to increase fivefold and for parks and green areas to expand by 250 per cent. The development of the road system (ring roads) prompted new growth, although thoroughfares were also common. The PGM involved an important agreement between, on the one hand, the more 'pro-development' visions – with large-scale road layouts – and those of 'local movements', on the other, which were joined by the 'progressive technocrats'. From here, some consider there to be certain continuities between the urban development of the 'development policy' years and that initiated at the end of the 1980s. In any case, it seems evident that the democratic City Council continued with this policy of responding to the serious urban development shortfalls in a climate that continued to be characterized by widespread economic crisis (Esteban, 1999; Calavita and Ferrer, 2000).

During the 1980s, a series of economic, political and urban development processes coincided. The first, as noted, was that of economic crisis. The second was the democratization of the municipal government with the advent of a left wing majority in the elections of 1979, 1983, 1987 and 1991. The third was the adoption of new urban development strategies, backed by the PGM and new urban projects. In this context, a programme for the creation of public spaces and small local amenities was established. The availability of land occupied by former industries, railways or port installations enabled their re-use for new leisure facilities, parks or amenities. It is not difficult to find similarities between the ideas that dominated Barcelona's most distinctive schemes in the 1980s and those of other cities, particularly Paris's 'Grand Projects' and those linked to the IBA in Berlin (Rowe, 1997; Sokoloff, 1999; Monclús, 2003).

The so-called 'culture of the urban project' was highlighted in the City Council's first publications, albeit being presented empirically. However, it is in the well-known book by Oriol Bohigas,[4] Director of Planning between 1980 and 1984, significantly titled *Reconstruction of Barcelona*, in which the principles of a new architectural and contextualized form of urban planning are put forward (Bohigas, 1985). In this book, the efficacy of small-scale projects of urban reform as an alternative to the abstraction of conventional planning was vindicated. The message was simple but strong: to overcome the limitations of planning, one has to give way to architecture. At the same time, the public spaces of the historic city, the squares and streets are recovered. It is not necessary to think in literal terms about the adoption of the principles of the 'reconstruction of the European city'. However, a number of convergent elements are clear. Above all, understanding the city to be essentially architecture is required, as well as an extraordinary emphasis on its morphology. This conception also struck a chord with the visions of the fragmentary construction of the city or 'collage city' put forward by Colin Rowe (Rowe and Koetter, 1978), or with the ideas that dominated the transformation of other cities during the 1980s. Bohigas himself cited Berlin as the clearest reference: a city in which 'a reconstruction of the centre starting from the absolute respect for the road and the traditional form of the street' (Bohigas, 1985, p. 118). It was a strategy based on the relative effectiveness of the specific project compared to the abstraction of the traditional general plan.

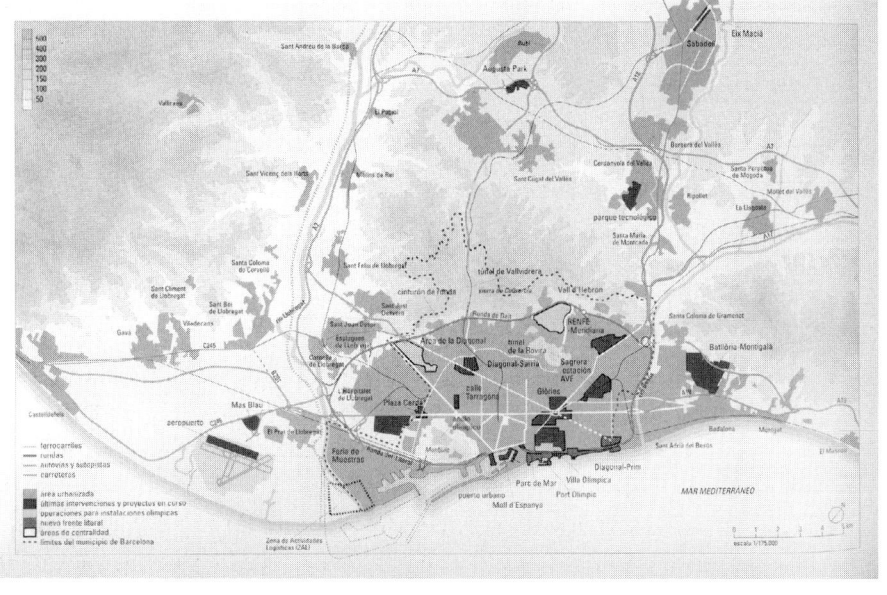

Figure 13.3. Barcelona urban growth and strategical projects (1980–1992) (M. Guárdia *et al.,*
1994).

Based on these principles, development in Barcelona focused on a series of
schemes that sought to recover public spaces. These schemes, developed within
areas in continuity with the existing neighbourhoods, involved more than 150
projects in parks, squares and amenities during the 1980s. However, it comes as
no surprise that a 'reconstruction' model was promoted in these years of scarce
resources, with modest interventions of a public nature with regard to open spaces
and amenities (Barcelona City Council, 1983).

This entire experience led the School of Urban Design at Harvard University
to award Barcelona the 1991 Prince of Wales Prize for architecture in recognition
of the modernity and rationality which had guided the planning of the new spaces
created during the first years of municipal democracy. Prior to this, in 1987, the
city had achieved the Harvard Prize for its good design. In 1999, the Royal Institute
of British Architects' Gold Medal for Architecture was given to the politicians and
professional architects of the City Council, for their 'commitment to planning',
including 'the combination of spectacular urban projects and of small-scale
improvements to squares and streets'. In addition, the widely publicised report
Towards an Urban Renaissance (DETR, 1999; see Hebbert, 2000), prepared by a
group of experts and co-ordinated by Richard Rogers at the request of the then
newly-elected Labour government, contained significant references to the case of
Barcelona (see also chapter 9). In the report, attention is focused on two types of
planning intervention: the capacity to regenerate or treat central spaces through
small operations of urban reform; and the 'strategic' projects that characterize later
intervention. Of particular significance is the fact that Pasqual Maragall, the former

mayor of Barcelona (between 1982 and 1997), was asked to provide the Foreword to that publication (Maragall, 1999a). The message was clear: 'It is critical to understand that improving public spaces is relevant to solving social and economic problems'. However, Maragall stressed the leap to a more ambitious strategy in the mid-1980s, when the initial small-scale operations were followed by large-scale strategic urban planning projects: 'The trick in Barcelona was quality first, quantity after' (see the epigram at the start of this chapter).

From Quality to Quantity

In this context of economic crisis and 'strategic urban development', the candidature of Barcelona to host the Olympic Games was launched in 1981. The shift 'from quality to quantity' evolved at that time, with the Games as a pretext. It was a strategy to attract public and private investment (therefore, not so different to the Expo 82, although now in a democratic version), but also an instrument capable of generating consensus and action in a depressed economy. All this in a few years in which the transition to a service-based, rather than an industrial-based, economy was assumed to be inevitable.

In 1981, the Mayor of Barcelona, Narcís Serra, and the Deputy Mayors (Josep Miquel Abad, Josep Maria Cullell and Pasqual Maragall), began to carry out a study of the possibility of holding the Olympic Games in the city. From the debate which took place on 30 June 1981 among the representatives of these parties, the first agreement was adopted unanimously by the new democratic council: namely, to present the Barcelona Olympic Candidature again.[5] Work began on the ideas and dossiers for the first Candidature and by 1982, the 'Cuyas Report' or the Preliminary Project had already been drafted. Over the following four years, the '92 Programme' was drawn up.

The choice of Barcelona in October 1986 emerged against intense competition. Eight years earlier, Los Angeles had been the sole candidate. For the 1988 Games, Seoul only had to compete with Nagoya. In contrast, there were six candidates for the 1992 Games, among them cities of importance such as Paris, Amsterdam and Brisbane. The Olympic nomination marked the difference between Barcelona and other Spanish and European cities, which were then also experiencing a change in their urban dynamics as a result of widespread economic recovery. However, when Barcelona obtained the nomination, the economic circumstances had already changed, with full integration in the European Economic Community (which reached completion in 1993) and a climate favourable for the rebirth of the city. The Olympic euphoria was soon unleashed with the exhibition of projects under way.[6] By 1986, it was not difficult to realize that the urban development strategies that characterized the early 1980s were giving way to others with similar, but more ambitious, criteria. As Bohigas (1999) later explained 'the new urban development programme corresponded to simple and rapidly applied premises'. Deep down, they were the same conditions that had been applied in the specific actions at the beginning of the 1980s. With reference to the planning of the four Olympic areas, three fundamental criteria were used. First of all:

> locate the four main Olympic areas within the municipality of Barcelona, in strategic points – the edges of the consolidated city and the first periphery – which will directly affect the problematic areas and at the same time accelerate the surrounding osmotic regeneration processes. Secondly, apply the same methods in this area as those which had been used in the specific actions of the neighbourhoods; in other words, the formula for urban projects. Thirdly, ensure that all the buildings and public spaces constructed have a clear use following the Games and represent fundamental pieces in the transformation of the city. (*Ibid.*)

The four Olympic areas were therefore designed and presented, with qualitative criteria similar to those of the previous small projects, but incorporating objectives corresponding to the new scale of the Olympic urban development interventions. One such objective was to contribute to continuous urban promotion and the creation of new centralities through these four areas.

In reality, two key areas were considered for the sporting facilities (with a third of less importance) and a strategic location for the Olympic Village. The main venue was planned in the Montjuïc Mountain. In 1929, a park with cultural and sporting facilities had been planned here. The second Olympic area was that of 'Valle de Hebrón', which was planned in a semi-developed area of the first periphery, surrounded by diverse amenities, a strategy in which the wish for urban

Figure 13.4. Olympic Ring (M. Guárdia, 2002).

regeneration was clearly shown.[7] In addition to these two venues, and in contrast to the aforementioned, another was reorganized around the most prestigious route of the city – the 'Diagonal' – with the objective of taking advantage of the existing installations. Finally, the Olympic Village was located on the waterfront, with the objective of its regeneration and the 'opening of the city to the sea'.

The Preliminary Project listed the venues for the competitions and described the Barcelona Olympic Games. In the first phase, the general criteria had to be developed and the process of transformation of the city to host the event specified. The Candidature Preliminary Project took six months to draft, and during that time a team of specialists outlined the matters that would have to be dealt with: the sporting and technological requirements, town planning, residences and financing. Experiences from previous Olympics and contacts with the organizers of the Los Angeles Games were a primary source of information and comparison. The conclusions of the Preliminary Project followed the line traced in *Primeres Aproximacions*. It was stressed that the figures for the budget were merely indicative, corresponding to detailed estimates based on data from previous Games. They were therefore a useful reference point for the administration when it came to estimating the financing for the infrastructure required to organize the Games. There was also an analysis of the cost to the city in comparison with that of previous host cities and the conclusion reached was that it was within its means. The Preliminary Project defined fundamental questions for the later development of the Candidature and the organization of Barcelona 1992: the demarcation of the four Olympic areas (Montjuïc, Diagonal, Vall d'Hebron and Parc de Mar); the participation of other cities as venues for sports competitions; the establishment of a mixed model of financing, which included contributions from public administrations and the support of private enterprise; and the programming of a cultural Olympiad lasting four years (COOB, 1992, p. 237).

The 'areas' were an attempt to concentrate a series of activities at sites which, in the tradition of the Olympic parks, would provide suitable conditions for holding the great festival of the Games. At the same time, the intention was to avoid packing all the sports facilities into a single place, which would have meant that they were useful for the sixteen days of the Olympic competition, but would have been of little social value afterwards. Another consideration was ease of access to all the venues, which were located at reasonable distances to avoid transport problems and other inconveniences for the Olympic Family and spectators. The competitions in 19 of the 24 planned sports would be held in the four chosen areas. The areas were all near junctions with main city thoroughfares and easily accessible by public transport. All four were in a circle with a radius of 5 kilometres and travelling time between them would not exceed twenty minutes, either by public or private transport. The Dossier stated that of the 37 competition venues required for the Games, 27 had already been built (of which five would need to be converted and seven adapted for the occasion), five were under construction and five more at the planning stage (COOB, 1992, p. 271).

Figure 13.5. Olympic Village and Parc de Mar area (M. Guárdia *et al.*, 1994).

The most ambitious and innovative urban project associated with the Olympic Games was the regeneration of the 'seafront' or 'maritime façade' which, under the slogan of 'opening the city to the sea', was the prime sector for attracting investment (with housing for the Olympic Village through VOSA [Vila Olímpica Societat Anonimà] as part of the Olympic Holding). The aim of the town planning initiatives in this area was to provoke a radical reshaping of the city's entire seafront; not just the Olympic Village sector but also 6 kilometres of coastline immediately to the north. It is important to point out that the decision to locate the Olympic Village on abandoned industrial land was part of a much wider operation, namely, the regeneration of the whole coastline or 'seafront' of Barcelona in line with other international experiences of *waterfronts*. In this way, continuity with previous initiatives can be better understood. In 1987, the redevelopment of the Bosch and Alsina wharf – popularly known as the Moll de la Fusta – and its connection to the area of the old city was the first step in the renovation of the central area of Barcelona's seafront and the beginning of an extensive redevelopment of the old port with the object of turning it into a recreational and sporting area. This process of renewing the city's seafront was complemented by improvements to the district of Barceloneta and the conversion of the old industrial and warehousing zone of Poblenou into a residential area.

Within the strategic plan for the location of the Olympic installations proposed in the Barcelona Candidature, two options were considered for the Olympic Village. In keeping with the aim of building all the facilities on the periphery, somewhere in the suburbs, Vallès would have been the safest and the cheapest bet. In the end, however, it was the opportunity for the city to benefit from the Olympic Village that effectively determined the decision. As McKay (2000, p. 5) noted:

> The site chosen was a practically abandoned industrial triangle, between the curve in the railway line bordering the Parc de la Ciutadella and the diagonal of the Bogatell storm water channel, which meant that the city could finally be opened to the sea. The reward was that, after the Games, Barcelona would have 4.5 kilometres of beaches with an urban front open to the Mediterranean.

The Parc de Mar, the proposed location for the Olympic Village, was undergoing a process of deindustrialization; the beaches were in an extremely degraded state and railway lines separated the district from the sea. The redevelopment of the area changed all this. An alteration in the route of the railway was already envisaged in a project to reorganize the Barcelona railway system, with two new stations planned on the outskirts of the city. The design for the residential area was to follow the pattern of streets in the Eixample, something which would also allow the Diagonal to be extended as far as the sea and would integrate the new area of the Olympic Village into the fabric of the city. Finally, the development of the Poblenou seafront and the construction of the coastal ring road entailed the redesign of the system of main drains. A plan was drawn up in 1988 which covered the municipality of Barcelona and its entire hydrographic area and provided for a 100 kilometre extension of the sewer network.

The Parc de Mar was the district of Barcelona that underwent the greatest change as a result of hosting the Games. The Olympic nomination made it possible to recover more than 100 hectares of industrial land for residential areas and public facilities through a large-scale redevelopment project. The Parc de Mar area contained the Olympic Village, with 2,400 housing units for more than 15,000 people, both athletes and officials, and the Parc de Mar Village, for referees and judges. Competitions for four of the sports in the Barcelona 92 programme were held there: yachting (based in the Olympic harbour), badminton (in the Pavelló de la Mar Bella), table tennis (in the Polisportiu Estació del Nord, 2 kilometres from the Olympic Village, in the Eixample district) and some events of the Basque pelota competition (in the Frontó Colom, in the lower part of the Rambla). The Olympic Village, as noted, was built in an area which shortly before had been occupied by declining industries, separated from the rest of the city and from the sea by two railway lines. This, in turn, restricted access to beaches affected by pollution, caused by an industrial sewer outflow as well as a less polluted ground water drain. The Special Town Plan,[8] approved in June 1986, provided the instrument that made it possible to turn the Olympic Village into a new district, integrated into an urban fabric graced with public spaces and endowed with sports facilities.

The complex operation of transforming the whole of this large area of the city and integrating it into the urban structure implied the execution of a large number of projects, which can be summarized as follows:

- Regeneration of the coast-line and the restructuring of the sewage network.

- Restructuring the railway network, with the elimination of the two lines that crossed the area.

- Construction of the semi-covered stretch of the Ronda del Litoral which passes. through the area, so that parks could be laid out over it and the streets of the Eixample district could be extended to reach the sea.

- Widening the Passeig Marítim to 30 metres.

- Building a new marina, the Olympic Harbour.

- Construction of hotel, commercial and leisure facilities between the Ronda del Litoral and the Passeig Marítim.

- Continuation of the morphology of the Eixample district, with the creation of 'super-blocks'. These super-blocks include commercial spaces, a sports hall and cultural, religious and health care centres.

- Provision of a network of green spaces throughout the area, with the Parc de Mar Area covering 130 hectares, of which 45 are occupied by the Olympic Village.

The town planning operation made it possible to recover 5.2 kilometres of the coast-line for the use of the people of Barcelona and of all the inhabitants of the metropolitan area.[9]

The Olympic Village represented the flagship of the new urban development in Barcelona and the culmination of the previous discourse on the reconstruction of the city. In its architectural and urban development configuration, the influence of some historical models of modern urban development can be observed (especially that of south Amsterdam). The 'reconstruction' discourse turned out to be particularly appropriate for an updated version of the traditional morphologies of the Ensanche (Solá-Morales, 1992).

The jump in scale involved in the strategic or major urban projects linked to the Olympics was in keeping with the extension of the new strategies based on the so-called 'new areas of centrality', although the principles of the 'new strategic planning' were as simple as in the first phase of 'pragmatic planning and public spaces'. These projects were now developed and formalized as part of the new category of 'strategic urban projects' (Barcelona City Council, 1987b; Busquets, 1992) and included the so-called 'areas of new centrality', the interventions in the

Figure 13.6. Forum of Cultures 2004 (Barcelona City Council).

city road system and other projects centred on major infrastructure, highlighting the implementation of the ring roads and road accesses.[10] The four Olympic areas were promoted by the public sector. The rest relied on private initiative, were under the management of the public sector, or were funded according to mixed formulae, determined by the rate of private investment.

Catalyst for Strategic Urban Projects

Analysing the nature of the urban development strategy at the time of the Olympic nomination needs to consider international progress in 'city entrepreneurialism', which was being developed in association with the proliferation of strategic urban projects in the United States and later in diverse European cities. This urban planning transformation which Peter Hall identified in the 1970s also occurred in Barcelona, although some years later. As Hall (1988, p. 355) observed: 'Planning turned from regulating urban growth to encouraging it by any and every possible means. Cities, the new message rang loud and clear, were machines for wealth creation; the first and chief aim of planning must be to oil the machinery'.

In the first volume of the Official Report, published just prior to the start of the Games, Josep Miquel Abad made the significant point that the 16 days of competition would merely be 'the climax of a process which has taken years and that many of our objectives – the reactivation of the city and the country, the town planning works, the boost to the economy – will have already been more than accomplished before the magic date' (COOB, 1992, p. 1). However, as was seen later, the development of the Olympic Games took place at a time when clear priority was given to the economic promotion strategy. In this way, the main sources of urban policy in Barcelona centred on the attempt to become a more competitive and dynamic city, using the Olympic Games as the agent for the strategic projects.

The level of continuity between the Olympic initiative and the projects developed at the beginning of the 1970s is questionable. However, it is not difficult to see how new more strategic approaches were imposed compared with the visions of conventional urban development, based on zoning and control of urban growth. Although the Expo 82 initiative could now be registered in these visions, it was in the mid-1980s when Barcelona definitively absorbed the message of 'leverage' – the reorientation of urban policy towards 'entrepreneurial urban development' based on the use of public capital to stimulate private capital investment.

After the 1980s, the leaders of Barcelona understood the need to adapt the city to the pressures and opportunities arising from economic globalization, a process from which the city could not opt out. From here came the implementation of strategic plans designed as part of a new urban impulse for the economic re-launch of the city. The experience of the North American strategic plans, particularly San Francisco in 1984, contributed to the preparation of the 'Barcelona 2000 Economic and Social Plan', a document produced from the consensus between the different urban agents (including institutions, companies and trade unions). This took place in 1987, when the 'strategic' decisions were under way for the important urban projects associated with 1992 (Barcelona City Council, 1999*a*). The strategic plans approved in the 1990s were less characterized as 'antidotes' against a situation of crisis and urban stagnation, than tools to ensure urban growth beyond the Olympic event (Santacana, 2000). Barcelona was less original with regard to the aims and objectives of the Games: place promotion and urban regeneration. The Barcelona 2000 Plan identified three goals: improving communications; improving the quality of life with reference to the environment, training, research, social opportunities for housing and cultural infrastructure; and supporting industry and advanced services to business with particular reference to telecommunications and technological innovation. It was a long-term strategy for modernization, aimed at regenerating the city's economy and more generally its central urban fabric. In relation to the city's strategic modernization process, there was continuity in the developments connected with the Olympics (Roche, 2000, p. 144).

With the Olympic programme already developed, the picture presented in the post Olympic situation raised the need to agree on a new set of actions which would enable the continuation and extension of the initial strategy of 'extracting investment from the central government'. The promotional objectives were becoming increasingly more explicit, *city marketing*. It was no longer just a case of guaranteeing state public funds (as with the Expo 82 or in the first versions of the Olympic programme, when this was justified to finance the infrastructural work that the city had pending since the 1960s). Rather, it was a case of using them appropriately, together with advanced business management formulae, with a view to increasing the city's prestige and image at an international level and hence attracting private investment for the 'new Barcelona' (Borja and Castells, 1997; McNeill, 1999).

Analysing the effect of the Olympic Games, the fact that the majority of operations had been considered an adaptation of previous projects to the specific needs of the event has already been mentioned. Therefore, the improvement of the road network was connected to the need to link the different Olympic areas appropriately, but it served as an unquestionable driving force to a project which had already been planned much earlier. The construction of the new ring roads (planned since the beginning of the twentieth century) produced a decisive impact on urban structure. Similarly, the burying and remodelling of railway lines and the modernization of the sanitation network can be considered as important infrastructure projects arising from investment associated with the Olympics. Likewise, new sports facilities and large-scale telecommunications works were the main actions carried out courtesy of the Games.

In this respect, a key aspect which is not easily quantifiable is the relative importance of projects which were not directly linked to the Olympic areas. Indeed, the most important investments were generated in parallel and outside these areas, with investments strictly related to the event representing a mere 15 per cent of the total cost of 'approved' investment (Clusa, 1999, p. 93). This is probably the most relevant aspect of the Barcelona experience and helps to explain the scope of other schemes linked, to a greater or lesser degree, to new infrastructure, such as ring roads and the remodelling of the railways. It is not easy to measure the economic impact of the Games, as their planning and preparation coincided with Spain joining the European Community (1986). However, between 1986 and 1991 employment rose by 20 per cent in the municipality, 45 per cent in metropolitan Barcelona, and 30 per cent in the rest of the metropolitan region. The economic impact was most notable: between 1986 and 1992 'Barcelona would go from depression to economic boom'. Finally, the impact of other operations linked even more indirectly to the Olympic project has to be taken into consideration, including the remodelling of the port, the airport, the 'Diagonal Mar', the high-speed train and the Sagrera area (Barcelona Regional, 1999). In this process, public and private investment associated with the Olympic Games was a determining factor – almost $10 billion – which contrasts with the costs of $1.3 billion strictly associated with the event (Brunet, 1995).

No less decisive were other repercussions in the sense of new ways of running the city, which became increasingly business-like and less controlled by the traditional city council departments. New methods of intervention and management of urban planning were introduced, as with the creation of Olympic Holding (1987–1993, managed by Josep Acebillo, transformed in 1994 into the Agencia Metropolitana Barcelona Regional, SA). This was a 'joint venture' between the local administration and the central government that would not have been possible without exceptional circumstances such as those arising from the Olympic Games. It is well known that cooperation between institutions is usually more difficult than between companies.[11]

Perhaps above all else, it seems evident that the most important effects were related to the so-called 'map effect' – the desire 'to stamp Barcelona's image on the map'. The wish had been repeatedly expressed 'to stamp Barcelona's image on the map'. It is not an exaggeration to suggest a direct relationship between the Olympic Games and the notable increase in tourism: from 4.1 million tourists in 1991 to 6.3 million in 1995. The adoption of 'cultural urban development' strategies, with the construction of museums and cultural facilities, must also be noted in this respect. In fact, the centrality of the cultural strategies was reinforced a few years after the Olympic Games, with the decision to organize a new international event, the Forum of the Cultures 2004. This event, unique in the field of large-scale urban celebrations, adopted the 'dialogue between cultures' as an excuse for intense urban renewal in a problematic and strategic area of the city. Once again, Barcelona placed its trust in the use of international celebrations as the engine of important urban development transformations – a formula used repeatedly in Barcelona, as in many other cities (Monclús, 2006).

Epilogue

'When the Olympic flame has been quenched, everyone, and particularly the generations to come, will be left with a city transformed, with a new urban weft and a new loom'. In the Foreword to the Official Report (COOB, 1992), Mayor Maragall summarized the main achievements of the Olympic programme, prior to the celebration of the Games, with references to the extraordinary urban transformation of the city. However, following the enormous success of the Games, the city's ability to organize the Games also contributed to improving the image of the city, another fundamental objective although somewhat less explicit. Linked to this new urban image, the use of the 'leverage opportunities' also shows the success of the Olympic bid, as mentioned in relation to the economic impact of the Games and its multiplier effect on the tourist industry.

As with other major events, assessment of the 1992 Barcelona Olympic Games must be undertaken in accordance with the level of compliance with the main objectives, both officially stated and those which were not so explicit, but also in accordance with the eventual costs and social and cultural benefits. This is where the limits of the 'Barcelona model' are shown. Among the most important criticisms are the references to the excessive, almost obsessive, concern to improve the image of the city, with the resulting trivialization process of urban methods and a certain loss of its historic identity. Rem Koolhaas (1995) pointed out that a unique city like Barcelona could become a 'generic city', by oversimplifying its identity',[12] sentiments echoed by other noteworthy critics (Tello, 1993; Delgado, 2005; Capel, 2005).

This concern contrasts with the necessity of interventions in areas as essential as public transport and housing. As far as the former is concerned, it seems that the main advances have been in private rather than public transport, with repercussions for the new road networks in the restructuring of the metropolitan area of Barcelona. Admittedly, however, it is also true that the responsibility for the suburban and metropolitan dispersion processes cannot be attributed solely to the Olympic projects rather than other factors (Monclús, 1998). As far as the weakness in housing policy is concerned, the urban land revaluation and the property boom that coincided with the 'Olympic years' made the consequences more serious and negative. In addition to the rise in housing prices, the excessive importance given to hotels and offices and the 'over-development' of real estate markets have been criticized. Here, the strong dependence on short cycles of the economy shows one of the limits of this type of event, with the high revaluation of central areas resulting in the displacement of public sector housing and the young towards the metropolitan periphery.

Nevertheless, the Barcelona Olympic Games were extraordinarily successful in catalysing plans and projects and stimulating the urban economy. There was decisive and consensual public intervention and the event was used to improve extensive areas of the city. The project for 'Greater Barcelona' – thought about for decades but developed in the 1980s – became a reality in the 1990s. The city is now an international point of reference for architects and international investors alike and the Olympic Games were the instrument used for private-led developments. There is a 'before' and 'after' effect of the Olympic Games, although for some, the change produced in the 1990s would have involved greater importance of private capital in urban development, far from the initial 'Barcelona model' (Montaner and Muxí, 2002; Bohigas, 1999). Although it may seem contradictory, Barcelona may have become a victim of its own success. As in other cities, the success of the strategic urban development in the city may have been the root of problems arising from the revaluation of certain urban areas. The quickening of decentralizing tendencies and the exponential increase in metropolitan mobility correlates with considerable costs in energy, land and commuting times, in other words, the quality of urban life.

Perhaps it could be concluded that the 'new urban development' of Barcelona, following the Games, has decisively opted for quantity, taking the quality of the interventions for granted – although this conclusion may not be so clear, if one includes other parameters associated with urban development quality: for example, housing characteristics (price and quality), reasonable mobility, and environmental aspects. The Olympic Games, however, have a limited responsibility for these trends, if they are considered, first, as a logical conclusion to a process initiated far earlier than the celebration of the event and, secondly, as a Barcelona version of 'international global urban development', which here had greater support and was more 'domesticated' than in other cities affected by the phenomenon of globalization.

Notes

1. Maragall (1999*b*, p. 5).

2. Josep Porcioles was appointed Mayor of Barcelona by the Franco regime in 1957, a post he did not leave until 1973.

3. The 'Riverside Plan' – which had the poetic sub-title 'Barcelona. A city which can no longer live with its back to the sea' – was a project promoted by a group of important companies with land and factories in this sector. In 1968, the City Council approved the project, made up of a strip separated from the old 'Poble Nou' by a ring road. Local resistance paralysed the project in 1973.

4. Oriol Bohigas was born in 1925. He became an architect at the Barcelona School of Architecture (Escola Técnica Superior d'Arquitectura de Barcelona – ESTAB) in 1951, Town Planner in Madrid in 1961, Professor at the ETSAB in 1966, and its Director from 1977 to 1980. In 1980 he was appointed Planning Director at the Barcelona City Council, a position he held until 1984 when he became Personal Advisor to the Mayor.

5. The City Council, democratically elected for the first time in 40 years, had councillors from five parties: PSC, PSUC, CiU, UCD and ERC (COOB, 1992, I, p. 219).

6. Exhibition held in October 1988 in the Edifici de les Aigües under the title *Barcelona, the City and 92*. It was a comprehensive account of the town planning projects in progress which were related directly or indirectly to the organization of the Games. The exhibition was an unprecedented success and received over 350,000 visitors (COOB,1992, II, p. 347).

7. The objective of the action was to structure an urban space located in an under-privileged area. In the Vall d'Hebron Area, the Candidature Dossier could point to an Olympic venue completed well before the city was nominated to host the 1992 Games: the velodrome, which had been inaugurated for the World Cycling Championship in 1984. The area, which occupies 160 hectares, has other facilities, such as the Llars Anna Gironella de Mundet, the Club Esportiu Hispano-Francès and the Unió Esportiva d'Horta (COOB, 1992, II, p. 247).

8. Drawn up by the team of architects: Josep Martorell, Oriol Bohigas, David MacKay and Albert Puigdomènech.

9. In contrast, what happened in Barcelona's Old Harbour (Port Vell) was the generalized renovation of port and industrial facilities into something approaching a thematic park. This was done by the Port Authority, outside of the control of the City Council. Indeed, the remodelling of the Port Vell reflects these influences: the conversion of former port facilities for recreational, leisure and tourism uses in the 'Rouse style' (after the developer of Baltimore and Boston). It is now a part of a new city image. Some similarities can be found with the 'Baltimore model' (Ward, 2006).

10. From the twelve new 'poles' or 'areas of centrality' four were for the Olympics, four for the waterfront, and four other places. There were two main objectives: 'decentralizing central land uses' (tertiary uses: offices); and regenerating the seafront. If we look at the seafront, we can understand that those objectives were complementary. These areas benefited from special planning conditions in order to attract the new types of directional and tertiary uses corresponding to the services and facilities sectors, in spaces with obsolete uses but with good accessibility (Barcelona City Council, 1987b; Esteban, 1999).

11. This formula allowed 40 per cent of public investment from the central administration, 32 per cent from the regional government and 18 per cent from Barcelona City Council to be managed (Brunet, 1995, p. 103).

12. 'Sometimes an old, singular city, like Barcelona, by oversimplifying its identity, turns generic. It becomes transparent, like a logo' (Koolhaas, 1995).

Chapter 14

Sydney 2000

Beatriz García

This chapter studies Sydney's experience as an Olympic city from the perspective of cultural policy and planning. In previous work I have argued that culture and the arts play a critical role in defining the Games' symbolic dimensions and are determining factors in the sustainability of event legacies (see García, 2002*b*, 2003, 2004; Moragas 1992). In this context, interpreting Sydney's cultural discourse is fundamental to understanding how the city was experienced during the Olympic fortnight and the kinds of images that it projected to the rest of the world in its lead-up and aftermath.

Sydney's cultural discourse offers a good example of the internal contradictions that underpin many examples of city-based events that try to be everything for everyone: locally meaningful, nationally engaging and globally impacting. The problem of such a multi-layered approach is that it tends to lead to overly simplistic and tokenistic cultural representations, an issue best reflected in the often confused narratives of Olympic Opening and Closing Ceremonies (see Tomlinson, 1996). Despite claims to the contrary (Cashman, 2006), Sydney 2000 was no exception as its ceremonies failed to depart from established narratives about Australia dominated by a white and Western sense of aesthetics where indigenous and multicultural cultures are an exotic addition rather than a core component (García and Miah, 2000). However, Sydney promised a comprehensive programme of cultural activity over four years and presented an unprecedented programme of street activity during the Olympic fortnight, which provided additional opportunities to explore and demonstrate the worth of its cultural discourse.

This chapter offers a detailed analysis of how Sydney's cultural discourse came about and influenced its profile as an Olympic city. It builds on the current debate about event-led cultural regeneration in urban environments (Chalkley and Essex, 1999; Burbank *et al.*, 2002; Monclús 2004; Richards and Wilson, 2004; Gold and Gold, 2005) to provide critical scrutiny of existing definitions and guidelines for cultural engagement within the Olympic Movement. Its key argument is that the positioning of the Olympic Games as a city-based, nationally-framed and globally embracing cultural event presents important challenges for those that make cultural policy, yet has rarely resulted in sustainable cultural legacies. Sydney had an opportunity to question established practices and overcome the trend towards using cultural activity as a platform for global media spectacle at the expense of meaningful local representation. However, existing Olympic structures, particularly media and sponsorship agreements, prevented this ambition from fully coming to fruition.

Bringing the Games to Sydney

Sydney was the third consecutive Australian city to present a candidature for hosting the Olympic Games between 1992 and 2000. Brisbane, capital of the state of Queensland and host city of the 1988 World Expo, had bid for the 1992 Games, while Melbourne, capital of the state of Victoria and host of the 1956 Olympic Games, bid for 1996. Farrell (1999) argued that Australia's continuing interest in staging the Games cannot be explained on the grounds of expected economic benefits and international exposure alone. Rather, there is a rooted passion for sports manifested by the day-to-day practices of most Australians and a widespread acceptance and interest in the Olympic Movement, as shown by Australia's uninterrupted participation in the Games despite its geographical isolation (*Ibid.*). Sydney's Olympic promotional material claimed that, with Greece, Australia is the only other country to have participated in every Olympic Games since their revival in 1896 (see SOBL, 1992; SOCOG, 1999*a*, 2000*a*).

The Sydney Olympic Bid Limited (SOBL) emphasized these cultural factors to show the deep commitment and support of Australians for the Olympic Games (McGeoch and Korporaal, 1994). Further, SOBL (1992) argued that in Australia there was no organized group opposed to the Games. Tony Veal noted that not even Aboriginal communities, initially feared for the threat of boycotts, were strongly opposed to the Olympics as the opportunity to participate and win Olympic medals had converted many of their members into national heroes.[1] Despite some opposition from academics and community leaders (Frankland, 2000; Waitt, 2003, 2004), the notion of a nationally and culturally cohesive Olympic proposal was to emerge as a key selling point in the bid, particularly at an international level. As such, once key operational arguments, such as sound infrastructural and environmental strengths, had been won among national stakeholders, two cultural arguments became a distinctive factor of Sydney's bid discourse among IOC members and the global media: the celebration of Sydney's and Australia multiculturalism, and the advancement of Aboriginal reconciliation (Hanna, 1999; García, 2002*b*).

The Australian bid organizers realized that the multicultural composition and, most importantly, the presence of Aboriginal cultures, made Australia a unique place to explore exemplary ways in which the Olympic ideals of universal understanding could foster and promote the respect of human rights (Hanna, 1999). Accordingly, the Sydney bid incorporated references to Australia's indigenous cultures and emphasized the advances made by the Australian government in supporting them. An example of the centrality given to Aboriginal cultures is found in the social component of the bid presentation during the last night preceding the IOC final vote in Monaco. McGeogh and Korporaal (cited in Hanna, 1999, p. 28) observed that 'indigenous musicians played outside the Hôtel de Paris' with 'the haunting sounds attracting [IOC] members to [the Sydney 2000 Bid Committee's] hospitality suite'. This cultural presentation was criticized by Australian scholars Booth and Tatz (1999, pp. 6–7) who considered that the SOBL 'flooded Monaco with black dancers and performers, but ... they were tourist curios like koalas and kangaroos'. By contrast, Hanna (1999, p. 28) claimed that 'although used tokenistically, the significant inclusion of Indigenous culture created the impression of a national culture that values the contributions of its minority groups' and resulted in renewed debates about this issue throughout Australia.

Furthermore, McGeoch and Korporaal (cited in Hanna, 1999, p. 29) argued that Sydney presented its official cultural programme as an important part of the bid strategy and noted that 'it was promoted at the July 1993 opening of the Olympic Museum in Lausanne [while] other cities, by contrast, focused primarily on the sporting festival'. Reinforcing this argument, Donald McDonald, chairman of the Cultural Committee for the Bid and subsequent chairman of the Olympic Cultural Commission, emphasized the unique characteristics of the Sydney proposal by claiming that 'Sydney was the only city to have produced a special publication on the Cultural Olympiad and presented an extensive programme of activities to be held in the four years leading to the Games' (McDonald, 1994). In his words, the use of the Sydney Opera House as the main cultural venue and the emphasis given to Aboriginal reconciliation were considered 'issues crucial' to the success of Sydney's bid (*Ibid.*).

International Expectations and Brand Images

Sydney's emphasis on Aboriginal issues and multiculturalism must be understood within a particular climate of international expectations strongly concerned with human rights abuses. The Sydney bid was in close competition with that from Beijing, with the latter being the favourite. An important limitation of the Beijing bid was China's dubious human rights record, a factor accentuated by the killing of pro-democracy demonstrators at Tiananmen Square in 1989, only three years before the IOC vote. In order to gain some advantage over Beijing, Sydney and Australia needed to address areas likely to raise similar international concern. Accordingly, the promotion of a harmonic and progressive view on the Aboriginal and multicultural composition of the country became a top priority.

The emphasis on reconciliation and multiculturalism was also a response to the pressures faced by the promoters of the bid to present an image of the host city and country that is distinctive and easy to understand. The use of simplified cultural themes to define the idiosyncrasy of a given place has been widely discussed within events and Olympic-specific literature. Berkaak (1999, p. 68) argues that 'an Olympic event is an opportunity to be focused on – with an assured benefit' and an opportunity for the host city or nation to 'choose which aspects [it wants to] showcase to the world'. Moragas (1992, p. 32) adds that it is necessary that the Olympic city or nation 'synthesize[s its] complex reality in an image [or] brand image' in order to suit global media production processes, thus maximizing its communication impact and avoiding misunderstandings. This makes the Games 'a laboratory of incalculable value to understand the logic behind the commercialisation of nowadays culture' (*Ibid.*, p. 34). The use of Aboriginal reconciliation and multiculturalism as Australia's international brand images were well adapted to the requirements of the mass media during the bid period and thus received extensive publicity worldwide (García, 2002*b*).

In order to strengthen its cultural case, Sydney decided to follow the example of Barcelona 1992 and present a four-year Cultural Olympiad fully engaged with these themes. However, as discussed below, at the time of winning the bid, the celebration of multiculturalism and Aboriginal reconciliation was not as established and clearly defined in Australian cultural policy terms as the chosen brand images of previous Olympic cities, notably Mediterranean culture in Barcelona 1992 and Southern and African-American cultures in Atlanta 1996 (see Australian Democrats, 2001; Bottomley, 1994; NSW Ministry for the Arts, 1997). This would be a cause of conflict and disagreement over the management and implementation of the cultural programme and was, arguably, a reason for the inconsistent support that the programme received over the years.

Reviewing Sydney's Chosen Brand Images

Despite the apparent strengths of multiculturalism and reconciliation as brand images, a closer look at these motives reveals a contradiction between their cultural potential and their essentially problematic political dimensions. The emphasis placed on the concept of 'multiculturalism' or 'multicultural society' was aimed at acknowledging the diverse first or second generation migrant communities composing Australia's and, particularly, Sydney's population. However, Jakubowicz (1981, 1994) discussed the uses and abuses of the term multiculturalism within the Australian government rhetoric, questioning its promotion as an official state ideology. In line with this, Cunningham argued that the multicultural discourse in Australia has never been taken from a cultural policy perspective but only from the perspective of social policy:

> this discourse is focused on solving the social problems of immigration in terms of language, education, jobs, health services etc. but not in consistently promoting a presence of ethnically and culturally diverse people in the media or the arts world. [Thus], it is unlikely that relevant multicultural components are included within the Games cultural programme beyond a token presence in the event promotional or marketing discourse.[2]

Accordingly, it can be argued that the use of a multicultural discourse in Sydney's cultural programme was not an effect of the host city or Australia's priorities in cultural policy but rather a strategic decision associated with the country's policies in communication and international relations (see also Wilson, 1996).

At a different level, the promotion of Aboriginal culture was shaped around the term 'reconciliation'. Reconciliation was meant to signify the commitment of Australian society towards a full acceptance and acknowledgement of Aboriginal and Torres Strait Islanders cultures within its national discourse and sense of self. However, Tatz (1999) has contested the use and meaning of the term reconciliation and has accused the Olympic organizations and those government bodies supporting them of masking an extremely delicate and largely unsolved issue behind a public relations game. For Tatz, this game 'has always been conceived from a white sense of aesthetics' which prevents the public from genuinely understanding the situation (*Ibid.*). In support, Aboriginal film-maker Frankland (2000) states that the way Aboriginal questions were dealt with in Olympic discourses tended to be superficial and tokenistic. He argues that they were aimed at exploiting their most appealing side for both governments and the media to present a harmonious Australia to the world, but were not consistent in the process to create truly significant cultural projects and offer Aboriginal peoples a representative voice.

The suspicion arising over the Olympic bid's brand 'images' within the Australian academic and arts communities did not prevent Games' promoters and organizers from using the terms as core elements of their Olympic discourse for the enjoyment of foreign audiences. Nevertheless, in common with previous Olympic bids, the key words that were used to attract the investment of national stakeholders and promote the key benefits of the Olympic project were terms such as 'trade' and 'tourism', which had little to do with pursuit of cultural identity.[3] This is indicative of a conflict between the image that was projected abroad and the beliefs or aspirations of the Australian population, in particular, the stakeholders that were to fund the Olympic experience.

There remained a contradiction between what was 'sold' or promised to international audiences and the interests of national audiences and stakeholders. This resulted in the planning of a remarkably ambitious cultural programme which was to be produced almost without any formal support from Australian organizations that, ultimately, had a marginal role within the Olympic city atmosphere.

Managing Culture at the Olympics

The Sydney Organizing Committee for the Olympic Games (SOCOG) was established in 1993 with responsibility to prepare and present the Games and work in close coordination with the Olympic Coordination Authority (OCA). The latter was in charge of managing infrastructures and the overall Games legacy, while SOCOG retained control of all aspects of the Games implementation, including both the sporting competitions and the IOC-required cultural and educational programmes. In previous Games, this programme had been subject to varied policies and strategies, as some cities feel that the mission of an Organizing Committee does not necessarily respond to the priorities and agendas of the host city or country but rather the established IOC global regulations and the demands of other global partners such as sponsors and media. Consequently, cities such as Barcelona and Athens retained control of their cultural programmes through separate organizations.[4] Sydney's decision to keep its cultural programme within SOCOG meant that it was integrated within the main Olympic structures and, theoretically, able to benefit from common resources. Yet, it also ran the risk of losing visibility within the highly demanding and multi-faceted Olympic project.

Sydney's official cultural programme took the form of four annual 'Olympic Arts Festivals' and was located within SOCOG's division of Marketing and Image, which incorporated a wide range of programmes including marketing, design and special events. Despite its positioning within an influential division, the Festivals' management team was rather marginal within SOCOG structure (García, 2002b; SOCOG, 1999b). Beyond the lack of interaction within their own overarching marketing division, the Arts Festivals were isolated from other programmes with a clear focus on cultural matters and an emphasis beyond sport, such as the torch relay, the education programme, community relations and the ceremonies programme. Furthermore, there was no direct interaction with the committees in charge of addressing and collaborating with Aboriginal and multicultural communities at a local or national level.[5] Ultimately, the cultural programme missed an important association with one of the most relevant Olympic programmes in 'city' terms, based at the same division. This was the 'look of the Games', a programme with a major impact on the feel of the city during the Olympic fortnight through the creation of banners and other decorative devices dedicated to locate key venues and embellish urban public spaces.

A further negative effect of this managerial isolation was the lack of strong strategies to approach and lobby external stakeholders. SOCOG had specific programmes to approach government, sponsors and the media. However, the Festivals were not a central part of their agenda and rarely benefited from established agreements. The lack of clear and convincing strategies to approach stakeholders indicates that the cultural programme was not in a strong position to secure the full accomplishment of all its objectives. Instead, it relied on the willingness and particular interests of specific partners (see section on stakeholders, below).

In sum, nothing indicates that SOCOG's management structure responded to or supported a defined cultural policy. The organization's top decision-making was based on economic imperatives with a view to supporting tourism, business and sporting achievements rather than guaranteeing a coherent cultural strategy. The most evident effect of this situation was the lowering of standards in Sydney's Olympic cultural discourse, with generic entertainment and branding devices dominating over the more distinctive and representative messages devised at the bid stage. Some clear examples are found in the merchandise and 'look of the Games' design which, although effective in media terms, failed to establish a clear message about contemporary Sydney and instead used similar techniques to previous and subsequent Games – a clear case of global standards dominating over place-specific trends.

Designing the Games' Cultural Dimension

Despite its marginal position, Sydney's culture team decided to go ahead with its original proposal of a four-year Cultural Olympiad, following the example of Barcelona and Atlanta. The programme manager argued that it was important to

Figure 14.1. Olympic Games design: global branding versus local representation. The 'Look of the Games' city banners used similar techniques in Sydney 2000 and Athens 2004.

use the Olympics to project ambitious cultural events regardless of the subsequent difficulties in implementing them. In her view, 'a four-year period is better than just three weeks, and national and international presentations, exhibitions and collaborations are more challenging and stimulating for the arts in Australia than a short Sydney-based festival'.[6]

However, the cultural programme suffered a radical budget cut in the first year after winning the bid, from A$51 million to A$20 (SOCOG, 1999c, 1999d) and many of the early proposals for implementation had to be cancelled or reframed, which limited their impact on Sydney and Australia. Furthermore, the lack of resources led to reallocating the responsibility for some of the designed Olympic cultural activities to other departments, including the plan for an Olympic Village Cultural Programme and liaisons with the Olympic Youth Camp.[7]

The final programme of activity retained the original concept of Australia-wide and international Arts Festivals. In this context, all generic and festival-specific cultural references were about Australia as a nation rather than Sydney as an Olympic city, as detailed in table 14.1.

The overly ambitious nature of the Festivals, combined with limited resources and a marginal structural position made it very difficult for this cultural discourse to have a direct impact on the city, the rest of Australia and, indeed, the world, as was originally intended. As noted below, the final Olympic communications strategy focused on a generic Olympic discourse that celebrated the Games and Australia's way of life but was not finely tuned to the original bid discourse of multiculturalism and aboriginal reconciliation – and did little to advance the cause for greater cultural understanding and direct representation of cultural minorities, as reflected in recent reports of racial violence in the city (Greer, 2005, pp. 12–13). Arguably, the decision to focus on the representation of Australia as a nation rather than Sydney as a city was an additional challenge, limiting the programme's ability to make a difference, as its purpose became too vague and difficult to implement.

Promoting the Games, Promoting the City

As discussed earlier (see chapters 6 and 7), Olympic marketing and communications is a priority for the IOC and respective Olympic organizers. The IOC is in charge of the world-wide dimension of Olympic communications by retaining direct control of global sponsorship programmes such as The Olympic Partners (TOP), the negotiation of television rights, worldwide merchandizing and the distribution of generic advertising campaigns about the ideals of Olympism. Contrasting with the global dimensions of the Olympic brand, the design and management of local campaigns to promote particular messages about a specific Games – and, indeed, the host city – is the sole responsibility of respective OCOGs.

The structure of marketing and communications at SOCOG exemplified the need to reconcile the global aspirations of the IOC with the locally based needs of an Olympic host (see Wilson, 1996). Within its sponsorship programme,

Table 14.1. Olympic Arts Festivals length, themes, objectives and main components.

Year, Name, Length and Location	Theme/Mission	Objectives	Programme Components
1997 The Festival of the Dreaming, September to October (Sydney)	Celebration of the world's indigenous cultures, in particular those of Australian Aborigines and Torres Strait Islanders	*General*: expand a greater awareness and appreciation of Australian indigenous heritage *Specific*: ensure indigenous authorship and control of the work presented	30 exhibitions, 14 dance and theatre productions, eight performance troupes, 50 films, a literature programme, three concerts and special commissions involving overseas indigenous artists Every state and territory of Australia was represented
1998 A Sea Change, June to October, (Australia-wide)	A 'snapshot' of Australia's diverse migrant cultures	*General*: Create a time capsule of Australian culture in the end of the Millennium for generations to come *Specific*: Help people across the nation learn more about the arts in their country and demonstrate the importance of its geographic and cultural diversity	92 presenting companies and 122 dance, theatre, visual arts, literary, music and education events. *Highlights*: lighthouse and harbour concerts; touring exhibition *Sculpture by the Sea* *Publications*: 1998 Anthology of Australian writing and photography
1999 Reaching the World, November 1998 to January 2000 (five continents)	Events by Australian companies and artists touring to countries in each of the five regions represented by the Olympic symbol	*General*: bring Australian arts and culture to the international stages; *Specific*: establish collaboration with foreign governments and arts organizations	70 events travelling to 50 countries and 150 cities or towns including dance, music, theatre, visual arts, literature, films, architecture and design Publication of *Australia on Show*, a guide to Australian Arts Broadcasting
2000 The Harbour of Life, August to October (Sydney)	The culmination of the Olympiad, 'a festival on a scale to match the grandeur of the Olympic Games'	*General*: define the finest elements of Australian culture; present a number of works on grand scale, unlikely to be seen again in a lifetime; establish artistic legacies	75 day-event focused in the harbour and Opera House – opera, theatre, dance and classical concerts; 30 visual arts exhibitions in key galleries and museums

Source: Information extracted from Olympic Arts Festivals fact sheets (SOCOG, 1997–2000).

SOCOG had to address the needs of TOP partners at the same time as the needs of domestic partners. Furthermore, the marketing programmes had to reach local audiences while securing a world-wide impact that was coherent with established IOC strategies. Finally, within its diverse communications programmes, SOCOG had to cover the needs of a wide range of local communities while, at the same time, integrating all Games communications into a joint Olympic promotional plan (SOCOG, 1998).

There is insufficient space here to offer an in-depth study of Sydney's communication plans, but it can be argued that SOCOG's main priority was to ensure the success of the Games rather than Sydney's projection as an Olympic city. Accordingly, it is possible to observe certain imbalances in the levels of support provided to different Olympic dimensions. While programmes such as the torch relay, the Opening and Closing Ceremonies and naturally the sports competitions were placed centrally on the agendas of marketing and communication divisions, the Arts Festivals and educational programmes were rarely mentioned in the mainstream communication and marketing strategies and were excluded from the coverage of the official media centres – the Main Press Centre and International Broadcasting Centre (García, 2001, 2002*b*).

Arguably, the global aspirations and commercial needs of the IOC resulted in a strong emphasis on marketing imperatives at the expense of communication policies that could have leveraged the meaning and implications of the Olympic cultural programme for the city. This situation forced the Olympic cultural programme to develop its own communication strategy, practically in complete isolation from mainstream Olympic marketing. The strategy involved the creation of a new logo for the final Festival in 2000, and the positioning of the Festival within an emerging phenomenon within the Games hosting process, the non-accredited media centre (see García and Miah, 2004) in coordination with a new arts information service, *ausarts2000*, funded by the Arts Council (National Library of Australia, 2000). These factors helped the 2000 Festival gain more visibility within the cultural sector, but also contributed to disassociating it from previous Festivals and the notion of a four-year Olympiad (García, 2002*b*). Given that the final Festival was focused on the celebration of world class artists in 'world class venues' such as the Sydney Opera House, this also meant that the original themes of reconciliation and multiculturalism, explored at length in 1997 and 1998, were ultimately lost (*Ibid.*).

Overall, the main limitation of Sydney's Olympic communication strategy in cultural policy terms was the focus on entertainment rather than cultural representation. The main problem was the lack of interaction between the more sophisticated cultural (arts) messages and generic Olympic marketing. As such, overall Games promotions went back to established image stereotypes that marginalized many ethnic communities, while the Arts Festival promotion was limited to the cultural sector through minority or specialized media outlets.

Involvement of Key Stakeholders

Following the practice of most Olympic cities since Los Angeles 1984, the Sydney Games were managed via a public-private partnership led by SOCOG and OCA. Key Olympic stakeholders included the Australian government at local, state and federal levels; corporate sponsors and supporters at national and global levels; and the media at international and Australian local and national levels. The involvement of different stakeholders in Sydney's cultural programme evolved throughout the four-year period of the Olympiad. For the most part, stakeholders who showed interest in the first Festival, became vague or reticent to support the two central ones, but increased their contributions in time for the Olympic fortnight in year 2000 (García, 2002b).

Overall, there is no evidence to suggest that the support provided by the average cultural stakeholder led or contributed to strengthening a coherent cultural policy for the event. Stakeholders' interests were often ambiguous or contradictory and so were their strategies for involvement, which combined the search for spectacle and media appeal with the often overstated ambition to guarantee local representation. In general, it can be argued that Olympic stakeholders were unable to prevent the imbalances and limitations provoked by the weak position of the official cultural programme within SOCOG.

Public Sector

Government bodies were fully supportive of the Olympic programme but were divided in their interests and expectations towards the Games' cultural dimension. Local and state bodies viewed the Games – and indeed, the associated Arts Festivals – as an opportunity to expand tourism and trade opportunities. In this sense, their Olympic cultural policy was dominated by a rationalist and market-oriented approach, in line with overall trends in Australia (Caust, 2003; DCITA, 1994; Radbourne and Fraser, 1996; Wilson, 1996) and their priority was to support those activities most likely to have an international impact. In contrast, Federal bodies such as the Arts Council were committed to revisiting notions of Australian culture and fighting established stereotypes of white colonialism. Their emphasis was on exploring and supporting the notions of multiculturalism and Aboriginal reconciliation that had been presented as Australia's brand images since the bid stage and, with them, an image of tolerance and pride in diversity that was best represented by the *ausarts 2000* programme. Both approaches had common goals and used similar techniques but the first welcomed the use of pure entertainment and spectacle while the second placed an emphasis on maximizing representation and a shared vision of Australia's and Sydney's cultural discourse.

Until 2000, public support for the Olympic cultural programme was vague and limited. Several observers explain this by pointing at the conflict over government 'ownership' of the Games.[8] The Games had been awarded to Sydney, so they were the responsibility of the state of New South Wales (NSW), with Federal government having only a secondary role in terms of decision-making and resource allocations. This resulted in a lack of coordination between state and Federal bodies and a certain sense of competition between states wanting to benefit from the Games with priorities and interests differing from those of Sydney and NSW. SOCOG and NSW often reacted to the situation with defensive or protective measures, as was the case in their relationship with Queensland over its contribution to the cultural programme, which was lower than the figure for which state agencies had wished. The limited contributions of Federal arts funding bodies during the first three years of the Olympiad could also be understood as a measure to avoid conflicts among states.

However, in preparation for the Olympic fortnight, local, state and Federal bodies joined their efforts in a common initiative that became one of the greatest catalysts for the promotion of the Olympic cultural programme. This was the creation of a non-accredited media centre, the Sydney Media Centre (SMC). This complemented the established Main Press Centre and International Broadcasting Centre and was managed according to IOC regulations. The SMC had the mission to serve all media, regardless of their access to official IOC accreditation, by providing stories about Sydney and Australia not related to the sporting competitions. The SMC was managed by Tourism NSW and the Department of State and Regional Development (state bodies) in conjunction with the Sydney Harbour Foreshore Authority (local government), the Australian Tourism Commission and the Department of Foreign Affairs and Trade (Federal government). Tourism, trade and culture were the focal points of most press conferences at the SMC. Accordingly, the final Arts Festival became a key beneficiary and gained a strong SMC presence with regular press conferences. Furthermore, the Festival had its own media information office in partnership with the Arts Council-funded *ausarts2000*.

Beyond these generic government programmes, in the context of the Olympic city it is of particular relevance to consider the involvement of the main local authority, the City of Sydney. The City had a direct association with the Arts Festivals: the Lord Mayor was a board member of the Olympic Cultural Commission and the City became official presenter of the 2000 Festival, which resulted in the operational authorship of all outdoors arts and entertainment programmes for that year.[9] In addition, the City of Sydney offered A$2.25 million value-in-kind support by presenting Arts Festival banners, bus advertising and brochure placement in official booths and all main city streets and squares. This suggests that local government used the Festival as part of the city's cultural policy strategy.

However, the City of Sydney's interest in the Olympic period went well beyond the official arts programme. The City created a year-long Olympic project including an ambitious programme of city beautification, service upgrading and the provision of entertainment during the Olympic fortnight. The latter was aimed at coordinating the efforts by the City, SOCOG, OCA and the Olympic Roads and Transport Authority (ORTA) which only functioned during the Olympic fortnight. The objective was to provide a mechanism for crowd management during all major events in 2000 including the New Year's Eve celebrations and the Sydney Festival. During the Olympics, the project was named *Olympic LiveSites!*. This was an entertainment programme distributed at six popular locations in the city centre 'at times when Olympic venues were filling and spilling simultaneously and transport would be at its most stressed'.[10] The *LiveSites!* offered simultaneous coverage of the sporting competitions via giant screens and also included concerts, acrobatic shows, and street theatre. However, these activities were not linked

Figure 14.2. Olympic LiveSites. Sydney's *LiveSites* created a festive atmosphere throughout the city but failed to integrate the progressive and culturally meaningful messages embedded within the official Olympic Arts Festivals.

to the 2000 Arts Festival. In fact, the popularity and visibility of the *LiveSites!* overshadowed the indoor and somehow elitist nature of most official Olympic cultural activities that year. This led many journalists, tourists and Sydneysiders to believe that the Games cultural programme was the former and not the latter (García, 2002*b*).

Overall, the City of Sydney's involvement in the final Olympic Arts Festival must be understood in the context of other plans and activities for year 2000, where the Olympics and the arts programme were not the only priority. The City's interest in the 2000 Festival was not the exploration of Sydney's cultural values, but rather the projection of a contemporary and lively image of the central business district (CBD) to attract foreign visitors and corporations. This affected the nature and emphasis of the *LiveSites!* outdoors activity which, though highly entertaining and widely popular, were poorly related to the bid promise of a multicultural, all embracing and representative cultural celebration.

Sponsors

The corporate sector plays a key role in funding the Games and is also an important element in the look and feel of any Olympic city. Due to the strict IOC ban on any commercial advertising inside the Olympic sport venues, sponsors tend to focus their investment on alternative Olympic activities within outdoor spaces, from the route of the torch relay, to key host city locations involving, typically, the covering of buildings with Olympic-themed corporate messages. In Sydney, the main sponsorship programmes were the IOC-led worldwide TOP programme and, at a national level, the Team Millennium partners, Sydney 2000 Supporters and Sydney 2000 Providers which, together, generated over $492 million (IOC, 2002). The distribution of funding is linked to negotiations over 'core properties', that is, direct associations with specific Games components. Many of these corporate-owned 'core properties' have particular significance at a local rather than global level and thus have a strong impact on the workings of the Olympic city. Table 14.2 lists cultural and entertainment programmes either funded or organized, or both, by specific Olympic sponsors in 2000, most of which took place in Sydney exclusively.

An interesting aspect of table 14.2 is the emphasis on youth programmes. Children and youngsters are a priority in the Olympic context due to the specific connotations of the Olympics as a 'youth movement' (IOC, 2004*a*). Indeed, this approach also has a lucrative appeal, as it provides good opportunities to reach out and engage with potential consumers at an early stage. The other notable element is the emphasis on entertainment over cultural activities – including standard popular activities such as light and sound shows, or pop concerts – over city-specific offerings. Only 20 per cent of the activities in table 14.2 presented the work of locally based artists or performers or stories or work representative of Sydney's diverse communities. As such, even at a local level and for the benefit of mainly

Table 14.2. Olympic sponsors involvement on cultural and entertainment programmes in year 2000.

TOP Sponsors (World-wide)	Cultural/Entertainment Programme	Description
Coca Cola	Coca Cola Olympic Club Sydney & POWERADE Training Camp	300 teenagers from around the world experience the Games
McDonald's	Olympic Youth Camp	400 teenagers from around the world share two weeks of cultural exchange in Sydney and Australia
Panasonic	Olympic LiveSites!	Six giant screens displayed in six popular city locations to showcase Games coverage
Samsung	World of entertainment at the Olympic Rendez-vous@Samsung	Cultural performances by traditional folkloric groups at Samsung tent, Olympic Park
UPS	Aqua Spectacular	Nightly laser and water show in Darling Harbour
Visa	Olympics of the imagination	A world-wide arts contest for kids between 9 and 13 years olds from 25 countries. 36 winners attend the Games

Team Millennium Partners	Cultural / Entertainment Programme	Description
Swatch	Olympic LiveSites!	Six countdown clocks, one at every site
AMP	Torch Relay Official Sponsor	Funding and promotional support for the relay
Energy Australia	Energy of Australia by Marc Newson	Nightly light show over the sails of the Opera House (Olympic Arts F.)
Fairfax	Olympic Arts Festivals, Education Programme, Volunteer Programme	Regular brochures highlighting key arts, education and volunteer activities; special events for programme participants
Holden	Hospitality Community Project	Assistance to the Chinese community
	Concert at the Domain (2000)	Sydney Symphony Orchestra open air free concert
News Corp	Ticketing programme presenter	Regular paper inserts following the Torch route and listing torch bearer names, support to the torch bearer selection scheme; regular brochures highlighting ticketing promotions
	Torch Relay presenter	
Telstra	National Aboriginal and Torres Strait Islanders Art Award	Australia's most prestigious prize for indigenous art, presented at Sydney's Customs House
Westfield	The Olympic Journey (1997–1999)	Olympic-related activities, focus on children
	Hosting the Kids 2000 Olympic Arena	
Westpac	2000 Pacific School Games	Youth–oriented educational Olympic programmes
	Westpac Olympic Youth Programme	
	National Education Programme	
	The Olympic Journey (1997–1999)	

Sydney 2000 Supporters	Cultural / Entertainment programme	Description
Nike	Kids interactive sport park	Entertainment park at the Domain and Fox Studios
	Radio Free Sydney	Underground radio station featuring athletes' interviews combined with youth-oriented house, techno, acid jazz and World Beat music

Source: Extracted from sponsors media news releases.

local audiences, Olympic sponsors saw more value-for-money and thus focused on supporting global entertainment rather than local cultural representation.

Interviews with Sydney sponsors indicated that current Olympic regulations did not make it worth investing in the official cultural programme. Part of the reason is the high cost compared with the limited profile and visibility of Olympic cultural activities. In Sydney, the ambiguous and, at times, elitist character of the cultural programme also diminished its corporate appeal. Olympic sponsors such as Swatch, Telstra and the Seven Network suggested that the programme – particularly in 2000 – was not able to engage with general audiences in the way that ceremonies and free street entertainment could. Thus, as seen in table 14.2, they saw greater benefit in developing an association with the sporting competitions, Olympic rituals or their own specially designed community fun programmes.[11]

Additional factors limiting potential corporate investment in cultural activity are the IOC exclusivity agreements (only one product category per sponsor, thus excluding brand competitors) and the strict protection of the Olympic rings, which can only be used by official Olympic sponsors. While these regulations have increased the lucrative value of sponsorship agreements, they have had a negative effect on cultural programming as it prevents non-Olympic sponsors from contributing to the Arts Festivals. Furthermore, it prevents existing arts companies and cultural groups from establishing an official and branded association with the Games if they receive funding and intend to acknowledge the support of any non-Olympic corporate sponsor.

Media

Together with Olympic sponsors, the media are the other key determinant of the Games' success at a global level. Moragas *et al.* (1995) argue extensively about the Games being first and foremost a 'media event' – their size and global impact being the direct result of the involvement and daily following of media networks representing more than 200 nations and reaching a potential global audience of 2–3 billion people (*Ibid.*; see also Dayan and Katz, 1994; Wilson, 1996). The Sydney 2000 Games presented the unique situation of two competing publishing companies (Fairfax and News Ltd) being Team Millennium Partners simultaneously. SOCOG's marketing negotiations with both groups secured the publication of special supplements on their respective 'core properties'. News Ltd owned the right to associate its national paper, *The Australian,* with Olympic ticketing and the torch relay. Fairfax owned the right to describe the *Sydney Morning Herald*, Sydney's main paper, as the 'official presenter' of the four Olympic Arts Festivals and owned the right to present official information about the Education Programme and the Volunteer Programme through its national tabloid, the *Sun Herald.* The Olympic official broadcaster was the Seven Network, which did not establish any special outlet for the coverage of Olympic cultural activity and instead focused almost exclusively on the sporting competitions and most popular symbolic dimensions of the Games.

During a series of personal interviews, journalists, press editors and broadcasters representing a range of Australian media expressed the view that, although the official Arts Festivals might be an interesting addition to the Games, they lack the public appeal and uniqueness that characterizes other Olympic elements, from infrastructure developments to the sport competitions.[12] In their view, the only exception was the 1997 Aboriginal Festival, which was viewed as a key point of reference for future festivals all over Australia (Eccles, 1997). All interviewees agreed that the concept of an indigenous festival impacted on and was relevant to Australia, but they thought subsequent festivals lost that momentum, a factor accentuated by the growing presence of more easily recognizable Olympic news stories. Despite the wide coverage offered by major papers such as the *Sydney Morning Herald* and *The Australian*, the 2000 Festival was not seen as a distinctive event capable of engaging the average Olympic fan and was generally excluded from Olympic stories and specially-designed Olympic sections.

Living the Games

Helen Wilson (1996, p. 603) has asked the question, 'what is an Olympic city?' and noted the required 'dual function' that any Games host city must perform, is as a 'stand-in for the nation' and as a 'worldly city'. Wilson claims that 'the Games are as much about the "city as spectacle" as they are about sport' which 'emphasiz[es] the way that television manipulates and "theatricalizes" their urban sites' (*Ibid.*). The latter reflects the notion of the Games as a media event, which ultimately transforms the Olympic city into a space that is essentially understood through its representations in the media. Wilson stresses the impact of the Games experience on urban centres that must become 'sites of cultural consumption' (*Ibid.*, p. 607) according to international standards. This argument is consistent with the findings discussed in previous sections: in Sydney, like many other Olympic cities, the emphasis of key stakeholders was on image rather than representation. Wilson claims that this trend often leads the Olympic city to be 'similar looking' to all its predecessors, with 'world class com[ing] to mean just the standards of facility and kinds of entertainment that affluent international travellers expect anywhere' (*Ibid.*, p. 608).

Olympic versus Public Spaces

One of the most notable aspects of Sydney's Olympic urban planning was its emphasis on environmental sustainability. After various attempts at promoting the 'Athletes' and 'Millennium' Games, SOCOG focused on the promotion of the 2000 Olympics as the 'Green Games', and used its approach to remodelling formerly derelict Homebush Bay into the official Olympic Park as its most iconic environment-friendly development (SOCOG, 1999e; see also chapter 2). Sydney's emphasis on its green policies and credentials was accentuated by the IOC's decision to make the 'environment' the third main strand of Olympism, after sport and culture (IOC 2000b).[13]

The promotion of a Green Games came not without controversy, as local activists denounced what they saw as an opportunistic top-down strategy that failed fundamental environmental standards but succeeded in creating a perception of success thanks to the 'questionable' or bought-in support of media partners (Waitt, 2004, pp. 398–397). McManus (2004, p. 164) corroborated the view of Sydney's environmental strategy as flawed by referring to what he considered a direct negative effect of becoming an Olympic city:

> [T]he concept of an Olympic city influenced many parts of Sydney. While it was visible in the beautification of routes from the airport and the motorway to the Homebush Olympic facilities, the notion that an Olympic city could not be a 'place of shame' was most noticeable in the decision to relocate the cycling road races from Bankstown in the south-west of Sydney to the more affluent eastern suburbs… In the case of Rozelle Bay, it was possible to appeal to the discourse of the Olympic city in order to gain support for a project such as a 'temporary' super-yacht marina that otherwise may have been considered unnecessary or politically sensitive. The text, in this case plans showing the 'temporary' moorings and even the proposed uses beyond the Olympic Games, were embedded in a frantic haste to prepare Sydney to become the Olympic city… Approval was likely to be more forthcoming under such circumstances.

Despite these concerns, the 'Green Games' became the strongest line of communication by SOCOG and continued to be used within official documentation and government funded post-Games evaluation reports (PriceWaterhouseCoopers, 2002). However, during the Olympic fortnight itself, the environmental debate was progressively confined to the walled and ticketed official Olympic areas and lost prominence in the perception of what the Olympic city was really about. While a privileged few had access to the new facilities and environmental transformation of the Homebush Olympic Park and other sporting arenas, most Sydneysiders experienced the Olympics simply by living the street. In this context, a fourth, unofficial line became prevalent: the notion of the 'Friendly Games', which had been the most recognizable by-line to the Melbourne Olympics in 1956. It is interesting to consider the implications of the 'Friendly Games' tag over the official denominations as it emerged, rather spontaneously, out of the city's atmosphere and can thus be considered more representative of the sort of Olympic city that Sydney became for those experiencing it first hand.

This situation suggests that despite the many arguments concerning the overarching 'media-space' inhabited by any mega-event (Dayan and Katz, 1994; Wark, 1994; Wilson, 1996), the lived experience of the Games offers an added value and is a fundamental element in understanding how an Olympic host city

Figure 14.3. Sydney 2000 Volunteers. Sydney's Olympic volunteers became the city's most popular ambassadors and were key to the perception of the 'Friendly Games'.

operates. There are many interesting examples of Olympic street experience prior to year 2000, yet Sydney was able to advance the case further and set a precedent for subsequent Olympic hosts. This came courtesy of a combination of established Games practices (open air and free sport competitions such as the marathon; Olympic decorations or 'look of the Games') and the introduction of unprecedented interventions with the aid of new technologies (*LiveSites!*).

Traditionally, the role of the street and other urban public spaces during the Olympic fortnight is to offer a distinctive experience, rooted in the culture of the local host but supported by world-class services and entertainment. In this aspiration, Olympic cities must balance the tension between offering a culturally meaningful and representative experience and satisfying the expectations of international visitors with global standards. Sydney was particularly successful with its 'world-class' entertainment provision, using both public and private spaces in its CBD to present a wide range of food, drink, accommodation, shopping and related entertainment, both through free and paying programmes of activity. The Olympic city's core spaces were concentrated in two main areas: the spectacular Circular Quay, home to the Sydney Opera House and Sydney Bridge, and the recently developed Darling Harbour, presenting the range of services characteristic of festival marketplace developments (see Stevenson, 2003, p. 101). The latter was also home to key cultural venues such as the Maritime Museum and the

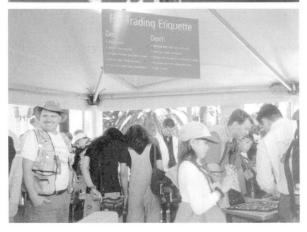

Figure 14.4. The Feeling of the Street. The Olympic rings in feathers to decorate a trendy hair salon window; restaurant special 'Olympic deals'; and the ever popular Olympic-pin trading tents.

Powerhouse Museum, the Sydney Media Centre and several Olympic National Houses. The Olympic city feel was at its core the result of the combination of the 'Look of the Games' programme, managed by SOCOG, and the innovative *LiveSites!* by the City of Sydney. However, the emergence of alternative and often unplanned manifestations was also central to its success. These ranged from the unofficial creation of Olympic-themed shop motifs (see figure 14.4) to the extreme popularity of some Olympic National Houses such as The Netherlands House, sponsored by Heineken and host to some of the loudest all-night parties in the city.

However, the buzz and vibrancy of the city centre was not equally distributed throughout Sydney and did not extend to the suburbia surrounding key Olympic venues. The town of Parramatta, at the outskirts of Homebush, can be considered the only notable exception, as the authorities supported the setting up of large tents for Olympic pin-trading, which has emerged as one of the most popular hobbies of Olympic fans around the world. Other neighbouring communities were largely deprived of special activity other than the isolated efforts of local authorities to welcome the torch relay on the final days leading to the opening of the Games.

Impacts on Local Creative Communities

At this point, it is relevant to understand the reactions of Sydney's creative communities. Even though general opinion polls reveal high levels of satisfaction from average Sydneysiders (Waitt, 2003), research into the impressions of special interest groups suggests a different picture. Previous work on the cultural dimensions of the Sydney Olympics indicates that some of the strongest levels of dissatisfaction are found within the city's diverse creative communities, in particular, ethnic minorities including Aboriginal groups (García, 2002b).

As often the case with any mega-event hosting processes and the Olympics in particular, a relevant section of Sydney's creative community felt that the Olympics were a threat to innovative and representative cultural manifestations. This feeling was expressed when Sydney won the bid in 1993 and was accentuated after learning about the existence of an official Olympic cultural programme that was underfunded and unable to guarantee open access and participation (García, 2002b, 2004). In 2000, the worst impressions were found amongst multicultural arts representatives and small companies from suburban Sydney. The latter claimed to be doubly disappointed: first, as they could not become an active component of a festival 'exclusively designed to showcase high art' and, secondly, for their exclusion as potential venues of the event.[14] Cases deserving special consideration were the suburbs of Auburn (which administratively incorporates Homebush, site of the Olympic park), Parramatta (adjacent to Homebush) and Liverpool (host of sporting competitions). Despite their geographical proximity to the principal sporting events, none of these suburbs hosted Olympic Arts Festival events. Another remarkable case was that of Rosehill, an area adjacent to

Olympic Park and home to some sporting competitions, which was supposed to host 'Australians All', the only Festival event 'taking place out of the city centre' (SOCOG, 1999f). After a year of promoting the commitment to reach suburban Sydney with Olympic arts activities, the initiative was cancelled and the concert was transferred to a popular park in the heart of the CBD, where all other events were taking place.

Sydney's multicultural arts representatives denounced the lack of a genuine interest by SOCOG to embrace the existing diversity of the city despite its being a focal point of the Games' mission statement. To substantiate this impression, representatives of Carnivale, the most comprehensive multicultural festival in Sydney which takes place annually in September and was expected to coincide with the Olympic fortnight, repeatedly denounced the barriers placed in the way of integrating Carnivale into the 2000 Olympic programme.[15] After unclear discussions, it was decided to delay the start of the 2000 Carnivale until the end of the Games. The Festival was finally held in parallel with the Paralympic Games without being allocated any special Olympic funding.

Interestingly, the Premier of NSW proposed the creation of a street festival during the Olympic period with the aim of reflecting aspects of Sydney's multicultural society at a grassroots level. The NSW Ethnic Council obtained a grant for this project and local ethnic councils were invited to present proposals (McMill, 1999). In the event, neither Carnivale nor the Olympic Arts Festival team were included in the negotiations. The Street Festival project was thus designed independently of established ethnic and multicultural arts groups to focus instead on populist events without the direct input of local artists or grassroots cultural organizations. The frequent confusions and misunderstandings between different factions of Sydney's ethnic arts community and government bodies suggests a poorly devised multicultural arts policy which led to noticeable shortcomings within the Olympic programme and prevented the establishment of clear legacies.

Sydney's mainstream cultural institutions had a greater role within the Arts Festivals and insisted on the value of including an official cultural programme as part of the Olympic hosting process. One of the main benefits identified was potential national and global media exposure. In contrast, very few established cultural institutions expressed a belief in the long-term legacy and sustainability of the experience. In their view, the Olympic extravaganza was made for bold and spectacular statements rather than the more subtle or complex cultural messages that would have been required to represent contemporary Sydney or indeed Australian cultures properly.[16]

The Sydney Opera House was one of the main venues presenting Olympic art work in August 2000 and the sole official performing arts venue during the Games. To maximize exposure, the management team created 'Opera House 2000', a public relations programme starting on New Year's Eve with an acrobatics show and a large fireworks display on the building's rooftop. The 2000 programme continued throughout the Sydney Festival in January with a roof light design show every night in addition to the established performance programme. These activities were enhanced during the Games in order to emphasize the key role of the building in Sydney's lifestyle. In fact, most of the limited range of Olympic art outdoors events in 2000 took place in the Opera House forecourt, including a Torch Relay Opera Gala; a free performance by New Zealand Maori dancers, and the nightly lighting of the Opera rooftop.

According to the Sydney Opera House's Media Relations Officer, these events, combined with the international dance, music and opera programme taking place indoors, ensured the prominence of the venue throughout the Games and provided great opportunities for national and international media coverage.[17] Nevertheless, the interest of the international media was focused on its role as an architectural icon of Sydney, rather than its sophisticated indoors cultural programming. While the building was often used as a backdrop to media reporting, references to the Arts Festival programme were practically non-existent, particularly within broadcast media.[18] Furthermore, the levels of coverage of the building as a background to outdoors sporting competitions, from the sailing to the men's and women's triathlon and marathon, clearly outstripped any coverage of outdoor arts events. The only events to rival the sports competitions were the arrival of the torch to Sydney and the Closing Ceremony fireworks spectacular.

The involvement of the Opera House in the official Olympic cultural programme also had some negative consequences, such as a significant increase in ticket prices that, arguably, prevented the average public from attending events during the Games (Morgan, 1999, p. 15). Many shows were sold out but, off-the-record, observers have suggested that it was due to Olympic sponsor functions and other pre-arranged Olympic family evenings, rather than public interest. Indeed, this brings into question the extent to which the Sydney Opera House played a relevant role for the general public during the Olympic period other than as emblematic background.

Besides the Sydney Opera House, the only arts venues with a strong presence during the Olympic fortnight were Sydney's public arts galleries and museums, which offered one of the most extensive visual arts programmes ever presented alongside the Games. The Art Gallery of New South Wales and the Powerhouse Museum were particularly committed to the Olympics and agreed to finance hallmark exhibitions responding to both local and international demands.[19] As such, they combined the presentation of Australian work[20] with prestigious world collections.[21] Venues such as the Australian National Maritime Museum saw the Games as an opportunity to attract extra revenue and complemented its exhibition programme with rent deals for sponsor and athletes' functions, which proved to be the most lucrative strategy (Scott, 2004). An interesting addition to their involvement in the official cultural programme was the development of an ambitious visitor research project by the Powerhouse Museum and the Australian National Maritime Museum. As mentioned earlier, these institutions are located in the surroundings of Darling Harbour, which became an Olympic sports site and entertainment location, so both museums were interested in assessing whether the Olympic experience brought any change to their visitor profile. The visitor research project compared qualitative and quantitative visitor data from September 1999, 2000 and 2001 and provided evidence of the benefits (e.g. visitor increase)

Figure 14.5. Sydney Opera House. Elitist or inclusive? Contrasting sights. An exclusive Olympic Arts Festival function within the Opera House sails (above) and the popular forecourt just before the women's marathon.

of having cultural institutions physically near the site of hallmark sporting events and presenting event themed exhibitions (*Ibid.*). This was one of few initiatives promoting the Games' impact on host city cultural venues and has contributed to a better understanding of the role and potential of the Games cultural programme.

Successes and Failures

Seven years on, Sydney is still remembered with fondness by the general media and Sydneysiders in particular and criticism remains muted compared with either Atlanta 1996 or Athens 2004. Even though Homebush has not become the environmental hallmark promoters tried to sell, and despite growing references to the 'white elephant' syndrome in Olympic Park (see Searle, 2002), the complaints, outside strict academic circles (see Lenskyj, 2002; Waitt, 2003, 2004), have not been particularly loud. London, confirmed host of the 2012 Games, is relying on Sydney's experience over any other previous host city, which probably indicates that, despite inevitable failings, Sydney managed the Games in the right way (see also chapter 2).

Official Reports emphasize Sydney's success in financial terms, claiming that the city managed 'the most comprehensive business development program ever held in association with an Olympic Games' with a clear focus and unprecedented benefits for 'industry development, investment attraction and national tourism' (PriceWaterhouseCoopers, 2002, pp. 1–6).[22] The IOC corroborates this impression of success by claiming that SOCOG established the 'most financially successful domestic sponsorship programme to date' (*Ibid.*, p. 40) and 'the largest television broadcast operation in history' reaching an unprecedented 3.7 billion viewers (*Ibid.*, p. 11). Beyond the positive business impacts, it can be claimed that the Games have left a significant image legacy through presenting contemporaneous Australia, and making the case for Sydney as a 'world city' in the sense argued by Sassen (1994, pp. 85–89), that is, with the ability to attract foreign investment in real estate and finance. The official Arts Festivals, with assistance of the *ausarts2000* programme and, particularly, the popular *LiveSites!,* contributed to the establishment of such images and further strengthened the city's leisure and business tourism markets in areas such as Darling Harbour.

However, the claim that the Games helped the cause of Aboriginal reconciliation and multicultural understanding is harder to prove. This is because it is difficult to dispute Wilson's (1996) claim that the Games were not used to advance the cultural case beyond image terms. As such, many of the groups that were struggling to get their voices heard before the Games, despite brief appearances at ceremonial and entertainment programmes, are still struggling today. Notably, the reputed Carnivale multicultural festival ceased to exist in 2004, with only one of its elements, Café Carnivale, coincidentally inaugurated during the Paralympic Games, surviving to this day.

So what kind of city is Sydney today, and what is the main cultural legacy of having hosted the Olympics? Regardless of the limited progress towards 'reconciliation' in political terms, an unquestionable cultural legacy is the dramatic growth in demands and expectations about Aboriginal arts and culture both nationally and internationally. The 1997 Olympic Arts Festival established an important precedent to ensure that all future festivals and events in Australia include Aboriginal work and that this is presented in mainstream venues with corresponding levels of funding rather than just as fringe activities.[23] Furthermore, Hinkson (2003) argued that, in terms of tourism, Sydney now has a marked 'Aboriginal' profile, which has obliged Tourism NSW to revise their generally outdated promotion of Aboriginal culture as 'traditional' and non-metropolitan and start highlighting urban Aboriginal sites and contemporary cultural expressions to satisfy visitors' demands. Beyond the Aboriginal case, the Festivals also contributed to the long-term sustainability of other cultural initiatives. One of the most successful examples is the 'Sculpture by the Sea' programme, an open air sculpture circuit connecting Bondi and Tamarama Beaches which started in 1997 with minimal funding. This became a core component of the 1998 Festival and, 10 years on, is one of Sydney's most popular annual events with regular spin-offs across Australia. At another level, the Olympic cultural programme helped make the case for City of Sydney to invest in a more ambitious and relevant public art programme in the city, which now counts as the Games' most important cultural physical legacy (see Best, 2000).

Overall, the main limitation of Sydney's Olympic cultural dimensions was the emphasis on succeeding at a global rather than local level. This is a fundamental tension that remains unresolved within the Olympic hosting process and requires much more careful attention in the future. As such, while Sydney is presented as the most successful Games host to date by the IOC and Australian government, the question remains: how is success measured in the Olympic city? Should the priority be satisfying the demands of global partners or addressing the concerns of local communities? Sydney opted for the first and reaped important business benefits for local stakeholders as well. However, for the general public, the main benefit was a feeling of pride and renewed confidence in their city and nation. How these elements are taken forward will depend on the vision of current and future opinion leaders. It will be up to them to recover the original bid promises of multiculturalism and Aboriginal reconciliation and to try to embed them further in the day-to-day practices of the post-Olympic city, this time not for the sake of global spectacle but as a regular practice which is perhaps less glamorous but more meaningful and empowering to all.

Notes

1. Interview with Tony Veal, Associate Professor, Department of Sport, Tourism and Leisure Studies, University of Technology of Sydney, 15 April 1999; see also Thompson (2000).

2. Interview with S. Cunningham, Head of School, Media and Journalism, Queensland University of Technology, 25 August 2000.

3. At a local level, the promoted and perceived strengths of Sydney's candidature were a compact Olympic plan guaranteeing minimal travel to the venues for athletes, the Australian climate, the country's political stability and security, the large community support, the fact that it was Australia's third consecutive bid and, overall, 'a government with a strong commitment to sport, as evidenced by the fact that around 70 per cent of the required sports facilities would be available prior to the IOC vote in 1993, regardless of winning the Games' (McGeoch and Korporaal, 1994, p. 38). None of these arguments were directly related to culture.

4. In the case of Barcelona, this was 'Olympiada Cultural Sociedad Anonima' (OCSA), a private society separated from the Games Organizing Committee but associated with it through the shared responsibilities of board members representing key public agencies. In Athens, this was the Hellenic Culture Company, a sub-branch of the Hellenic Ministry of Culture acting independently from the Organizing Committee, and is currently trying to establish itself as a permanent Cultural Olympiad Foundation.

5. Interview with L. Marinos, Director, Carnivale and member SOCOG Multicultural Advisory Committee, 13 September 1999.

6. Interviews with K. Brown, Olympic Arts Festivals Programme Manager, SOCOG, 15 May and 6 August 1999.

7. The Youth Camp is an optional requirement described under Rule 58 of the Olympic Charter. It is aimed at bringing together young people in the host city from each participating country. The Charter recommends that they are accommodated together during the duration of the Games in order for them to learn about the Olympic movement and the host city Culture (IOC, 2004b).

8. Interviews with E. Louw, Senior Lecturer in Communications, University of Queensland, 25 August 2000 and G. Turner, Department of English, University of Queensland, 25 August 2000.

9. These included, 'The Sculpture Walk', a permanent public art project featuring outdoor sculptures at Sydney Botanic Gardens and other popular city locations; 'Sunscreen Sydney 2000', an open-air film festival produced in collaboration with Tourism NSW and the corporate sector, and the 'Olympic Park Exhibition', a miniature display of Olympic venues held at Sydney's Customs House Exhibition Centre (SOCOG, 2000b).

10. Interview with B. Powell, General Manager of Major Projects, City of Sydney, 8 October 2000.

11. Interviews with A. Jeffrey, National General Manager, Special Events and Olympics 2000, Telstra, 2 September 1999; L. Bits, Public Relations Manager, Swatch, 2 October 2000; and F. Hammond, Olympic Sponsorship Officer, Seven Network, 2 October 2000.

12. Interviews with J. Christey, Olympic Sponsorship Manager, Sydney Morning Herald, 23 August 1999; K. Lyall, Olympic Editor, The Australian, 28 September 1999; K. Strickland, Arts Editor, The Australian, 13 September and 5 October 2000.

13. Previously, the three main dimensions of Olympism had been termed 'sport, culture and education' but with the arrival of the environment as a top priority, education has been placed under the generic umbrella of 'culture' (IOC, 2004b).

14. Interview with C. Gouriotis, Director, Casula Powerhouse Regional Arts, 14 September 1999.

15. Interviews with J. Díaz, NSW Multicultural Music Coordinator and Carnivale Musical Coordinator, 15 November 1999; and L. Marinos (see above, note 5).

16. Interviews with B. Barnes, General Manager, State Theatre, 18 August 1999; J. Dyer, General Manager, Bangarra Dance Theatre Company, 16 September 1999; and E. Capon, Director, The Art Gallery of New South Wales, 22 February 2000.

17. Interview with G. Coste-Paul, Olympic Media Relations, Sydney Opera House, 5 October 2000.

18. Interview with F. Hammond, Olympic Sponsorship Officer, Seven Network, 2 October 2000.

19. Interview with E. Capon, (see note 15) and C. Scott, Manager, Evaluation and Visitor Research, Power House Museum, 4 October 2000.

20.   National Art Gallery: *Papunya Tula,* a highly praised Aboriginal exhibit; *Australian Icons* an exhibition presenting some of the greater Australian names in painting; Powerhouse: display of items from the Opening Ceremony and other Sydney Olympic memorabilia.

21.   National Art Gallery: *The Dead Sea Scrolls* a rare and internationally renowned collection; Powerhouse Museum: exhibition of the first-ever overseas import of Greek antiquities; Korean art works exhibit; exhibit of the *Codex Leicester* by Leonardo da Vinci.

22.   PriceWaterhouseCoopers (2002, pp. 1–2) pointed out 'some $3 billion in business outcomes', 'injection of over $6 billion in infrastructure developments' and 'over $1.2 billion worth of convention business for NSW between 1993 and 2007', 'over $6 billion in inbound tourism spending during 2001', 'greatly enhanced business profile for Sydney, NSW and Australia through the equivalent of up to $6.1 billion worth of international exposure', 'greater expertise and confidence in tendering, both domestically and overseas, on large-scale projects', 'new and improved business programs including strong collaboration with the private sector'.

23.   Indeed, many Aboriginal and Torres Strait Islanders do still prefer to act independently from the mainstream and keep engaging in grassroots alternative or marginal work, but having a 'mainstream' option is generally regarded as an important step forward (interview with J. Diaz: see note 15).

Chapter 15

Athens 2004

Margaret M. Gold

In 2004 the Olympics will return to the place where they were born, where they were revived and where they will be renewed. The ATHENS 2004 Olympic Games are more than an opportunity to participate in the greatest celebration of humanity. They are an opportunity to be part of a story as old as history itself. And when it comes to making history, there is really no place like home.

ATHOC (2004, p. 31)

The relationship between Greece and the Olympic Games is like no other. The slogan 'There's no Place like Home', used in all the advertising for the 2004 Games, resonated with Greek identity, collective memory and historical experience. As home to the classical Olympics, the Games go to the very heart of Greek culture. Indeed, from the point at which Greece regained its independence in 1830, the possibility of reviving the Games, along with the drive to rebuild Athens as a worthy successor of the grand city of Antiquity, became key themes for those seeking to restore Greek values and identity. While not inseparable, there would always be a close link between staging the Olympics and the regeneration of Athens – always likely to be the host city whenever the Games returned to Greece.

This chapter looks at the 2004 Summer Olympic Games against this background. Its early sections briefly chart the growth of the Olympic movement in Athens alongside attempts to regenerate the city, a period that culminated in the first Olympiad of 1896 and the 1906 Intercalated Games. The subsequent sections analyse the decision to bid for the centenary 1996 Games and its failure, the successful bid made in 1997 to stage the 2004 Games, and the urban planning strategy associated with that event. Finally, there is an assessment of the urban legacy bequeathed by Athens 2004.

An Immature Metropolis

Athens at the start of the nineteenth century was far from the grand city of classical imagining, as 'filtered through European scholarship and imagination' (Waterfield, 2004, p. 29). The handful of more adventurous visitors that made their way to this corner of the Ottoman Empire were confronted by a small provincial centre with a population of around 10,000. The upper town on the Acropolis contained the Turkish garrison with barracks, housing, shops and a mosque intermingled with the remains of the Parthenon and other classical structures. A lower town on the northern and eastern slopes of the Acropolis housed the Greek, Albanian and Turkish civilian populations. The city itself fared badly in the fight for independence (1821–1830). Although Greece gained its independence after the signing of the London Protocol in February 1830, the Turkish garrison did not leave finally until 1833. By this time the population had fallen to 6,000 and the city was described by the traveller Christopher Wordsworth in 1832 as: 'lying in ruins. The streets are almost deserted: nearly all the houses are without roofs. The churches are reduced to bare walls and heaps of stones and mortar. There is but one church in which the service is performed' (cited in Bastéa, 2000, p. 10). At this time, it was not even the Greek capital, with Nauplion, a strategic Venetian fortress on the east coast of the Peloponnesus, serving that function until 1833.

Understandably, thinking soon turned to finding readily recognizable symbolic strategies through which to reassert the sense of nationhood, of which the two that most readily came to the fore were the reconstruction of Athens and the revival of the Olympics. Two German-trained architects Stamatios Kleanthes and Eduard Schaubert, for example, had visited Athens in 1830–1831 and produced a plan for a city for 35–40,000 people. It featured a baroque-inspired layout based on radial axes (meeting at present day Omonia Square) where the Royal Palace, Parliament and Senate would be placed, and a series of grids creating nodal points for other key buildings (Travlos, 1981, pp. 393–394). The opposition to the necessary demolitions to implement the plan, the lack of resources to carry it through and the immediate pressure of population influx as the functions of government were established in Athens and exiles returned, meant that the plan needed almost immediate amendment. Instead, the new Athens developed gradually rather than by radical reconstruction, with an approach that sought to respect the classical archaeology, while creating a new neo-classical townscape.

The idea for the revival of the Olympic Games developed around the same time as the initial schemes for replanning Athens, although not without fierce debate between those that believed their restoration was essential for reviving Greek culture, values and identity and those who saw the Games as a cultural irrelevance and practical impossibility. The Greek poet Panagiotos Soutsos, for instance, launched a campaign in 1835 based around a series of poems that featured figures from the past calling on present-day Greeks to reinstate the Olympic Games. As early as January 1837, a Royal Decree established a 'national gathering' with competitions in agriculture, industry and athletics, with the specified athletic events being those associated with the ancient Games – discus, javelin, long jump, foot races, wrestling, and chariot racing (Young, 1987, p. 273; 2004, p. 141). The ancient Panathenian Stadium formed a natural focus for such activity and was restored to serve as the setting for two of the three Zappas Games (1870 and 1875; see chapter 2).[1] Various attempts were made to revive that series, notably in 1892, but they were thwarted by financial difficulties. The initiative of the Coubertin-led IOC in reviving the Olympics and choosing Athens as the site for the 1896 Games, therefore, served the interests of both Greece and the Olympic movement. Athens gained a new Olympic Games with international recognition and participation, whereas the revived Games benefited from the imprimatur of being held on Greek soil. However, the IOC's preference for an ambulatory festival and fierce resistance to giving the Games a permanent home in Greece meant that, apart from the Intercalated Games of 1906, Athens would not receive another Olympic festival until the next Millennium.

Bidding

By 1990, when the city next formally sought the Games, Athens was a byword for problems characteristic of many Mediterranean cities (Wynn, 1984; Leontidou, 1990). A plethora of further plans commissioned from foreign architects and planners had come and gone in the face of military conflict and political and economic problems, with none adopted (Sonne, 2003, p. 146). Athens experienced rapid growth in the 1960s and 1970s, driven by industrial investment, rural-urban migration, a building boom and spontaneous development at the urban fringe – much of it illegal and unplanned. Public transport was poor and the city suffered severe environmental pollution and congestion. Although a capital city, Athens was not competitive with other major centres in Europe (Leontidou, 1990, p. 263) and was unable to offer inducements to counteract its relatively isolated position. Certainly, the idea of seeking the modern Olympic Games, with its inevitable financial burden, appeared implausible before Los Angeles 1984 established the new financial model.

Athens's first, and unsuccessful, bid for the return of the Games between 1987 and 1991 should be seen against this background. The city's reasons for its campaign reflected a mixture of the general and specific. Like most potential host cities, there was a broad place promotional message that sought to offset negative features (e.g. stereotypes about the Greek economy and culture) with positive images of a 'new face for Greece, outward looking and ready to take-up the challenges of globalisation'.[2] The city looked to the mega-event to make Athens ready to compete in a world market for jobs and investment, while simultaneously enhancing Greek sporting infrastructure and helping to solve urban problems. As Vissilis Harissis, Director of the Organization for Athens, the body responsible for coordinating the Athens city plan, noted forcefully: 'Getting the Olympics is the best chance we'll ever have to save Athens. It'll be like fighting a war: there will be money and an incentive' (Hope, 1990).

Yet behind these broader objectives lay another set of ambitions that emanated from Greece's special relationship with the Olympics. The Greeks looked to the Olympics to help the nation recapture its soul; linking the ancient and modern in a meaningful and contemporary way for the twenty-first century. At the same time the Greeks wanted to reassert traditional values, especially as a reaction to the politicized and commercialized Games of the 1970s and 1980s when calls periodically surfaced that the Games might be able to regain their core values by returning to their geographical roots (Pound, 2004, p. 4). There was a strong sense that Greece wanted to 'correct the course' of the Modern Olympic Movement (ATHOC, 2005, I, p. 63). While talk of a permanent home for the Games had long since subsided, there seemed an incontestable logic in a Greek bid to host the Twenty-Sixth Olympiad in 1996 to celebrate the centenary of revival.

The bid achieved Parliamentary approval in April 1986, with the Bid Committee presenting Athens's candidacy to the IOC in 1988 and the final Bid File in March 1990 for the IOC meeting in Tokyo the following September. The case was put that 70 per cent of the sports facilities were already in place or would be completed for the planned Eleventh Mediterranean Games in 1991. The documentation trumpeted Athens's experience in organizing international sporting competitions, listing 12 events hosted between the European Athletics Championships of 1982 and the Men's World and European Weightlifting Championship in 1989. Three of these, it was noted, had won awards from the International Press Association for the best organized press facilities. However, its publicity of course failed to mention the twin disasters of 1982 – the IAAF Golden Marathon when police failed to close the last 5 kilometres of the course to traffic, with runners encountering rush hour traffic, or the fact that the track in the new Olympic Stadium had not been laid by the time athletes were arriving for the European Athletics Championships (Payne, 2006, p. 258).

The strategic plan sought to concentrate the sports facilities in two centres. The first, the Athens Olympic Sports Complex (AOSC), would be at Maroussi, a suburban municipality 9 kilometres north-east of central Athens. This would build on existing facilities, most notably the stadium constructed between 1980 and 1982 for the European Athletic Championships, which was always seen as providing Greece with a facility of international standing that would allow Athens to compete for international events. AOSC would feature the stadium, velodrome, swimming complex, multi-purpose sports hall, an indoor hall and tennis centre, the Press Village, Main Press Centre and International Broadcasting Centre. The second complex, on the coast south of Athens at Faliro Bay and the nearby Karaiskaki Stadium,[3] would make use of the existing Stadio Erinis end Filias (Peace and Friendship Stadium) and new facilities to accommodate basketball, wrestling, judo, boxing, handball, baseball and yachting. Existing facilities in Athens would be used for sports such as archery and shooting, while the city centre would be the focus of the cultural festivities, making use of the classical legacy such as the Panathenian Stadium and Herodeion. The centre would house IOC members, the Olympic Family and official guests, with the Olympic Village scheduled for construction on the northern fringes of the Athens Metropolitan Area on the slopes of Mount Parnitha. The Olympic Ring promised travel times of only 12 minutes between the Olympic Village and stadium and 18 minutes to Faliro Bay. Road projects, new metro lines, a new tram line, improvements to the existing Helleniki International Airport on the coast east of Faliro Bay and a new international airport at Sparta were also planned.[4]

The eventual decision to award the centenary Games to Atlanta came as a shock. Melina Mercouri, the Greek Culture Minister, protested that 'Coca Cola won over the Parthenon' and the Prime Minister, Andreas Papandreou, called it 'an injustice against Greece' committed by the international community (Senn, 1999, p. 250). Rather later, the official Report from Athens 2004 (ATHOC, 2005, I, p. 65) placed part of the blame for the bid's failure on the perception of political instability that was created by the three general elections in eight months leading up to the IOC decision – a factor noted in the IOC Evaluation Commission's report. The Athens team was also accused of taking an arrogant approach towards endorsement, but the real stumbling block was the size of the task needed to provide the required infrastructure and setting for the Games. Even the Mayor of Athens had recognized in 1987 that a radical transformation was required to deal with the city's atmospheric pollution, traffic congestion, noise, lack of parking, shortage of open space, new sports facilities, outmoded media facilities and deficiencies in the public transport network. Such was the scale of the problems that although he supported the government's plan to host the Games, he stated that 'if we are in danger of looking ridiculous, I will not go along with it, and I will stand up and tell the public the truth' (quoted in *Anon*, 1987).

Greece's wish to stage the Games quickly resurfaced after the disappointment of the award to Atlanta. In 1995, the government toyed with the idea of seeking the 2008 Games outside the customary bidding procedure by requesting 'a direct award' of the Games as 'an honour' recognizing the special status of Athens. This was pursued for a while but the impracticality of obtaining the support of two-thirds of the IOC for the necessary change in the IOC Charter led the Hellenic Olympic Committee, in December 1995, to canvass vigorously for a conventional bid for the 2004 Games. Athens's candidature was submitted on 6 January 1996, five days before the official deadline, joining a group of cities already well ahead with their preparations. These comprised Rome, regarded as the favourite, along with Buenos Aires, Cape Town, Istanbul, Lille, Rio de Janeiro, St Petersburg, San Juan (Puerto Rico), Seville and Stockholm (ATHOC, 2005, I, pp. 67–68).

Not wholly surprisingly, Athens's final bid document for the 1997 IOC decision bore similarities to the failed 1990 bid, but with a less strident tone in the presentation (AOBC, 1997). The accompanying statements from politicians and officials now stressed the profound economic changes in Greece and Athens, particularly in the context of membership of the European Union. The Mayor, Dimitris Avramopoulos, wrote about the need to:

> give renewed impetus to the Olympic Ideal and to help the Olympic Movement start afresh at the beginning of a new century. Athens is ready, and we Athenians – all of us – are sensible of the responsibility that stems from the supreme and noble honour that, we hope, awaits us.

The Minister of Sport, Andreas Fouras, assured the IOC that the:

> long-term programme of construction and installation of equipment which will ensure that long before 2000 – and regardless of whether Athens is awarded the Games – the city will have made good the few shortcomings it still displays in the facilities necessary for all the Olympic sports.

The Master Plan sought to concentrate the Games in a small number of locations while making use of existing sport infrastructure. Indeed, the bid claimed that 75 per cent of the competition venues and 92 per cent of the training venues were already in place. The backbone of the strategy remained to use the locations identified in the earlier bid – the Olympic Village on the slopes of Mount Parnitha; AOSC at Maroussi to host seven events (athletics, basketball, cycling, football, gymnastics, swimming and tennis); central Athens (cultural Olympiad and accommodation for Official Visitors); and the Faliro Coastal Zone, designated as a major regeneration project for Athens's Riviera, which would house baseball, boxing, fencing, handball, hockey, judo, wrestling, softball, taekwondo and volleyball.

The plan envisaged four further sites within the Athens conurbation – the Nikaia indoor hall for weightlifting and the Peristeri indoor hall for badminton (both in the west); in the north the Galatsi gymnasium for table tennis; and in the east, Goudi for the modern pentathlon. Beyond the conurbation, the equestrian and archery events were located at Tatoi in the north on Mount Parnitha; rowing, canoeing and kayaking at Schinas on the coast north-east of Athens near the ancient battlefield of Marathon; shooting at Markopoulo south-east of Athens; and sailing and the triathlon along the coast at, respectively, Kosmas and Glyfada. The Olympic Ring project remained as before to link the conurbation sporting venues. Investment in roads and in metro, tram lines and suburban railways would improve movement throughout the metropolis and provide access to the other venues. A new international airport at Sparta had become a central part of the planning strategy, although for the period up to and including the Games it would work in conjunction with the existing airport at Elliniko. The latter was proposed for closure in late 2004 (AOBC, 1997). A four-year Cultural Olympiad was planned, with events taking place in Greece and abroad to 'restore the Olympic Ideal' in the opening years of the new millennium. The estimated budget was $1.607 billion with the principal sources of income being television rights, sponsorship, licensing, official suppliers, donations, ticket sales and lotteries (*Ibid.*, p. 162). The non-OCOG budget, however, was $7.35 billion, which included expenditure on roads, airport construction and landscaping.

Planning Athens 2004

The IOC's decision in September 1997 to award the 2004 Games to Athens reflected the quality of the campaign run by the Greek bidding team led by Gianna Angelopoulos-Daskalaki. Despite assurances that the same team would lead the planning and organization of the Games, they were replaced on return to Athens (Payne, 2006, p. 259). Moreover, instead of immediate implementation of the Master Plan, the government instigated a review in early 1998 'to eliminate potential problems that might arise during the implementation phase due to the existing zoning and town planning legislation' (ATHOC, 2005, I, p. 143). These considerations, coupled with rethinking on the logistics of the festival and community views on site decisions, led to considerable and time-consuming changes to the original strategy.

The AOSC complex remained the heart of the scheme, but the government decided to concentrate less activity in the Faliro area while retaining it as a 'pole' of the Games and an important urban regeneration site. After exploring the idea of moving some events to Aspropyrgos, west of the Athens conurbation – which proved unacceptable to both the IOC and the International Federations (*Ibid.*, p. 144) – it was decided to use a site at the much criticized Athens International Airport at Helleniki.[5] Faliro now only staged four rather than 11 sports (volleyball, beach volleyball, handball and taekwando), Helleniki would handle baseball, fencing, hockey, softball, basketball, some of the handball matches from Faliro and, after a court case (see below), the canoe and kayak slalom centre (*Ibid.*). Boxing and badminton were moved to, respectively, Peristeri and the Goudi complex. Two sports were moved to sites with classical connotations to assert the sense of Greek ownership of the Games: archery to the Panathenaic Stadium and the shot put to Olympia. The decision on Olympia was controversial. The first suggestion was to stage the javelin or discus there because these were events that featured in the Ancient Games. This encountered opposition from the archaeologists due to potential damage to the site (see chapter 2). The shot put was finally selected as likely to create fewer problems, but the Archaeological Service insisted that no electronic equipment could be used, the throwing circle was to be portable, and that 15,000 free tickets could be issued for spectators to sit on the grass, obviating the need to build a temporary grandstand.[6]

These changes to the original strategy set back the timetable. Some locations needed planning from scratch, with the transport strategy requiring revision to take into consideration the new sites and relocated sports. The process of rethinking, with associated debates, contributed to the now infamous delays in the completion of venues and infrastructure that Payne (2006, p. 261) called the 'three lost years'. Although it was claimed that 75 per cent of the venues already existed, the renovation work envisaged for some was ambitious; for example, amounting to demolition and rebuilding of the swimming complex and tennis centre at AOSC. Additional problems arose from the presence of multiple and often conflicting agencies (Beriatos and Gospodini, 2004, p. 193), the difficulties of gaining cooperation from officials from different political parties, the bureaucratic planning system, and from archaeological discoveries made during construction that required excavation and recording before work could continue. In some instances plans had to be adjusted in order to preserve structures, such as the re-siting of the Olympic Village site to avoid archaeological remains (see below). Matters were not helped by the increased security concerns that inflated costs and caused a review of the layout of venues.

The resulting delays in finalizing venues or in sites becoming available for development caused alarm at the IOC, with Samaranch warning Greece in April 2000 that they might lose the Games if action was not forthcoming. The sense of crisis was fanned by the press, although some observers (e.g. Waterfield, 2004, p. 372) felt that there was insufficient recognition of the complexities of operating in an ancient city such as Athens. The government reacted by bringing Gianna Angelopoulos-Daskalaki back to the development team (Payne, 2006, pp. 261–262), making available emergency funds and introducing new legislation and mechanisms to speed up the development process (Pyrgiotis, 2003, p. 417). This all added substantially to the cost of the Games, with 'speed bonuses' offered by government as an incentive to improve completion, coupled with threats of loss of licences to contactors that failed to complete on time.

The final plan for the Games was described by Beriatos and Gospodini (2004, p. 197) as a 'scattered model' suggestive of a strategy for promoting 'multi-nucleus urban regeneration and development' (Ibid., p. 192), in contrast to cities like Barcelona which focused investment on a few key locations. The plan diluted the logic of concentrating development in major nodes by a policy that suggested post-Games use, in which facilities were more widely spread in the community. In reality, however, there was no proper strategic planning for the period after 2004, with the plan containing apparent contradictions. Despite espousing the desire to protect and create open space, development focused primarily on greenfield sites and overlooked possible brownfield locations. Emphasis was placed on gaining spectacular buildings and monuments to create a sense of place and to signify the 2004 Games, yet these structures are outside the main tourist areas.

Broadly speaking, the plan proposed three approaches to preparing the city for the Games. The first concerned the permanent structures: the sports venues, transport infrastructure, city renovation and arts infrastructure that were designed to be a physical legacy for the city. The second involved a series of temporary interventions designed to house additional sports capacity, visitor accommodation and traffic movements. This also included measures to shape the 'look' of the city to provide it with a festive atmosphere that clearly identified it with the Olympics. The third comprised attempts to encourage volunteering and change the behaviour of the population by tackling issues such as litter and smoking.

Olympic Facilities

AOSC was the spectacular centrepiece of the Olympics, eventually developing into a focus that went far beyond simple renovation of the complex created for the 1982 European Athletic Championships. Having decided that it wanted an 'architectural landmark of international recognition', the Ministry of Culture approached the Spanish architect Santiago Calatrava in March 2001 to submit a Master Plan. The result was a series of projects, including equipping the Olympic stadium with an innovative two leaf, laminated glass roof to protect spectators from the fierce sunlight, roofing the velodrome, bringing about the aesthetic unification of the various structures and plazas of the site by means of landscaping and an installation – the sinuous 'Wall of Nations' – that could also double as a giant video screen (Tzonis, 2005). The stadium roof in particular was a complex design and was only moved into position on the day that the IOC set as a deadline for the project to be either in place or abandoned (Payne, 2006, p. 269). Even so, shortage of time meant that only 9,000 of the projected 17,000 trees were planted around the stadium.

In the original plan, Faliro Bay was recognized as a prime candidate for regeneration. This area had developed in the 1870s as an elegant resort serving the Athenian middle class but a century later, cut off from adjacent residential districts by the coastal highway, it had declined into a virtual no man's land, degraded, polluted, and an illegal dumping ground. The nearby low-lying housing districts of Moschato and Kallithea were also subject to flooding. The Olympics provided a unique occasion for upgrading this area, again opening Athens to the sea and supplying much needed public open space. The downgrading of Faliro from the second most important Games complex to one staging just four events none of which had any great importance within Greek sporting culture meant there would be no legacy of specialized sports facilities here. Most construction work involved renovation of the two existing stadia – the Peace and Friendship Stadium for volleyball and the Karaiskaki for part of the football competition.

Having said this, the area did receive a moderate amount of remodelling. The race course at the east end of the site was moved and the land cleared. The Illissos River was canalized as part of the flood protection works, a marina was constructed in the east of the site and the area landscaped. An 800-metre-long esplanade was built from the old race track over the coastal highway to the new indoor sports hall and marinas. This connected the residential area with the renovated coastal zone, with walkways radiating westwards towards the beach volleyball arena. Improvements to roads and a new tram network linked the site to the centre of Athens and to the other Olympic venues. This was to be a prelude to planned post-Games projects intended to continue the anti-flooding work and move the coastal highway into a cutting allowing new bridges to the park beyond.

Of the two new buildings constructed for the Olympics, the beach volleyball centre would become an open-air theatre and the indoor sports hall for handball and taekwando would convert into a Metropolitan Convention Centre taking advantage of its proximity to major hotels, the city centre and the coast (Romanos et al., 2005, p. 6). Landscaping the area to the west of the theatre would create a 'green zone', with an environmental centre and communal sports facilities.

The old race track would become open space with water sports at the end of the esplanade. More tentative plans foresaw an Opera House on the race course site, an archaeological park to display classical structures from the regeneration project (*Ibid.*, pp. 4–6) and a heritage park including the Military Museum in the Syngrou villa, the Naval Museum and a new contemporary art museum (Sykianaki, 2003, p. 21). In total, the Coastal Leisure Park would provide 100 hectares of accessible open space (Sykianaki and Psihogias, 2006, p. 12).

The principle of coastal revitalization was continued further south with the redevelopment of the airport site at Helleniki. This entailed conversion of hangars to create indoor halls for fencing and basketball as well as provision of facilities for softball, baseball, hockey, canoeing and kayaking (ATHOC, 2005, p. 144). Not surprisingly, conversion of this site tended to produce a sports centre with a ground plan dominated by the exiting geometry of the airport. Suggestions for post-Games usage hazily envisaged the conversion of the East Airport Terminal, designed by Eero Saarinen in 1960, into a Conference and Exhibition Centre and luxury hotel, with the surrounding area touted as the largest metropolitan park in Europe. The question of how many Convention Centres Athens actually required scarcely entered the equation.

The extraordinary retreat from the original concentrated approach led to a scattering of other centres throughout the region. These included sailing at Aghios Kosmas, the modern pentathalon at the Goudi Olympic Complex at the foot of Mount Ymittos, weightlifting at Nikea, and the equestrian centre at Markopoulo (a significant archaeological site). Perhaps the most difficult location was the Schinas Rowing Centre, which attracted international controversy. Originally a wetland area, this coastal site had been partly drained for agriculture in the 1920s and had been used for civil and military aviation since the 1950s. The official viewpoint was that this was a degraded wetland in need of protection and the removal of existing installations. The 2.25 kilometre rowing course would be on the line of the old runway, along with practice facilities, an adjacent 400-metre slalom course for canoes and kayaks, grandstands for 10,000 spectators with space for 40,000 more along the course, associated start and finish towers, car parks, boathouses and visitor facilities. By contrast, environmentalists saw it as a rare ecological habitat with a delicate freshwater wetland habitat used by 176 bird species, and with a rare stone pine forest on the coastal dunes. Archaeologists and historians saw it as the site of the battle of Marathon and an important cultural landscape. The Greek government was criticized for removing the area from a list of sites to be submitted for Natura 2000 status – the European Union's initiative to guarantee the maintenance, or reestablishment, of important habitats (Metera *et al.*, 2005, p. 7).

When the Greek government ignored the European Commission's request for it to be reinstated, four environmental groups took the government to court.[7] Archaeological and heritage groups joined the protest, arguing that the Battle of Marathon had raged though the area and the development was akin to building a sports complex on the Gettysburg Battlefield. The government countered by saying that the area was previously under the sea and that there was no evidence of archaeological importance. The outcome did not prevent use of the site for the Olympics, but did produce concessions. The area received National Park status, the facilities were moved to the western end of the site, provision of visitor facilities were curtailed, and the slalom course was re-sited at Helleniki (see above). There was also a commitment to restore the wetlands and create an environmental zone and archaeological park.

The site of the Olympic Village was chosen partly because the government already owned half of the site, thereby reducing the need for compulsory purchase, and partly because the development, with its associated services, would 'upgrade the neglected area of the north-west section of the Greater Athens area' (AOBC, 1997, p. 26). The bid document had claimed the housing would be built to the highest environmental standards using solar energy, water management systems, planting of indigenous species and landscaping to create an ecological park. It was designed to accommodate 17,428 participants, with the maximum occupation level during the Olympics being 14,243 and 7,166 during the Paralympics (ATHOC, 2005, II, p. 49). In addition, the Village was intended to be self-financing, with the accommodation sold after the Games to middle-income families (*Ibid.*, p. 26).

From the outset, the authorities were criticized for lack of progress, although discovery of the remains of Hadrian's aqueduct on the site caused delay for excavation and redesign to protect the archaeology. Rather more criticism came from environmentalists, initially because the development encroached into an environmentally sensitive area and later due to the failure to implement the environmental elements as originally planned. The World Wildlife Fund, for example, criticized the lack of inbuilt water-saving measures, the irrigation of plantings in the surrounding areas from tap water, the lack of photovoltaic cells or solar heating systems in the design, and the failure to use environmentally friendly materials such as certified timber or ozone friendly cooling systems (WWF, 2004, pp. 8, 9).

Infrastructure

The Olympics provided an opportunity to take a fresh and comprehensive look at transport within Greater Athens, with its attendant problems of congestion, parking, slow travel times, pollution and the unpopularity of the public transport system (comprising bus, trolley bus, metro and suburban railway networks). The metro consisted of a single line dating back to the 1860s which by 1957 ran from Piraeus to Kifissia. By this time, however, the city had long since expanded into Attica, with large swathes reliant on trams (until 1961), trolleybuses (from 1949), diesel buses and the private car. Investment in improving public transport and creating an integrated transport system for the first time, therefore, was paramount.

A proportion of the investment was scheduled before gaining the Games; for example, contracts for two new metro lines were signed in 1991. Nevertheless, early progress was extremely slow due to bureaucratic problems, geological difficulties and delays for archaeological excavations ahead of station construction. Lack of progress on line 3, which connected with the airport, particularly concerned the IOC, with one observer commenting in 2002 that 'there are plans to extend this line all the way to the airport, but work has yet to start on this' (Dubin *et al.*, 2002). It remained incomplete at the time of the Games but, in reaching Doukaissia Plakentias by July 2004, it was possible to run services to the airport using a suburban rail line. Concerns over pollution led to replacement of the aged bus fleet, with environmentally-friendly vehicles that also offered greater accessibility for the disabled. Developments specifically for the Games included a new tram network that connected central Athens with the coastal Olympic venues – with one branch serving the Faliro Coastal Zone and the other heading south to Helleniki, Agios Kosmas and ending at Glyfada. It met with limited success however, given that traffic lights, frequent stops and vehicles obstructing the lines caused it to be 'strangely sluggish' (Sales, 2005, p. 29). The road network received investment to improve connections between Athens and other major centres and to create an outer ring road interlinking the Olympic venues, the international airport and the city. AOSC gained a ring road that operated during the Games as a clockwise one-way system reserved for Olympic traffic (ATHOC, 2005, p. 173). Elsewhere, a new Traffic Management System meant that traffic flows could be managed to prioritise Olympic traffic, with appropriate signage and dedicated lanes. In the final event, the free-moving traffic was a public relations coup for a city where congestion and traffic jams were regarded as endemic.

Cultural infrastructure also benefited from the Olympics. Major Athenian museums such as the National Archaeological Museum, Byzantine Museum and the National Gallery were renovated for the Games, although in the case of the National Archaeological Museum the task was made more challenging by damage from the 1999 earthquake (it was not fully opened until 2005). The Olympics were also a vehicle for developing contemporary art. This led to the foundation of two complexes, both housed in former industrial premises: Technopolis, an arts and performance space that also houses a small Maria Callas Museum; and the Athinais, a restored silk factory that contains a theatre, cinema, music space, museum space, restaurants, bars and cafés, and conference facilities. These have acted as exemplars for further developments, most notably the Hanson Building in Metaxourgio, which is to be converted into the new Athens Art Gallery, and the National Museum of Contemporary Art, which opened in 2005 in a converted brewery.

Beautification

As was seen with the examples of Mexico City 1968 (chapter 11) and Atlanta 1996 (chapter 2), beautification of a city is a contentious issue, prioritising impressing visitors over the interests of the poor, whether through redistribution of resources or displacement of previous residents. These issues arose in the case of Athens, but in the context of the longstanding desire to remake it as a city in keeping with the splendours of its august past. The return of the Games in 2004 witnessed a flurry of activity to beautify the city centre – the focus of the festivities and cultural activities that accompanied the Games, as well as the venue for the cycling road race and the finish of the marathon at the Panathenian Stadium (Sykianaki, 2003, p. 11). Perhaps the most important of the measures taken in relation to the Games was the unification of archaeological sites – a project that dated back to the 1832 plan which suggested that, when cleared and planted, the 'whole would be a museum of ancient building-art second to none in the world' (quoted in Bastéa, 2000, p. 219). The idea of a unified cultural-historic area resurfaced periodically over the next century and a half, but financial and practical problems hindered progress (Papageorgiou-Ventas, 1994, p. 28). In 1993, a formal scheme to link the key classical sites by landscaped pedestrian routes and green open spaces received European Union funding. Its rationale rested in part on romantic nationalism, partly on a wish to marry together the old and the new into a functional whole, and partly on creating a unique tourist amenity that could compete with the great European tourist cities (*Ibid.*, p. 398).

The city's planners considered it imperative to complete a major part of this project in time both to receive Olympic visitors and accommodate the road race which was planned to use the newly-pedestrianized streets around the Acropolis. By the Games, for instance, it was possible to walk from the Panathenian Stadium to the ancient cemetery at Kerameikos, via the Olympieion, the south side of the Acropolis, the Theatre of Dionysus and the ancient agora. By contrast, other projects such as the restoration of the Parthenon and the development of the new Acropolis Museum proved impossible to complete before the Games, due particularly to archaeological and conservation issues.

The programme for improving central Athens also encompassed improvements to street lighting, the refurbishment of city squares, restoration of façades, floodlighting monuments and key buildings, planting and landscaping, renewal of street furniture, repaving roads and improving pavements. Work was also carried out to upgrade the waste management systems of the city. The staging of the Paralympic Games had an important impact in improving access for the disabled, with installation of more than 7,000 wheelchair ramps (Bokoyannis, 2006, p. 6), modifications to public transport, and encouragement from ATHOC for businesses to cater for the needs of the disabled (see chapter 5).

Besides the regeneration schemes and other projects that made a permanent contribution to the quality of life of residents and visitors, there were also the temporary measures that announced that the city was *en fête*. The notion of giving the city a distinctive 'look' during the Olympic festival, a recurrent theme since Tokyo 1964 (see chapter 2), was again observed at Athens. Like its predecessors, this involved the careful selection of colours, logos, decorations and artwork, with the creation of a Kit of Parts that could be applied to all the venues and arranged so that athletes, visitors and television audiences could see the legend 'ATHENS 2004' and the Olympic Rings at all venues and along significant routes. This creation of 'visual identity' (ATHOC, 2005, I, p. 331) involved specification of a twenty-colour palette, centring on blue (sky and sea), yellow and oranges (summertime), red and fuchsia (flowers), green (landscape) and grey (stone) (*Ibid.*, p. 319). Construction sites and ugly buildings disappeared behind large building wraps, with images of ancient Olympia and photographs by Greek artists. Conscious of the over-commercialism of Atlanta – about which the Greeks had made considerable reference when bidding for the Games – attempts were made to control advertising displays throughout the city. By the summer of 2004, 5,000 billboards had been removed and official sites given over to sponsors and used for messages promoting the Olympic ideal. In the process, the Organizing Committee effectively enhanced the value of the investment made by sponsors in offering them 'a whole new level of protection against ambush marketing', comprising 'the most tightly controlled' marketplace to date (Payne, 2006, pp. 262–263, 266).

Legacy

Ensuring that Olympic sports facilities have viable alternative uses is a challenge with which many cities have struggled once the Games are over and Athens certainly made much of the idea that it was creating permanent facilities that would have post-Olympic use. Over the seven-year preparation period, official statements constantly speculated on the post-Games legacy, with the city clearly looking for a multifaceted outcome (ATHOC, 2005, II, p. 525). Leisure, cultural, sporting and conference uses were typically mentioned, but unless there is state involvement (as in the case of a government ministry using premises for offices) or end-users are directly identified and involved in construction (e.g. the Press Villages were funded by the universities for halls of residence), it is not so easy to dictate use.

In terms of immediate effect, there was the reality of a city which, with little margin for error, completed the facilities in time for the Games despite the scepticism of journalists who, only weeks earlier, described the rubble on building sites and listed the work still outstanding. There was spectacular television footage of the Opening Ceremony and the striking backdrop of the city. All this confirmed that the 'smoggy Aegean backwater' had indeed been 'transformed' (the most common adjective used) into a city of beautiful boulevards, clear and azure skies, a growing number of art centres, a vibrant and cutting edge spirit and the finest metro in Europe (Correspondent, 2004). Sadly for the organizers, the drug scandal involving Greek athletes on the eve of the Opening Ceremony was a public relations disaster both in the context of Athens promising a return to the core values of the Olympics and in diverting attention away from the city.[8] By the end of the Games however, attention had re-focused on the Games, with consensus being that the Games had been run well, with praise for the scheduling, transport and the athletes' facilities.

The longer term impact of the Games remains contentious. The Official Report (ATHOC, 2005, II, p. 525) outlines their legacy in terms of transport improvements, reduced pollution, land reclamation, sports facilities, beautification of the city, a culture of cooperation, civic spirit and job training, concluding:

> The Games were a 17-day advertisement for our competence and sophistication, potential investors discovered that Greece has the talent, attitude and infrastructure – and the EU membership – to compete internationally. Finally we Greeks proved to ourselves that we can do whatever we set ourselves to doing, under extraordinary pressure, with a global audience. After the Olympic Games, we know we can compete with anybody.

The Director for the Organization for the Planning and Environmental Protection of Athens, Catherine Sykianaki and her colleague Sakis Psihogias (2006, p. 11) maintained that the physical legacy of the Games in terms of 'renewal and regeneration' represented a 'catching up process after some decades of inertia had eroded the competitiveness and quality of life of Athens'. Athens now had an infrastructure conducive to economic growth. IOC marketing specialist Michael Payne (2006, p. 271) believed that the Games helped 're-brand Greece as a country' and that they had successfully managed to combine the mythological and traditional images with modern, dynamic designs. The Athens communication team even talked of 'just in time delivery' as if 'it was something that had been planned all the time so that the country could showcase its efficiency and ingenuity at the last minute' (*Ibid.*, p. 269) to counteract the press view that it was in fact a 'last minute approach'.[9] However, notwithstanding such promotional gloss, there is no doubt that corners were cut, plans cancelled and tasks left incomplete – issues which impacted on post-Games planning.

Popular tourist literature applauds the changes made in connection with the Games that transformed Athens into a more attractive tourist destination. This has occurred through the transformation of the city centre, the creation of the Archaeological Park, renovated museums, new galleries and improvements to public transport. Hotels and catering have improved and there is now a modern cultural sector in addition to the classical heritage. The Games were praised for placing disability on the agenda, although some warn that the city lags behind other capitals and more needs to be done.[10] By contrast, and despite the frequency with which images of the iconic Olympic complex are reproduced as symbols of the new Athens, their peripheral locations are far removed from the normal tourist circuit and, although easily reached by public transport, are fenced off and kept locked.

Environmentalists, as mentioned previously, were particularly critical that the rules laid down in the tender for the Olympic Village were largely ignored when reducing construction costs became the priority. In more measured tones, commentators from the United Nations Environment Programme noted that while there had been undoubted achievements in the areas of transport, coastal rehabilitation and improvements in public awareness of environmental issues, in the matter of energy consumption and the building of eco-friendly facilities standards had fallen 'below expectations'. They regretted that there had not been more consultation at the preparation stages with 'key stakeholders, particularly environmental NGOs'.[11] For its part, the environmental assessment of the Games by the World Wildlife Fund (WWF) in July 2004 evaluated 18 environmental performance indicators with a score from 0 (very disappointing) to 4 (very positive). As table 15.1 shows, Athens's average was just 0.77, scoring zero on no less than 11 of the criteria, including protection of natural habitats, protection of open spaces, siting of Olympic venues, use of green technologies, green energy, water saving, integrated waste management and recycling, and respect for environmental legislation. The highest scores were for public awareness (4), improvement of the built environment (3) and public transport (3). The WWF's assessment was that there had been no effort to integrate the environment into the planning of the Games and that opportunities to use systems in areas where Athens is vulnerable – water and energy supply and waste disposal – were missed. Nothing was done to promote renewable energy or water conservation or to tackle waste management other than to purchase a new fleet of dust carts.

Finding other worthwhile uses for Games facilities, another canon of sustainable Olympic development, frequently became a political issue, with the two major national political parties accusing each other as to which bore more blame for the lack of post-Games strategy. The New Democracy Party, in power since March 2004, claimed that PASOK, their Socialist predecessors, had no proper business plans for the Olympic sites. PASOK countered that facilities are being allowed to deteriorate.[12] The New Democracy government established a state-owned holding company, Hellenic Olympic Properties (HOP), to which it transferred 22 venues. These included all the Athens sports facilities, the Media Press Centre and the International Broadcasting Centre but not the AOSC complex, the Olympic Village or Press Villages. AOSC is to remain an international sports complex and the Villages have post-Games plans in place. HOP's brief is to achieve 'sustainable commercial development' in areas of activity compatible with government strategy, with a general framework of permitted uses laid down in legislation passed in 2005–2006 (HOP, 2006). HOP will manage the remaining sites until lease-holders can be found in the form of foreign or domestic investors or public-private partnerships, thus helping to recoup building costs, avoid the costs of maintaining the venues (estimated at $100 million per annum) and benefit local communities in terms of cultural amenity and jobs.

Understandably, HOP faces the problem that the locations of the venues reflected political, landownership and pragmatic considerations rather than planning for post-Games commercial use. A stated aim for the free-standing venues is to improve the infrastructure of the unplanned suburbs, but the

Table 15.1. Olympic Environmental Assessment, Athens 2004.

Issue	Score	Highlighted Examples
Overall Planning		
Environmental planning	0	Principles of the Environmental Policy of ATHOC published 2001 – more a communications tool than an environmental strategy.
Environmental assessment	0	Absence of concrete and measurable environmental commitments
Natural Environment		
Protection of natural habitats	0	Schinas Rowing and canoeing centre. Fragile environmental areas trapped by the expansion of the urban web
Urban Environment		
Protection of open spaces	0	Use of open space for venues: Galatsi,Maroussi Press facilities, Olympic Village; failure to complete the ecological park at Faliro
Increase of urban green	0	Failure to plant Mediterranean species; planting out of season and requiring irrigation
Improvement of the built environment	3	Façades, removal of billboards, pedestrian network, unification of archaeological sites, street cleaning
Transport		
Public transport	3	Metro, gas powered buses, urban rail and tram network, public awareness campaign to reduce car usage. No cycle facilities.
Constructions		
Siting of Olympic venues	0	Lack of public consultation over sites
Use of existing infrastructure	1	Olympic Stadium and Peace and Friendship Stadium used
Use of green technologies	0	Failed to include environmental obligations in the contracts for the Olympic Village: use of solar power, water saving systems, ozone-friendly cooling systems, certified timber. Debris abandoned at constructions sites
Energy		
Green energy	0	Solar and wind energy options not considered for the Olympic sites
Water		
Water saving scheme	0	Tap water used for irrigation of Olympic Village site; 16 km pipeline supplies tap water to Schinais competition reservoirs in dry periods
Waste		
Integrated waste management and recycling	0	No integrated waste management strategy. Recycling bins provided at Olympic venues
Public Participation		
Social consultation	1	No stakeholder consultation. Opposition to the sites for Schinas Rowing Centre, Galatsi, Olympic Village, Press Centre
Transparency	1	Poor information; NGOs with an international base had more success in obtaining information than other groups
Public information	1	Website used as a promotional rather than an information tool. Central role therefore played by the press in highlighting issues
General Issues		
Respect for environmental legislation	0	Existing legislation bypassed, for example in the case of the Press Village Maroussi.
Public awareness	4	Good environmental education and awareness to reduce car usage and water consumption
Total Score	0.77	

(4 = very positive; 3 = positive; 2 = fair; 1 = disappointing; 0 = very disappointing)
Source: Compiled from World Wildlife Fund Greece (2004) *Environmental Assessment of the Athens 2004 Olympic Games*, July 2004.

municipalities cannot afford to maintain them (MSNBC, 2004). The Faliro and Helleniki complexes are meant to generate critical mass since they contain a number of attractions but it is estimated, for example, that the cost of running Faliro is 5–7 million euros as against an income from the Marina and Indoor Hall of 2–4 million euros (Romanos *et al.*, 2005, p. 6).

Therefore, progress towards realizing a new life for the venues has been patchy. Tenders were invited for the Badminton Hall at Goudi, the International Broadcasting Centre and the canoe-kayak slalom course at Helleniki in July 2005; for the sailing centre at Agio Kosmas and the Galatsi Olympic Indoor Hall in August 2005; and the beach volleyball centre at Faliro in March 2006. At the time of writing, a private-public partnership has been approved for the work required to adapt the Faliro Pavilion for use as an International Conference Centre and for facility management and maintenance for a 25-year period, but no operator for the Centre has yet been selected. In May 2006, a consortium signed a 25-year lease on the Badminton Hall for 12.5 million euros with a plan to convert the structure into an arts, theatre and entertainment centre.[13]

AOSC raises a familiar problem for Olympic cities, namely, the future of a very large stadium that is scarcely used on any regular basis. As elsewhere, there has been usage for football, with the ground now shared by Panathinaikos and AEK Athens, but stadia essentially built for athletics rarely provide ideal conditions for football. Panathinaikos has the long-term aim of developing its own stadium complex, a plan backed by the Athens Municipality which sees this development as spearheading the regeneration of the Votanikos/Alexandros Avenue area to provide open space, cultural, sporting and commercial facilities in a part of Athens lacking good infrastructure (Bokoyannis, 2006, p. 18). AEK Athens, which moved to the Olympic stadium in 2003 when their Nikos Goumas Stadium was demolished, have average gates of only 27,500. Apart from match days, the complex is locked and Calatrava's landscaped spaces are not part of the local amenities or accessible to visitors.

Aside from the Olympic venues, the Games were also seen as a means of achieving place promotional goals and the 'soft legacy' of support services, training, employment, attitudinal changes, and organizational knowledge that comes from the successful planning and management of a hallmark event (METREX, 2006, p. 6). In the case of Athens, this included the 'positive climate of opinion within which continued progress could be made' (*Ibid.*, p. 7). Greek politicians quickly latched on to these ideas. Prime Minister Costas Karamanlis, for example, stated at the start of the Games that 'Greece will be a more experienced, a more optimistic and self-confident country' (Beard, 2004). In attempting to learn what such assertions meant in practice, Sykianaki and Psihogias (2006, p. 13) identified four important areas in which Athens 2004 created new working practices that might profoundly affect the city's future development. The first was in pioneering private-public partnerships as a new way of generating development funds. The government introduced legislation in 2005 to provide a framework for such partnerships, then new to Greek practice. This was seen as central to economic policy, something that would support entrepreneurship and make the Greek economy internationally oriented and competitive.[14] Secondly, it was argued that the Games had highlighted the problems of bureaucracy and encouraged a more flexible approach to problem solving. Thirdly, the Games were seen as a vehicle that showed how the city could use major events to lever investment, modernize the built environment and expand Athens's international role. Finally, the Olympics were felt to have mobilized citizens in the affairs of the city.

Conclusion

Calculating the costs and benefits of an Olympic Games is a daunting task given the powerful indirect as well as direct effects of staging the Games for the domestic economy and society. They also depend on political viewpoint. As noted in chapter 1, radical critics on the Left argued that, quite apart from impact on civil liberties, the long-term consequences of the staging the Games included reinforcement of trends towards the militarization of urban space, environmental damage and destruction of heritage. Each could have costs for society beyond those that can be imputed in economic terms. Moreover, assessments of costs also depend on the accounting procedures adopted, particularly judgments as to whether or not investment was purely related to the Games or would have happened anyway (e.g. transport improvements and urban beautification). At the end of 2004, for example, the Economy and Finance Minister George Alogoskoufis assessed the cost of the Games as 8.954 million euros but consciously omitted costs of the airport and metro, even though their development was expedited for the Games, and the continuing costs of maintaining venues until occupiers can be found.[15]

When looked at in narrow economic terms, ATHOC balanced its books and is eventually expected to declare a profit thanks to larger-than-expected contribution from IOC broadcast and sponsorship revenues. Games spending helped the sluggish Greek economy to record a 4 per cent annual increase (Payne, 2006, p. 271), but most of the revenue benefited the Athens region. Regional politicians argue that Athens sucked in investment at the expense of other regions, reinforcing the city's primacy and undoing 'past tendencies for decentralisation' (Coccossis *et al.*, 2003, p. 3). There is, however, consensus that the Games were expensive and over-budget, with infrastructural projects costing 37 per cent more than in the original plan. Greece was the smallest nation to host the Games since Finland in 1952, and there is no doubt that the scale of expenditure expected by the start of the twenty-first century was a strain for a small economy. In Greece's case European Union membership and access to its funds were of central importance – in particular the Cohesion Fund (for which Greece was one of the major beneficiaries) and the access to loans from the European Investment Bank. European ties, however, also impose costs. The conditions attached to membership of the European Economic and Monetary Union (EEMU) meant that steps were needed to lower Greece's deficit, which, at 6.1 per cent of Gross Domestic Product in 2004, was more than double the limit set by the terms of the EEMU. This resulted in Greece requiring increased taxes, cuts in public spending and wage restraint measures to realign its economy.[16]

Yet notwithstanding the cost calculations, Athens 2004 is popularly remembered within Greece as a success that confounded journalistic critics and came as a relief to those with any measure of responsibility for staging the Games. After the negative publicity surrounding the delays and descriptions of building sites that were relayed to television viewers and newspaper readers in the weeks leading up to the Olympics, the hurried completion of the sites (even if the landscaping and planting was incomplete), the new public transport and the spectacular Opening Ceremony created the aura of success. The city gained a tangible legacy of infrastructure that can provide the basis for the hoped for cultural, convention and business tourism trade. The centre of Athens is pedestrian friendly and guidebooks wax lyrical on the transformation of the city, although few short break visitors will see the Olympic venues themselves. The cultural sector has benefited from new performance spaces, exhibition spaces and renovated museums. The Games undoubtedly accelerated urban renewal and brought investment in transport and telecommunications. In turn, as Sykianaki and Psihogias (2006, p. 11) argued, these developments produced a more 'conducive environment for economic growth', which would be consolidated in a new Structural Plan for the Athens Metropolitan Area. Whatever costs have been incurred, it is scarcely plausible that the range of changes experienced would have occurred without being driven by the approach of an Olympic Opening Ceremony. Certainly most Greek politicians would have settled for this outcome if they had been offered it before the event.

Notes

1. The first Zappas Games of 1859 were held in Loudovikou Square (Plateia Eleftheris).

2. Yannis Pyrgiotis, Executive Director of the Organizing Committee for the Olympic Games (Pyrgiotis, 2003, p. 414).

3. It was built on the site of the velodrome constructed for the 1896 Games.

4. Information from a poster entitled 'Athens 96: Return to the Future', produced by the Executive Committee for the Candidacy of Athens for the 1996 Olympic Games.

5. In the bid document this airport was to be replaced by the new Elefthenos Venizelos International Airport near Sparta, but Helliniki was to continue in operation until the Games were over.

6. Even so the site manager Xenia Arapogianni was quoted as saying 'We still have misgivings about the sanctuary being used in this way. Ancient Olympia isn't a film or television set', but the local mayor hoped that the television coverage would spur tourist development (Special Correspondent, 2004). Olympia also benefited from renovation and three new museums.

7. These were the World Wildlife Fund Hellas; Greek Society for the Protection of the Environment and Cultural Heritage; Hellenic Society for the Protection of Nature; Hellenic Ornithological Society.

8. Two of Greece's athletic stars, Kostas Kenteris and Ekaterini Thanou, failed to report for

a drugs test on the eve of the Opening Ceremony and ended up in an Athens hospital under somewhat confused circumstances.

9. Smith, H. (2003) 'Athens prays to Zorba to rescue its "shambolic" Olympic Games', *The Observer*, 13 July.

10. Information compiled from Dubin *et al.* (2004), Facaros and Theodorou (2005) and Sales (2005).

11. UNEP Press Release 2004/37, August, http://www.unep.org, accessed 26 September 2006.

12. Hellenic Republic Embassy of Greece, press releases, 12 October and 13 November 2004.

13. Three companies were involved Adam Productions (event organizers), Half Note Jazz Club (club owners and event organizers) and Allou Fun Park (Greece's largest Amusement park). Information from Hellenic Republic Embassy of Greece, press release, 16 May 2006.

14. Information from Ministry of Economics, press release, 4 August 2006.

15. Information from Hellenic Republic Embassy of Greece, press release, 14 November 2004.

16. The aim was to get it down to 3 per cent by the end of 2006 (Church, 2005).

Chapter 16

Beijing 2008

Ian G. Cook

Anyone who has travelled frequently to Beijing since the early 1990s will have witnessed enormous changes, with the city rapidly metamorphosing into an 'internationalized metropolis' (Cook, 2006). This period has seen Beijing make not one, but two, bids to host the Summer Olympics. The first bid was submitted in 1992–1993 and was eventually rejected, with Sydney winning the race to host the 2000 Olympics. 'Human rights' were cited as a major reason for the rejection of this bid, unsurprising given that Tiananmen was fresh in the memory, with the tanks being sent in to clear the square on 4 June 1989. Environmental issues, however, were also a major factor. Beijing had hosted the Asian Games in 1990, and so the city had already spent a considerable sum on stadia, a Games Village, and on transport infrastructure. Foreign observers noted how most schoolchildren in 1992 seemed to sport the bright yellow baseball cap bearing the Asian Games logo. There was an air of expectancy that China would be awarded the 2000 Summer Olympic Games. The disappointment at rejection was palpable.

In contrast, the announcement in June 2001 that Beijing would host the Olympics in 2008 was greeted by mass rejoicing. Even Shanghai, often cast as a rival of Beijing, witnessed warm celebrations when the result was announced, not least because Shanghai is due to co-host the soccer tournament (figure 16.1). The announcement provided a sense of vindication of China's improved standing in the world. When the People's Republic of China (PRC) was founded on 1 October 1949, Mao Zedong said in his address to the new nation that China had stood up and would never be humiliated again. After many years of effort, of marked successes and notable failures, the opportunity to host the 2008 Olympics was proof that China had not only stood up, but that it was no longer a pariah state and was ready to take its rightful place as one of the leading countries on earth. To analyse the Beijing Olympics, therefore, is not only to analyse the urban dimension of this Olympic City, but also to contextualize Beijing's successful bid within the rise of the New China, a China that is proud of its past and increasingly proud of its present.

This wider contextualization highlights negatives as well as positives concerning the Beijing Olympics. This chapter, therefore, first examines China's uneven

Figure 16.1. Shanghai joins in the celebrations: Sofitel Hotel, central Shanghai after the announcement of the successful bid.

transformation, before considering Beijing's development path. The ensuing sections consider the bidding process and the relationship between the Olympics and urban regeneration. The final part considers the range of controversies that remain, including the environment, resettlement, human rights, corruption, and obesity.

China's Uneven Transformation

The dramatic changes in China that took place in the second half of the twentieth century are well known (Cannon, 2000; Cook and Murray, 2001). The establishment of the PRC as a communist state led by the Chinese Communist Party (CCP) led to three alternative models of development: first the Soviet model in which centralization and heavy industry were key features; then the Maoist model in which the decentralized commune was a major element; and finally the Dengist model of market socialism, or 'socialism with Chinese characteristics'. The Dengist model took China, probably irrevocably, down the capitalist road – albeit under strong direction from the Chinese state. It was based on an Open Door for foreign direct investment (FDI), with the objective of modernizing China's agriculture, industry, defence, science and technology. Under the market reforms unleashed by Deng and his successors, China's 'Gold Coast' has opened up to global connections and China is now in rapid transition from being a closed, poverty-stricken rural society towards being open, wealthy and, for many, urban. In brief, the Chinese state sets the preconditions for investment to enter, the local state (at province, city or town level) provides the infrastructure, and foreign companies provide the necessary investment through which China's resources of land and labour can be fully exploited. The scale and pace of change are phenomenal, especially in China's emerging cities, where the processes of globalization and urbanization interlock so dramatically (Wu, 2006, 2007).

China has 29 Provinces, plus four cities run directly by central government (Beijing, Shanghai, Tianjin and Chongqing). Initially, most FDI flowed via Hong Kong into the neighbouring Guangdong Province. In 1997, Guangdong experienced $12.6 billion of actually utilized FDI. Although the annual total dropped slightly in 1998–1999 due to the combined effects of the Asian financial crisis and a degree of investment saturation in the Pearl River delta, by 2003 FDI in Guangdong was still high at $7.8 billion (National Bureau of Statistics, 1999, 2006). Shanghai and neighbouring provinces in the 'arrowhead' of the Yangtze River delta are fast developing as an alternative attraction for FDI, with the corresponding figures for actually utilized FDI in Shanghai in 1997 and 2003 being $4.2 billion and $5.5 billion, respectively. As for Beijing itself, the corresponding data show that by 1997 $1.6 billion FDI was utilized, rising to $2.2 billion in 2003. Part of the 'China miracle', this type of investment is ploughed into export-oriented manufacturing, the property market, the retail sector and other activities, fuelling the dramatic transformation noted above. Multinational and transnational companies such as Volkswagen, Renault, McDonalds, KFC, Motorola, Nokia, Microsoft, BP, B & Q and many more are engaged in this continuing struggle to enter the lucrative China market.

This investment, however, is spatially uneven. It is clear that the cycle of circular and cumulative causation, to use the old terminology associated with Gunnar Myrdal (1968 and elsewhere), is very much oriented towards the coast. Chai (1996, p. 57), for instance, in his analysis of East-West income differentials from 1978 to 1991, found that regional income disparity had increased significantly over this period:

> The trend of concentration of investment resources along the Eastern seaboard was reinforced by the export-led growth and FDI policies adopted during this period. The Eastern seaboard had ports facilitating the imports of raw materials and exports of manufacturing. Consequently, most of the export processing facilities tended to concentrate in the coastal areas. Furthermore its proximity to the potential foreign investors as well as the special investment incentives created by the central government had attracted most of China's foreign investments into these areas.

Many other studies have similarly indicated the deeply embedded nature of these spatial contrasts (see Cook and Murray, 2001). They are also found with regards to urban-rural differentials and can vary, as would be expected, at the local scale within provinces, perhaps reflecting upland-lowland contrasts, for example. The new Chinese leadership under Hu Jintao seems particularly concerned to tackle such disparities, emphasizing the importance of investment in the western provinces, and of tackling rural deprivation. However, whether the government can redress these imbalances in the light of the massive attraction of development in the eastern seaboard remains to be seen. Investment in the Beijing Olympics, of course, will add still further to this attraction, and thus to the imbalance of development at the national scale.

Beijing's Development Path

Despite a long and distinguished history, under communism Beijing became an austere, drab producer city, full of steel mills and petrochemical works (Cook, 2006). It was heavily influenced by the Soviet style of planning with wide thoroughfares, mid-rise flats on a large scale, occasional grand buildings, and the expansion of Tiananmen Square to become the new heart of the city. The population of 1.2 million in 1949 within the old boundaries by the early 1980s was probably 4.14 million within its expanded boundaries, including 1.76 million specifically classified as 'urban' (Dong, 1985). In the western outskirts, the Shihjingshan Iron and Steel Works (also known as Shougang, or the Capital Iron and Steel Works) became one of China's largest. The city was worthy but dull, and by the 1970s an increasing proportion of its population were beginning to complain of the endless diet of revolutionary dramas and operas. The average family would aspire to own a radio, watch and bicycle and there was little in the way of luxury available to the mass of the population. As for externalities, Zhou (1992, p. 30) observed that:

> over a rather long period, Beijing put undue emphasis on heavy industry at the expense of light industry, which was underdeveloped. The excessive heavy industry created a shortage of water, electricity and transport capacity, and worsened environmental pollution. Little attention was paid to housing and public facilities... The urban population expanded while the commercial service network decreased.

Today, Beijing is worlds apart from this brief sketch. The reform period has ushered in a period of massive urban change, with new hotels, banks, high-rise residences, ring roads, new subway lines, the largest shopping mall in Asia (Oriental Plaza) and the whole paraphernalia of a city that is seeking to internationalize (Cook, 2006). The total population was officially estimated at 14.93 million in 2004, which includes the *liudong renkou*, or 'floating population', who do not have resident status. These are the migrants who are usually tolerated by the authorities, if not by the long-term residents themselves who see the newcomers as 'new urban outcasts' (Solinger, 1995), and supply, for instance, the cheap labour on which the rapid pace of construction is based, work which is '3D' – difficult, demanding and dangerous (Shen, 2002).

Contemporary Beijing often seems to resemble a giant building site. All around, huge new buildings are in various stages of construction, often cloaked in large nets to prevent tools falling on passers-by. The streets are hazardous due to the trenches which have been dug for pipes and cables, the pavements which are being laid, the trees that have been knocked down or are being replanted, and the trucks and workers' buses which cut across the flows of pedestrians and bicycles into the corrugated iron fortresses which surround the sites. By early 1999, with the advent of the fiftieth anniversary of the PRC, there were an estimated 5,000 building sites in the city (Cook, 2000).

Adoption of the trappings of modern consumer society accompanied this transformation of the built environment. Supermarkets carry Western-style red wines and beer, bread and cakes. The streets have American fast food chains (e.g. McDonalds, Kentucky Fried Chicken and Dunkin' Donut). Chinese tastes now extend to Western motor vehicles (Cherokee Jeep, Audi, Volkswagen, and even Ferrari), clothing (Benetton, Adidas or Wranglers), perfumes (Estée Lauder or Nina Ricci), electrical goods (Sony, Phillips and Panasonic), and housing, with executive-style estates of detached houses complete with nearby golf courses and private schools, perhaps within the complex itself. For the growing middle class, material goods are in full supply. For the working class, too, the department stores are rapidly expanding their size and product range. A night out is increasingly to a Hard Rock Cafe, pub or disco, usually featuring Western music. It is in the light of such changes that Beijing made its bids for the Olympics.

The Bidding Process

As in other Communist societies, sport became an important element in promoting the nation and patriotism. The annual *China Statistical Yearbook* on 'Culture, Sports and Public Health' routinely tabulates such outputs as 'Visits between Chinese and Foreign Sports Delegations', 'Activities of Mass Sports', 'World Records Chalked up by Chinese Athletes by Events' and 'World Championships won by Chinese Athletes'. Dong (2005, p. 533) shows that 'Chinese political and sports officials openly acknowledged that they viewed sport as an instrument for the promotion of national pride and identity... Contemporary competitive sport in China is motivated by nationalism and in turn contributes to the enhancement of patriotism'. From the mid-1980s, a strategy was developed to maximize gold medals, with an interesting feature being the success of female athletes, and the high proportion of females relative to males in the Chinese team. This has not always been unproblematic. There have been well publicized defections of top athletes plus question marks over the training methods and unprecedented success of 'Ma's Barmy Army' (after their trainer) of female marathon runners in recent years. Dong shows that the first time that the question as to when China could actually host the Olympics was raised as far back as 1908 in the *Tianjin Youth Magazine*, but it was at the end of the successful Asian Games in 1990 that a huge banner was unfurled, stating 'With the success of the Asiad, we look forward to hosting the Olympic Games' (cited by Dong, 2005, p. 538).

As noted above, Beijing failed on this occasion, losing to Sydney by only two votes for the right to host the Millennial Olympics in 2000. There were suggestions (e.g. GamesBids.com, 2007) that there was a vote scandal at this time, but there was also strong opposition from Human Rights groups and the 'Free Tibet' movement, who were vehemently opposed to a successful bid from China. Although the Asian Games had been successful, the shadow of Tiananmen still loomed large as far as many Western governments were concerned (see Broudehoux, 2004), but Beijing continued to be a severely polluted city at that time, with relatively poor infrastructure. It was certainly no surprise to most observers that the 1990s bid was unsuccessful.

By 2001, however, much had changed. China had decided to bid, primarily as part of the drive to modernize and internationalize Beijing. The city, one of five short listed, prepared for the final visit of the bidding panel in February 2001 with great care. *Inter alia*, the short- and longer-term measures were taken with the 2008 bid in mind, including, for example, illuminations in Olympic colours, billboards, magazines in taxis, the Millennium Museum showing Olympic films and displays, street signs in English, investment in infrastructure (notably the fourth and fifth ring roads), development of new hotels; painting of older buildings to improve appearances; spraying the grass green; establishment of parks, green and silver bins to increase awareness of environment (i.e. waste recycling), removal of older cars from the city to reduce air pollution, banning people burning coal in the city, and the closure of the Shougang factory (steel plant).

The bid adopted the overarching slogan of the 'New Beijing: Great Olympics', with subsidiary themes of delivering a 'high-tech Olympics', a 'green Olympics' and a 'people's Olympics'. It featured a plan to construct an Olympic Park and strategies to address the serious environmental issues faced by the Chinese capital. The commitments included:

◆　An Olympic Park covering an area of 1,215 hectares. It would include an 80,000 seat stadium, 14 gymnasia, an athletes' Village and an international exhibition centre, surrounded by a 760-hectare forest and greenbelt.

◆　During the tenth Five-Year Plan period (2001–2005) Beijing would build three green ecological belts, aiming to raise its green coverage to 48 per cent. By 2005, 'the city will realize the complete and safe disposal of treated waste and 96 per cent of waste water will also be treated'.[1]

◆　If Beijing gained the nomination 'there will be 5,750 sports venues by 2008 with 23 major stadia to hold events. And last year a new airport was opened that can move three million passengers a month. Beijing will have 72,000 rooms in 241 quality hotels and there are plans to build a $500 million national theatre on the edge of Tiananmen Square, to hold cultural events during the Games'.[2]

◆　'The government plans to spend the equivalent of $15 billion on anti-pollution efforts through 2008, roughly nine times what China's Olympic committee organizers estimate the Games would cost'.[3]

Beijing's long-term plan for environmental protection to 2010 had its time-scale reduced to ensure readiness for the 2008 games. From 1998 to 2007, the plan envisaged such features as:

♦   total expenditure of $12.2 billion on protection and enhancement of the ecological environment;

♦   fourteen new wastewater treatment plants to be built to improve the sewage treatment rates to 90 per cent from 42 per cent;

♦   240 square kilometres of trees and grass to be planted around Beijing to create a 'green coverage' area of more than 50 per cent;

♦   200 industrial enterprises to change production or to be moved out of the downtown area altogether to reduce pollution levels;

♦   completion of the fourth and fifth ring roads, five new subway lines, 90 per cent of buses and 70 per cent of taxis to use natural gas.[4]

In all, it was forecast at the time that 280 billion yuan ($33.8 billion) of investment would be made in the period to 2008, mainly in stadia and gymnasia, increasing China's annual GNP growth by 0.3–0.4 per cent and Beijing's by 2.5 per cent (Xin, 2001). With these and other activities, the potential impact of the Olympics would be enormous, adding further to China's growing power and prestige on the international stage, and contributing significantly to Beijing's urban development *per se*. The city would move away from being a producer city towards being a city of consumption, of knowledge-based activities, and a city with an enhanced international profile.

For their part, the visiting panel was impressed by these and other evidence not just of the commitment of Beijing's residents to the Olympic ideal but also that of the nation as a whole. By May 2001 the Olympic Evaluation Commission Report was summarized[5] as:

This is a government-driven bid with considerable assistance of the NOC (National Olympic Committee). The combination of a good sports concept with complete government support results in a high quality bid.

The Commission notes the process and pace of change taking place in China and Beijing and the possible challenges caused by population and economic growth in the period leading up to 2008 but is confident that these challenges can be met.

There is an environmental challenge but the strong government actions and investment in this area should resolve this and improve the city.

It is the Commission's belief that a Beijing Games would leave a unique legacy to China and to sport and the Commission is confident that Beijing could organize an excellent Games.

Beijing's success soon afterwards (13 July 2001) was the climax of a series of celebrations, beginning with the return of Hong Kong in 1997, Macao in 1999, the fiftieth Anniversary of the PRC in 1999 and the eightieth Anniversary of the founding of the CCP in July 2001. Later, China unsuccessfully bid for the 2010 FIFA World Cup and successfully for a World Exposition in Shanghai in 2010. It is difficult to underestimate the symbolic nature of these successes for China's people, the CCP and the leadership of the nation.

Urban Regeneration

In the six years since the bid's success, Beijing has seen considerable work and investment towards realizing the Olympic dream. In many respects, the Olympics are a national rather than just a city-based event. Parts of the Olympics will be staged away from Beijing, notably, sailing (Qingdao, Shandong Province), equestrian (Hong Kong), and football (Tianjin, Shanghai, Shenyang and Qinhuangdao). In the case of Qingdao, Shanghai and Hong Kong these cities are located hundreds, one thousand and two thousand miles, respectively, from Beijing itself.[6] Most of the effort and investment, however, is being expended in Beijing itself. In 2003, work was begun on four Olympic venues, with a further 11 begun in 2004. By mid-2006, 44 major projects were underway. The Olympic Village lies to the north of the central city (figure 16.2), and the main stadium is in the shape of a 'bird's nest' lattice-work structure; in the environs are the inevitable sheets of corrugated iron surrounding related construction activities (figure 16.3). Beijing International Airport has been considerably modernized and expanded through the building of Terminal 3. New subway lines are being built, and a new loop line was opened to the north of the city in 2002.

Figure 16.2. The Olympic stadium, designed by Herzog & de Meuron, under construction.

Figure 16.3. Corrugated iron sheets surround the stadium construction site.

The Beijing Organizing Committee for the Games of the XXIX Olympiad (BOCOG) held its first plenary session in January 2004 at which it was announced that the first phase of development was complete (Cook, 2006). The second phase would run from 2004 to 2006, leaving the time from 2007 until the Games' Opening Ceremony for test events and fine-tuning. Construction of new hotels, road infrastructure and other essential facilities continued apace, including parks and water recycling centres. The new Opera House (Beijing National Theatre) behind the Great Hall of the People is now complete, notwithstanding the controversies over its huge cost and 'jelly-fish' or 'blob' architectural design (see Broudehoux, 2004). On the symbolic side, the new Beijing Olympic logo – 'Chinese Seal, Dancing Beijing' – was unveiled in August 2003, combining 'elements of engraving, calligraphy, painting and poetry' and bringing together elements of the ancient and the modern.[7]

BOCOG 'is requiring all proprietors … to follow "green" environmental guidelines in the construction of Olympic venues' (Lei, 2004). Sustainable development is a key element with the main tasks identified by the Executive Vice President of BOCOG as 'controlling air pollution, especially reducing the coal and industrial pollution and vehicle discharges, effective disposal of municipal sewage and municipal refuse, raising the green land acreage to 50 per cent' (*Ibid*.). As an indication of success in these endeavours, in March 2006 Chaoyang District became the first urban area in Beijing to be named a 'model ecological zone', following three suburban districts of Yanqing, Pinggu and Miyun (Li, 2006). Over 60 square kilometres of green zones have been created since 2004, and according to the municipal authorities: 'Greenbelts cover 43.5 per cent of the district, and green public space has reached an average of 15 square meters per person. Meanwhile, air and water quality has improved' (*Ibid.*). The Capital Iron and Steel Works is being gradually moved to a coastal location some distance from the capital in Shandong Province. The regular visitor can vouch for the fact that Beijing's environmental quality is often better than it was, with more blue sky days (one of the set targets), more tree planting, more green spaces, increased use of LPG in buses, and greater restrictions on pollution via industry or vehicles. Nevertheless, there still remains much to be done before the vision of 'Olympic Green' is realized.

Continuing Controversies

Despite the environmental improvements noted above, data from the European Satellite Agency in October 2005 stress that Beijing remains the most polluted city in the world, while it and neighbouring provinces have the world's worst levels of nitrogen dioxide (Watts, 2005). Despite the immense amount of tree planting in recent years, China's plans were disrupted by a huge sandstorm that hit the city on 16 April 2006. Around 330,000 tons of dust was estimated to have fallen on Beijing that day, while the next saw most of north and north-west China enveloped in sandstorms. This was chastening for the authorities, given that it coincided with the Sixth National Conference on Environmental Protection. Addressing the conference, Premier Wen Jiabao commented: 'Repeated sandstorms should send a warning to us all, we should feel heavy loads on our shoulders while meeting here to discuss environmental problems'.[8] Yet while the government views claims to take environmental issues seriously, the pace of social and economic change often outstrips the ability to regulate and control environmental pollution. For example, in 2003 the level of car ownership in Beijing reached the anticipated level for 2010. Much higher taxation rates have been announced for large vehicles with rates on small engined cars being reduced, but in a society with such a fast rate of wealth creation and where social status is increasingly a product of conspicuous consumption, it is probable that most people will not be deterred from buying larger vehicles unless punitive measures are taken. It is said that the authorities will severely restrict vehicle use during the Olympics which means, since Beijing is a city the size of Los Angeles, that the impact of any restrictions may be considerable.

Another controversial aspect of the Olympics schedule is demolition to make way for the new structures associated with the Olympics. The set target was 9 million square metres of 'dilapidated housing', replaced by new houses that would provide a living area of 18 square metres per capita (Xin, 2001). This is part of an ongoing process of demolition across the whole city, which particularly threatens the old *hutong* and *siheyuan* areas (Cook, 2000, 2006; Cook and Murray, 2001). In brief, these old, often dilapidated, single-storey houses arranged along narrow lanes, originally with access to the 'Hong Tong' or water well, are in areas that ill befit the dreams of planners and developers concerned with creating the grand structures of an internationalized Olympic metropolis. Between 1991 and 2003, 1.5 million people were relocated from such areas out to the high-rise residential blocks in the suburbs. The previous Mayor admitted that the difficult problem of resettlement of families affected by this demolition process 'remains to be solved', while the new Mayor, Wang Qishan, although admitting that some of these relocation projects violate the law, states that older parts of the city will still continue to be demolished to make way for the Olympics projects (cited in Cook, 2006). Estimates suggest that approximately 300,000 people have been evicted specifically because of the Olympics, although the government of the PRC denies this (Acharya, 2005).

The last point is a reminder that the issue of human rights refuses to disappear. Organizations such as Amnesty International or Human Rights Watch Asia continue to deplore human rights violations by the Chinese authorities. These crystallize around a number of broad themes, such as the overall lack of democracy, use of the death penalty, the occupation of Tibet, Muslim insurgency in Xinjiang Province and the treatment of the Falun Gong (a Buddhist sect). Security in China, including Internet security, is tight so the likelihood of violence marring the Olympics in 2008 is probably low, but there remains the possibility of public protests concerning these and other potential issues. Indeed, as in other countries previously, the upheaval created by the Games may actually *contribute* to protest and dissent. For their part, the Chinese authorities retaliate by defending their human rights record by pointing to the lack of basic rights in countries such as the United States and maintaining that the current war on terrorism and the involvement of the US and UK in Iraq, complete with examples of human rights abuse by American and British soldiers, shows the operation of double standards.

Corruption is another issue. As shown above, vast sums of foreign investment have entered the country in recent years. Perhaps inevitably, corruption has become a problem for the government, and some would point to the lack of democratic controls as rendering it very difficult to root out corruption among officials and CCP members. Reports of the first Beijing Olympic official to be sacked over corruption surfaced recently (Watts, 2006*b*). According to these reports, Liu Zhihua, a vice-mayor of Beijing responsible for overseeing construction of sporting venues for the Olympics was removed by the Standing Committee of the Beijing Municipal People's Congress for 'corruption and dissoluteness'. He could face the death penalty for financial crimes if found guilty of taking an alleged 10 million yuan as a bribe from developers. The huge amount of money that has been budgeted for the various events and venues means that this may well not be the last such case.

Finally, Dickson and Schofield (2005) have noted certain contradictions that apply to the Beijing Olympics in particular. The main sponsors for the event include 'calorie-dense beverages (Coca-Cola) and food (McDonalds) as well as motorized transportation (Volkswagen)' (*Ibid.*, p. 170). Such sponsorship will exacerbate China's growing obesity problem. Other sponsors such as Samsung or Panasonic produce goods that further contribute to a sedentary lifestyle. They argue that 'the world's most populous nation is at the beginning of an explosion in lifestyle-related disease' (*Ibid.*, p. 177), a point supported by Cook and Dummer (2004) who observed that the first 'fat camp' was opened in Beijing in 1994. This, they argued, reflected 'a growing problem of obesity as Western "junk food" becomes increasingly popular in the cities … obesity in young children increasing by over 50% from 1989 to 1997' (*Ibid.*, p. 338). Although the Olympics will help encourage a proportion of China's population to take more exercise, as has happened in previous Olympic cities, Dickson and Schofield (2005, p. 177) maintained that this will be insufficient to offset 'the opportunities for massive multinational globalization and ultimately, globesity'. This would surely be the ultimate irony that the Beijing Olympics might contribute to the couch potato syndrome in China and in the rest of the globe. Whatever the outcome, one can readily agree with Broudehoux (2004, p. 200) in observing that 'one thing is sure: the Games will leave a deep mark on Beijing and its inhabitants'.

Notes

1. www.china.org.cn/english/11125.htm, accessed 17 April 2001.
2. *Ibid.*
3. www.GamesBids.com/archives/2008/Beijing.htm, accessed 12 June 2006.
4. www.beijing-olympic.org.cn/xbxa/ztzt/gree/gree-index.shtm, 2001, accessed 5 May 2001.
5. www.GamesBids.com/archives/2008/Beijing.htm, accessed 12 June 2006.
6. http://en.beijing2008.com/21/65/column212006521.shtml, accessed 9th June 2006.
7. *Ibid.*
8. *Ibid.*

Chapter 17

London 2012

Graeme Evans

On Wednesday, 6 July 2005, the International Olympic Committee's meeting in Singapore decided to award the 2012 Summer Olympics to London. The decision represented a combination of Eurovision-style partisanship, tactical voting,[1] global schmoozing and last minute surprises. London's *coup de grâce*, another steal from the French, was a multicultural-faced group of excited East End children, in contrast to the sombre suited Parisian messieurs. Celebrations began in Stratford, the nondescript town centre of the London borough of Newham, and the heart of the prospective Olympic Park. The next day, four suicide bombers killed fifty-six people, including themselves, in attacks on underground trains and a bus in London. The 2012 celebration party was cut short and thinking inevitably started to focus on the size of the task ahead, with all its attendant problems.

This chapter provides a critique of the London 2012 Olympic project in its post-award, development phase. The first of its four sections provides an analysis of the urban three 'Rs' – regeneration, renaissance and renewal – in thinking about the Olympics. The second discusses how the Games are to be financed, with the third focusing on the designation of the Olympic sites in the Lea Valley and their implications for regeneration. The conclusion adds final thoughts about the potential legacy of London 2012.

The Urban Three 'R's

It is interesting to note that a recent review of literature on the Olympics (Veal and Toohey, 2005) found only two out of over 1,500 entries were specifically on 'regeneration' or 'renewal'. Articles and reports, and a growing number of edited collections, are dominated by 'impacts' – economic, physical, political and tourism (Hughes, 1993) – and themes of marketing, image and place-making. By contrast, analyses of long-term regeneration effects are notable by their absence. Olympic effects are subsumed into wider redevelopment and competitive city narratives. This makes it problematic to measure the true impact of the Games, which become a symbolic but highly temporal event in a city's evolution and another chapter in the Olympic history book.

Notwithstanding the extensive development of facilities undertaken to host even the least ambitious Olympic Games, it is important to distinguish between the now ubiquitous urban renewal attached to Olympic plans and genuine regeneration (see also chapter 9). *Regeneration* has been defined as the renewal, revival, revitalization or transformation of a place or community (Evans and Shaw, 2004). Regeneration is both a process and an outcome. By definition, it is a response to decline (or *de*-generation). The decline could be physical, economic or social, although the three commonly coexist. This instrumental approach which now underlies public urban policy initiatives, presumes that such decline can be reversed from the outside by 'breathing new life and vitality into an ailing community, industry and area [bringing] sustainable, long-term improvements to local quality of life, including economic, social and environmental needs' (LGA, 2000).

At a wider scale, entire cities and city-regions are said to be capable of undergoing a *Renaissance* through the process of making towns, cities and other areas 'liveable' and rediscovering city pride (ODPM, 2003b). The view of the UK government is that regeneration should now be a 'holistic process of reversing economic, social and physical decay in areas where it has reached a stage when market forces alone will not suffice' (*Ibid.*). This market failure analysis presents an interesting case for the rationale of being the Olympic host. Neither market nor state can afford (politically and financially) to take the full risk and burden of the Games, and both city and national government must front and act as guarantor to the bid, and demonstrate a degree of public and cross-party political support.

A third 'R' – *Renewal* – is also applied by the government in its basket of public intervention objectives. Renewal is 'the improvement in the situation of the most disadvantaged places and their communities, including the level and quality of the services they receive. Renewal objectives may be wide ranging but will seek to deliver improved work and business opportunities, improved residential attractiveness and improved public services' (*Ibid.*). The distinguishing characteristics are that they have a strong spatial focus and often, as a result, distributional impacts, both positive and negative. They tend to aim at, or contribute to, the overall goals for sustainable development of target areas and groups, and have the specific objective of improving outcomes in social, economic and environmental terms (ODPM, 2003b). Spatial and distributive effects are therefore vital in any assessment of the regenerative benefits and impacts arising from the Games. If the ultimate aim of '3R' interventions is to achieve thriving, inclusive and sustainable communities in all regions by raising levels of social inclusion, promoting neighbourhood renewal and fostering regional prosperity, these aims demand a suitably integrated assessment, but such a holistic and balanced approach is still a utopian prospect rather than utilitarian practice (Evans, 2005a).

In London's bid, the greatest emphasis is placed on the legacy and after-affects of the Olympic leverage opportunity, rather than the event, its content and purpose. As (Allen, 2006, p. 3) indicated:

> Talk of the 'Olympic Legacy' is so common that it has started to sound like a tautology; shorthand for the perceived wisdom that the Olympics has everything to do with urban regeneration and only a passing concern with patriotism, athletics or public spectacle.

This presents a fundamental problem to the national Olympic and city delivery agencies. The financial, land ownership and usage, constructional, and related infrastructural and promotional efforts are of necessity dominated by the event delivery objectives and cost pressures. National performance in the competition itself, i.e. in the final medal league table, is the test of sporting success.[2] It is here that compromises in community benefits (social, local economy and procurement), design quality and after-use, are most likely to be made:

> it's now becoming clear that the idea is something of a smokescreen. In practice, it's becoming apparent that this legacy involves putting the narrowly technical demands of the 17 days of the games above everything else, and then trying to adapt the site for long-term use afterwards. (Sudjic, 2006)

The visionary masterplans, artists' impressions and promises at the bidding and consultation stage are just that – promises. Barcelona's Olympic Village housing, for example, was privately sold but not 'affordably' as promised (Nel-lo, 1997). The final form and function will therefore be dictated by budget and contractual realities, political stamina and consensus, as it has been in other regenerating Olympic cities.

No regeneration programme for London's major Olympic sites at Stratford in London's East End, of course, could ignore the lessons of two major regeneration schemes that lie on the periphery of the Olympic zone and influence both the political culture and economy surrounding London 2012. The first is the Docklands regeneration for which the symbolic and economic heart is Canary Wharf and the cluster of newer office towers that have grown up alongside (figure 17.1). This was carried out under the aegis of the London Docklands Development Corporation (LDDC), which was formed by the previous Conservative government in 1980 and which, until it was wound up in 1998, served to fast track physical regeneration of the declining areas of the inner and outer docklands (see Brownhill, 1990; Colenutt, 1988; and DCC, 1990). Through the granting of planning permission, the LDCC took control of land-use development away from incumbent local authorities in the London Docklands. Shortly afterwards, London also had no city-wide authority with the winding up of the Greater London Council (GLC) in 1984. As a result, there was neither strategic nor local area planning in this regeneration zone at the time of its peak development. Coupled with property boom and bust cycles (Canary Wharf's Canadian developers, Olympia and York, went into receivership) and delays to the vastly over-budget Jubilee Line Underground Extension which links Canary Wharf and the Greenwich peninsula to central London, regeneration of the wider Docklands area, including the Olympic zone, had been limited. The

Figure 17.1. The distant skyline of Canary Wharf looking south from the site of the future Olympic Park (May 2007).

viability of the inner Docklands office city relied on public investment, and only when the costly Jubilee Line underground extension (JLE) reached Canary Wharf in 1999 just in time for the Millennium celebrations in Greenwich, did the so-called private-led development become financially secure. What is of importance here is that this model of urban development is intrinsic to preparing for London 2012. Urban Regeneration Companies are being used to accelerate development, over and above local planning authorities in the London Thames Gateway and wider region, and the Olympic Delivery Authority and the Mayor's London Development Agency have taken over compulsory land purchase and strategic planning powers in place of the locally elected authorities.

The second, more recent public project was the Millennium Dome across the river from Canary Wharf on the Greenwich peninsula (figure 17.2). Built as the centre of the nation's celebration of the new Millennium in 2000, its vague purpose and escalating capital cost cast a cloud over such public *grand projets* in Britain. This has been exacerbated by the failure to secure its after-use and disposal. Over five years on, the costs of annual insurance and security for the vacant facility were put at £1 million. The site was sold in December 2001 to Meridian Delta Ltd. (backed by Philip Anschutz, American billionaire oil, rail, sport and telecoms entrepreneur), with plans for a 20,000 seat sports and entertainment (i.e. casino) venue, and a housing and office development on the surrounding land of 150 acres (60 hectares). In May 2005 Anschutz sold the rights to the Dome

Figure 17.2. The Millennium Dome, north Greenwich (December 2000).

to O$_2$, a mobile phone company. The refurbished Dome is due to re-open in 2007, with incongruous opening events, the Festival of Scouting Centenary and the 'Tutankamun and the Golden Age of the Pharaohs' exhibition. For the 2012 Olympics, the Dome is designated for use as a venue for the artistic gymnastics, trampolining and basketball finals.

In the memories of the public and politicians, as well as the media, the Dome is an exemplar of poor planning and financial profligacy and a ghost that inevitably haunts London's Olympic vision.[3] The main criticisms of the project were the escalating cost and unclear purpose and content, as well the problem of promoting the event as a national celebration in a non-central London location (Evans, 1996b, 1999a). The final cost of the Dome was £790 million, of which £600 million was funded by the National Lottery and the balance from ticket sales. This was £200 million or 50 per cent over the original budget estimate, due to a shortfall in visitor numbers – around 6.5 million people came, compared with 12–18 million ('mid-high' range) in the original business plan (Price Waterhouse, 1994; Evans, 1996a). Like the Olympics (2005 award and event in 2012), the Millennium year actually took place after a general election, and in 1997 the transfer from a Conservative to a Labour government, which optimistically expanded the scope of the event. The four criteria for the Millennium Exhibition award, 'the best event of its kind in the world', is also echoed in London's Olympic vision (table 17.1).

Financing London 2012

The Olympic events are, of course, known quantities, and ticket sales will

Table 17.1. Millennium Festival 2000 and London2012 visions.

Millennium Festival	London2012
The environment	'Green', sustainable Games, Lower Lea Valley regeneration
Art, culture	Cultural Legacy, Olympic festivals, Creative Hub
Community activity	Participation in Sport and Culture
Improved access to the natural and technological world	Park, environmental and transport improvements, site reclamation and Olympic Institute and Media Centre

doubtless be enthusiastically promoted and taken up (82 per cent ticket yield is forecast). Britain is a keen spectator sporting nation. British spectators were highly visible at team events at Athens 2004. Association football and major sporting events regularly draw large crowds, albeit with ticket prices for premier events outside of the reach of lower income groups. A strong cultural programme is also promised, with a Festival of World Youth Culture, Olympic Proms and Carnival and an 'Olympic FriendShip' to be launched at the Beijing Games in 2008 which, it was proposed,[4] will sail around the world before arriving in London in 2012. Over 250,000 Volunteers are to be recruited, with London Student Pledge, Olympic Language and Young Ambassadors programmes planned.

The issues of capital and running cost overruns are the main concern in this development phase, as well as security and terrorism risks. Like the Millennium Dome, the Olympics are reliant upon National Lottery ticket sales of £1.5 billion (via a special Olympic lottery) and £300 million in ticket revenue, with 75 per cent of all Olympic Game tickets costing £48, with 25 per cent above this level.[5] The British public, of course, has choice whether to buy lottery tickets or to attend the Olympics. By contrast, London rate payers have no choice. A £20 per annum or 38p per week extra tax will be levied on each household to raise a further £625 million towards the Games. The London Mayor, Ken Livingstone, has pledged that Londoners will pay no more than £240 each towards the Games, despite the rising costs. However in a BBC London poll of the public's attitude towards the London Olympics, nearly 80 per cent believed that the Games would end up costing Londoners more than this levy. Surveys conducted for the Olympic organizers (LOCOG) indicate increasing public support at this stage.[6] In December 2006, 79 per cent were in favour (47 per cent 'Strongly Agreed'; 32 per cent 'Agreed'), up from 75 per cent three months earlier. Nevertheless, the strongest English support came from *outside* of London. Wales and the West of England showed the highest support (87 per cent).[7]

With the history of cost overruns and unrealistic and unrealized budget and visitor forecasts, the modern Olympics have a major credibility problem. Nevertheless, learning from the past is not high on the agenda. Previous Olympic experiences are seen as 'atypical', even the much heralded example of Barcelona (Experian, 2006), and the planning process adopted is all too familiar. The firm of consultants used to prepare the visitor forecasts and impact assessment for the Millennium 'Dome' ten years earlier (Price Waterhouse, 1994) has again been used for London 2012! Distancing the project from its precursors also allows the promoters to ignore warnings and claim immunity when history repeats itself. The *post hoc* reviews that governments tend to commission are more about attributing blame and non-compliance (e.g. National Audit Office), rather than implementing a real change in organizational behaviour and assessment regimes. Experience with the Dome, major public facilities such as the Scottish Parliament building (Sudjic, 2005), Jubilee Line Extension and recent sporting stadia – for example, the new Wembley Stadium[8] – suggests that publicly procured mega-event facilities are uncontrollable and guaranteed to degenerate into cost and contract disputes and political controversy (see the discussion of megaprojects in chapter 9). The French *grand projects* experienced similar cost spirals, with similar criticisms, but were ultimately driven through by political will or, perhaps, arrogance, in the case of Pompidou and Mitterand:

> The French system is said to be a 'cultural monarchy', where he pleases, the minister in office defines his options and takes his decisions in the fashion of a sovereign, according to the principles of 'enlightened despotism'. (Wangermée, 1991, p. 35)

However, private sector-led major infrastructure projects offer no guarantee of cost restraint either. The joint UK-French EuroTunnel capital cost was two-thirds higher than budgeted and the company remains technically insolvent over ten years on. When combined with major transport and regeneration projects, the capital risk therefore multiplies. In the case of the Olympics, this risk ultimately is underwritten by the state and municipal authorities, with the maximum impacts falling on local communities.

Attempting to apply a cost-benefit analysis to an Olympic Games impact assessment initially requires estimating capital and revenue costs, but, like the bidding and national campaigning processes, this aspect is also confused and fluid. In the first place, the income and costs of the event from bidding to staging, are distributed between international, national and city-regional organizations and sponsors, and budgeting is not transparent.[9] Whether state-led or heavily private sponsor oriented, much investment and expenditure is 'off-balance sheet', understating the true resource costs and impacts. Secondly, there is the challenge of attributing expenditure to the Olympic event itself. Strictly, commitments made prior to the decision to bid for the Games for, say, transport and other environmental improvements, as well as for sporting, hospitality and media facilities should be discounted. Governments, however, often anticipate bidding for future mega-events as part of place-making and regeneration strategies and investment is also planned, but not necessarily implemented, as part of the competitive bidding process, as putative hosts 'talk up' their capacity to host the future Games.

In practice, winning cities use the Games to accelerate, 'divert' and expand infrastructural investment, pulling proposals off the shelf as the heightened Olympic prospect offers sources of finance and political opportunities for fast-tracking projects not feasible under 'normal' conditions. Schemes that would otherwise encounter resistance from politicians, the public and local communities may be attached to the Olympic project, with the hope of finding added value (e.g. the 'feel good' factor or 'legacy'). Losing cities also provide examples of the 'additionality test' – investment still made in the absence of the Olympic effect. Regional capital cities such as Birmingham (1992), Manchester (1996, 2000) and Toronto (1996, 2008) have staked the regeneration of major sites on such failed bids, often despite popular resistance, whilst others have been burdened by the financing and failure associated with undeveloped post-event sites, in some cases long after they occurred (e.g. Montreal for Expo 67 and the 1976 Olympics).

Evidence of incentives and their effect on investment decisions, indicates that when withdrawn (e.g. expiry or cessation of grant funding), some projects are cancelled or deferred, but many go ahead with alternative finance and at a smaller scale (PACEC, 1990b; Evans, 1999b). Comparing and attributing Olympic Games and related regeneration expenditure, therefore, is as much of an art as a science (Preuss, 2004). When major transport improvements, site clearance and security considerations are taken into account, total investment rises substantially. In the case of Beijing, the estimated costs are $40 billion to get the Chinese capital's infrastructure ready for 2008, with $23 billion for the Games themselves (BBC Sport, 2006). London 2012 is no exception to this conflation and the credibility gap between bid estimates, promises and naïve assumptions, and the realities of the land acquisition, construction and delivery package. The line between Olympics and regeneration becomes impossible to detect.

Table 17.2 summarizes the capital and operating costs and financing included in the Candidate File submitted to the IOC in 2005 (LOCOC, 2004). A £2.375 billion capital budget and £1.5 billion operating budget were supplemented by the additional financing of transport and site infrastructure, the Athletes' Village and investment in sport at community and elite levels. Post-award, the messy process of procurement and the vagaries of construction and materials (e.g. steel prices) have been fuelled by 'oversights' in cost estimates, which included omitting Value Added Tax on construction and not allowing for inflation. London is also spending £7 billion on rail infrastructure (CTRL, East London line) and £1.5 billion on regeneration programmes in the Lower Lea Valley, largely over and above the Olympic budget. This is already increasing from the bid stage, with the £1.5 billion operating budget now estimated at £2 billion; land compulsory purchases and compensation rising from £478 million to £1 billion; and with construction inflation running at 7 per cent (versus 3 per cent in the budget) the £2.375 billion capital cost was forecast by late-2006 to rise by £900 million to £3.3 billion.

The spectre of the Athens 2004 Games hovers over London. This eventually produced expenditure of $10–12 billion, more than double the budget, with

Table 17.2. London 2012 Olympic capital and revenue budget (£ million).

Capital and Operating Budget (Lead authority)	London 2012 Bid July 2005	Funding Source	Estimate, December 2006	Variation
New facilities (ODA)				
Olympic Stadium;	250	} 1500 Special Lottery	300	'Inflation'
Aquatic Centre, Velodrome, Arenas;	310			Higher security costs
International Broadcasting Centre/ Main Press Centre;	130			
Transport improvements around Olympic Park;	*380	250 LDA	3000	250 VAT on construction 'omitted'
Bridges, Tunnels;	350	625 Londoner's Council Tax		
Security, Elite sport, Contingencies	955			
Agreed Funding Package	*2,375*		*3300*	*39 per cent*
Athletes Village (ODA)	650	Privately financed housing development	1050	300 subsidy, 100 'rent'
Security (ODA)	200	ODA	220	Higher costs
Running cost (LOCOG)	1,500	560 IOC TV/ marketing	2000	33 per cent 'Inflation'
		450 sponsorship/ official suppliers		
		300 ticket from venues		
		60 Licensing		
Lower Lea Valley Regeneration (LDA) – site preparation, infrastructure	800	750 LDA on acquisitions/ relocations to date	1000	'Inflation'
Transport – Channel Tunnel Rail Link (CTRL), East London Line Extension (DCLG, DfT, TfL)	6,620	Central government and Transport for London. Of which *380 from the Olympic budget, above		
Athlete preparations (BOA, UK Sport). Target = 4th place in medal table	300	200 Treasury over 7 years 100 raised by private sponsorship		
Legacy Trust fund 2007–2012	40	34 Lottery 6 Central government		

Abbreviations: ODA – Olympic Delivery Authority; LOCOG – London Organizing Committee of the Games; BOA – British Olympic Association; Lottery – National Lottery; LDA – London Development Agency; DCLG – Department for Communities and Local Government; DfT – Department for Transport; TfL –Transport for London; IOC – International Olympic Committee.

Source: London Candidacy File.

security costs (post-9/11) and poor ticket sales adding to the deficit. Before that, Sydney 2000 cost over $2.8 billion against an initial budget of $1 billion (Cashman, 2006). Beijing expects a small profit on the 2008 Games and London still aims to make a surplus of £100 million to be reinvested in sport (LOCOC, 2004). Given the post-event accounting and attribution problems, however, these small surpluses represent, at best, creative accounting.

Winning Ways

London and more so, the outside world, never expected to win the 2012 bid. Land acquisition and relocations had, not surprisingly, been taken less than seriously. The planning, IOC review visit and press support, built up a momentum in the last few months, as credibility and confidence grew – but second place was regarded as the 'best' outcome. The regeneration legacy was not reliant upon the Olympics; this would be the icing on the cake and provide the international cachet, even to an established world city and cultural capital. The countdown was, however, marked by an installation in Trafalgar Square, hoardings, and banners along key road routes. In the run up to the IOC vote in Singapore, London was still ranked third after Paris, the clear favourite, and Madrid. No city had hosted the Games more than twice (London and Paris) and London had never won by competition, only hosting by default in 1908 and 1948. New York was originally the obvious choice for the 2012 Olympics due to sympathy over 9/11, but much of this support had ebbed away, leaving New York as an unlikely choice. Moreover, public opposition to the city's first location of the Olympic stadium complicated its bid, compounded by protracted disputes over the design and rebuilding of the World Trade Centre and post-9/11 site, and the deferral of schemes such as the proposed Gehry-designed Guggenheim museum over the Hudson River. Madrid and Moscow planned city centre sites. By contrast, Paris had most facilities in place, having hosted the FIFA World Cup in 1998.

London's bid therefore rested pragmatically on both broader regeneration and legacy plans, including an explicit 'with' and 'without' Games scenarios. This formed the consultation roadshow that rolled out to the East London communities who would be most affected by the regeneration games. The master-planning team, led by the US-UK firm of EDAW plc, with stadium architects HOK and urban designers Allies and Morrison, also employed a firm of community architects, Fluid, to undertake the community consultation on the Olympic and Legacy plans. The Community Engagement included over 30 public events, the distribution of 400,000 public information leaflets to incumbent households and the requisite website. The Lower Lea Valley site used for community consultation is now subsumed into the London Development Agency (the Mayor's economic development agency and the government's regional development body for London) and London2012 official websites.[10]

An estimated 5,000 people participated in the event programme held in various community venues in the five Olympic boroughs. Local businesses (around 300 firms) and 'hard to reach' groups were also targeted to ensure their voice was at least heard. The firm undertaking the consultation also worked with the Lea Valley Matrix Group, but this group had been established and led by the London Development Agency itself, comprising businesses, boroughs and local regeneration partnerships. It was not a representative or independent community organization (Harskamp, 2006). Organized opposition to the Olympics was evident locally. Based on experience from other Olympic cities and mega-events, residents, environmentalists, businesses, cultural groups and others were anxious about the negative impacts, spiralling costs and displacement arising from the development. Ideological resistance was also apparent, but the Olympic good news story and the outsider status of the London bid lessened the negative press. Most observers did not expect the city to win and so opposition was not coordinated. Following the award in July 2005, organized resistance has focused on monitoring the development process[11] and on campaigning against land and premises relocation as the pace of issuing compulsory purchase orders intensifies.

Local Impacts

Not all sports venues will be concentrated in East London's Olympic complex. World-class facilities for specialist events are already available elsewhere, such as Wimbledon for tennis, and football matches will be staged at Wembley and other United Kingdom football stadia (Cardiff, Glasgow, Birmingham, Newcastle and Manchester), with sailing at Weymouth on the south coast of England. Temporary facilities will be made available for volleyball in Horseguards Parade and riding events in Hyde Park.

The heart of the Olympic developments and associated regeneration, however, will be at Stratford. The initial Olympic site plans showed a Park and associated zone of development situated in a linear strip measuring roughly 2 kilometres from north to south, in the valley of the River Lea – a small river that flows south from the Chiltern Hills to meet the River Thames at Bow Creek. By 2011, when trial events begin, this will contain the main Olympic Stadium and Village, together with the Paralympic tennis and archery facilities, hockey centre, velopark, fencing hall, handball arena, aquatic centre, basketball arena, media centres and warm-up facilities. These are to be served by a major transport interchange, located 1 kilometre to the east of the stadium at Stratford and served by underground, national rail, Eurostar and bus services.

When designated, however, the area presented a wholly different picture to the observer. Criss-crossed by a maze of river channels and canals, the area contained a mosaic of undeveloped flood plain (figure 17.3) and industrial land (figure 17.4). Some of the latter was long derelict, but other sites involved active manufacturing plant which needed to be relocated (figure 17.5). In some cases, regeneration had already started before designation. This area of London has been undergoing

Figure 17.3. The Pudding Mill River, tributary of the River Lea, bisecting the southern part of the future Olympic Park. The 80,000-seater Olympic stadium will be located to the left and the warm-up athletics tracks to the right (May 2007).

Figure 17.4. Industrial land in the south of the Olympic zone (May 2007).

piecemeal and selective regeneration for over ten years and reflects successive urban programmes under Conservative and Labour governments which have collectively produced a 'patchwork' of regeneration funding schemes (Audit Commission, 1989). It is perhaps ironic that the new demands made by the 2012 Games have had the result of seeing previously proposed areas of regeneration

Figure 17.5. The factory of H. Forman and Son, the oldest salmon smokery in the United Kingdom and the last of thirty such businesses in East London, lies in the zone to be cleared to make way for the stadium. The firm awaits relocation (May 2007).

Figure 17.6. The rundown Marshgate Lane Trading Centre, which was home to 300 businesses and a notable centre of resistance to London 2012, had launched a regeneration programme before the bid. A written announcement supplying notification of a Compulsory Purchase Order is appended to the sign (May 2007).

Figure 17.7. The Compulsory Purchase Order, served by the London Development Agency (May 2007).

themselves subsequently subject to compulsory purchase orders (figures 17.6 and 17.7).

There were two main reasons for locating the Olympic Park in this area of East London. The first, which needs little emphasis, was the availability of brownfield land and existing transport extensions to rail and underground systems, including EuroStar (Evans and Shaw, 2001). The second was the disadvantaged profile of incumbent communities in Newham and the adjoining 'Olympic boroughs'. Relative 'deprivation' is measured in England by a number of economic, environmental and social (including education) factors, weighted towards employment and economic participation (ODPM, 2004). These include individual domains such as income, education and skills, health, and housing and environment producing a composite standard by which local areas are ranked nationally, with the score of 1 representing the most deprived area in a national 'Index of Multiple Deprivation' (IMD). This therefore provides a national league table which is used as the prime criterion for regional and other regeneration assistance programmes (i.e. public funding). Table 17.3 shows the ranking of the income factor in the IMD, comparing the Olympic zone neighbourhoods with Olympic sub-region boroughs, and with London and England as a whole. This confirms that 62 per cent of the Olympic zone neighbourhoods (and 39 per cent of the five boroughs) are ranked in the top ten most income-deprived areas in England, and 48 per cent in the worst five.

The legacy plan shows the key after-use facilities, excluding the temporary facilities which will be removed after the Games. This includes downsizing the main sports stadium from approximately 80,000 seats to 25,000 and converting the Olympic Village to promised mixed-income housing. Environmental improvements (including transport access) will be the main physical features of the Olympic legacy. However, it is the economic regeneration and consequent social benefits – given the association of poor housing, health, education and crime with poverty and lack of work – that have been used to justify the sustainability of London 2012, and ultimately the longer term benefits to offset the explicitly stated and indeterminate direct and indirect costs, as outlined in table 17.2. Event and post-event economic impacts also rely on maintaining increased tourism flows, with 15,000 additional hotel rooms to be available within 50 kilometres of the Olympic zone, as well as on employment from growth sectors such as the creative industries, with a 'creative hub' centred on Stratford (Evans, 2006c) and post-event usage of the Media Centre and Press Centre.

It is hoped that new housing will also attract residents to 3,600 apartments in

Table 17.3. Ranking of Super Output Areas (SOAs) on Income Deprivation Domain of Index of Multiple Deprivation (per cent of SOAs, IMD 2004).

Ranking on IMD (% of all SOAs)	Olympic zone (%)	Five Olympic boroughs (%)	London (%)	England (%)
> 10–15	13	17	8	5
> 5– 10	20	19	9	5
> 1–5	38	18	6	4
Up to 1	4	2	1	1

Note: Super Output Areas (SOAs) are spatial units used for the collection and publication of small area statistics in the 2001 British Census. They contain an average of 1500 residents and are coterminous with ward boundaries.

Source: PriceWaterhouseCoopers (2005).

the Olympic village and 9,000 in the Olympic Park area as a whole. However, the masterplan for the swathe of east London along the Lea Valley allows new housing and amenities to be designed with facilities that are less than the accepted national standards. This runs the risk of reinforcing a lower quality of life on this historically poorly served community and environment, which has seen its docklands, manufacturing and smoke-stack industrial base (with concomitant pollution and land contamination), irrevocably decline. The Olympic zone borough of Newham had reduced the percentage of new dwellings built on brownfield land from an average of 85 per cent (1997–2000) to 75 per cent (2001–2004). This countered the upward trend elsewhere, although the density of housing development increased dramatically during the same period, from 58 to 94 dwellings per hectare (DCLG, 2006). This reflects the pace of new development already taking place in the borough, and the drive, supported by the London Mayor and central government, for higher density in the shape of so-called 'compact' living and working (ODPM, 2003a). Sustainable compact living requires quality and levels of amenity, urban design and local employment to counter outward commuting and car use (Evans, 2005b). Post-event employment and economic development is rather less apparent in the Olympic-related regeneration plans (Experian, 2006; Kornblatt, 2006). Estimates of the contribution of the Games to the *national* economy prior to the Olympic city award was put at only 0.34 per cent over seven years (Patrick, 2005), with a net gain of £82 million (Crookson, 2004).[12] It is the wider *distributive* effects that are attributed to the Olympic regeneration impact, particularly in employment. However, in the government's own impact appraisal (PriceWaterhouseCoopers, 2005), projected employment is highly concentrated in pre-event construction activity and benefits the London region more than the local economy (see table 17.4).

The broader regeneration growth strategy relates to the Thames Gateway, of which the Olympic zone forms a north-western segment. The Thames Gateway stretches from east and south-east London, further south and east to the counties of Essex and Kent, out to the Medway estuary. It is the subject of large-scale house-building plans (200,000 new homes) and forms a key plank of the government's Sustainable Communities strategy (ODPM, 2003b, 2003c). The annual housing targets required to meet this growth have to date not been met, and the pace of development has been slow. The Olympics therefore provide an investment leverage opportunity to accelerate development. However, this is taking place in

Table 17.4. Summary of expected impacts on employment.

Area	Pre-event (2005–2011)	During event (2012)	Legacy/post-event (2013–2016)	Overall (2005–2016)
UK (excluding London)	2,955	3,261	1,948	8,164
London	25,824	3,724	9,327	38,875
North-east London	7,344	311	311	7,966

Source: PriceWaterhouseCoopers (2005).

the Thames Gateway *London* region, rather than the exurban segment, reinforcing London's development preference and capacity for population growth (an estimated 700,000 increase by 2016) and creating a shadow effect over the outer Thames Gateway region. In contrast, Barcelona's expansion has not been limited to the Diagonal and new Forum zone linking the old city to the Olympic Village and beyond (Monclus, 2003), but housing and employment growth is now greater in the outer metropolitan area and Catalonian region, whilst the city's density is reducing (Evans, 2006*a*).

Two issues dominate the capital phase impacts on host communities. The first is cost inflation and 'crowding out' of employment and other resources, as the mega-development sucks resources and productive capacity out of the economy. The second stems from the employment effects which are again driven by skills levels and capacity. The United Kingdom, and London and the South-East, have already been experiencing a development boom. This is revealed in a lively housing and office market (although, as noted above, not necessarily where it is 'needed') and massive public facility building programmes – notably, in transport with Network Rail's ten-year £4 billion strategy for the redevelopment of six London mainline and 50 regional stations; public health care (the largest hospital rebuilding programme in the world); and education. This investment has been substantially funded outside the public spending balance sheet, under the government's private finance initiative (PFI). The PFI, however, has not been used to finance Olympic capital projects. This is an indication of the poor viability of such facilities, since PFI contractors earn their considerable returns on facility management and leaseback to the public sector, in return for risk capital investment in the development phase.

At the same time, major sports facilities such as the new national football stadium at Wembley (public) and Arsenal Football Club's Emirates Stadium (commercial) have been under construction in London, involving some of the same Olympic contractors. This boom in facility provision must be seen in the context of an industry which has an endemic lack of capacity and skills, as highlighted in the Egan Review (ODPM, 2004), the Urban Task Force's identification of a 'design skills deficit' (CABE, 2001), and regional assessments of regeneration skills (Bagwell *et al.*, 2005). Nationally, an extra 348,000 workers are forecast to be needed by 2010, with the highest demand from east and south-east London regions (CITB, 2006). It is no surprise therefore that foreign contractors and workers have migrated to fill this gap. This pattern is long established, particularly in this area of London – where Huguenot, Jewish, Irish and Bangladeshi immigrants, among others, have gone before. Today, East European economic migrants underpin the construction and other service activities. What these groups share historically is resistance from incumbent communities (competition for jobs, housing and amenities) and some of the worst discrimination and stigma attaching to their unglamorous and unromantic contribution to London's infrastructure (Evans and Foord, 2005). Ironically, it is members of these residual communities in the East End that now represent some of the highest groups of economic inactivity, and the targets of the Olympic trickle down effect. As Vigor (2006, p. 14) noted:

> If the Lower Lea Valley is to be transformed – socially as well as physically – then these are the people who need to access new employment opportunities. Sustainable regeneration will require a genuine increase in the local employment rate – not just the result of highly skilled population moving in and displacing the indigenous lower skilled one.

A sobering fact is that nearly 20 per cent of the adult population in the Thames Gateway has no formal qualifications and half of the children live in workless households. As the incoming chief executive of the Thames Gateway Partnership, Judith Armitt said: 'educational attainment in the region [is] very depressing, and [is] often overlooked because of a focus on more tangible regeneration such as transport and infrastructure' (*Building Design*, 2006, p. 5)

As Vigor (2006, p. 14) also pointed out:

> past Olympics have focused too closely on hard infrastructure concerns. Organizers have automatically assumed that the people and places most in need of any lasting benefits will receive them. There is little evidence of this.

This scenario is therefore worrying, and a response from the London Mayor has been the creation of a London 2012 Employment and Skills Task Force, which aims to train low-skilled residents 'so they can compete for any new jobs that arise *and* work with employers to change their recruitment procedures, which have sometimes discriminated against such individuals' (*Ibid.*) The notion that the least 'skilled', or more accurately, those whose skills are now redundant in a post-industrial city, and with the highest barriers to employment participation will be transformed into the construction and service workers required to deliver the Olympics 'on time, on budget', to use the mantra, is unrealistic (Kornblatt, 2006). Public procurement legislation requires contracts of £100,000 and over to be advertised EU-wide, and combined with the labour market challenge: 'at present there's no reason why London 2012 should not provide more of a skills legacy for Gdansk (Poland) than Newham' (LCC, 2005).

Conclusion

In contrast to mega-events such as the World Fairs, which provided a flexible format that addressed a wide range of goals, today's Olympics have developed into a homogenous and highly controlled form. By closing down and effectively monopolizing the Olympic brand and globalizing the media contracts, local and regional economies stand little chance of economic engagement with the Games, and risk lawsuits if they attempt to capitalize on its brand images, such as the five-rings or the London 2012 logos (Culfe, 2006). This raises a serious challenge to the regeneration aims and legacy plans of the host city, with employment generation and economic impacts concentrated in imported construction activity during the development phase. Plans to regenerate east London formed a key part of the capital's successful bid to host the games, but as the Chamber of Commerce observed: 'That objective can only be met if the games itself benefits local businesses' (LCC, 2005).

Writing on an Olympic host city only two years on from designation, prior to detailed planning submission and five years before the big event, makes any assessment of London 2012 contingent and speculative, but the accumulating mega-event experience (Evans, 2005a and b) suggests a predictable path and outcome. The history, as Baudrillard once said of the impending entry to the new Millennium, has already been written (Evans, 1999a). The alternative to the Olympic development machine rolling inexorably on would require a leap of imagination and facing off of the 'political consequences of creating a blueprint for a less costly, less cumbersome Olympics, without the endless decision-making that permanent buildings demand'.[13] As Allen (2006, p. 3) went on to ask:

> Which would be the most meaningful Olympic legacy? A blueprint that makes hosting the Olympic games a viable aspiration for developing countries? Or a host of mega-structures that have outlived their primary use?

In the absence of this radical departure from the Olympic hegemony, an independent Commission for the Olympic Legacy will therefore need to convene permanently in London to ensure that the promises and regeneration aspirations are also delivered. Poetry and dance might have been integral to the Olympics of classical Greece, but without this legacy guarantee, it will be hard to avoid Kunzmann's (2004, p. 2) gloomy prediction that: 'Each story of regeneration begins with poetry and ends with real estate'.

Notes

1   A misplaced vote might have helped London win the 2012 Olympics. An International Olympic Committee member (President of the Greek Olympic Committee) had mistakenly voted for Paris rather than Madrid. Paris received 33 votes to Madrid's 31 in the third round, eliminating the Spanish capital. Moscow and New York were eliminated in the first two rounds. Had Madrid received the vote rather than Paris, the cities would have tied with 32 each, seven fewer than London, and entered a tiebreaker. London beat Paris 54–50 in the final round.

2   According to the Chief Executive of the British Olympic Association, Simon Clegg: 'The sole measurement of the Games won't be on how efficient the organizing committee is, or how beautifully architectured the design of the stadiums are – it'll be decided on how many British athletes stand on the podium and collect medals' (http://ukolympics.org.uk, accessed 1 December 2006). The official target is to improve the place in the Olympic medal table from tenth in 2004 to fourth in 2012.

3   Although the experience of visitors was generally positive – 88 per cent said that they had a 'fun day' (BBC 'Vote on the Dome').

4   This 'journey of discovery' project has been queried by the ODA due to the cost and associated risks, proposing instead, a 'virtual vessel' (*Anon*, 2007). Whether the project takes place or not, this is an example of the Olympic bid promises and visions being downgraded as budget and operational realities take over.

5   It is estimated that there will be 9.6 million tickets on sale for the London 2012 Games.

6   'Poll shows strong support for London Games', www.bbc.co.uk/London, 2006.

7   London 2012 'Favourability Research', www.london2012.com, December 2006.

8   Massively over-budget and failing to complete to agreed timetables, Wembley left the Australian Multiplex developer near-bankrupt.

9   Government claims for 'transparency' in decision-making and financing of the Olympics are able to be side-stepped under the mask of 'commercial confidentiality' in the procurement process.

10   www.london2012.org.

11   Games Monitor: debunking the Olympic myths (see www.gamesmonitor.org/uk).

12   In the case of another iconic regeneration project, Guggenheim Bilbao, the contribution to the Basque regional GNP was estimated at 0.47 per cent in 1997, similar to London 2012, with substantial prior public investment in transport infrastructure (Evans and Foord, 2003). As Cerro (2006) concluded 'Bilbao's economic performance since 1994 was not fundamentally due to Gehry's Guggenheim building'.

13   Allen (2006, p. 3) suggests that 'the business of temporary public spectacle would be better left to the professional event designers; to those who know how to do it best'. In an effort to produce spectacular buildings, the Olympic commissioning agencies have selected star architects such as Zaha Hadid, whose Aquatic Centre design has been substantially scaled back. ODA Chief Executive David Higgins claimed that 'Design is at the Heart of what we are doing here' (*Building Design*, 1 December 2006) and the Culture Minister Tessa Jowell said that the ODA must: 'ensure design is as much of a pre-occupation as cost control' – the ODA had no architect on its board, but in late-2006 appointed design advisers Ricky Burdett (ex-London School of Economics, Greater London Authority Architecture and Urbanism Unit); Peter Cook (University College London and the 1960s group Archigram); and the Tate Gallery director, Nicholas Serota. None has a significant track record of design practice, or of major sports buildings (primarily academic or curatorial careers).

Chapter 18

Afterword

John R. Gold and Margaret M. Gold

Legacy: *A sum of money, or a specified article, given to another by will…*
transf. and fig.; esp. = anything handed down by an ancestor or predecessor.[1]

On 15 March 2007 Tessa Jowell, the Secretary of State for Culture, Media and Sport, stood up in the British House of Commons to deliver a statement about the costs of the 2012 London Summer Olympic and Paralympic Games. The readily apparent strain on her face suggested that this was not an occasion that she had been anticipating with much pleasure. As shown in the previous chapter (see table 17.1), the Olympic bid document outlined a £2.375 billion capital budget and £1.5 billion operating budget, which would be supplemented by the additional financing of transport and site infrastructure. The subsequent steady drip of information, undoubtedly stage managed to prepare the way for an eventual (and accurate) reckoning, had revealed the various items not previously included in the costings. Policing and security, conspicuously absent from the original costings now weighed in at £600 million. Value-added tax, somehow omitted from earlier calculations, was estimated as £836 million. A hefty programme contingency cost of £2.747 billion had appeared at the Treasury's bidding to cover cost overruns. The headline figure was now £9.325 billion.[2]

The response from the political opposition was cautious. Had the subject in question been anything other than the Olympics, the reaction to such apparently damning information would have been loud, sustained and probably decisive for the Minister's future career. The Olympics, however, demanded a different response. The project remained popular in a country where enthusiasm for sport runs deep. Despite fulminating about incompetence and mismanagement, politicians were only too aware that 'winning' the Games was seen as a major British success story and one which confirmed the re-emergence of London as a world city of the first order. Jowell herself tried to swat criticism by wrapping herself in the flag and, somewhat implausibly, stating that disapproval amounted to a 'vote for Paris' – the city that London had defeated in the final round of IOC voting in July 2005. To attack the project was apparently tantamount to disloyalty.

A true assessment of whether the huge underestimates were products of incompetence or a careful massaging of the figures to win the bid may well have to wait for the release of official papers in the National Archives some three decades hence. In the mean time, the suspicion remains that the London bid committee faced up to the challenge of staging the 'bloated beast' that is now the Summer Olympics (Tomlinson, 2004, p. 158) in a similar manner to many predecessors. This comprised first producing an initially conservative figure as part of a package designed to impress the grandees of the IOC and then slowly allowing the real costs to emerge to those footing the bill. Whatever the final costs, it is certain that they will be met just as they were for the two previous Summer Games in Sydney and Athens. Notwithstanding cost overruns, cancellation or withdrawal are simply not options. In such circumstances, it is inevitable that the prime area for discussion will focus less on costs than the nature of the benefits, long-term or otherwise, thought likely to accrue.

That debate, as we have seen at so many points in this book, focuses around the nebulous concept of legacy; an idea that was not part of the original vision behind the revival of the Games. The exact time when the term 'legacy' entered Olympic discourse is difficult to determine with any precision. The IOC archive holdings in Lausanne suggest that the first significant mention occurred in 1956 in relation to the Melbourne Games (McIntosh, 2003, p. 450). Prior to that, the idea of impact did not really extend to a physical legacy. Rather, the emphasis was on the honour of holding the Games, for which the host provided suitable premises and facilities. This is not to say that earlier hosts were not aware of the potential the Games might have, particularly in the area of tourism. Yet given the IOC's attachment to amateurism and antipathy to profit, it was considered inappropriate to glory in what the Games would do for the city rather than for sport and the pleasure of the citizens (*Ibid.*, pp. 450, 452).

The trend towards emphasizing planned outcomes, which we have charted in this book, brought about a situation in which preoccupation with infrastructural change and city rebranding seemed to erode the attention paid to the sporting dimension. Scale exerted an intoxicating appeal. Certainly the IOC seemed to develop a partiality for supporting comprehensive interventions that somehow mirrored, and possibly served to justify, the steadily increasing size and demands of the Games. A proposal that offered a striking regenerative transformation such as Sydney's Homebush Bay or London's Lea Valley might serve as a symbol of the positive virtues of staging the Olympics and act as a fig leaf for the enormous expenses required and incurred.

Admittedly, the IOC is not entirely happy with the over-identification of notions of legacy with purely the interests of the host city and the instrumentalist approach that this appears to embody. One of the most effective elements of London's final bid presentation to the IOC was widely held to be its emphasis on the children of the world and the Games as an inspiration for participation in sport and striving for excellence. The Olympic movement's ruling circles would also recognize the importance of the intangible legacy of the Games. This might variously find expression in terms of encouraging the development of skills, changing attitudes, inculcating new ways of working, and reinforcing a still-potent internationalism. In keeping with the spirit of an age that, at least superficially, pays lip service to the goal of transferring assets in a sustainable manner to succeeding generations, the Olympics have taken on new qualities of encouraging good environmental practice in the built environment and fostering long-term change in sporting culture. The close connection with the Paralympics has placed the Olympic movement centre stage in driving the disability agenda. Each of these elements testifies to the fact that this is a supremely flexible festival that has been repeatedly invented and reinvented to address the needs of the time.

In coming to terms with the diversity of what is termed 'legacy', a symposium meeting under IOC auspices in 2002 considered the relevant theory and practice. After extensive deliberations, it concluded that:

> the effects of the legacy have many aspects and dimensions, ranging from the more commonly recognised aspects – architecture, urban planning, city marketing, sports infrastructures, economic and tourist development – to others ... that are less well recognised ... the so called intangible legacies, such as production of ideas and cultural values, intercultural and non-exclusionary experiences (based on gender, ethnicity or physical abilities), popular memory, education, archives, collective effort and voluntarism, new sport practitioners, notoriety on a global scale, experience and know-how. (IOC, 2003b, p. 2)

The point, however, is that, thus construed, thinking about legacy tends to be predisposed towards accenting the positive. The contrary evidence supplied by the experience of, say, Berlin or Montreal, seemingly represent aberrations from the norm. It is not part of the function of this book to debunk the Games or attempt to gainsay the real contributions that the Olympic movement has made. What is apparent from the standpoint of Olympic cities, however, is that staging the Games is now divorced from the conventional rationale that surrounds almost all other festivals. The right to host the Olympics represents the ultimate accolade that a city can earn on the world stage. To surrender that right would invite universal ridicule and inflict a mortal blow on the standing of the host city in the international urban pecking order. Expenditures might be disputed and lower priority events, such as the Cultural Olympiad or associated youth programmes, might have their budgets slashed, but the prestige element of the expenditure will go ahead. Ways will be found to finance the Games regardless of the logic of the balance sheet, probably with the nation as a whole rather than the Olympic city picking up the bulk of the bill. Without cost as an effective constraint, debate inevitably centres on the seductive promise of legacy to sustain popular enthusiasm and drive the project ahead. What is certain is that the circus will have left town long before the day of reckoning arrives.

Notes

1. Oxford English Dictionary, vol. 9, p. 183.
2. National Audit Office figures, reported in *Financial Times*, 16 March 2007.

References

The references listed in this bibliography include both the primary and secondary sources used in writing this book. Full publication details are not always given for the small number of sources listed here that were published before 1900, since some were privately published and bear only the names of their printers.

Acharya, S.K. (2005) Urban development in post-reform China: insights from Beijing. *Norsk Geografisk Tidsskrift*, **59**, pp. 229–236.

ACOG (Atlanta Committee for the Olympic Games) (1990) *Welcome to a Brave and Beautiful City*. Atlanta: Atlanta Committee for the Olympic Games.

Alibés, J.M.R., Campo, M.J., Giral, E., Huertas Claveria, J.M., Pradas, R. and Tarragó, S. (1975) *La Barcelona de Porcioles*, 2nd ed. Barcelona: Editorial Laia.

Allen, I. (2006) Should regeneration be based on a fleeting and extraordinary event? *Architects' Journal*, **224**, 30 November, p. 3.

Altshular, A. and Luberoff, D. (2003) *The Changing Politics of Urban Mega-Projects*. Washington DC: Brookings Institution Press.

Andranovich, G., Burbank, M.J. and Heying, C.H. (2001) Olympic Cities: lessons learned from mega-event politics. *Journal of Urban Affairs*, **23**, pp. 113–31.

Anon (1904) *Universal Exposition, Saint Louis 1904: Preliminary Programme of Physical culture, Olympic Games and World's Championship Contests*. St. Louis: Organizing Committee.

Anon (1910) Dover, Robert. *Encyclopaedia Britannica*, 11th ed., vol. 8. Cambridge: Cambridge University Press, p. 453.

Anon (1963) Two cities battle to host the Olympics. *Business Week*, 23 February, p. 36.

Anon (1987) The future of Athens: a city in transition. *Financial Times*, 6 May.

Anon (2003) Athens prays for Zorba to rescue its 'shambolic' Olympic Games. *Observer*, 13 July.

Anon (2004) Securing the Olympic Games. *Wall Street Journal*, 22 August.

Anon (2005) How the bid financing breaks down. *Daily Telegraph*, 4 July.

Anon (2006) Don't make grassroots pay for Olympics. *The Observer*, March 26.

Anon (2007) Olympic FriendShip may run aground. *thelondonpaper*, 4 January, p. 5.

AOBC (Athens 2004 Olympic Bid Committee) (1997) *Athens Candidate City*. Athens: AOBC.

Arbena, J.L. (1991) Sport, development, and Mexican nationalism, 1920–1970. *Journal of Sport History*, **18**, pp. 350–364.

Arbena, J.L. (1996) Mexico City 1968: The Games of the XIXth Olympiad, in Findling, J.E. and Pelle, K.D. (eds.) *Historical Dictionary of the Modern Olympic Movement*. Westport, CN: Greenwood Press, pp. 139–147.

Arnold, B. (1992) The past as propaganda. *Archaeology*, **45**(July/August), pp. 30–37.

Askew, K. (2006) Debt sinks Stadium Australia: ANZ to take control for $10m. *Sydney Morning Herald*, 16 November.

Aso, N. (2002) Sumptuous re-past: the 1964 Tokyo Olympic Arts Festival. *Positions*, **10**, pp. 7–38.

ATHOC (Athens Organizing Committee for the Olympic Games) (2004) Archery in the shadow of the Acropolis (advertisement), in Konstandaras, K. *Greece: The Ideal Destination*. Athens: Hellenic Sun Editions.

ATHOC (Athens Organizing Committee for the Olympic Games) (2005) *Official Report of the XXVIII Olympiad*, 2 vols. Athens: Liberis Publications Group.

Audit Commission (1989) *A Review of Urban Programme and Regeneration Schemes in England*. London: HMSO.

Auditor General (2002) Cost of the Olympic and Paralympic Games, *Auditor General's Report to Parliament*, vol. 2. Sydney: New South Wales Auditor General.

Auf der Maur, N. (1976) *The Billion-Dollar Game*. Toronto: James Lorimer.

Augustin, J.-P. and Gillon, P. (2004) *L'Olympisme: Bilan et enjeux géopolitiques*. Paris: Armand Colin.

Australian Democrats (2001) *An Australian Cultural Plan*. http://www.democrats.org.au/policies/#, accessed 21 January 2007.

Baade, R.A. and Matheson, V. (2002) Bidding for the Olympics: fool's gold, in Baros, C.P., Ibrahimo, M. and Szymanski, S. (eds.) *Transatlantic Sport: The Comparative Economics of North America and European Sports*. Cheltenham: Edward Elgar, pp. 127–151.

Bagwell, S., Foord, J. and Lewis, J. (2005) *Regeneration Skills and Training Needs Survey*. London: Cities Institute for the Higher Education Innovation Fund (HEIF2), London Metropolitan University.

BALASA (British Amputee and Les Autres Sports Association) (2007) Les Autres Athletes. http://www.patient.co.uk/showdoc/26739787/, accessed 12 March 2007.

Bandy, S.J. (1988) The Olympic celebration of the arts, in Seagrave, J.O. and Chu, D. (eds.) *The Olympic Games in Transition*. Champaign, IL: Human Kinetics, pp. 163–169.

Barcelona City Council (1971) *Barcelona 2000*. Barcelona: Ayuntamiento de Barcelona.

Barcelona City Council (1983) *Plans i projectes per a Barcelona, 1981–1982*. Barcelona: Ajuntament de Barcelona.

Barcelona City Council (1987*a*) *Arees de nova centralitat*, Barcelona: Ajuntament de Barcelona.

Barcelona City Council (1987*b*) *Plans cap al 92*. Barcelona: Ajuntament de Barcelona.

Barcelona City Council (1996) *Barcelona: La segona renovació*. Barcelona: Ajuntament de Barcelona.

Barcelona City Council (1999*a*) *Barcelona 1979–2004: del desenvolupament a la ciutat de qualitat*. Barcelona: Ajuntament de Barcelona.

Barcelona City Council (1999*b*) *Urbanisme a Barcelona*, Barcelona: Ajuntament de Barcelona.

Barcelona Regional (1999) *Barcelona New Projects*. Barcelona: Ajuntament de Barcelona.

Barkham, P. (2005*a*) Chirac's reheated food jokes bring Blair to the boil. *The Guardian*, 5 July.

Barkham, P. (2005*b*) Spielberg (ET, Jaws) and Besson (Nikita, Léon). The winner: Goodrich (Travelex ads). *The Guardian,* 7 July.

Barker, P. (2006) London 1948. *Journal of Olympic History*, **14**(2), pp. 65–69.

Barkin, D. and King, T. (1970) *Regional Economic Development: The River Basin Approach in Mexico*. Cambridge: Cambridge University Press.

Barnett, C.R. (1996) St. Louis 1904: the Games of the 3rd Olympiad, in Findling, J.E. and Pelle, K.D. (eds.) *Historical Dictionary of the Modern Olympic Movement*. Westport, CN: Greenwood Press, pp. 18–25.

Barney, R.K., Wenn, S.R. and Martyn, S.G. (2004) *Selling the Five Rings: The International Olympic Committee and the Rise of Olympic Commercialism*, revised ed. Salt Lake City, UT: University of Utah Press.

Bastéa, E. (2000) *The Creation of Modern Athens: Planning the Myth*. Cambridge: Cambridge University Press.

Bataillon, C. and Rivière d'Arc, H. (1979) *La Ciudad de México*. Mexico City: Sep Diana.

BBC News 24 (2006) London's Olympic victory. Broadcast 1 January.

BBC Sport (2006) Beijing eyes Games profit in 2008. www.news.bbc.co.uk/go/pr/fr/-/sport1/hi/other_sports/4559728stm, accessed 26 December 2006.

Beard, M. (2004) The Greek heroes, a missed drugs test and a 'motorbike accident' that upset the Games. *The Independent*, 14 August.

Bergmann, B. (1999) Introduction: the art of ancient spectacle, in Bergmann, B. and Kondoleon, C. (eds.) *The Art of Ancient Spectacle*. Washington, DC: National Gallery of Art, pp. 8–35.

Beriatos, E. and Gospodini, A. (2004) 'Glocalising' urban landscapes: Athens and the 2004 Olympics. *Cities*, **21**, pp. 187–202.

Berkaak, O.A. (1999) In the heart of the volcano: the Olympic Games as mega drama, in Klausen, A.M. (ed.) *Olympic Games as Performance and Public Event: The Case of the XVII Winter Olympic Games in Norway*. New York: Bergham Books, pp. 49–75.

Berlin, P. (2003) What did Olympics bring Sydney? *International Herald Tribune*, 24 December. http://www.iht.com/articles/2003/12/24/t1_2.php, accessed 26 December 2006.

Bernstein, A. (2000) Globalisation, media, and the Olympics. *Journal of Sport and Social Issues*, **24**, pp. 351–369.

Best, S. (2000) Public art in the Olympic city. *Architecture Australia*, **89**(5), pp. 80–85.

Bianchini, F. and Parkinson, M. (eds.) (1993) *Cultural Policy and Urban Regeneration: The West European Experience*. Manchester: Manchester University Press.

Bijkerk, A.T. (2006) Amsterdam 1928. *Journal of Olympic History*, **14**, pp. 29–31,

Blair, T. (2004) A message, in Anon, *A Vision for the Olympic Games and Paralympic Games*. London: London2012, p. 1.

BOBICO (Beijing 2008 Olympic Bid Committee) (2001) *Beijing Candidature File*, vol. 1. http://en.beijing2008.com, accessed 13 February 2006.

Bohigas, O. (1985) *Reconstrucció de Barcelona*. Barcelona: Edicions 62.

Bohigas, O. (1999) Valorización de las periferias y recuperación del centro: recuperación del frente marítimo, in Maragall, P. (ed.) *Europa próxima: Europa, regiones y ciudades*. Barcelona: Edicions de la Universitat Politècnica de Catalunya, pp. 199–214.

Bokoyannis, D. (2006) Athens: The Making of a Contemporary and Friendlier City. Speech, 9 February, Athens Concert Hall. http://www.cityofathens.gr/files/pdf/highlights/apologismos_omilia_en.pdf, accessed 1 September 2006.

Booth, D. (1999) Gifts of corruption? Ambiguities of obligation in the Olympic movement. *Olympika*, **8**, pp. 43–68.

Booth, D. and Tatz, C. (1999) *One-Eyed: A View of Australian Sport*. Sydney: George Allen and Unwin.

Borges, W., Lennartz, K., Quanz, D.R. and Teutenberg, W. (1995) *Deutsche Olympiade Kalender. Daten zur Olympischen Bewegung in Deutschland, Teil 1: I. bis XIII. Olympiade (1896–1945) mit Interludium (393–1889) und Praeludium (1889–1996)*. Kassel: Agon-Sportverlag.

Borja, F. (1992) *The Winter Olympic Games. Albertville 1992: A Case Study*. Paris: American University of Paris.

Borja, J. (ed.) (1995) *Barcelona: A Model of Urban Transformation 1980–1995*. Quito: Urban Management Series (PGU-LAC).

Borja, J. and Castells, M. (1997) *Local y Global: La gestión de las ciudades en la era de la informació*. Madrid: Taurus.

Bottomley, G. (1994) Post-multiculturalism? The theory and practice of heterogeneity. *Culture and Policy*, **6**, pp. 139–152.

Bourne, C. (2006) *A Future for Presentism*. Oxford: Oxford University Press.

BPA (British Paralympic Association) (2007) Sydney 2000. http://www.paralympics.org.uk/paralympic_games.asp?section=000100010003&games_code=00010003000300010003, accessed 11 February 2007.

Bradby, D. and McCormick, J. (1978) *People's Theatre*. London: Croom Helm.

Brewster, K. (2005) Patriotic pastimes: the role of sport in post-revolutionary Mexico. *International Journal of the History of Sport*, **22**, pp. 139–157.

Brichford, M. (1996) Munich 1972: the Games of the 20th Olympiad, in Findling, J.E. and Pelle, K.D. (eds.) *Historical Dictionary of the Modern Olympic Movement*. Westport, CN: Greenwood Press, pp. 148–152.

Broudehoux, A.-M. (2004) *The Making and Selling of Post-Mao Beijing*. London: Routledge.

Brown, D. (1996*a*) Pierre de Coubertin's Olympic exploration of modernism, 1894–1914: Aesthetics, ideology and the spectacle. *Research Quarterly for Exercise and Sport*, **67**, pp. 121–135.

Brown, D. (1996*b*) Revisiting the discourses of art, beauty, and sport from the 1906 Consultative Conference for the Arts, Literature and Sport. *Olympika*, **5**, pp. 1–24.

Brown, D. (2001) Modern sport, modernism and the cultural manifesto: de Coubertin's *Revue Olympique*. *International Journal of the History of Sport*, **18**, pp. 78–109.

Brownhill, S. (1990) *Developing London's Docklands*. London: Paul Chapman.

Browning, M. (2000) Olympics under the gun. *The Guardian*, 8 March. http://www.cpa.org.au/gachive2/991games.html, accessed 1 April 2000.

Brundage, A. (1951) Report of Commission appointed by the IOC at its meeting in Copenhagen in 1950 to study conditions in Latin America. *Bulletin of the International Olympic Committee*, 27 June, pp. 37–39.

Brunet, F. (1995) An economic analysis of the Barcelona '92 Olympic Games: resources, financing and impact, in Moragas, M. de and Botella, M. (eds.) *The Keys of Success: The Social, Sporting, Economic and Communications Impact of Barcelona '92*. Barcelona: Bellaterra, pp. 203–37.

Buchanan, I. and Mallon, B. (2001) *Historical Dictionary of the Olympic Movement*. Lanham, MD: Scarecrow Press

Buchanan, P. (1984) Regenerating Barcelona: projects versus planning – nine parks and plazas. *Architectural Review*, **175**(6), pp. 32–46.

Buchanan, P. (1992) Barcelona: a city regenerated. *Architectural Review*, **191**(August), pp. 11–14.

Building Design (2006) Gateway skills crisis highlighted. *Building Design*, 15 December, p. 5.

Burbank, M.J., Andranovich, G.D., and Heying, C.H. (2001) *Olympic Dreams: The Impact of Mega-Events on Local Politics*. Boulder, CO: Lynne Rienner.

Burbank, M.J., Andranovich, G.D. and Heying, C.H. (2002) Mega-events, urban development, and public policy. *Review of Policy Research*, **19**, pp. 179–202.

Burroughs, A. (1999) Winning the bid, in Cashman, R. and Hughes, A. (eds.) *Staging the Olympics: The Event and Its Impact*. Sydney: University of New South Wales Press, pp. 35–45.

Busquets, J. (1992) *Barcelona: evolución urbanística de una capital compacta*. Madrid: Mapfre.

CABE (Commission for Architecture and the Built Environment) (2001) *Urban Design Skills Working Group: Report to the Minister for Housing, Planning and Regeneration*. London: DTLR.

Calavita, N. and Ferrer, A. (2000) Behind Barcelona's success story: citizens movements and planners' power. *Journal of Urban History*, **26**, pp. 793–807.

California Olympic Commission (1960) *VIII Olympic Winter Games Squaw Valley, California, Final Report*. Squaw Valley: Organizing Committee.

Calvert, P. (1973) *Mexico: Nation of the Modern World*. London: Ernest Benn.

Campbell, D. (2005) The day Coe won gold. *The Observer*, 10 July.

Campbell, T. and Wilk, D. (1986) Plans and plan-making in the valley of Mexico. *Third World Planning Review*, **8**, pp. 287–313.

Cannon, T. (2000) *China's Economic Growth: The Impact on Regions, Migration and the Environment*. London: Macmillan.

Capel, H. (2005*) El modelo Barcelona: un exámen crítico*. Barcelona: Edicions del Serbal.

Carisbroke, Lord, Porritt, A., Webb-Johnson, Lord, Heyworth, Lord, Templer, E.M., Londin, H., Summers, S., Bannister, R., Faure, J.C.A. and Guttmann, L. (1956) Games for the paralysed. *The Times*, 20 March, p. 11.

Cashman, R. (1999) The greatest peacetime event, in Cashman, R. and Hughes, A. (eds.) *Staging the Olympics: The Event and Its Impact*. Sydney: University of New South Wales Press, pp. 3–17.

Cashman, R. (2006) *The Bitter-Sweet Awakening: the legacy of the Sydney 2000 Olympic Games*. Sydney: Walla Walla Press.

Caust, J. (2003) How has the discourse about cultural policy been captured by the economists and the marketers and what should be done about it? *International Journal of Cultural Policy*, **9**, pp. 51–63.

Cerro, G. del (2006) *Bilbao: Basque Pathways to Globalization*. Oxford: Elsevier.

Chai, J.C.H. (1996) Divergent development and regional income gap in China. *Journal of Contemporary Asia*, **26**, pp. 46–58.

Chalkley, B. and Essex, S. (1999) Urban development through hosting international events: a history of the Olympic Games. *Planning Perspectives*, **14**, pp. 369–394.

Chandler, R. (1776) *Travels in Greece; or, an Account of a Tour made at the Expense of the Society of Dilettanti*. Dublin.

Chappelet, J.-L. (1997) From Chamonix to Salt Lake City: evolution of the Olympic Village Concept at the Winter Games, in Moragas, M. de, Llines M. and Kidd, B. (eds.) *Olympic Villages: A Hundred Years of Urban Planning and Shared Experiences*. International Symposium on Olympic Villages. Lausanne: Documents of the IOC Museum, pp. 81–88.

Chappelet, J-L. (2002) *A Short Overview of the Olympic Winter Games*. Barcelona: Centre d'Estudis Olimpics I de l'Esport, Universitat Autònoma de Barcelona.

Charmetant, R. (1997) Albertville: Olympism and architecture, in Moragas, M. de, Llines M. and Kidd, B. (eds.) *Olympic Villages: A Hundred Years of Urban Planning and Shared Experiences*. International Symposium on Olympic Villages. Lausanne: Documents of the IOC Museum, pp. 109–115.

Chernushenko, D. (2004) Sustainable Urban Development in the Beijing Olympic Bid. Speech given during a private presentation to the Beijing Deputy Mayor and the Beijing Olympic Organizing Committee. http://www.ottawagreens.ca/ottawa-centre2/about/trackrecord/speech-sud_e.php, accessed 13 December 2006.

Church, B. (2005) Forgotten games. *Houston Chronicle*, 13 August.

CIIC (China Internet Information Centre) (2004) Beijing subways improve access for handicapped. *China Daily* (English language edition), 17 August. http://www.china.org.cn/english/2004/Aug/104219.htm, accessed 11 February 2007.

CITB (Construction Industry Training Board) (2006) *Construction Skills Network Report*. London: CITB.

Clancy, M.J. (1999) Tourism and development: evidence from Mexico. *Annals of Tourism Research*, **26**, pp. 1–20.

Clusa, J. (1999) La experiencia urbanística de Barcelona 1986–1992 y las expectativas del Forum 2004. *Ciudades*, **5**, pp. 85–102.

Clusa, J. (2000) The Barcelona Olympic Experience (1986–1992) and the 2004 Forum Expectations. Paper given to the World Direct Investment Forum, Lisbon, 5–6 June.

Coaffee, J. and Shaw, T. (2005) The liveability agenda: new regionalism, liveability and the untapped potential of sport and recreation. *Town Planning Review*, **76**(2), pp. i–v.

Coaffee, J. and Wood, D. (2006) Security is coming home: rethinking scale and constructing resilience in the global urban response to terrorist risk. *International Relations*, **20**, pp. 503–517.

Coccossis, H., Deffner, A. and Economou, D. (2003) Urban/regional Co-operation in Greece: Athens, a Capital City under the Shadow of the State. Paper presented to 43rd European Congress of the Regional Science Association (ERSA), University of Jyväskylä, 27–30 August. http://www.jyu.fi/ersa2003/cdrom/papers/358.pdf, accessed 1 March 2007.

Cochrane, A., Peck, J. and Tickell, A. (1996) Manchester plays games: exploring the local politics of globalisation. *Urban Studies*, **33**, pp. 1319–1336.

COCO (Commission d'Enquête sur le Coût de la 21e Olympiade) (1980) *Rapport*, 3 vols. Quebec: Éditeur Officiel.

CODA (XV Olympic Winter Games Committee/Calgary Olympic Development Association) (1988) *XV Olympic Winter Games: Official Report*. Calgary: Organizing Committee.

COJO (Comité d'Organisation des Xemes Jeux Olympiques d'hiver) (1968) *Official Report Xth Winter Olympic Games*. Grenoble: Organizing Committee.

Colenutt, B. (1988) Local democracy and inner city regeneration. *Local Economy*, **3**, 119–125.

Colvin, S. (1878) Greek Athletics, Greek Religion and Greek Art at Olympia: An Account of Ancient Usages and Modern Discoveries. Paper given to the Liverpool Art Club, 4 February.

CONI (Comitato Olimpico Nazionale Italiano) (1956) *VII Giochi Olimpico Invernsali: Cortina d'Ampezzo. Rapporto Ufficiale*. Rome: CONI.

COOB (Barcelona Olympic Organizing Committee) (1992) *Official Report of the Games of the XXV Olympiad*, 3 vols. Barcelona: COOB.

Cook, I.G. (2000) Pressures of development on China's cities and regions, in Cannon, T. (ed.) *China's Economic Growth: The Impact on Regions, Migration and the Environment*. London: Macmillan, pp. 33–55.

Cook, I.G. (2006) Beijing as an 'internationalized metropolis', in Wu, F. (ed.) *Globalisation and China's Cities*. London: Routledge.

Cook, I.G. and Dummer, T.J.B. (2004) Changing health in China: re-evaluating the epidemiological transition model. *Health Policy*, **67**, pp. 329–343.

Cook, I.G. and Murray, G. (2001) *China's Third Revolution: Tensions in the Transition to Post-Communism*. London: Curzon.

Cook, T.A. (1909) *International Sport: A Short History of the Olympic Movement from 1896 to the Present Day, containing the Account of a Visit to Athens in 1906 and of the Olympic Games of 1908 in London together with the Code of Rules for 20 Different Forms of Sport and Numerous Illustrations*. London: Archibald and Constable.

Correspondent (2004) Going for gold: the Olympics can pay off, but only if you have a city to sell. *Financial Times*, 14/15 August.

COWGOC (Calgary Olympic Winter Games Organizing Committee/Calgary Olympic Development Association) (1988) *XV Olympic Winter Games: Official Report*. Calgary: Organizing Committee.

Crookson, M. (2004) Making the Games work: a sustainable employment legacy, in Vigor, A., Mean, M. and Tims, C. (eds.) *After the Gold Rush: A Sustainable Olympics for London*, London: IPPR, pp. 51–68.

Crowther, N.B. (2003) Elis and Olympia: city, sanctuary and politics, in Phillips, D.J. and Pritchard, D. (eds.) *Sport and Festival in the Ancient Greek World*. Swansea: Classical Press of Wales, pp. 75–100.

Culfe, A. (2006) Five-ringed circus comes under unfriendly financial fire. *The Guardian*, 19 May.

Daley, R. (1963) Lyons makes a lavish pitch to be site for 1968 Olympics. *New York Times*, 17 October, p. 47.

Davenport, J. (1996) Athens 1896: the Games of the 1st Olympiad, in Findling, J.E. and Pelle, K.D. (eds.) *Historical Dictionary of the Modern Olympic Movement*. Westport, CN: Greenwood Press, pp. 3–11.

Dayan, D. and Katz, E. (1994) Media *Events: The Live Broadcasting of History*. Cambridge, MA: Harvard University Press.

DCC (Docklands Consultative Committee) (1990) *The Docklands Experiment: A Critical Review of Eight Years of the London Docklands Development Corporation*. London: DCC.

DCITA (Department of Communications Information Technology and the Arts) (1994) *Creative Nation: Commonwealth Cultural Policy*. Canberra: DCITA.

DCLG (Department for Communities and Local Government/Office for National Statistics) (2006) *Land Use Change in England: Residential Development to 2005* (LUCS21). London: DCLG.

Delgado, M. (2005) *Elogi del vianant: del 'model Barcelona' a la Barcelona real*. Barcelona: Edicions de 1984.

de Pauw, K.P. and Gavron, S.J. (2005) *Disability Sport*, 2nd ed. Champaign, IL: Human Kinetics.

DETR (Department of Environment, Transport and the Regions) (1999) *Towards an Urban Renaissance: The Report of the Urban Task Force chaired by Lord Rogers of Riverside*. London: Office of the Deputy Prime Minister.

Dickson, G. and Schofield, G. (2005) Globalisation and globesity: the impact of the 2008 Beijing Olympics on China. *International Journal of Sport Management and Marketing*, **1**, pp. 169–179.

Diem, C. (1912) *Die Olympischen Spiele 1912*. Berlin: Ausgabe.

Diem, C. (1942) *Olympische Flamme: Das Buch vom Sport*. Berlin: Deutscher Archiv.

Dong, J. (2005) Women, nationalism and the Beijing Olympics: preparing for glory. *International Journal of the History of Sport*, **22**, pp. 530–544.

Dong, L. (1985) Beijing: the development of a socialist capital, Sit, V.F.S. (ed.) *Chinese Cities*. Oxford: Oxford University Press, pp. 67–93.

Drees, L. (1968) *Olympia: Gods, Artists, Athletes* (trans. G. Onn). London: Pall Mall Press.

Dubin, M.S., Ellingham, M., Fisher, J. and Jansz, N. (2002) *The Rough Guide to Greece*. London: Rough Guides.

Dunn, K.M. and McGuirk, P. (1999) Hallmark Events, in Cashman, R. and Hughes, A. (eds.) *Staging the Olympics: The Event and Its Impact*. Sydney: University of New South Wales Press, pp. 18–34.

Eccles, J. (1997) Smart individuals are no match for the clever people. *The Australian Financial Review*, 4 October, p. 14.

Eckert, R. and Schäche, W. (1992) *Zu Geschichte und Bestand des ehemaligen Reichssportfeldes in Berlin-Charlottenburg: Expertise im Auftrag der Senatsverwaltung für Stadtentwicklung und Umweltschutz*. Berlin.

Editor (2004) Securing the Olympic Games. *Wall Street Journal*, 22 August.

Emery, P.R. (2002) Bidding to host a major sports event: the local organising committee perspective. *International Journal of Public Sector Management*, **1**, pp. 316–335.

Espy, R. (1979) *The Politics of the Olympic Games*. Berkeley, CA: University of California Press.

Essex, S. and Chalkley, B. (1998) Olympic Games: catalyst of urban change. *Leisure Studies*, **17**, pp. 187–206.

Essex, S. and Chalkley, B. (1999) Olympic locations and legacies: a study in geography and tourism. *Pacific Tourism Review*, **3**, pp. 185–200.

Essex, S. and Chalkley, B. (2002) Il ruolo dei Giochi Olimpici nella trasformazione urbana, in Bobbio, L. and Guala, C. (eds.) *Olimpiadi e Grandi Eventi*. Rome: Carocci, pp. 57–76.

Essex, S. and Chalkley, B. (2004) Mega-sporting events in urban and regional policy: a history of the winter Olympics. *Planning Perspectives*, **19**, pp. 201–232.

Esteban, J. (1999) *El Projecte Urbanístic: valorar la perifèria i recuperar el centre*. Barcelona: Aula Barcelona.

Evans, G.L. (1996a) Planning for the British Millennium Festival: establishing the visitor baseline and a framework for forecasting. *Journal of Festival Management and Event Tourism*, **3**, pp. 183–196

Evans, G.L (1996b) The Millennium Festival and urban regeneration: planning, politics and the party, in Robinson, M. and Evans, N. (eds.) *Managing Cultural Resources*. Newcastle: Business Education Publishers, pp. 79–98.

Evans, G.L. (1999a) Last chance lottery and the Millennium City, in Whannel, G. and Foley, M. (eds.) *Leisure, Culture and Commerce: Consumption and Participation*, Publication 64. Eastbourne: Leisure Studies Association, pp. 3–22.

Evans, G.L. (1999b) Leisure investment incentives in the European Community: changing rationales, in McPherson, G. and Foley, M. (eds.) *Sustainability and Environmental Policies*, vol. 1, Publication 50. Eastbourne: Leisure Studies Association, pp. 1–27.

Evans, G.L. (2005a) Measure for measure: evaluating the evidence of culture's contribution to regeneration. *Urban Studies*, **42**, pp. 959–984.

Evans, G.L. (2005b) Mixed-use and urban sustainability. *Planning in London*, **52**(January–March), pp. 43–46.

Evans, G.L. (2006a) *Creative Spaces: Case Study Barcelona*. London: London Development Agency, www.creativelondon.org.uk/upload/pdf/SFCS_Barcelona_Case_Study_Nov_2006.pdf, accessed 20 April 2007.

Evans, G.L. (2006b) Evidence-based or Instrumentalist? Urban Policy and Wicked Problems. Paper presented to Annual Conference, Royal Geographical Society, London, September.

Evans, G.L. (2006c) *Creative Spaces: Case Study London*. London: London Development Agency, www.creativelondon.org.uk/upload/pdf/SFCS_London_Case_Study_Nov_2006.pdf, accessed 20 April 2007.

Evans, G.L. and Foord, J. (2000) European Funding of Culture: promoting common culture or regional growth? *Cultural Trends*, **36**, pp. 53–87

Evans, G.L. and Foord, J. (2003) Cultural planning in East London, in Kirkham, N. and Miles, M. (eds.) *Cultures and Settlement: Advances in Art and Urban Futures*, vol. 3. Bristol: Intellect Books, pp. 15–30

Evans, G.L. and Foord, J. (2005) Rich mix cities: from multicultural experience to cosmopolitan engagement, *Journal of European Ethnology*, **34**(2), pp. 71–84.

Evans, G.L. and Shaw, P. (2004) *A Review of Evidence on the Role of Culture in Regeneration*, London: Department for Culture, Media and Sport.

Evans, G.L. and Shaw, S. (2001) Urban leisure and transport: regeneration effects. *Journal of Leisure Property*, **1**(4), pp. 350–372.

Experian (2006) *Hosting the 2012 Olympics: Skills and Employment Challenges*, Draft Final report, version 2. Prepared for Learning and Skills Council and London Development Agency, April.

Facaros, D. and Theodorou, L. (2005) *Athens and Southern Greece*, Cadogan Guides 84. Guildford: Globe Pequot Press.

Farrell, F. (1999) Australian Identity, in Cashman, R. and Hughes, A. (eds.) *Staging the Olympics: The Event and Its Impact*. Sydney: University of New South Wales Press, pp. 59–69.

Fellmann, B. (1973) The history of excavations at Olympia. *Olympic Review*, Nos. 64/65, pp. 109–118, 162.

Fischer, D.H. (1971) *Historians' Fallacies: Toward a Logic of Historical Thought*. London: Routledge and Kegan Paul.

Flyvbjerg, B., Bruzelius, N. and Rothengatter, W. (2003) *Megaprojects and Risk: An Anatomy of Ambition*. Cambridge: Cambridge University Press.

Frankland, R. (2000) Media Briefing, 26 November. Sydney: Indigenous Unit, Australian Film Commission.

French, S.P. and Disher, M.E. (1997) Atlanta and the Olympics. *American Planning Association Journal*, **63**, pp. 379–392.

GameBids.com (2006) Review of Olympic Bid news and information. http://www.gamesbids.com/english/index.shtml, accessed 30 January 2007.

García, B. (2001) Enhancing sports marketing through cultural and arts programmes: lessons from the Sydney 2000 Olympic Arts Festivals. *Sport Management Review*, **4**, pp. 193–220.

García, B. (2002a) The concept of Olympic cultural programmes: origins, evolution and projections, Paper. Centre d'Estudiis Olimpics I de l'Esport, Universitat Autònoma de Barcelona.

García, B. (2002b) *Towards a Cultural Policy for Great Events: Local and Global Issues in the Definition of the Olympic Games Cultural Programme. Lessons from the Sydney Olympic Arts Festivals 1997–2000.* Barcelona: Universitat Autònoma de Barcelona.

García, B. (2003) Securing sustainable legacies through cultural programming in sporting events, in Moragas, M. de, Kennet, C. and Puig, N. (eds.) *The Legacy of the Olympic Games 1984–2000: International Symposium (14–16 Nov 2002).* Lausanne: Olympic Museum, 314–320.

García, B. (2004) Urban regeneration, arts programming and major events: Glasgow 1990, Sydney 2000 and Barcelona 2004. *International Journal of Cultural Policy*, **10**, pp. 103–118.

García, B. and Miah, A. (2000) Olympic Ideals and Disney Dreams: cultural representation during Sydney's Opening Ceremony. *Culture @ the Olympics*, **2**(4), pp. 15–20, www.culturalolympics.org.uk, accessed 21 January 2007.

García, B. and Miah, A. (2004) Non-Accredited Media, the Olympic Games and the host city: The British Academy 2004 project. *Culture @ the Olympics*, **6**(1), pp. 1–7, www.culturalolympics.org.uk, accessed 21 January 2007.

Garcia-Espuche, A., Guárdia, M., Monclús, F.J. and Oyon, J.L. (1991) Modernization and urban beautification: the 1888 Barcelona World's Fair. *Planning Perspectives*, **6**, pp. 125–138.

Garcia-Ramon, M.D. and Albet, A. (2000) Pre-Olympic and post-Olympic Barcelona: a model for urban regeneration today? *Environment and Planning A*, **32**, pp. 1331–1334.

Gardiner, J. (2005) The spoils of victory. *Regeneration and Renewal*, 15 July, pp. 18–19.

Garrido, M. (2003) The Olympic Ideal. *Property People*, 19 June, pp. 8–9.

Gehl, J. and Gemzoe, L. (2001) *New City Spaces*. Copenhagen: Danish Architectural Press.

Gehl, J. and Gemzoe, L. (2004) *Public Spaces, Public Life: Copenhagen 1996*. Copenhagen: Danish Architectural Press and Royal Academy of Fine Arts.

Georgiadis, K. (1996) Olympic ceremonies in the Athens Games of 1896 and 1906, in Moragas, M. de, MacAloon, J.J. and Llinés, M. (eds.) *Olympic ceremonies: Historical Continuity and Cultural Exchange*. Lausanne: IOC, pp. 81–91.

Giniger, H. (1968a) Mexicans rushing Olympics' complex. *New York Times*, 21 July, V, p. 5.

Giniger, H. (1968b) Olympic building is behind schedule. *New York Times*, 8 September, V, p. 10.

GLA (Greater London Authority) (2006) *Lower Lea Valley Opportunity Area Planning Framework*, Consultation Draft for Mayor of London. London: Greater London Authority.

Glancey, J. (2004) Comment and analysis: the games have already started: don't let the Olympic bid serve as an excuse for another gimcrack redevelopment scheme. *The Guardian*, 23 January, p. 28.

Gleeson, B. (2001) Disability and the open city. *Urban Studies*, **38**, pp. 251–265.

Glendinning, M. (2006) Finance: NSW still paying for Olympics. *Sport Business International*, No. 112, April, p. 51.

Gold, J.R. and Gold, M.M. (2005) *Cities of Culture: Staging International Festivals and the Urban Agenda, 1851–2000*. Aldershot: Ashgate.

Gold, J.R. and Gold, M.M. (2007) Access for all: the rise of the Paralympics within the Olympic movement. *Journal of the Royal Society for the Promotion of Health*, **127**(3), pp. 133–141.

Gold, J.R. and Revill, G. (2003) Exploring landscapes of fear: marginality, spectacle and surveillance. *Capital and Class*, **80**, pp. 27–50.

Gold, J.R. and Revill, G.E. (2006) Gathering the voices of the people? Cecil Sharp, cultural hybridity and the folk music of Appalachia. *GeoJournal*, **63**, pp. 55–66.

Golden, M. (1998) *Sport and Society in Ancient Greece*. Cambridge: Cambridge University Press.

Goldstein, E.S. (1996) Amsterdam: the Games of the 9th Olympiad, in Findling, J.E and Pelle, K.D. (eds.) *Historical Dictionary of the Modern Olympic Movement*. Westport, CN: Greenwood Press, pp. 68–83.

Good, D. (1999) The Cultural Olympiad, Cashman, R. and Hughes, A. (eds.) *Staging the Olympics: The Event and Its Impact*. Sydney: University of New South Wales Press, pp. 159–169.

Goodman, S. (1986) *Spirit of Stoke Mandeville: The Story of Sir Ludwig Guttmann*. London: Collins.

Gordon, B.F. (1983) *Olympic Architecture: Building for the Summer Games*. New York: John Wiley.

Gratton, C., Shibli, S. and Coleman, R. (2005) Sport and economic regeneration in cities. *Urban Studies*, **42**, pp. 985–999.

Gratton, C. and Taylor, P. (2000) *Economics of Sport and Recreation*, 2nd ed. London: E. and F.N. Spon.

Green, D.A. (2003) *Olympic Impacts: Should We Expect An Employment Boom?* Vancouver, BC: Canadian Centre for Policy Alternatives.

Green, M. (1986) *Mountain of Truth: The Counter Culture begins, Ascona, 1900–1920*. Hanover, NH: Tufts University/University Press of New England.

Greer, G. (2005) Two tribes go to war. *The Guardian*, G2, 15 December, pp. 12–13.

Grey-Thompson, T. (2006) The Olympic Generation: How the 2012 Olympics and Paralympics can create the Difference. Inaugural Lecture, Staffordshire University, 26 October. http://www.staffs.ac.uk/news/article/dame_tanni.php, accessed 2 February 2007.

Grose, T. (2001) White City Stadium. *UK Running Track Directory 2001*. http://www.runtrackdir.com/uk/london(wc).htm, accessed 30 November 2006.

Guárdia, M., Monclus, F.J. and Oyon, J.L. (eds.) (1994) *Atlas Histórico de Ciudades Europeas*, vol.1: Península Ibérica. Barcelona: CCCB-Salvat.

Guillain, J.-Y. (2005) The end of the Olympic Arts contests: when art and sport became strangers to each other. *Journal of Olympic History*, **13**(3), pp. 24–30.

Guillain, J.-Y. (2006) Paris 1924. *Journal of Olympic History*, **14**, special edition, pp. 22–43.

Guttmann, A. (1984) *The Games Must Go On*. New York: Columbia University Press.

Guttmann, A. (2002) *The Olympics: A History of the Modern Games*, 2nd ed. Urbana, IL: University of Illinois Press.

Guttmann, L. (1976) *Textbook of Sport for the Disabled*. Aylesbury: H.M. & M. Publishers.

Halifax plc (2004) Houses go for Gold in Olympic Host Cities. Press Release, 18 October.

Hall, C.M. (1989) The definition and analysis of hallmark tourist events. *GeoJournal*, **19**, pp. 263–268.

Hall, C.M. (1992) *Hallmark Tourist Events: Impacts, Management and Planning*. London: Belhaven.

Hall, P. (1980) *Great Planning Disasters*. London: Weidenfeld and Nicolson.

Hall, P. (1988) *Cities of Tomorrow: An Intellectual History of Urban Planning and Design in the Twentieth Century*. Oxford: Basil Blackwell.

Hall, T. and Hubbard, P. (eds.) (1998) *The Entrepreneurial City: Geographies of Politics, Regime and Representation*. Chichester: John Wiley.

Hanna, M. (1999) *Reconciliation in Olympism: The Sydney 2000 Olympic Games and Australia's Indigenous People*. Sydney: Walla Walla Press.

Harlan, H.V. (1931) *History of Olympic Games: Ancient and Modern*. Topanga, CA: Athletic Research Bureau.

Hargreaves, J. (2000) *Freedom for Catalonia? Catalan Nationalism, Spanish Identity and the Barcelona Olympic Games*. Cambridge: Cambridge University Press.

Harskamp, M. van (2006) Lost in translation. *Rising East*, No. 3, January, www.uel.ac.uk/risingeast/currentissue/essays/vanharkskamp.htm, accessed 20 September 2006.

Hart Davis, D. (1986) *Hitler's Games: The 1936 Olympics*. London: Century.

Harvey, D. (1989) From managerialism to entrepreneurialism: the transformation of governance in late capitalism. *Geografiska Annaler, Series B*, **71**, pp. 3–17.

Haynes, J. (2001) *Socio-Economic Impact of the Sydney 2000 Olympic Games*. Lucerne: Olympic Studies Centre/Universitat Autònoma de Barcelona.

Haynes, R. (1999) There's many a slip 'twixt the eye and lip': an exploratory history of football and running commentaries on BBC Radio, 1927–1939. *International Review for the Sociology of Sport*, **34**, pp. 143–156.

Hebbert, M. (2000) El Grupo de Trabajo – *Task Force* – y el nuevo enfoque del urbanismo británico. *Urban*, **4**, pp. 82–90.

Hill, C.R. (1992, 1996) *Olympics Politics: Athens to Atlanta, 1896–1996*. Manchester: Manchester University Press.

Hiller, H.H. (1989) Impact and image: the convergence of urban factors in preparing for the 1988 Calgary Winter Olympics, in Syme, G.J. Shaw, B.J., Fenton, D.M. and Mueller, W.S. (eds.) *The Planning and Evaluation of Hallmark Events*. Aldershot: Avebury, pp. 119–131.

Hiller, H.H. (1990) The urban transformation of a landmark event: the 1988 Calgary Winter Olympics. *Urban Affairs Quarterly*, **26**, pp. 118–137.

Hiller, H.H. (2000) Mega-events, urban boosterism and growth strategies: an analysis of the objectives and legitmations of the Cape Town 2004 Olympic bid. *International Journal of Urban and Regional Research*, **24**, pp. 439–458.

Hinkson, M. (2003) Encounters with aboriginal sites in Metropolitan Sydney: a broadening horizon for cultural tourism? *Journal of Sustainable Tourism*, **11**, pp. 295–306.

Hoffmann, H. (1993) *Mythos Olympia: Autonomie und Unterwerfung von Sport und Kultur*. Berlin: Aufbau-Verlag.

Hofstadter, D. (ed.) (1974) *Mexico 1946–73*. New York: Facts on File.

Holt, R. and Mason, T. (2000) *Sport in Britain, 1945–2000*. Oxford: Blackwell.

HOOWI (Herausgegeben vom Organisationskomitee der IX Olympischen Winterspiele in Innsbruck) (1967) *Offizieller Bericht der IX Olympischen Winterspiele Innsbruck 1964*. Vienna: Österreichischer Bundesverlag für Unterricht, Wissenschaft und Kunst.

HOP (Hellenic Olympic Properties SA) (2006) Hellenic Olympic Properties: public real estate & sustainable commercial development. http://www.olympicproperties.gr/, accessed 7 August.

Hope, K. (1990) A chance to save Athens. *Financial Times*, 27 February.

Hornbuckle, A.R. (1996) Helsinki 1952: the Games of the 15th Olympiad', in Findling, J.E. and Pelle, K.D. (eds.) *Historical Dictionary of the Modern Olympic Movement*. Westport, CN: Greenwood Press, pp. 109–118.

Howell, R.A. and Howell, M.L. (1996) Paris 1900: the Games of the 2nd Olympiad, in Findling, J.E. and Pelle, K.D. (eds.) *Historical Dictionary of the Modern Olympic Movement*. Westport, CN: Greenwood Press, pp. 12–17.

Huber, M. (2003) Review of *Megaprojects and Risk*. *British Journal of Sociology*, **54**, pp. 594–596.

Hughes, H.L. (1993) Olympic tourism and urban regeneration. *Journal of Festival Management and Event Tourism*, **1**, pp. 157–162

Hughes, R. (1996) *Barcelona*. New York: Alfred A. Knopf.

IMC (Independent Media Centre) (2005) 18 Dead Workers make a Good Olympic City. http://thessa loniki.indymedia.org/front.php?lang=el&article_id=21326, dated 8 November 2005.

Imrie, R. (1996) *Disability and the City: International Perspectives*. London: Sage.

Intervistas Consulting (2002) *The Economic Impact of the 2010 Winter Olympic and Paralympic Games: An Update*. Vancouver: Intervistas Consulting.

IOC (International Olympic Committee) (1997) *Marketing Matters*, No. 11, special issue, August.

IOC (International Olympic Committee) (1999) Final Recommendations for IOC Reform Published. Press release, 24 November, Lausanne: IOC.

IOC (2000a) IOC and IPC Sign Cooperation Agreement. Press release, 20 October, Lausanne: IOC.

IOC (2000b) The Environment: The Third Dimension of Olympism. http://www.olympic.org/uk/organisation/missions/environment_uk.asp, accessed 21 January 2007.

IOC (2001) IOC and IPC Sign Agreement on the Organisation of the Paralympic Games. Press release, 10 June. Lausanne: IOC.

IOC (2002) *Sydney 2000 Sponsorship*. Sydney 2000 Marketing Report. http://multimedia.olympic.org/pdf/en_report_253.pdf, accessed 21 January 2007.

IOC (2003a) IOC and IPC sign Amendment to 2001 Agreement. Press release, 25 August, Lausanne: IOC.

IOC (2003b) The Legacy of the Olympic Games 1984–2000: Conclusions and Recommendations. http://multimedia.olympic.org/pdf/en_report_635pdf, accessed 16 March 2007.

IOC (2004a) *2012 Candidature Procedure and Questionnaire: Games of the XXX Olympiad in 2012*. Lausanne: Lausanne: IOC.

IOC (2004b) *The Olympic Charter*. Lausanne: International Olympic Committee.

IOC (2005a) *A Report of the IOC Evaluation Commission for the Games of the XXX Olympiad in 2012*. Lausanne: IOC.

IOC (2005*b*) Olympic Broadcasting. http://www.olympic.org/uk/orgnaistion/facts/broadcasting/index_uk.asp, accessed 2 January 2005

IOC (2006*a*) IOC and IPC sign Agreement Extension for 2014 and 2016. Press release, 22 June, Lausanne: IOC.

IOC (2006*b*) *Marketing Fact File*. Lausanne: IOC Press.

IOC (2007) Olympic Winter Games. http://www.olympic.org/uk/games/index_uk.asp, accessed 15 March 2007.

IPC (International Paralympic Committee) (2005) *Annual Report 2004*. Bonn: IPC.

IPC (2006*a*) *About the IPC*. Bonn: IPC. http://www.paralympic.org/release/Main_Sections_Menu/IPC/About_the_IPC, accessed 29 October 2006.

IPC (2006*b*) *Annual Report 2005*. Bonn: IPC.

IPC (2006*c*) *IPC Strategic Plan 2006–2009*. Bonn: IPC.

Iton, J. (1977) *The Economic Impact of the 1976 Olympic Games: A Study undertaken for the Organizing Committee of the 1976 Olympic Games*. Montreal: McGill University Industrial Research Centre.

Jakubowicz, A. (1981) State and ethnicity: multiculturalism as ideology. *Australian and New Zealand Journal of Sociology*, **17**, pp. 4–13.

Jakubowicz, A. (1994) Australian (dis)contents: film, mass media and multiculturalism, in Rizvi, F. and Gunew, S. (eds.) *Arts for a Multicultural Australia: Issues and Strategies*. Sydney: George Allen and Unwin, pp. 86–107.

Jenkins, S. (2006) Let's have commonsense games, not an extravagant festival of chauvinism. *The Guardian*, 24 November, p. 37.

Jennings, A. and Sambrook, C. (2000) *The Great Olympic Swindle: When the World wanted Its Games back*. London: Simon and Schuster.

Jessop, B. (1997) The entrepreneurial city: re-imaging localities, redesigning economic governance, or restructuring capital? in Jewson, N. and McGregor, S. (eds.) *Transforming Cities: Contested Governance and New Spatial Divisions*. London: Routledge, pp. 28–41.

Johnston, C. (2005) Olympic ad director speaks of delight. *The Guardian*, 7 July.

Kasimati, E. (2003) Economic aspects and the Summer Olympics: a review of related research. *International Journal of Tourism Research*, **5**, pp. 433–444.

Kidd, B. (1992*a*) The culture wars of the Montreal Olympics. *International Review for the Sociology of Sport*, **27**, pp. 151–161.

Kidd, B. (1992*b*) The Toronto Olympic commitment: towards a social contract for the Olympic Games, in Barney, R.K. and Meier, K.V. (eds.) *Proceedings of the Second International Symposium for Olympic Research*. London, Ontario: Centre for Olympic Studies, University of Western Ontario, pp. 67–77.

Kidd, B. (1996) Montreal 1976: the Games of the 21st Olympiad, in Findling, J.E. and Pelle, K.D. (eds.) *Historical Dictionary of the Modern Olympic Movement*. Westport, CN: Greenwood Press, pp. 153–160.

Killanin, Lord (1983) *My Olympic Years*. London: Secker and Warburg.

Kim, J. and Choe, S.-C. (1997) *Seoul: The Making of a Metropolis*. Chichester: John Wiley.

Koolhaas, R. (1995) What ever happened to urbanism? in Sigler, J. (ed.) *Small, Medium, Large, Extra-Large*. Rotterdam: 010, pp. 958–971.

Kornblatt, T. (2006) *Setting the Bar: Preparing for London's Olympic Legacy*, IPPR Discussion Paper 8. London: IPPR.

Krauze, E. (1997) *Biography of Power: A History of Modern Mexico 1810–1996*. New York: Harper Collins.

Kunzmann, K. (2004) Keynote Speech, Intereg III Mid-Term Conference. London, 19 November.

Kyrieleis, H. (2003) The German excavations at Olympia: an introduction, in Phillips, D.J. and Pritchard, D. (eds.) *Sport and Festival in the Ancient Greek World*. Swansea: Classical Press of Wales, pp. 41–60.

Lane, P. (2006) The Paralympics 2012. Unpublished lecture, symposium on 'Profiling London', London Metropolitan University, 26 April.

Lappo, G., Chikishev, A. and Bekker, A. (1976) *Moscow, Capital of the Soviet Union: A Short Geographical Survey*. Moscow: Progress Publishers.

Larson, R. and Staley, T. (1998) Atlanta Olympics: the big story, in Thompson, P., Tolloczko, J.J.A.

and Clarke, J.N. (eds.) *Stadia, Arenas and Grandstands: Design, Construction and Operation*. London: Spon, pp. 276–283.

Law, C.M. (1994) Manchester's bid for the Millennium Olympic Games. *Geography*, **79**, pp. 222–231.

LCC (London Chamber of Commerce) (2005) *Meeting the Olympic Skills Challenge*. London: LCC.

LDA (London Development Agency) (2004) *Statement of Participation: Introduction – Context Document for the Lower Lea Valley Olympic and Legacy Planning Application*. London: London Development Agency.

Leake, W.M. (1830) *Travels in the Morea*, 3 vols. London: John Murray.

Lee, J.K. (2005) Marketing and promotion of the Olympic Games. *The Sport Journal*, **8**(3), reproduced at www.thesportjournal.org/2005Journal/Vol 8-No3/lee-aug1.asp, accessed 28 January 2007.

Lei, L. (2004) Beijing evolves into Olympic 'Green'. *China Daily*, 1 March, www.chinadaily.com.cn, accessed 17 April 2006.

Lennartz, K. (2006*a*) Stockholm 1912. *Journal of Olympic History*, **14**, pp. 10–11.

Lennartz, K. (2006*b*) Antwerp 1920. *Journal of Olympic History*, **14**, p. 18.

Lenskyj, H. J. (1992) More than Games: community involvement in Toronto's bid for the 1996 Summer Olympics, Barney, R.K. and Meier, K.V. (eds.) *Proceedings of the Second International Symposium for Olympic Research*. London, Ontario: Centre for Olympic Studies, University of Western Ontario, pp. 78–87.

Lenskyj, H.J. (2000) *Inside the Olympic Industry: Power, Politics and Activism*. Albany, NY: State University of New York Press.

Lenskyj, H.J. (2002) *The Best Olympics Ever? The Social Impacts of Sydney 2000*. Albany, NY: State University of New York Press.

Leontidou, L. (1990) *The Mediterranean City in Transition: Social Change and Urban Development*. Cambridge: Cambridge University Press.

Levin, M. (2001) London 1908. http://www.lib.umd.edu/ARCH/honr219f/1908lond.html, accessed 10 February 2004.

Levy, C.J. (2004) Uneasy Greece focus on Olympic security. *New York Times*, 7 April.

LGA (Local Government Association) (2000) *A Change Of Scene: The Challenge of Tourism in Regeneration*. London: DCMS/Local Government Association.

Li, Y. (2006) Green Chaoyang part of Olympic preparations. *Beijing Today*, 24 March.

Littlewood, A.R. (2000) Olympic Games, in Speake, G. (ed.) *Encyclopaedia of Greece and the Hellenic Tradition*, vol. 2. Chicago: Fitzroy Dearborn, pp. 1176–1179.

LOCOC (London Organizing Committee for the Olympic Games) (2004) *London 2012: Candidate File*. London: LOCOC. http://www.london2012.com/en/news/publications/Candidatefile/Candidatefile.htm, accessed 14 April 2006.

Logan, J.R. and Molotch, H. (1987) *Urban Fortunes*. Berkeley, CA: University of California Press.

Loland, S. (1995) Coubertin's ideology of Olympism from the perspective of the history of ideas. *Olympika*, **4**, pp. 49–78.

Lorey, D.E. (1997) The Revolutionary Festival in Mexico: November 20 celebrations in the 1920s and 1930s. *The Americas*, **54**, pp. 39–82.

Lovett, C. (1997) *Olympic Marathon: A Centennial History of the Games Most Storied Race*. Westport, CN: Praeger.

LPOOC (Lake Placid Olympic Organizing Committee) (1932) *Official Report III Olympic Winter Games, Lake Placid*. New York: III Olympic Winter Games Committee.

LPOOC (1980) *XIII Olympic Winter Games, Lake Placid New York, Final Report*. Lake Placid: Lake Placid Olympic Organizing Committee.

MacAloon, J.J. (1981) *This Great Symbol: Pierre de Coubertin and the Origins of the Modern Olympic Games*. Chicago, IL: University of Chicago Press.

MacAloon, J.J. (1984) Olympic Games and the theory of spectacle in modern societies, in MacAloon, J.J. (ed.) *Rite, Drama, Festival, Spectacle: Rehearsals towards a Theory of Cultural Performance*. Philadelphia, PA: Institute for the Study of Human Issues, pp. 241–280.

MacAloon, J.J. (1989) Festival, Ritual and TV (Los Angeles 1984) in Jackson, R. and McPhail, T. (eds.) *The Olympic Movement and the Mass Media*, part 6. Calgary: Hunford Enterprises, pp. 21–40.

Macko, S. (1996) Security at the Summer Olympic Games is ready. *EmergencyNet NEWS Service*, **2**, p. 191.

Macleod, G. and Goodwin, M. (1999) Space, scale and state strategy: rethinking urban and regional governance. *Progress in Human Geography*, **23**, pp. 503–527.

Magdalinski, T, and Nauright, J. (2004) Commercialisation and the modern Olympics, in Slack, T. (ed.) *The Commercialisation of Sport*. London: Taylor and Francis, pp. 185–204.

Mahne, C. (2004) Did the Sydney Olympics pay off? *BBC Online*. http://newbbc.co.uk/1/hi/business/3549580.stm, accessed 10 August 2004.

Mallon, B. (1998) *The 1900 Olympic Games: Results for All Competitors in All Events with Commentary. Results from the Early Olympics 2*. Jefferson, NC: McFarland and Company Inc.

Mallon, B. (1999a) *The 1904 Olympic Games: Results for All Competitors in All Events with Commentary. Results from the Early Olympics 3*. Jefferson, NC: McFarland and Company Inc.

Mallon, B. (1999b) *The 1906 Olympic Games: Results for All Competitors in All Events with Commentary. Results from the Early Olympics 4*. Jefferson, NC: McFarland and Company Inc.

Mallon, B. and Buchanan, I. (2000) *The 1908 Olympic Games: Results for All Competitors in All Events with Commentary. Results from the Early Olympics 5*. Jefferson, NC: McFarland and Company Inc.

Mallon, B. and Widland, T. (1998) *The 1896 Olympic Games: Results for All Competitors in All Events with Commentary. Results from the Early Olympics 1*. Jefferson, NC: McFarland and Company Inc.

Mallon, B. and Widland, T. (2002) *The 1912 Olympic Games: Results for All Competitors in All Events with Commentary*. Jefferson, NC: McFarland and Company Inc.

Maloney, L. (1996) Barcelona 1992: the Games of the 25th Olympiad, in Findling, J.E. and Pelle, K.D. (eds.) *Historical Dictionary of the Modern Olympic Movement*. Westport, CN: Greenwood Press, pp. 185–193.

Mandell, R.D. (1976) *The First Modern Olympics*. London: Souvenir Press.

Maragall, P. (ed.) (1999a) *Europa Próxima: Europa, regiones y ciudades*. Barcelona: Edicions de la Universitat de Barcelona and Edicions de la Universitat Politècnica de Catalunya.

Maragall, P. (1999b) Foreword, in Department of Environment, Transport and the Regions, *Towards an Urban Renaissance,* London: E. and F.N. Spon, pp. 5–6.

Marrs, C. (2003) The benefits of believing. *Regeneration and Renewal*, 13 June, p. 23.

Marsan, J.-C. (1994) *Montréal en Évolution*, 3rd ed. Montreal: Éditons Le Méridien

Marshall, T. (1996) City entrepreneurialism in Barcelona in the 1980s and 1990s. *European Planning Studies*, **4**, pp. 147–165.

Marshall, T. (ed.) (2004) *Transforming Barcelona*. London: Routledge.

Martins, L. (2004) *Bidding for the Olympics; A Local Affair? Lessons Learned from the Paris and Madrid 2012 Olympic Bids*. Marne-La-Vallée: Laboratoire Techniques, Territoires et Sociétés, École nationale des Ponts et Chaussées.

Masterson, D.W. (1986) The modern Olympic Games and the arts, in International Olympic Committee. *Report of the 26th International Academy 3–18 July 1986*. Lausanne: IOC, pp. 104–115.

Matheson, V.A. (2006) *Mega-Events: The Effect of the World's Biggest Sporting Events on Local, Regional, and National Economies*, Faculty Research Series, paper 06–10. Worcester, MA: Department of Economics, College of the Holy Cross.

Matthews, G.R. (1980) The controversial Olympic Games of 1908 as viewed by the *New York Times* and *The Times* of London. *Journal of Sports History*, **7**, pp. 40–53.

Matzerath, H. (1984) Berlin, 1890–1940, in Sutcliffe, A. (ed.) *Metropolis, 1890–1940*. London: Mansell, pp. 289–318.

May, V. (1995) Environmental implications of the 1992 Winter Olympic Games. *Tourism Management*, **16**, pp. 269–275.

McCann, B. (2005) Complete the street! *Planning*, **71**(5), pp. 18–23.

McDonald, D. (1994) Interview. *Arts Today*, December.

McGehee, R.V. (1993) The origins of Olympianism in Mexico: the Central American games of 1926. *International Journal of the History of Sport*, **10**, pp. 319–323.

McGeoch, R. and Korporaal, G. (1994) *The Bid: How Australia won the 2000 Games*. Melbourne: William Heinemann Australia.

McGuirk, P.M. (2003) Producing the capacity to govern a global Sydney: a multiscaled account. *Journal of Urban Affairs*, **25**, pp. 201–223.

McGuirk, P.M. (2004) State, strategy, and scale in the competitive city: A neo-Gramscian analysis of the governance of 'global Sydney'. *Environment and Planning A*, **36**, pp. 1019–1043.

McIntosh, M.J. (2003) The Olympic bid process as a starting point of the legacy development, in Moragas, M. de, Kennett, C. and Puig, N. (eds.) *The Legacy of the Olympic Games 1984–2000*. Lausanne: IOC, pp. 450–456.

MacKay, D. (2000) *La Recuperació del Front Maritim*. Barcelona: Quaderns de Gestió.

McManus, P. (2004) Writing the palimpsest, again: Rozelle Bay and the Sydney 2000 Olympic Games. *Urban Policy and Research*, **22**, pp. 157–167.

McMill, E. (1999) NSW Ethnic Communities, Advocacy and Lobbying: Past, Present and Future, in Multicultural Arts Alliance, Conference on 'The Future of Multicultural Arts', 7 November, Australian Museum, Sydney.

McNeill, D. (1999) *Urban Change and the European Left: Tales from the New Barcelona*. London: Routledge.

Merrow, E.W. (1988) *Understanding the Outcomes of Megaprojects: A Quantitative Analysis of Very Large Civilian Projects*. Santa Monica, CA: RAND Corporation.

Metera, D., Pezold, T. and Piwowarski, W. (2005) *Implementation of Natura 2000 in New EU Member States of Central Europe: An Assessment Report*. Warsaw: The World Conservation Union.

METREX (The Network of European Metropolitan Regions and Areas) (2006) *The Legacies from Major Events: Findings and Conclusions*. Symposium on 'Planning for Major Events', Turin, 25–26 March. Glasgow: METREX. http://www.eurometrex.org/Docs/Expert_Groups/Major_Events/Torino_Report_2003.pdf, accessed 1 March 2007.

Meyer-Künzel, M. (2002) *Der planbare Nutzen: Stadtentwicklung durch Weltausstellungen und Olympische Spiele*. Hamburg: Dölling and Galitz.

MIC (Melbourne Invitation Committee) (1948) *The Melbourne Invitation Committee extends a Most Cordial Invitation to the Esteemed International Olympic Committee to celebrate the XVI Olympiad in Melbourne, Australia in 1956*. Melbourne: G.W. Grant and Sons.

Miller, D. (2003) *Athens to Athens: The Official History of the Olympic Games*. Edinburgh: Mainstream.

Miller, S.G. (2003) The organization and functioning of the Olympic Games, in Phillips, D.J. and Pritchard, D. (eds.) *Sport and Festival in the Ancient Greek World*. Swansea: Classical Press of Wales, pp. 1–40.

Molotch, H. (1976) The city as growth machine: towards a political economy of place. *American Journal of Sociology*, **82**, pp. 309–332.

Monclús, F.J. (ed.) (1998) *La Ciudad Dispersa: Suburbanización y nuevas periferias*. Barcelona: Centre de Cultura Contemporània de Barcelona.

Monclús, F.J. (2000) Barcelona's planning strategies: from 'Paris of the South' to the 'Capital of West Mediterranean'. *GeoJournal*, **51**, pp. 57–63.

Monclús, F.J. (2003) The Barcelona Model: an original formula? From 'reconstruction' to strategic urban projects (1979–2004). *Planning Perspectives*, **18**, pp. 399–421.

Monclús, F. J. (2004) International Expos and Planning Culture: Innovation and Tradition in Strategic Urban Projects. Paper presented to 11th International Planning History Conference, Barcelona, 14–17 July.

Monclús, F.J. (2006) International exhibitions and planning: hosting large-scale events as place promotion and as catalysts of urban regeneration, in Monclús, F.J. and Guardia, M. (eds.) *Culture, Urbanism and Planning* Aldershot: Ashgate, pp. 215–239.

Montaner, J.M. (1990) El modelo Barcelona. *Geometría*, **10**, pp. 2–19.

Montaner, J.M. and Muxí, Z. (2002) Los modelos Barcelona: de la acupuntura a la prótesis. *Arquitectura Viva*, **84**, pp. 28–32.

Moragas, M. de (1992) *Cultura, Símbols i Jocs Olímpics*. Barcelona: Centre d'Investigació en Comunicació, Generalitat de Catalunya.

Moragas, M. de, Rivenburgh, N.K. and Larson, J.F. (1995) *Television in the Olympics*. London: John Libbey.

Moreno, E. and Vazquez-Montalban, M. (1991) *Barcelona, cap a on vas?* Barcelona: Llibres de l'index.

Morgan, J. (1999) Opera to ask its audiences for top notes at Games. *Sydney Morning Herald*, 30 July, p. 15.

Morin, G.R. (1997) *La Cathédrale Inachevée: l'histoire rocambolesque des installations Olympiques de Montréal … et des idées pour en finir*. Montreal: Éditions XYZ.

Morse, J. (2001) The Sydney 2000 Olympic Games: how the Australian Tourist Commission leveraged the games for tourism. *Journal of Vacation Marketing*, 7, pp. 101–107.

Moss, M. L (1985) Telecommunications and the Future of Cities. Paper presented to 'Landtronics' Conference, London, June 1985.

MSNBC (Microsoft/National Broadcasting Corporation) (2004) No concrete plans for Greek athletics venues. 30 August. http://www.msnbc.msn.com/, accessed 26 September 2006.

Müller N. (1994) *One Hundred Years of Olympic Congresses, 1894–1994*. Lausanne: IOC.

Müller, N. (ed.) (2000) *Pierre de Coubertin, 1893–1937: Olympism, Selected Writings*. Lausanne: International Olympic Committee.

Muñoz, F. (1997) Historic evolution and urban planning typology of the Olympic Village, in Moragas Spà, M. de, Llinés, M. and Kidd, B. (eds.) *Olympic Villages: a Hundred Years of Urban Planning and Shared Experiences*. Lausanne: International Olympic Committee, pp. 27–51.

Myrdal, G. (1968) *Asian Drama: An Inquiry into the Poverty of Nations*. New York: Pantheon Books.

National Bureau of Statistics (1999) *China Statistical Yearbook 1998*. Beijing: China Statistical Publishing House.

National Bureau of Statistics (2006) *China Statistical Yearbook 2005*. Beijing: China Statistical Publishing House.

National Library of Australia (2000) ausarts2000, in *Pandora. Australia's Web Archive*. http://pandora.nla.gov.au/nph-arch/2000/Z2000-Sep-12/http://www.ausarts2000.com/index.html, accessed 21 January 2007.

Nel-lo, O. (1997) *The Olympic Games as a tool for urban renewal: The Experience of Barcelona'92 Olympic Village*. Barcelona: Centre d'Estudis Olimpics, Universitat Autònoma de Barcelona. http://olympicstudies.uab.es/pdf/wp090_eng.pdf, accessed 16 May 2006.

Ness, A. (2002) Blue skies for the Beijing Olympics. *China Business Review*, March.

Nikolaou, L.W. (1986) Olympism and art, in International Olympic Committee, *Report of the 26th International Academy, 3–18 July 1986*. Lausanne: IOC, pp. 77–82.

Nolan, M.L. and Nolan, S. (1988) The evolution of tourism in twentieth-century Mexico. *Journal of the West*, **27**(4), pp. 14–25.

NSW Ministry for the Arts (1997) *The Arts and Cultural Diversity*. Sydney: New South Wales Ministry for the Arts.

ODPM (Office of the Deputy Prime Minister) (2003*a*) *Assessing the Impacts of Spatial Interventions: Regeneration, Renewal and Regional Development. Main Guidance*. London: ODPM.

ODPM (2003*b*) *Sustainable Communities: An Urban Development Corporation for the London Thames Gateway*, Consultation Paper. London: ODPM.

ODPM (2003*c*) *Sustainable Communities: Building for the Future*. London: ODPM.

ODPM (2004) *The English Indices of Deprivation 2004: Summary (revised)*. London: ODPM.

Olds, K. (1998) Urban mega-events, evictions and housing rights: the Canadian case. *Current Issues in Tourism*, **1**, pp. 2–46.

Olson, L.L.K. (1974) Power, Public Policy and the Environment: The Defeat of the 1976 Winter Olympics in Colorado. Unpublished PhD thesis, Department of Political Science, University of Colorado.

Øresundstid (2003) History and Culture during the Past 1000 Years: The 19th Century. http://www.oresundstid.dk/dansk/engelsk/oresundstid/1800/index.htm, accessed 21 December 2006.

Organisasjonskomiteen (1952) *VI Olympiske Vinterleker Oslo 1952*. Oslo: Organisasjonskomiteen.

Organizing Commitee (1908) *The Fourth Olympiad: London 1908 Official Report*. London: British Olympic Association.

Organizing Committee (1924) *The Eighth Olympiad: Paris 1924 Official Report*. Paris: Organizing Committee.

Organizing Committee (1928) *The Ninth Olympiad, Amsterdam 1928: Official Report*. Amsterdam: R.H. de Bussig.

Organizing Committee (1936) *The Eleventh Olympiad, Berlin 1936*. Berlin: Amtlicher Bericht.

Organizing Committee (1948) *The Official Report of the Organising Committee for the XIV Olympiad: London 1948*. London: British Olympic Association.

Organizing Committee (1952) *The Official Report of the Games of the XV Olympiad*. Helsinki: Organizing Committee.

Organizing Committee (1960) *The Official Reports of the Olympic Committee for the Games of the XVII Olympiad*. Rome: Olympic Committee.

Organizing Committee (1964) *The Official Reports of the Olympic Committee for the Games of the XVIII Olympiad*. Tokyo: Olympic Committee.

Organizing Committee (1968) *The Official Report*, 2 vols. Mexico: Organizing Committee of the Games of the XIX Olympiad, Mexico.

Organizing Committee (1972) *The Official Report of the Olympic Committee for the Games of the XX Olympiad, Munich 1972*. Munich: Pro-Sport Munchen.

Organizing Committee (1976) *Official Report of the Games of the XXI Olympiad*. Ottawa: COJO-76.

Organizing Committee (1980) *Official Report of the Organizing Committee for the Games of the XXII Olympiad*. Moscow: Progress Publishers.

Organizing Committee (1984) *Final Report*. Sarajevo: Organizing Committee for the XIVth Winter Olympic Games 1984 at Sarajevo.

Organizing Committee (1989) *Official Report of the Games of the XXIV Olympiad*. Seoul: Seoul Olympic Organizing Committee.

Organizing Committee (1992) *Official Report of the XVI Olympic Winter Games of Albertville and Savoie*. Albertville: Organizing Committee.

Organizing Committee (1996) *Official Report of the Games of the XXVI Olympiad*. Atlanta: Atlanta Committee for the Olympic Games.

Ortloff, G.C. and Ortloff, S.C. (1976) *Lake Placid: The Olympic Years, 1937–1980*. Lake Placid: Macromedia.

PACEC (PA Cambridge Economic Consultants) (1990a) *An Evaluation of Garden Festivals*, Inner Cities Research Programme, Department of the Environment. Cambridge: PACEC.

PACEC (1990b) *Additionality in Section 4 Tourism Grants*. Cambridge: PACEC.

Paddison, R. (1993) City marketing, image reconstruction and urban regeneration. *Urban Studies*, **30**, 339–350.

Painter, J. (1998) Entrepreneurs are made, not born: learning and urban regimes in the production of entrepreneurial cities, in Hall, T. and Hubbard, P. (eds.) *The Entrepreneurial City: Geographies of Politics, Regime and Representation*. Chichester: John Wiley, pp. 259–273.

Papageorgiou-Ventas, A. (1994) *Athens: The Ancient Heritage and Historic Townscape in a Modern Metropolis*, Library Report 140. Athens: The Archaeological Society at Athens.

Patrick, A. (2005) Olympics offers little benefit for economy. *Daily Telegraph*, 21 May.

Payne, M. (2006) *Olympic Turnaround: How the Olympic Games stepped back from the Brink of Extinction to become the World's Best Known Brand*. Westport, CN: Westport.

Peek, L. (2004) How I strolled into the heart of the Games. *The Times*, 14 May, p. 4.

Portas, N. (1998) L'emergenza del progetto urbano. *Urbanistica*, No. 110.

Pound, D. (2004) *Inside the Olympics: A Behind-the-Scenes look at the Politics, the Scandals, and the Glory of the Games*. Toronto: Wiley Canada.

Prasad, D. (1999) Environment, in Cashman, R. and Hughes, A. (eds.) *Staging the Olympics: The Event and Its Impact*. Sydney: University of New South Wales Press, pp. 83–92.

Preston, J. and Dillon, S. (2004) *Opening Mexico: The Making of a Democracy*. New York: Farrar, Straus and Giroux.

Preuss, H. (2000) *Economics of the Olympic Games: Hosting the Games 1972–2000*. Sydney: Walla Walla Press.

Preuss, H. (2002) Economic Dimension of the Olympic Games. Lecture, Centre d'Estudis Olimpics i de l'Esport, Universitat Autònoma de Barcelona.

Preuss, H. (2004) *The Economics of Staging the Olympics: A Comparison of the Games, 1972–2008*. Cheltenham: Edward Elgar.

Price Waterhouse (1994) *Britain's Millennium Festival Project at Greenwich*. London: Price Waterhouse.

PriceWaterhouseCoopers (2002) *Business and Economic Benefits of the Sydney 2000 Olympics: A Collation of Evidence*. Sydney: NSW Department of State and Regional Development.

PriceWaterhouseCoopers (2004) *European Economic Outlook*. London: PriceWaterhouseCoopers.

PriceWaterhouseCoopers (2005) *Olympic Games Impact Study: Final Report*. London: Department for Culture Media and Sport.

Promyslov, V. (1980) *Moscow: Past and Present*. Moscow: Progress Publishers.

Proudfoot, P., Maguire, R. and Freestone, R. (eds.) (2000) *Colonial City, Global City: Sydney's International Exhibition 1879*. Darlinghurst, NSW: Crossing Press.

Purcell, S. and McKenna, B. (1980) *Drapeau*. Toronto: Clarke, Irwin and Co.

Pyrgiotis, Y. (2003) Athens 2004: planning and organising Olympic legacy, in Moragas, M. de, Kennett, C. and Puig, N. (eds.) *The Legacy of the Olympic Games, 1984–2000*. Lausanne: IOC, pp. 414–418.

Radbourne, J. and Fraser, M. (1996) *Arts Management: A Practical Guide*. Sydney: Allen and Unwin.

Readman, P. (2005) The place of the past in English culture, c. 1890–1914. *Past and Present*, **186**, pp. 147–199.

Redmond, G. (1988) Toward modern revival of the Olympic Games: the various pseudo-Olympics of the nineteenth century, in Seagrave, J.O. and Chu, D. (eds.) *The Olympic Games in Transition*. Champaign, IL: Human Kinetics, pp. 7–21.

Reeve, S. (2001) *One Day in September: The Full Story of the 1972 Munich Olympic Massacre and Israeli Revenge Operation 'Wrath of God'*. New York: Arcade.

Renson, R. (1996) Antwerp 1920: the Games of the 7th Olympiad, in Findling, J.E. and Pelle, K.D. (eds.) *Historical Dictionary of the Modern Olympic Movement*. Westport, CN: Greenwood Press, pp. 54–60.

Renson, R. and Hollander, M. den (1997) Sport and business in the city: the Antwerp Olympic Games of 1920 and the urban elite. *Olympika*, **6**, pp. 73–84.

Richards, G. and Wilson, J. (2004) The impact of cultural events on city image: Rotterdam, cultural capital of Europe 2001. *Urban Studies*, **41**, pp. 1931–1951.

Richie, J.R.B. (2000) Turning 16 days into 16 years through Olympic legacies. *Event Management*, **6**, pp. 155–165.

RICS (Royal Institution of Chartered Surveyors) (2004) Beijing Revolution Underway. News Release, 10 September.

Riding, A. (1987) *Mexico: inside the Volcano*. London: Hodder and Stoughton.

Roberts, P. and Sykes, H. (eds.) (2000) *Urban Regeneration: A Handbook*. London: Sage.

Roche, M. (1992) Mega events and micro-modernisation: on the sociology of the new urban tourism. *British Journal of Sociology*, **43**, pp. 563–600.

Roche, M. (2000) *Mega-Events and Modernity: Olympics and Expos in the Growth of Global Culture*. London: Routledge.

Rodríguez Kuri, A. (2003) Hacia México 68: Pedro Ramírez Vázquez y el proyecto olímpico. *Secuencia*, **56**, pp. 37–73.

Rognoni, G. (1996) The ideas and creativity of the Barcelona '92 Paralympic Ceremonies, in Moragas, M. de, MacAloon, J.J. and Llinos, M. (eds.) *Olympic Ceremonies: Historical Continuity and Cultural Exchange*. Lausanne: International Olympic Committee.

Romanos, A., Vellissaraton, J. and Liveris, K. (2005) Re-shaping Urban Environment through Major Events: The Athens Olympic Games. Paper presented to the 41st ISOCARP Congress 2005. http://www.isocarp.net/Data/case_studies/665.pdf, accessed 6 March 2007.

Rowe, C. and Koetter, F. (1978) *Collage City*. Cambridge, MA: MIT Press.

Rowe, P.G. (1991) *The Urban Public Spaces of Barcelona 1981–87*. Cambridge, MA: Graduate School of Design, Harvard University.

Rowe, P.G. (1997) *Civic Realism*. Cambridge MA: MIT Press.

Rürup, R. (ed.) (1996) *1936: Die Olympischen Spiele und der Nationalsozialismus: eine Dokumentation*. Berlin: Argon.

Salázar, R. (1968) Wonderland of colour welcomes Olympics. *Los Angeles Times*, 13 October, p. 8.

Sales, E. (ed.) (2005) *Time Out: Athens*, 2nd ed. London: Ebury.

Samatas, M. (2004) *Surveillance in Greece: From Anticommunist to Consumer Surveillance*. New York: Pella Publishing

Santacana, F. (2000) *El Planejament Estratègic*. Barcelona: Aula Barcelona.

Sassen, S. (1994) *Cities in a World Economy*. Thousand Oaks, CA: Pine Forge Press.

Schäche, W. (1991) *Architektur und Städtebau in Berlin zwischen 1933 und 1945: Planen und Bauen unter der Ägide der Stadtverwaltung* Berlin: Mann-Verlag.

Schäche, W. (2001) *Das Reichssportfeld: Architektur im Spannungsfeld von Sport und Macht*. Berlin: Bebra.

Schmidt, T. (1992) *Werner March: Architekt des Olympiastadions, 1894–1976*. Basel: Birkha user Verlag.

Schmitt, H.F. (1971) The Olympic Villages. *Olympic Review*, **44**, pp. 258–261.

Scott, C. (2004) The Olympics in Australia: museums meet mega and hallmark events. *International Journal of Arts Management*, **7**, pp. 34–44.

Scruton, J. (1998) *Stoke Mandeville: Road to the Paralympics: Fifty Years of History*. Aylesbury: Peterhouse.

Searle, G. (2002) Uncertain legacy: Sydney's Olympic stadiums. *European Planning Studies*, **10**, pp. 845–860.

Searle, G. and Bounds, M. (1999) State powers, state land and competition for global entertainment: the case of Sydney. *International Journal of Urban and Regional Research*, **23**, pp. 165–172.

Segrave, J.O. (2005) Pietro Metastasio's L'Olimpiade and the survival of the Olympic idea in eighteenth century Europe. *Olimpika*, **14**, pp. 1–28.

Séguillon D (2002) The origins and consequences of the first World Games for the Deaf: Paris, 1924. *International Journal of the History of Sport*, **19**, pp. 119–136.

Senn, A.E. (1999) *Power, Politics and the Olympic Games*. Champaign, IL: Human Kinetics.

Shank, M. (2005) *Sports Marketing*, 3rd ed. Harlow: Prentice Hall.

Sheil, P. (1998) *Olympic Babylon*. Sydney: Pan Macmillan.

Shen, J. (2002) A study of the temporary population in Chinese cities. *Habitat International*, **26**, pp. 363–377.

Simson, V. and Jennings, A. (1992) *The Lord of the Rings: Power, Money and Drugs in the Modern Olympics*. Toronto: Stoddart.

Smith, A. (n.d.) The Impact of Sports Events on City Images. London: University of Westminster, unpublished paper (c.2003).

Smith, H. (2004) Athens shows doubters it will hit games deadline. *The Guardian Online*. http://sport.guardian.co.uk/olympics/story/0,1278221,00.html, accessed 7 August, 2004.

SOBL (Sydney Olympic Bid Ltd) (1992) *Sydney Bid Books*. Sydney: SOBL.

SOC (Stockholm Organizing Committee) (1913) *The Fifth Olympiad; The Official Report of the Olympic Games of Stockholm, 1912: Issued by the Swedish Olympic Committee*, ed. E. Bergvall and trans. E. Adams-Ray. Stockholm: Wahlstrom and Widstrand.

SOCOG (Sydney Organizing Committee for the Olympic Games) (1997–2000) *Olympic Arts Festivals: Fact Sheets*. Sydney: SOCOG.

SOCOG (1998) *Olympic Marketing. Marketing Communications Manual*. Sydney: SOCOG.

SOCOG (1999a) Sydney 2000: A 'Total Olympic Experience'. Press release. Sydney: SOCOG.

SOCOG (1999b) *Games Time Structure*. Sydney: SOCOG.

SOCOG (1999c) *Summary Budget: Olympic Arts Festivals*. Sydney: SOCOG.

SOCOG (1999d) SOCOG Revised Games Budget. News release, 22 July. Sydney: SOCOG.

SOCOG (1999e) *Turning Green into Gold: Making an Environmental Vision a Reality*. Sydney: SOCOG.

SOCOG (1999f) *The Harbour of Life: Complete Guide to the Festival*. Sydney: SOCOG.

SOCOG (2000a) *Media Guide*. Sydney: SOCOG.

SOCOG (2000b) *Official Report of the XXVII Olympiad*. http://www.gamesinfo.com.au/postgames, accessed 19 August 2003.

Sokoloff, B. (1999) *Barcelone, ou comment refaire une ville*. Montreal: Les Presses Universitaires de Montréal.

Sola-Morales, I. (1992) Uso y abuso de la ciudad histórica: la Villa Olímpica de Barcelona. *A&V Monografías*, **37**, pp. 28–32.

Solinger, D. J. (1995) The floating population in the cities: chances for assimilation? in Davis, D.S. Kraus, R. Naughton, B. and Perry, E.J. (eds.) *Urban Spaces in Contemporary China: The Potential for Autonomy and Community in Post-Mao China*. Cambridge: Cambridge University Press, pp. 113–139.

Sonne, W. (2003) *Representing the State: Capital City Planning in the Early Twentieth Century*. Munich: Prestel.

Special Correspondent (1948) Games for paralysed archery tournament at Ministry Hospital. *The Times*, 30 July, p. 7.

Special Correspondent (2004) Olympia shot put aims to revive stadium of ancient Games. *Financial Times*, 18 August.

Speer, A. (1969) *Erinnerungen*. Berlin: Propyla en Verlag.

Spezia, G. (1992) *Eventi e Turismo*. Bologna: Editore Calderini.

Spivey, N. (2004) *The Ancient Olympics*. Oxford: Oxford University Press.

Stanhope, J.S. (1824) *Olympia: Or Topography Illustrative of the Actual State of the Plain of Olympia, and of the Ruins of the City of Elis*. London.

Stanton, R. (2000) *The Forgotten Olympic Art Competitions: The Story of the Olympic Art Competitions of the Twentieth Century*. Victoria, BC: Trafford.

Stevenson, D. (2003) *Cities and Urban Cultures*. Maidenhead: Open University Press.

Stone, C.M. (1989) *Regime Politics: Governing Atlanta 1946–1988*. Lawrence, KS: University of Kansas Press.

Stone, C.M. (1993) Urban regimes and the capacity to govern: a political economy approach. *Journal of Urban Affairs*, **15**, pp. 1–28.

Stump, A.J. (1988) The Games that almost weren't, in Seagrove, J.O. and Chu, D. (eds.) *The Olympic Games in Transition*. Champaign, IL: Human Kinetics, pp. 191–199.

Sudjic, D. (2005) *The Edifice Complex*. London: Allen Lane

Sudjic, D. (2006) Where are the Olympic building plans heading? *The Observer*, May 28.

Swyngedouw, E., Moulaert, F., and Rodrigues, A. (2002) Neoliberal urbanization in Europe: large-scale urban development projects and new urban policy. *Antipode*, **34**, pp. 542–577.

Sykianaki, C. (2003) Case Study: Athens and Olympic Games 2004. Paper given to symposium on 'The Legacies from Major Events', Turin, 25–26 March. http://www.eurometrex.org/Docs/Expert_Groups/Major_Events/Torino_Report_2003.pdf, accessed 1 March 2007.

Sykianaki, C. and Psihogias, S.(2006) Athens Case Study. Paper given to symposium on 'Planning for Major Events', Turin, 24–25 March. Glasgow: METREX. http://www.eurometrex.org, accessed 2 March 2007.

Taillibert, R. (1977) *Construire l'Avenir*. Paris: Presses de la Cité.

Talbot, J. (2003) Review of megaprojects and risk. *Geographical Journal*, **170**, pp. 172–173.

Tatz, C. (1999) Aboriginal Representation in the Olympics. Olympic lecture series, University of Technology, Sydney.

Teigland, J. (1999) Mega-events and impacts on tourism; the predictions and realities of the Lillehammer Olympics. *Journal of Impact Assessment and Project Appraisal*, **17**, pp. 305–317.

Tello, R. (1993) Barcelona post-olímpica: de ciudad industrial a escenario de consume. *Estudios Geográficos*, **212**, pp. 507–519.

Tenorio-Trillo, M. (1996) *Mexico at the World's Fairs: Crafting a Modern Nation*. Berkeley, CA: University of California Press.

Thamnopoulos, Y. and Gargalianos, D. (2002) Ticketing of large-scale events: the case of Sydney 2000 Olympic Games. *Facilities*, **20**, pp. 22–33.

Thompson, A. (1999) Security, in Cashman, R. and Hughes, A. (eds.) *Staging the Olympics: The Event and Its Impact*. Sydney: University of New South Wales Press, pp. 106–120.

Thompson, J. (2000) Aboriginal Tent Embassy set to stay. *Green Left Weekly*, No. 418, 30 August.

TOC (Tenth Olympic Committee of the Games of Los Angeles) (1933) *Tenth Olympiad: Los Angeles 1932 Official Report*. Los Angeles, CA: TOC.

Tomlinson, A. (1996) Olympic spectacle: opening ceremonies and some paradoxes of globalization. *Media, Culture and Society*, **18**, pp. 583–602.

Tomlinson, A. (1999) *The Game's Up: Essays in the Cultural Analysis of Sport, Leisure and Popular Culture*. Aldershot: Ashgate.

Tomlinson, A. (2004) The Disneyfication of the Olympics: theme parks and freak-shows of the body, in Bale, J. and Christensen, M.K. (eds.) *Post-Olympism? Questioning Sport in the Twenty-First Century*. Oxford: Berg, pp. 147–163.

Toohey, K. and Veal, A.J. (2000) *The Olympic Games: A Social Science Perspective*. Wallingford: CAB International Publications.

TOROC (Organizing Committee of the XX Turin 2006 Olympic Winter Games) (2005) *Italyart Cultural Olympiad Turin*. Turin: TOROC.

Townsend, M. and Campbell, D. (2005) London 2012 to be the greenest Games. *The Observer*, 13 February.

Travlos, J. (1981) Athens after the Liberation: planning the new city and exploring the old. *Hesperia*, **50**, pp. 391–407.

Tufts, S. (2001) Building the 'competitive city': labour and Toronto's bid to host the Olympic Games. *Geoforum*, **35**, pp. 47–58.

Tuppen, J. (2000) The restructuring of winter sports resorts in the French Alps: problems, processes and policies. *International Journal of Tourism Research*, **2**, pp. 327–344.

Tzonis, A. (2005) *Santiago Calatrava: The Athens Olympics*. New York: Rizzoli.

Ueberroth, P. (1986) *Made in America: His Own Story*. New York: Morrow.

Varley, A. (1992) Barcelona's Olympic facelift. *Geographical Magazine*, 64(7), pp. 20–24.

Vaubel, R. (2005) The role of competition in the rise of Baroque and Renaissance music. *Journal of Cultural Economics*, **29**, pp. 277–297.

Veal, A. J. and Toohey, K. (2005) *The Olympic Games: A Bibliography*. Sydney: School of Leisure, Sport and Tourism, University of Technology, www.business.uts.edu.au/lst/research.index, accessed 4 February 2007.

Videl, J. (2004) Village damned: Olympic hosts fail green test. *The Guardian*, 25 August.

Vigor, A. (2006) Olympic's legacy must focus on jobs. *Regeneration and Renewal*, No. 24, p. 14.

Vigor, A, Mean, M. and Tims, C. (eds.) (2004) *After the Gold Rush: A Sustainable Olympics for London*. London: IPPR/DEMOS.

Voeltz, R.A. (1996) London 1948: the Games of the 14th Olympiad, in Findling. J.E. and Pelle, K.D. (eds.) *Historical Dictionary of the Modern Olympic Movement*. Westport, CN: Greenwood Press, pp. 103–108.

Waitt, G. (2003) Social impacts of the Sydney Olympics. *Annals of Tourism Research*, **30**, pp. 194–215.

Waitt, G. (2004) A critical examination of Sydney's 2000 Olympic Games, in Yeoman, I., Robertson, M., Ali-Knight, J., Drummond, S. and McMahon-Beattie, U. (eds.) *Festival and Events Management*. Oxford: Elsevier Butterworth Heinemann, pp. 391–407.

Wangermée, R. (1991) *Cultural Policy in France, European Programme for the Appraisal of Cultural Policies*. Strasbourg: Council for Cultural Cooperation, Council of Europe.

Ward, P.M. (1990) *Mexico City: The Production and Reproduction of an Urban Environment*. London: Belhaven Press

Ward, P.M. (1998) Future livelihoods in Mexico City: a glimpse into the new millennium. *Cities*, **15**, pp. 63–74.

Ward, S.V. (1998) *Selling Places*. London: E. and F.N. Spon.

Ward, S.V. (2002) *Planning the Twentieth-Century City: The Advanced Capitalist World*. Chichester: John Wiley.

Ward, S.V. (2006) 'Cities are fun!': inventing and spreading the Baltimore model of cultural urbanism, in Monclús, F.J. and Guardia, M. (eds.) *Culture, Urbanism and Planning*. Aldershot: Ashgate, pp. 271–285.

Wark, M. (1994) *Virtual Geography: Living with Global Media Events*. Bloomington: Indiana University Press.

Waterfield, R. (2004) *Athens: A History from Ancient Ideal to Modern City*. London: Macmillan.

Watts, J. (2005) Satellite data reveals Beijing as air pollution capital of world. *The Guardian*, 31 October.

Watts, J. (2006a) Beijing to ban drivers for blue sky Olympics. *The Guardian*, 7 April.

Watts, J. (2006b) Beijing Olympic official sacked over corruption. *The Guardian*, 13 June.

Weaver, M. (2005) Livingstone promises green Olympics. *Guardian Unlimited*, 8 September, society.guardian.co.uk/communities/news/0,,1565373,00.html, accessed 4 April 2007.

Weirick, J. (1999) Urban design, in Cashman, R. and Hughes, A. (eds.) *Staging the Olympics: The Event and Its Impact*. Sydney: University of New South Wales Press, pp. 70–82.

Welch, P.D. (1996) Paris 1924: the Games of the 8th Olympiad, in Findling, J.E. and Pelle, K.D. (eds.) *Historical Dictionary of the Modern Olympic Movement*. Westport, CN: Greenwood Press, pp. 61–67.

Wendl, K. (1998) The route of friendship: a cultural/artistic event of the Games of the XIX Olympiad in Mexico City, 1968. *Olympika, 7*, 113–134.

Wenn, S.R. (1993) Lights! Camera! Little action: television, Avery Brundage, and the Melbourne Olympics. *Sporting Traditions*, **1**, pp. 38–53.

Wenn, S.R. (1995) Growing pains: the Olympic movement and television, 1966–1972. *Olympika*, **4**, pp. 1–22.

Whitelegg, D. (2000) Going for gold: Atlanta's bid for fame. *International Journal of Urban and Regional Research*, **24**, pp. 801–817.

Wilson, H. (1996) What is an Olympic city? *Media, Culture and Society*, **18**, pp. 603–618.

Wimmer, M. (1976) *Olympic Buildings*. Leipzig: Edition Leipzig.

Witherspoon, K.B. (2003) Protest at the Pyramid: The 1968 Mexico City Olympics and the Politicization of the Olympic Games. Unpublished PhD thesis, Florida State University.

Woodman, E. (2004) Stratford's glamour gameplan. *Building Design*, 30 January, p. 8.

WOS (Wenlock Olympian Society) (2006) Wenlock Olympian Society. http://www.wenlock-olympian-society.org.uk/, accessed 22 December 2006.

Wrynn, A. (2004) The human factor: science, medicine and the International Olympic Committee, 1900–70. *Sport in Society*, **7**, pp. 211–231.

Wu, F. (ed.) (2006) *Globalisation and China's Cities*. London: Routledge.

Wu, F. (ed.) (2007) *China's Emerging Cities*. London: Routledge.

WWF (World Wildlife Fund) (2004) *Environmental Assessment of the Athens 2004 Olympic Games*. Athens: WWF Greece.

Wynn, M. (ed.) (1984) *Planning and Urban Growth in Southern Europe*. London: Mansell.

Xin, Y. (2001) Olympic economy: a huge temptation. www.bjreview.com.cn/bjreview/EN/2001/200134/Nationalissues-200134(A).htm, accessed 7 February 2002.

Yarborough, C.R. (2000) *And They call Them Games: An Inside View of the 1996 Olympics*. Macon, GA: Mercer University Press

Yew, W. (1996) *The Olympic Image: The First 100 years*. Edmonton, Alberta: Quon Editions.

Yiftachel, O. (1994) The dark side of modernism: planning as a control of an ethnic minority, in Watson, S. and Gibson, K. (eds), *Postmodern Cities and Spaces*. Oxford: Blackwell, pp. 216–242.

Young, D.C. (1987) The origins of the modern Olympics: a new version. *International Journal of the History of Sport*, **4**, pp. 271–300.

Young, D.C. (1996) *The Modern Olympics: A Struggle for Revival*. Baltimore: Johns Hopkins University Press.

Young, D.C. (1998) Further thoughts on some issues of early Olympic history. *Journal of Olympic History*, **6**(3), pp. 29–41.

Young, D.C. (2004) *A Brief History of the Olympic Games* Oxford: Blackwell.

Zhou, S. (1992) *China: Provincial Geography*. Beijing: Foreign Languages Press.

Zimmerman, P. (1963) Financial nightmare ruins Detroit's Olympic Dream. *Los Angeles Times*, 10 March, D, p. 2.

Zolov, E. (1999) *Refried Elvis: The Rise of the Mexican Counterculture*. Berkeley, CA: University of California Press.

Zolov, E. (2004) Showcasing the 'land of tomorrow': Mexico and the 1968 Olympics. *The Americas*, **61**, pp. 159–188.

Index